Havana and the Atlantic in the Sixteenth Century

Envisioning Cuba

Louis A. Pérez Jr., editor

Havana and the Atlantic in the Sixteenth Century

Alejandro de la Fuente

With the collaboration of
César García del Pino *and*
Bernardo Iglesias Delgado

The University of North Carolina Press
Chapel Hill

This book was published with the assistance of the
William R. Kenan Jr. Fund of the University of North Carolina Press.

Manufactured in the United States of America
Set in Trinité by Tseng Information Systems, Inc.

The paper in this book meets the guidelines for permanence
and durability of the Committee on Production Guidelines
for Book Longevity of the Council on Library Resources.

Library of Congress Cataloging-in-Publication Data
Fuente, Alejandro de la, 1963–
Havana and the Atlantic in the sixteenth century /
Alejandro de la Fuente ; with the collaboration of
César García del Pino and Bernardo Iglesias Delgado.
p. cm. – (Envisioning Cuba)
Includes bibliographical references and index.
ISBN 978-0-8078-3192-2 (cloth : alk. paper)
ISBN 978-0-8078-7187-4 (pbk. : alk. paper)
1. Havana (Cuba) – History – 16th century.
2. Havana (Cuba) – Economic conditions –
16th century. I. García del Pino, César.
II. Iglesias Delgado, Bernardo. III. Title.
F1799.H357F84 2008
972.91'2303 – dc22   2007044528

cloth   12 11 10 09 08   5 4 3 2 1
paper   14 13 12 11 10   5 4 3 2 1

To three beloved friends, forever with me:

Manuel Moreno Fraginals:
here is the book that we discussed so many times

Ward "Su Majestad" Stavig,
for all the fun and for those bottles of mediocre wine

Manuel "Mano" Ferrero,
my brother in good and bad times

Contents

Acknowledgments xi

ONE
Introduction 1

TWO
The Port: Shipping and Trade 11

THREE
The Fleets and the Service Economy 51

FOUR
Urban Growth 81

FIVE
Production 118

SIX
Slavery and the Making of a Racial Order 147

SEVEN
The People of the Land 186

Epilogue 223

Notes 229

Bibliography 263

Index 281

Illustrations, Tables, and Figures

Illustrations

Wine consumption in sixteenth-century Europe, 23

"Die Grosse Insel Cuba" (The Great Island of Cuba), 68

Entrance to the Havana harbor, 75

Port city of Havana in the early seventeenth century, 76

Urban area of Havana around 1580, 109

Diagram of Havana by engineer Cristóbal de Roda, 1603, 115

Atlantic ships, 131

Sugar mill using Mediterranean technology, 139

Black servant in sixteenth-century Portugal, 155

Baptism of Africans, 163

Paying sailors before the transatlantic voyage, 216

Tables

2.1 Shipping Movement, 1571–1610, 13

2.2 Value of Imports and Exports (in Reales) by
Commercial Sector and Region, 1578–1610, 15

2.3 Value of Commodities, Percentage Distribution
by Commercial Sector, 1578–1610, 18

2.4 Fabrics Imported, 1578–1610: Quantity,
Average Prices, and Places of Origin, 33

2.5 Origin of Imported African Slaves,
Percentage Distribution, 1570s–1610, 41

3.1 Issues Discussed by the Cabildo,
Percentage Distribution, 1550–1610, 54

3.2 Currency Used, Percentage Distribution, 1578–1610, 59

3.3 The Fleets and Mercantile Activity, 1556–1610, 63

4.1 Origin of Immigrants, Percentage Distribution, 1585–1610, 87

4.2 Ethnonyms Applied to African Slaves,
Percentage Distribution, 1570–1610, 104

4.3 Average Prices (in Reales) of Real Estate, 1578–1610, 114

5.1 Average Prices (in Reales) of Rural Units, 1578–1610, 123

5.2 Sugar Mills, 1601–1615, 144

6.1 Race and Social Status of Baptism Godparents (1590–1610) and Marriage
Godparents and Witnesses (1584–1622), Percentage Distribution, 165

6.2 Origin of Spouses in Slave Marriages, 1584–1622, 167

7.1 Elite Dowries, Value and Composition, 1578–1610, 195

7.2 Apprenticeship Contracts by Trade and Average Learning Time,
Percentage Distribution, 1578–1610, 209

7.3 Average Wages (in Reales) of Seamen by Route
and Occupation, 1578–1610, 215

Figures

2.1 Monthly Shipping Movement, 1586–1610, 16

3.1 Monthly House Rentals (1579–1610) and Collection of Local Taxes (*Sisa*)
on Meat, Wine, and Soap (1566–1610), 56

3.2 Monthly Volume of Commercial Transactions (1579–1610)
and Land Petitions (1550–1610), 67

4.1 Estimated Free Population, 1520–1610, 85

4.2 Estimated Slave Population, 1540–1615, 102

4.3 Average Annual Number of Petitions for Urban Lots, 1551–1610, 113

5.1 Average Annual Number of Petitions for Rural Land, 1551–1610, 120

6.1 Average Prices for Healthy Slaves, 1578–1610, 160

6.2 Average Manumission Prices and Sale Prices for Women, 1585–1610, 175

Acknowledgments

My first note of thanks is to my collaborators, César García del Pino and Bernardo Iglesias Delgado, whose assistance made this book possible. They helped me with the endless process of gathering information from the notarial records, the town council records, the parish registries, and other sources. Bernardo also helped me enter some of this information into computerized databases. César, in turn, lent the project his prodigious knowledge of Cuban colonial history, his vast culture, and his remarkable memory. César is one of the most important historians of colonial Cuba.

The project had been born in the halls of the Archivo Nacional de Cuba a few years earlier as an attempt to study the formation of Havana as an Atlantic port city. My goal was simple: to gather all available information and to capture the life of this community in all its complexity. This is the sort of research project that a very young historian who has taken Braudel too seriously generates. A fellowship from the Spanish Institute of International Cooperation and a generous research grant from the Bank of Spain allowed me to do additional work at archives and libraries in Spain and England. I am forever indebted to these institutions, which opened the doors of the Archivo General de Indias, the Archivo Histórico Nacional, and the manuscript sections of the British Library and the Biblioteca Nacional de España to me. I am equally indebted to Manuel Moreno Fraginals for guiding me through the application process and for his mentorship.

I happily thank the personnel at all these archives and libraries for their help. Eusebio Leal Spengler, the Historian of the City of Havana and director of its museum, facilitated my access to the town council records. Leal has spent his adult life working to preserve Havana and its history. Monsignor Carlos Manuel de Céspedes authorized my using the books kept at the Havana Cathedral. The Archivo Nacional de Cuba was literally my second home. Archive director Berarda Salabarría even let me stay after hours so that I could conclude my work. The paleographers of that institution, Norma Roura, Nieves Arencibia, Luis Alpízar, and Magaly Leyva, taught me paleography, clarified doubts, and filled my life with a joy that I have never been able to replicate. I miss the Archivo Nacional.

Several colleagues helped along the way. Almost everything I know about Havana I learned from Leandro Romero Estébanez, a leading specialist of local architecture, art, and material culture who generously shared his notes, texts, and research materials with us. Arturo Sorhegui introduced me to the complexities of creole society. Pedro Deschamps Chapeaux taught me about slavery and Africans. Panchito Pérez Guzmán, Gabino La Rosa Corzo, Mercedes García, Enrique López, Israel Echevarría, and Olga Portuondo commented on my research, read drafts of early articles, or helped in other ways. The staff at Centro de Estudios Demográficos at the University of Havana taught me demography and computer skills; some staff members, particularly Luisa Alvarez Vázquez, became interested in my historical work.

In Europe, a truly remarkable group of scholars supported my research, helped me access funding, and commented on my work. I am profoundly grateful to Ruggiero Romano, John Lynch, Gabriel Tortella Casares, and Antonio Acosta for all their help. I also thank Consuelo Naranjo Orovio, Miguel Angel Puig-Samper, and Elena Hernández Sandoica for their support. Luis Miguel García Mora deserves a special mention for his help and friendship during all these years. A grant from the Cabildo Insular de Gran Canarias allowed me to research the links between Havana and the Canary Islands. The Fundación Sánchez Albornoz funded me to study historical demography with David Reher at the Centro de Estudios Históricos in Avila.

I was able to complement my work with early modern texts at the John Carter Brown Library. I thank Norman Fiering, former director at the JCBL, John J. TePaske, and Stuart B. Schwartz for supporting my work at this wonderful institution. My professor and friend Harold Sims read the entire manuscript and offered numerous suggestions. Susan Fernandez, Fraser Ottanelli, and Carmelo Mesa-Lago read parts of the manuscript as well. Three anonymous readers for the University of North Carolina Press made excellent suggestions, and editor Elaine Maisner embraced this project with generosity and enthusiasm. I have done most of the writing at the University of Pittsburgh, a place where it is very easy to work and learn. I thank my colleagues at Pitt for a friendly working environment and for letting me participate in some of the most bizarre meetings I have attended in my life.

The one constant element during all these years has been the love and support of my family and friends. The Castellary opened their house in Seville for me. I will be always grateful to Luigi and Maria Tatichi and to Humberto and Berta González for welcoming me into their lives when they barely knew me. Harry and Odalys Valdés were always there for me. Carmelo and Elena Mesa-Lago and Gena Wodnicki quickly became my Pittsburgh family; so did Victor and Carol Solomon. Back in the island, which was out of reach for many years, all the members of my extended family continued to find ways to express their love and confidence while sharing the hope that we would be reunited one day. In the meantime, my Isa was born and grew to be eleven. She and Patri, who has been by my side since before this project was even conceived, are the reason this book was not finished earlier: the temptation to be with them was simply too great to resist. For that, and for many other things, I thank them.

Havana and the Atlantic in
the Sixteenth Century

CHAPTER ONE

Introduction

On the morning of 10 July 1555, the guard at El Morro, an observation post at the entrance of Havana's bay, raised a flag indicating the approach of a vessel. As was customary in these cases, the commander of the town's small fortress reproduced the message by placing a flag in the fortress tower, where townspeople could see it. Commander Juan de Lobera also ordered artillery to fire. It was the sign for the eight or nine town residents who guarded the fortress to gather and for the populace to know that there was "a sail in the sea." The colonial governor arrived a few minutes later, accompanied by several residents on horseback. Nobody seemed to know the vessel or where it was coming from, although some residents suggested that it was the caravel of a merchant from Nombre de Dios, Panama, who paid frequent visits to Havana. To everyone's surprise, however, the ship did not enter the bay. It continued sailing westward, anchoring in a small inlet a quarter of a league to the west of the town, where two hundred men, with "their flags" and "in perfect order," landed.[1]

Commanding the ship was Jacques de Sorés, no stranger to Cuban waters. A lieutenant of François Le Clerc's, the French corsair known as Jambe de Bois, Sorés had probably accompanied his boss during the sacking of Santiago de Cuba in 1554. The "most heretic Lutheran," as local authorities referred to Sorés, had at his service a renegade Portuguese pilot who had lived in Havana for more than a year and who was familiar with the town and its port. Thanks to him, the corsair and his men managed to enter the deserted town undisturbed and to place the small fortress under siege. Inside, Commander Lobera prepared to protect His Catholic Majesty's artillery and honor with four harquebusiers and ten to fifteen men, including Spaniards, mestizos, and blacks. A few elders, women, and children who had been unable to flee the town were also inside the fort. The governor, Doctor Pérez de Angulo, and most of the residents found refuge in the nearby "Indian" village of Guanabacoa, where they plotted to recover the town.

Sorés's determined siege of the fort, which he set on fire, was based on false information: he had been told that it kept the treasury of a recent shipwreck. The attack could still be profitable, however. He seized the fortress, captured prisoners, including Lobera, and controlled the town. The corsair demanded a ransom of 30,000 pesos, 200 arrobas (5,000 pounds) of meat, and 100 *cargas* (5,000 pounds) of "bread" (that is, cassava) to relinquish the town. When the residents tried to bargain by offering 3,000 ducados (4,125 pesos), Sorés laughed at their emissary and replied "that he did not know there were crazies outside France." Either they paid the ransom or Havana would go up in flames.

Meanwhile, the governor prepared for a counterattack. With a force of 335 – 220 indigenous men, 80 blacks, and 35 Spaniards – Pérez de Angulo attempted a surprise attack. A lawyer with no military experience, the governor not only proved unable to defeat Sorés but also provoked the corsair's ire. Most of the prisoners were executed, although Lobera's life was spared in exchange for 2,200 pesos. Sorés's men set fire to the town before sailing out on 5 August. "They left this town in such a way, that the Greeks did not leave Troy worse," reported an observer.[2]

The attack could not have come at a worse moment. Like the rest of the island, by the 1550s the town of Havana had experienced several decades of stagnation and decline. Originally established by conqueror Diego Velázquez on the southern coast, the town, initially known as San Cristóbal, was supposed to serve as an advanced point in the process of conquest and colonization of the lands to the west and south of the island. Like most towns established by the Spaniards in Cuba, it faced the Caribbean, which was at the time the theater of Spanish expansion and trade. The king's order in 1515 to "ennoble" the settlements of the Cuban southern coast clarified that, in the eyes of the crown, the main function of these settlements was furnishing the expeditions that would continue the conquest and colonization of new lands.[3] Unlike the other towns established in Cuba, however, San Cristóbal lacked both mineral and demographic resources. Neither gold nor indigenous people, the two factors that defined the organization of the colonial economy between the 1510s and the 1530s, were available in the area. Since its creation, San Cristóbal had served mainly as a base to supply the expeditions of exploration and conquest. It was here that Hernando Cortés gathered his provisions before sailing to Mexico in 1519.[4]

By this time, however, the town was already in decline. At least some of its residents had moved to the northern coast, where they established what would eventually become the city of Havana. Neither process, the decline of the original San Cristóbal nor the establishment and slow growth of the northern Havana, can be explained without reference to the making of the Spanish empire in the

Indies, as the Americas were then called, or the organization of the Spanish Atlantic. Once the expeditions of conquest departed and the new settlements that San Cristobal and other Cuban towns were supposed to supply became organized and self-sufficient, Spanish interest in Cuba gradually declined. An important logistical base in the early 1500s, the island by the 1530s seemed to lack a purpose in the larger scheme of the emerging empire. Spanish residents left with every expedition, lured by the real or imaginary riches of new lands. As a resident of Santiago asserted in 1538, the island had been turned into "the mother to populate New Spain and to supply Tierra Firme."[5] In the 1530s, the conquest of Peru (1531-36) and the expedition of Hernando de Soto to Florida (1538) further contributed to the Spanish depopulation of the island. With the departure of "all the Spaniards," a contemporary asserted, the colony would be "lost."[6]

The magnitude of the decline in the Spanish population cannot be established with precision, but it approximated 80 percent between roughly 1520 and 1540. This decline was in turn linked to the demographic catastrophe of the native population. As French historian Pierre Chaunu has noted, the conquistador followed the American Indian and moved to those places where labor was available. As early as 1517, however, there were no "free" natives left on the island to distribute. Meanwhile, the production of gold also collapsed, from 112,000 pesos in 1519 to 8,000 in 1539.[7]

Thus by the 1540s Spain faced the threat of losing, through depopulation and abandonment, control over the colony. The island lacked gold. It lacked indigenous inhabitants. Unlike Santo Domingo, where the gold cycle had generated enough capital to launch the first sugar economy of the Caribbean, Cuba also lacked exports of commercial value. The island could produce large amounts of food supplies, but by the 1530s so did other colonies. That is why Governor Manuel de Rojas lamented the "abundance" of cattle in Mexico in 1534.[8]

Seeking to avert the depopulation of the colony, Spain granted important benefits and concessions to the remaining colonists. For the first time, in 1528 the crown allowed the *encomiendas*, an institution by which a group of indigenous people was allocated to a conquistador in exchange for religious indoctrination, to be hereditary in the island, a right that did not exclude the illegitimate children of the conquistadores.[9] More important, however, was the deferment of the application of the Leyes Nuevas (1542) to the colony. The Leyes Nuevas abolished the encomienda system in the Antilles and regulated other forms of exploitation of indigenous labor. But in the case of Cuba, the Council of the Indies advised against the implementation of this law "because the Spaniards are few" and the law would be "detrimental" to the population of the island. It was not until 1553, two years before Sorés landed in Havana, that this law was enforced in Cuba.[10]

Spain's efforts to maintain a presence in the colony were based on the gradual realization that the island would play a key role in the empire's system of communication and trade. With the organization of the great viceroyalties of Mexico and, later, Peru, the crown's emphasis shifted from Cuba's settlements on the southern coast to the Cuban northwest, particularly the Bay of Havana. Since 1519, when pilot Antón de Alaminos sailed from Mexico to Spain through the Straits of Florida taking advantage of the then unknown Gulf Stream, a stop in Havana or its environs became virtually mandatory for vessels returning to Spain. Alaminos himself called to port in the area to purchase cassava bread, meat, and other supplies before crossing the Atlantic.[11]

Apparently, the residents of the southern town of San Cristobal realized the advantages of the northern bay even before 1519. By the time Alaminos came through the area, he was assisted by some of the residents of the southern town who had moved north and established the town that would come to be known as San Cristobal de la Habana. Owing to the availability of fresh water from the Almendares River, the town was initially established west of the harbor of Carenas, as Havana's bay was initially known. But soon the residents realized that their future was linked to the magnificent harbor of Carenas, which could easily accommodate hundreds of ships and had a narrow mouth that could be easily defended. Fresh water would have to be brought to the new town, not the other way around.

Some sixteenth-century maps reflect this process of settlement by identifying two towns in western Cuba: San Cristobal in the south and Havana in the north. However, by the second half of the century the San Cristobal of the south began to disappear from maps and geographic accounts and was mentioned only in maps and descriptions that were clearly dated.

The strategic importance of Havana's port became evident to the crown and its enemies gradually, as the routes of oceanic shipping were being defined. To the royal officials of Cuba it was evident as early as 1532, when they described Havana as "a very good port where many ships from Castile and Yucatan come every year and disembark merchandise and trade." Conquistador Diego Velázquez had apparently realized the potential of the port, for in the 1520s he had appointed a lieutenant in the town, which he described as a "sea port" at "the end" of the island.[12] By midcentury the wonders of the port were becoming public knowledge, as European geographic and travel accounts began to mention Havana as an important maritime center in the New World. Some of these accounts were clearly distorted. In 1546 Martín Fernández de Enciso, for instance, included the "famous port of Havana" among the "most important and famous cities in the world," but writers like him reflected the initial knowledge that seamen and merchants were producing about the shipping routes of the Spanish Atlantic.[13]

Ultimately, it was foreign threats and attacks that made the crown fully realize the need to organize the Atlantic trade system and to protect its most important ports, such as Havana. Sorés's attack was not the first endured by the inhabitants of the town. A French corsair had sacked Havana earlier, in 1538, prompting the king to order the construction of a fortress for its protection and for "the ships that go and come from the Indies." This fortress proved useful to defend the harbor but failed to repel an attack by land, as the forces commanded by Jacques de Sorés demonstrated.[14]

Yet Sorés's attack also demonstrated that Havana's defense was not just a matter of proper fortifications. It was a demographic question as well, a point that local authorities had repeatedly made to the king.[15] Havana lacked the demographic resources needed to protect the town and its harbor. Governor Pérez de Angulo had been able to gather more than three hundred men in his failed attempt to expel the French, but only 10 percent of those men were characterized as Spaniards. Havana's defense rested primarily on its African and American Indian populations. Nor was the existing population capable of producing the supplies and rendering the services required by the growing number of ships, seamen, soldiers, merchants, priests, and travelers that came through town each year. Fleet commanders complained that they could not wait in the port for favorable weather because of the lack of supplies to sustain "so many people."[16]

The destruction of Havana by Sorés underscored the need to reconstruct and fortify the town. This reconstruction would proceed on new bases, however. As early as 1553 the king had ordered the governor of the colony to reside in Havana (as opposed to Santiago, then the capital of the colony), and after 1555 governors were always military men. Construction of the old Havana had depended mainly on indigenous labor. The new town would be built mostly by African slaves. Whereas the old Havana had relied mainly on its own meager resources for defense, the new Havana would rely increasingly on imperial moneys and garrisons. Within a few decades the town was transformed into a city protected by three capable forts staffed by a permanent garrison of at least 450. A new church was built. The old hospital, destroyed by Sorés, was rebuilt and a new one constructed. Three religious orders established monasteries in Havana. One of the most important shipyards in the Atlantic began operations. The population grew, making Havana the fastest-growing city in the Americas at the time.[17]

Changes were extensive, and studying this process of transformation is the main purpose of this book. In 1550, when our study begins, Havana was a sleepy town inhabited by a few hundred "Indians," Africans, and some forty *vecinos* (heads of households) of mostly Spanish descent. By 1610 it had become an impregnable port city and one of the most important shipping and trading entrepôts of the Spanish Atlantic with a permanent population of about six hundred vecinos, a garrison, several thousand slaves, and a sizable transient population that literally overflowed the city during the stay of the fleets.

The making of this Atlantic port city has been poorly studied, despite the growing attention that scholars have given to the creation and functions of port cities in the Americas and elsewhere.[18] Attention to port cities is not without merit. Historically, these settlements have displayed a great potential for growth, a process that is frequently associated with their pivotal role in colonial empires and in the making of the modern world economy, however defined. It is, of course, impossible to understand the European colonial expansion without reference to the great maritime centers of Europe, just as it is not possible to understand what Fernand Braudel called the Atlantic economy without reference to the port cities established by the Europeans in the Americas.[19]

These port cities linked colonial hinterlands with European metropolises and with other ports in the colonies. Indeed, some of these cities developed areas of influence that went well beyond the artificial boundaries fabricated by European geopolitical rivalries or administrative needs. Not only did they link local producers and entrepreneurs with distant merchant and credit houses in Europe, but they also linked peoples of dissimilar origins and cultural backgrounds through trade, services, consumption, and various labor arrangements. And they became centers of military innovation, as protecting shipping cargoes and sea routes became one of their main functions. Yet these attributes also turned them into visible targets, for people excluded from the emerging Atlantic trade were determined to participate in it either violently or surreptitiously. Conceived as fortified bastions of exclusion, colonial port cities represented in fact a permanent invitation for outsiders to intrude. As Sorés's attack on Havana shows, cultural exchanges were frequently mediated by gunpowder.

Relationships with the wider world are key to understanding port cities, but their inhabitants also have a history of their own. What makes a port city is the overwhelming influence of the port and its functions on the lives, occupations, opportunities, and experiences of the local community. These are not just human settlements by the shoreline. These are communities in which economic life and social life are intimately linked to the port, to its movement and demands.[20]

Because of their very nature, it is tempting to describe colonial port cities as mere appendages of the colonial powers, places whose history can be reduced to the colonial design. Many portrayals of Havana certainly fit this description, since modern historians have defined Havana as simply a service station for the fleets, a "factory" or a transient point in the Spanish system of communications and trade.[21] As a distinguished historian of urban colonial Latin America has stated, "colonial Havana, rendezvous port of the homegoing fleets, was not a mercantile but a service city with its port functions at the mercy of the erratic schedule of the fleet system."[22] A variant of the same argument is to emphasize the military importance of the city.[23]

These descriptions are essentially accurate, in the sense that the crown in fact designated Havana's port as the meeting point for the returning fleets. As scholars have noted, this designation, which gave proper legal form to patterns well established in navigation since the early sixteenth century, implied that Havana's role within the empire was that of a heavily fortified service station. The question, however, is whether such characterizations suffice to tell the story of the port city and its inhabitants.

As important as the fleet system was to Havana — and this study claims that it was crucial indeed — we need to evaluate its impact on local society and the opportunities and challenges it created for the various social groups that worked and lived in the city. As Allan Kuethe has noted, Havana's peculiar development was the result of "its unique maritime functions, its lucrative relationship to the colonial defense system and, in the long run, Cuba's own internal economic development."[24] Rather than treating the imperial vision of Havana as a descriptive end in itself, we treat it as a departing point to study the formation of this Atlantic community.

Such a change in focus requires the use of locally produced sources that allow us to get closer to the experiences and interactions of the many social actors that inhabited the Atlantic. The histories written from Europe and with European sources frequently privilege the activities of social actors with a systemic reach, such as big merchants and ship owners. The use of local colonial sources can help us identify less visible actors and study how they participated in the wider Atlantic and interacted with others. They can also help us escape the trap of the "telling example," life stories of cases that are atypical by definition.[25]

These sources have an additional advantage: comparability. They are "local" only in the sense that they were produced in a given administrative unit within the Atlantic, but their very existence and configuration were part of the process of imperial expansion and the creation of the Atlantic as a historical space. The kinds of sources that serve as the foundation for this study are available in many of the former colonial territories and in Spain. For instance, the notarial records, which contain information on mercantile transactions and juridical acts of various kinds, existed in most urban centers in the Iberian world. Parish registries varied from place to place depending on the composition of the population and the level of organization of the church, but their format was similar across the Spanish colonies. Each town had its council, which met more or less regularly and kept records of some kind.

Mining systematically the information contained in these local sources is daunting. In order to manage these sources and to facilitate the (inevitably partial) reconstruction of the lives and activities of individuals through nominal linkages, we organized our sources in computerized databases, as follows:

Source	Database	Number of Entries
Notarial Records	Merchandise	11,762
	Slaves	2,047
	Real estate	1,542
	Manumissions	161
	Apprenticeships	85
	Wills	153
	Dowries	134
Town Council Records	Land petitions	745
	Local taxes	654
	Topics and agreements	1,777
	Municipal offices	206
	Legal prices	143
Parish Registries	Baptisms	2,162
	Marriages	1,318
Treasury Registries	Import taxes	1,113

We have used these records to reconstruct aspects of the past that are otherwise difficult to study, particularly the activities of social actors that are rendered invisible in other sources. Wills, for instance, contain information about economic transactions and personal interactions that are difficult to detect elsewhere. Dowries contain information about the economic and social situation of women that is otherwise hard to obtain. The parish registries can be used to study the family and social strategies of the participants, their choices of spouses and godparents. The town council records are useful for analyzing the aspirations and concerns of the local elite, the process of distribution of lands, the assignation of public offices, the social worth of honorific appointments, and so on. Historians can use these sources to offer a reconstruction of the past that goes well beyond imperial sketches. That is what we try to do in this book.

The fleets impacted Havana in ways that are not always obvious. In contrast to other port cities that grew to serve the commercial needs of a vibrant agricultural or mining hinterland, in Havana it was the port that made the hinterland. Yet in the long term this process was reversed, with the agriculturally rich hinterland playing an increasingly important role in the life of the port city. As one would expect, the fleets generated a significant demand for maritime and human services – from ship repairs to hospitals, taverns, and lodging houses – and fueled the city's tertiary economy. These activities, in turn, influenced labor and social relations and facilitated the participation of even the most humble members of the community, such as slaves, in the monetary economy, giving local society a fluidity that in some cases defied imbedded notions of hierarchy and stratification. Furthermore, the fleets created opportunities and resources that the local residents seized in order to develop export activities that were not necessarily congruent with, and were at times in blatant opposition to, imperial plans for Havana. Local residents also used Havana's privileged reexport capacity to develop commercial and maritime networks in the circum-Caribbean area that were not necessarily ancillary to the needs of the fleets. In the process they turned the city into a colonial trading center, the "very mercantile town" that contemporaries so frequently celebrated and that modern historians have so frequently ignored.[26]

Through the port and its transactions local residents connected to an ever growing world in fairly concrete ways, as they traded and consumed commodities produced on several continents, including Europe, Africa, the Americas, and Asia. In some cases the place of origin of these products was so culturally meaningful that they designated the product itself, as with various European textiles such as the *ruan* or the *holanda* (linen fabrics from Rouen, France, and Holland). In other cases the origin was mentioned as a marker of quality, as with the "cinnamon from Ceylon" or the "wine of islands" produced in the Canary Islands.

Connections to that wider world took place at a more intimate level: colonial residents were part of that world, and many of their ideas, expectations, and consumption habits had been shaped by it. As they tried to organize colonial societies or adapt to new conditions, they had little choice but to turn to their home cultures for inspiration and information.[27] From Europe the Americas may have looked like a new world, but from the vantage point of the colonies, key elements of society and culture looked hardly new.

Furthermore, connections with the world economy and the world's cultures were renovated through the thousands of passengers, seamen, slaves, adventurers, merchants, and bureaucrats of various origins who came to town each year aboard the fleets. Some of these visitors stayed, strict royal prohibitions to the contrary notwithstanding. Indeed, when Sorés attacked Havana, the emissary of the local residents who negotiated with the corsair was a Frenchman who lived there. Designed by the crown to exclude and protect, Havana was particularly vulnerable to outside influences. The port city was a microcosm of Spain's failure to insulate the Spanish Atlantic from the influence and appetite of other Atlantic actors.

Nevertheless, with the organization of the fleet system, Spain was able to create sea lanes that were fairly secure despite the voracity of its European competitors. During the late 1500s the Spanish transatlantic shipping movement reached a volume that was not to be matched until the eighteenth century.[28] The making of Havana as an Atlantic port city corresponds to this golden age of the fleets, the period covered in this book.

To the residents of Havana the strategic importance of their port had another implication: leverage. They often reminded the crown that the port city was the "key" to the New World and demanded resources and concessions for its protection and growth. These resources were largely appropriated by an emerging, and progressively prosperous, landed and commercial elite. The members of this elite realized that the port was not only their main economic resource but also their most effective political argument. It was the engine of the local economy and therefore of their own prosperity. From their main institutional base of power – the local *cabildo*, or town council – they brought the point home in a letter to the king after the destruction of the town by Jacques de Sorés: "If Your Majesty is to have Indies [colonies] . . . it is necessary to protect this port. Otherwise, out of fifty ships that come from Castile to these lands very few or none will return."[29]

Increasingly aware of the fragility of its mercantile empire in the making, the crown listened. In the following decades millions of reales were poured into Havana to finance construction of its forts, supply its shipyards, and pay for its garrison. As a testament to the Atlantic character of the emerging port city, the orders came from Castile, but the silver came from Mexico and the workers from Africa. In a sense, it turned out, it had been almost a blessing that Jacques de Sorés, the Lutheran corsair, attacked the town on the morning of 10 July 1555.

CHAPTER TWO

The Port: Shipping and Trade

Before studying the town and its people, we must turn to the sea and consider the dozens of ships that came through every year. These ships gave life to Havana, which by the mid-sixteenth century was an Atlantic port city in the making. Ships brought consumers, merchants, products, and business to town. They were the engines that propelled the local economy and the reason that the crown spent millions of reales to fortify the port. Through these ships Havana was linked to the wider Atlantic, where peoples and products from virtually all corners of the globe were being constantly shuffled.

At first glance this movement of vessels may appear to have been chaotic. It was in fact a complex system of communications and trade that integrated several commercial circuits that were interconnected and mutually dependent. Because of its impact on the system as a whole, the first and most important circuit was transoceanic, which linked Havana with Europe (via Seville and the Canary Islands) and with Africa (through the Cape Verde Islands, São Tomé, and the various slave factories on the coasts of Guinea and Angola). This circuit was the largest commercial one, at least in terms of the value of products traded. The other two circuits, closely linked to the movement across the Atlantic, connected Havana to other colonial territories in the circum-Caribbean area (intercolonial) and to the settlements of central and eastern Cuba (insular or cabotage).

Each of these trade routes was distinctive in terms of the vessels used, the products and commodities traded, and the volume of capital required. Yet they shared a basic commonality: the sustainability and prosperity of each circuit was to some degree dependent on the fortunes of the others. Ships departing for Europe completed their cargoes in Havana with products that had been brought to town from other colonies or from what was already called the Cuban interior. Excess inventories of European manufactures and other commodities were left in town to be redistributed to regional markets not serviced properly by the fleets. Provisioning the fleets, their crews and passengers, created a market not only for local and regional producers of food but also for distant suppliers of wine, produce, and naval stores from Andalusia, the Canary Islands, and northern Europe. Havana was one of the few places in the Americas where these circuits converged and the only port where all the returning vessels came together before sailing back to Europe.

The available sources make it possible to reconstruct the shipping movement in Havana, but only after the 1570s.[1] By this time, however, the port was already known to be a transit point in transatlantic navigation and an important regional center of shipping and trade. Although the Carrera de Indias (fleet system) was not organized until the 1560s, we know from different sources that in the previous decade various fleets stopped in Havana, sometimes for an extended period of time while awaiting better climatic conditions. Such fleets are reported in 1550, 1551, 1556, and 1559. Indeed, in 1553 the Audiencia de Santo Domingo (the highest court of appeals in the Caribbean) ordered the governor of the island to reside permanently in Havana because of "the many ships" that came through its port every year from New Spain, Nombre de Dios, Cartagena, and Santa Marta in Tierra Firme. Havana, the *audiencia* asserted, had become "the key to all trading" in the New World.[2]

Some of these ships used Havana as a stopover, a base where they could complete provisions and make last-minute repairs before sailing across the north Atlantic. They neither brought nor took products from the local market and therefore do not appear in local records. Their very presence in the port generated economic opportunities for town residents, however, so we must take their existence into account when discussing the impact of the fleets on the local economy and society. But our discussion of the shipping movement refers to those vessels for which there are registered operations of import or export in the city, that is, to ships *trading* in Havana or purchasing services or supplies there.

According to every available source, this movement increased significantly in the second half of the sixteenth century. The number of vessels sailing between Havana and Seville with registered cargo for either place grew, according to the figures compiled by Chaunu, from less than 20 in the 1550s, to more than 50 in the 1560s, then to 181 in the 1590s. As impressive as these figures may be, they represented only a fraction of the total number of "trading" ships that visited the port town and an even smaller portion of total ships sailing through Havana with the fleets. The increase in transoceanic trade had an immediate effect on the intercolonial circuit, which shows a growth parallel to that of the transatlantic sector. In fact, in Havana's total shipping movement, most vessels were probably

Table 2.1. Shipping Movement, 1571–1610

Year	Incoming Ships				Outgoing Ships			
	Trans-oceanic	Inter-colonial	Cuban	Total	Trans-oceanic	Inter-colonial	Cuban	Total
1571–75	16	57	—	73				
1576–80	32	68	2	102				
1581–85	37	80	1	118				
1586–90	79	178	5	262	109	17	9	135
1591–95	117	265	5	387	94	19	3	116
1596–1600	88	77	10	175	54	24	6	84
1601–5	61	140	6	207	114	38	1	153
1606–10	64	140	9	213	139	47	3	189
Total	494	1,005	38	1,537	510	145	22	677

Sources: AGI, Contaduría, legs. 1088–1101, 1174–75; ANC, PNH, ER, 1578–1610.
Note: These figures refer to ships for which there are notarized or tax records in Havana. Since most reexports were not taxed and local products were frequently exempted from export duties, the number of outgoing vessels in this table is significantly lower.

devoted to trading with other colonial ports.[3] Among 1,537 ships entering the city between 1572 and 1610, those coming from other colonial territories represented a clear majority: 65 percent. A few additional vessels linked Havana with other ports and cities in Cuba's interior. Exchanges in this insular trade were not taxed, and therefore tracing the existence of these ships becomes an arduous task indeed.[4]

In the mid-1580s this shipping movement took off, growing at an astonishing rate for the next ten years. In the five-year period from 1591 to 1595, 387 "trading" vessels entered the port of Havana, compared with 118 between 1581 and 1585. The number of entries declined in the last few years of the sixteenth century but recovered again in the early 1600s. These changes took place in both the transoceanic and intercolonial circuits, suggesting the existence of important connections and linkages between them (see table 2.1).

Whereas the intercolonial movement dominated the entries, the vast majority of the outgoing ships, three-quarters of the total, went to San Lúcar de Barrameda, the gateway to Seville. This proportion remained basically unchanged between the 1580s and 1610. The convergence of the returning fleets of New Spain and Tierra Firme in Havana allowed the city to function as a regional collecting point from which it was possible to reexport colonial products to Europe. To a lesser degree, the opposite was also true. About a quarter of the outgoing vessels went to other colonial territories or to Cuba's interior, carrying with them European manufactures that had been previously registered as imports in the city. The growing number of "trading" ships entering the city from Seville – which more than tripled between the early 1580s and early 1590s – cannot be explained by population growth or by the needs of Havana's service economy. At least in part, this growth was conditioned by the city's ability to redistribute European products among colonial markets in the circum-Caribbean area. The intense exchanges that took place between Havana and other colonial areas gave local merchants access to accurate and timely information about neighboring markets, facilitating this regional traffic.

An analysis of Havana's trade based on values, instead of ships, confirms the existence of links between these complementary "circuits" of shipping and commerce (see table 2.2). The importance of the transoceanic sector in the city's total exports (70 percent) parallels the high proportion of vessels going to Seville among outgoing ships. Yet an analysis based on the shipping movement clearly overestimates the importance of the intercolonial sector in the provisioning of the local market. Most imports did come through the intercolonial trade, as the number of ships indicated, but the importance of the transatlantic sector in the imports is much greater than the number of vessels would suggest. Two factors account for this incongruence. One is related to the tonnage of the ships devoted to the transoceanic routes, which were on average larger than the *fragatas* used in the Caribbean sea lanes. The other factor is that some of the transatlantic imports commanded very high values – a factor that is particularly evident in the case of slave ships.

The most important point, however, is that these figures confirm Havana's role as a regional trading center, specialized in the reexportation of colonial commodities. Havana's significant trade surplus with Spain can be explained only in relation to its trade deficit with the colonies. Likewise, Havana's exports to the colonies and particularly to the towns of central and eastern Cuba cannot be understood without reference to the transatlantic imports, a good portion of which were reexported through cabotage, or coastal trade, and through the intercolonial sea routes. The town had few, if any, domestic products to offer to other colonial territories, many of which produced export commodities similar to those of Cuba. Although it is possible that some colonial products were moved within the Caribbean to satisfy the demands generated by the growing contraband practiced with the many enemies of the Spanish crown, European products were in fact a high proportion of Havana's intercolonial and insular reexports, goods that would compete with those offered by European smugglers. The king acknowledged the existence of these connections: "In the fleets and armadas that come to these kingdoms a large amount of all sorts of merchandise is brought in

Table 2.2. Value of Imports and Exports (in Reales)
by Commercial Sector and Region, 1578–1610

Region	Imports	Exports	Exports minus Imports
Transoceanic	5,563,328	7,063,699	1,500,371
Africa	521,106	0	−521,106
Spain	3,284,544	6,345,566	3,061,022
Canary Islands	1,616,623	536,685	−1,079,938
Portugal	141,055	181,448	40,393
Intercolonial	5,745,570	1,873,130	−3,872,440
Mexico	3,217,844	665,592	−2,552,252
Veracruz	2,035,229	330,587	−1,704,642
Yucatán	155,452	200,853	45,400
Unknown	1,027,163	134,153	−893,009
Honduras	593,455	37,983	−555,472
Guatemala	18,815	1,800	−17,015
La Española	150,996	103,951	−47,045
Puerto Rico	176,530	67,025	−109,505
Jamaica	40,282	11,461	−28,821
Margarita	31,624	5,274	−26,350
Florida	862,518	743,003	−119,515
Panama	164,841	2,892	−161,949
Colombia	433,282	172,356	−260,926
Peru	42,106	56,450	14,344
Other	13,278	5,342	−7,936
Insular	831,276	1,197,929	366,653
Trinidad	54,368	48,014	−6,354
Sancti Spíritus	115,416	64,756	−50,660
Remedios	54,960	47,467	−7,493
Puerto Príncipe	226,374	279,065	52,691
Bayamo	319,301	628,746	309,445
Baracoa	20,289	3,090	−17,199
Santiago de Cuba	18,312	115,892	97,580
Other/unknown	22,255	10,899	−11,356
Total	12,140,174	10,134,758	−2,005,416

Source: ANC, PNH, ER, 1578–1610.

return and in the port of Havana the passengers, masters, and seamen sell them covertly to residents and merchants."[5]

These linkages between the trading and shipping circuits, particularly between the Caribbean and the transoceanic, also had a seasonal dimension. The intercolonial trade was organized to facilitate the reexportation of colonial prod-

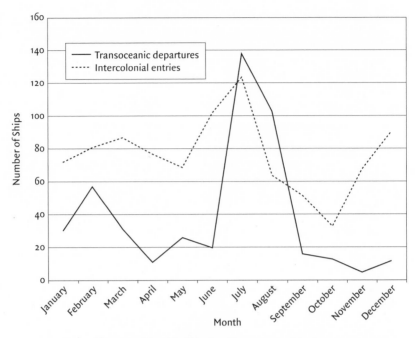

Figure 2.1. Monthly Shipping Movement, 1586–1610
Source: AGI, Contaduría, legs. 1088–1101, 1174–75; ANC, PNH, ER, 1586–1610.

ucts to Europe, so ships calling to Havana from the Caribbean did so during those months in which cargo capacity was at its highest point, that is, when one or both fleets were in town. The months with the largest numbers of departures for Europe were July and August; those with the largest number of entries from other colonial ports were June and July (see figure 2.1). There was clearly a shipping season in the summer months, when climatic conditions for navigation were optimal. As Louis A. Pérez has noted, efforts were made "to arrange the scheduled sailing of the annual treasure fleet around the Atlantic hurricane season."[6] Following the collapse of the transatlantic departures in September, in the midst of the hurricane season, the colonial entries reached their lowest point as well. They recovered partially between November and January, coinciding with an increment of the transoceanic departures in February, when the worst of winter was over.

The insular trade was also organized around the transatlantic movement. Most ships traveling between Havana and the settlements in central and eastern Cuba did so between July and September, just when most transatlantic departures took place. Yet the month with the highest number of insular entries was September, when very few Atlantic departures took place. Whereas it is possible to explain the high level of entries in July and August as a function of the fleets and of their cargo space for exports, the same is not true about September. However, this was the month with the highest number of transatlantic entries, when ships coming directly from Seville and the Canaries called to port. It may have been the availability of European products that was behind the relatively large number of cabotage vessels coming to Havana in September.

A characterization of Havana as just a station for the Carrera at the service of the empire cannot account for all this movement, much less for the ways in which the various trade routes related to one another. Historians of Spanish trade have rightly concentrated on the transatlantic movement, but as John Fisher states, such emphasis oversimplifies the complex intercolonial system of exchanges that came into existence around the fleets linking Seville with the colonial ports of Portobelo, Veracruz, and Havana.[7] Through this constant flow of vessels and commodities local merchants and residents got access to a large variety of goods. These goods came from production centers all over the world, from Amsterdam to Ceylon, and they were part of life in Havana and other Atlantic port cities. Local merchants, residents, and transients consumed and traded those commodities, shifting them from one sea route to another depending on the available information about local, regional, and distant markets and demands.

The "Ocean Sea": Seville and the Canary Islands

Despite all that is known about the Carrera de Indias and about the importance of American silver in the economic expansion of Europe, little is known about the European manufacturers and products that supplied the colonial markets. As economic historian Domenico Sella noted, "We know a great deal more, in fact, about what the Old World received from the New than about what the former sent to the latter." Yet we do know that a greater variety of products were imported into the colonies from Europe than were carried annually by the fleets from the colonies to Europe.[8] Taking a closer look at the commodities traded in each circuit not only helps us understand how these circuits worked but also contributes to our understanding of the formation of local markets and consumption patterns in the colonies.

It is not surprising, given Havana's capacity to export colonial commodities in the returning fleets, that its "exports" resemble those of the colonial territories as a whole (see table 2.3). This situation is clearly exemplified by the absolute predominance of bullion and specie in the total value of Havana's exports: 64 percent. The city received large amounts of silver, both minted and in bars,

Table 2.3. Value of Commodities, Percentage Distribution
by Commercial Sector, 1578–1610

Merchandise	Transoceanic		Intercolonial		Insular	
	Imports	Exports	Imports	Exports	Imports	Exports
Textiles	25.1	0.1	3.8	8.6	0.1	21.2
Fabrics	13.9	0.1	3.0	3.4	–	14.1
Clothing	6.2	–	0.5	1.5	0.1	6.0
Accessories	5.0	–	0.3	3.7	–	1.1
Footwear	0.2	–	0.1	0.1	–	0.5
Ironware	0.6	–	0.1	0.1	–	0.4
Weapons	0.4	0.2	–	8.3	–	–
Shipping supplies	3.3	0.7	–	0.4	0.1	0.3
Ships	3.6	6.5	1.0	4.7	4.8	3.9
Sugar mill supplies	2.0	–	–	–	–	–
Books, paper	0.2	–	0.1	0.1	–	0.9
Soap, candles	0.4	–	0.2	0.1	–	0.2
Houseware	0.2	–	–	0.1	0.1	0.1
Bullion, specie	7.2	64.2	53.4	30.7	35.1	12.9
Wine	26.4	0.9	0.2	8.6	–	8.5
Foodstuff	0.8	2.8	15.9	22.9	3.0	30.4
Oils	1.1	–	0.2	0.4	0.1	0.1
Spices, condiments	0.2	1.5	0.1	0.7	0.9	0.3
Hides	0.2	9.8	0.9	1.3	32.1	0.7
Wood	–	0.6	0.8	–	1.8	–
Dyes, medicinal	0.2	8.3	7.6	–	–	–
Slaves	13.6	0.2	8.3	6.3	12.5	11.5
Contract labor	0.8	1.8	1.4	0.4	–	0.5
Other	13.5	2.3	5.9	6.2	9.4	7.6

Source: ANC, PNH, ER, 1578–1610.

through the *situados* (allocations made by the crown to pay for various expenses) and through its own commercial activities. This silver financed local economic activities, as well as regional and long-distance trade.

Another colonial commodity, not produced locally, that was well represented in the city's transatlantic exports was *añil*, as the Spanish called it, or indigo. A blue dyeing material of vegetable origin, indigo was well known to European dyers and cloth producers since at least the Middle Ages. By the late sixteenth century, prices of this blue dye had declined, thanks to growing imports from Asia and the New World. Indigo from northern India represented about 6 percent of the total value of cargoes carried by the Portuguese Carreira da India between 1580 and 1640. Significant quantities came from the New World as well and were then distributed through the textile centers of Europe. Venetian drapers alone claimed in the 1590s that they dyed fifteen thousand bolts of cloth per year using colonial indigo. Most of this "costly color" came from Honduras, which was the main center of production in the Americas. Indeed, all the indigo exported from Havana to Seville had been previously imported from Honduras.[9]

Indigo alone accounted for more than 90 percent of all the goods listed under dyes and medicinal substances. The other great colonial dye, *grana*, or cochineal, had much less importance in the city's transatlantic trade, despite its value in the overall trade between the colonies and Spain.[10] A prized red dye obtained from an insect parasitic to the nopal cactus in Mexico, cochineal displaced some of the traditional and more expensive red dyes, such as the European kermes, and by the late 1500s had become one of the main coloring agents used by European cloth producers.[11] Its low representation in Havana's exports has a clear explanation. Unlike añil, most cochineal was produced in central and eastern Mexico, areas that had ready access to the fleets of New Spain via Veracruz.

Small amounts of logwood, or *palo de campeche*, were also exported from Havana to Seville. As with indigo and cochineal, palo de campeche was not obtained in Cuba but imported previously from the Yucatan Peninsula, an area with which Havana maintained an active commerce. Because of its low prices, the pigment obtained from this trunk became popular with European dyers, who used it to produce blue and black tones.[12]

Dyes were so valuable that authorities extended to indigo and cochineal the same level of protection that they gave to silver. When in 1600 the two fleets did not meet in Havana, the governor ordered that all the silver, cochineal, and indigo cargoes carried in the fleet of New Spain be deposited in Havana's fortresses until they could be moved safely to Spain. "They should not be ventured to the weakness of one fleet," he explained to the king.[13]

Another colonial commodity represented in Havana's exports, or reexports, to Seville is sarsaparilla, which was imported from Honduras. The roots of this plant were used to make infusions that were thought to have powerful curative effects. Sarsaparilla was used to treat a wide range of diseases, including "Gallic" or "French disease" (syphilis), tuberculosis, joint pains, and what, following the humoral pathology of the time, were described as malignant humors in the stomach and other parts of the body.[14]

It is much more difficult to establish the proportion that other intercolonial imports represented in city exports to Spain. For instance, foodstuffs, which accounted for about 3 percent of Havana's transoceanic exports, included both locally produced goods such as sugar and meat and colonial products such as biscuits and flour, which the city imported mainly from Mexico. The same is true concerning hardwoods. Havana exported small quantities of hardwoods, par-

ticularly ebony and mahogany, that either were produced locally or came from
producers in central and eastern Cuba.

Some export commodities, however, were clearly *products of the land* or *products
of the land's harvest*, as they were designated at the time. In addition to sugar and
woods, Havana exported to Spain significant quantities of ginger, which was
used as a spice and as a stomach medicine. It was by far the largest item under
the rubric of spices and condiments. Cuban exports of ginger to Spain were second only to those from La Española (Hispaniola). The same was true concerning
cañafístula, or cassia fistula, which was exported to Seville from both Cuba and La
Española. The dark and sweet pulp of this fruit was widely used as a laxative and
to "purge humors" of various kinds. Its medicinal virtues were so well known
that the author of a sixteenth-century pharmacopoeia deemed it useless to discuss its applications in any detail. "There isn't anyone who has not heard of this
medicine," he claimed.[15]

Small quantities of locally grown tobacco leaves also began to appear among
Havana's export products in the early 1600s. Although the consumption of tobacco was seen initially as a lowly and vulgar habit, "a thing of slaves and tavern
drinkers and people of little consideration," the seamen and passengers who
moved constantly across the Atlantic brought tobacco leaves and ground tobacco
to Europe, where demand was on the rise. As early as 1592 English sources referred to Cuban tobacco as "excellent." Besides, consumption was justified in
medical terms, for the plant was believed to have curative properties, its smoke
used to mitigate tiredness and pain. It should not be used in excess, physicians
argued, because its abuse may cause harm to the liver.[16]

Hides were the main export product of the land, in terms of both volume
and value. After 1580 the island typically exported between twenty thousand and
forty thousand legal units every year. "They keep a great number of oxen, more
to have the hides than the flesh," reported Samuel de Champlain, who visited
Havana in 1602.[17] In the period 1560–1620, Cuba was one of the leading suppliers
of hides to the Spanish market, second only to New Spain and followed by La Española and Honduras. In the early years of the seventeenth century, La Española
began to displace Cuba as the leading (legal) exporter of hides in the Caribbean.
The structure of each island's exports was rapidly evolving. In La Española the
expansion of the ranch economy was taking place at the same time that sugar
production was collapsing. In Cuba the opposite was true. The proportion of
sugar among its exports grew gradually in the 1600s, although hides continued
to be the leading export product of the island.[18]

Hides were a colonial commodity for which there was significant demand in Europe. Prices in Seville grew by 30 percent between 1580 and 1595, and hides were one of the most eagerly sought products by the French, English, and Dutch smugglers who traversed the waters of the Caribbean. Along with textile production, the leather industry represented a major economic activity in many urban centers of Europe. In Venice alone there were seven guilds related to the leather industry in the late sixteenth century.[19] In Spain leather making had developed under Muslim influence, expanding significantly during the sixteenth century. Some of the goods produced by Spanish leather artisans enjoyed a great reputation in European markets. "Anything Spanish was in fashion," reports Braudel. Among these items were gloves, shoes, and saddles. *Guadamecíes* or *guadameciles*, engraved and gilded leathers used for ornamental purposes, were reportedly "the most prized products of the industry."[20]

Ships of various kinds and sizes figured prominently among Havana's transatlantic exports as well. It is difficult to establish how many of the fifty-one ships that were sold in the city between 1579 and 1610 and taken to Seville or the Canary Islands had been produced domestically. Boats and small rowing vessels had been produced on the island probably since the 1520s, and there is concrete evidence of shipbuilding activity in Havana since at least the 1550s. Moreover, as we shall see later, shipbuilding in Havana increased significantly during the late 1500s. But the port town was also, for obvious reasons, an ideal place to trade vessels that had been built elsewhere, including in various European shipyards. In many cases owners sold a portion of the ship to finance trading, to pay for repairs and other expenses, or just to spread the risks associated with navigation. In Havana they found traders, local or transient, as well as fleet passengers willing to invest in the risky but potentially profitable shipping business. They also found workers, sailors who temporarily resided in Havana before signing on for a voyage. Masters and captains could find a good supply of men of the sea in Havana, from young apprentices and sailors to experienced pilots, caulkers, and ship carpenters. Although some of these seamen had become sailors to escape poverty in Europe, it seems that most of those in Havana wanted to sign on for work aboard a ship returning to Spain. The most common transaction in the local records involved payments to sailors coming from other colonial territories and labor contracts to serve in a fleet vessel going to Europe. Just as Havana reexported colonial commodities, it also served as a regional labor market for sailors waiting to sign on with the returning fleets. These sailors had come to the city on one of the many vessels traveling the intercolonial routes and used Havana as a transit station to find new employment. These labor contracts were significant enough to be included as a separate category in table 2.3. When payments were made for services rendered in ships coming to Havana, they were quantified as "imports." Conversely, advance payments made to seamen sailing out of Havana were quantified as "exports."

The city imported a much larger variety of goods from Spain and the Canary Islands than it exported. In contrast to the colonies as a whole, Havana's largest transatlantic import, in terms of both volume and value, was wine.[21] The city's large demand was of course related to its maritime and service functions. Wine was imported not only to cover the consumption needs of residents and visitors but also to provision the fleets and other colonial territories. About 20 percent of the imported wine was reexported later. One-fifth of these reexports went back into the transatlantic circuit, to serve the demands of fleet passengers and crews. The rest was redistributed through the sea routes of the Caribbean.

Daily consumption of wine, which was a major staple of the Spanish and Mediterranean diet, could reach fairly high levels. Wine was an inexpensive source of calories and a valuable stimulant for workers who had to perform hard labor, particularly in hot climates like the tropics. A sixteenth-century naval specialist considered it to be, along with bread, a major ingredient in the diet of sailors, who in his estimation should get about one and a half liters of wine daily. The crew of a 1568 armada received one liter per day, and historian Carla Rahn Phillips has estimated that wine provided about one-fourth of the total calorie intake for sailors in Spanish war ships in the early seventeenth century. The difficulties involved in preserving water for long periods, combined with the generous use of salt and spices in foods, stimulated wine consumption. Average consumption in southern Spain at the time may have been even higher than the figures mentioned above.[22]

Most of the wine consumed in Havana came from the Canary Islands, rather than from the peninsula. Thanks to a special tax imposed on this product, we have reasonably accurate figures about the volume and origin of wine imports in Havana. Between 1590 and 1608, according to fiscal sources, 11,699 *pipas* (pipes) of wine entered Havana legally. Out of this total 1,728 (15 percent) came from Seville, the rest from the Canary Islands, particularly from Tenerife (5,203 pipes) and La Palma (4,714), with Gran Canaria providing a negligible amount of the total.[23]

Conquered by the Spanish in the previous century, the Canary Islands by the mid-1500s had become renowned for the quality of their wines, which were consumed all over western Europe and were particularly appreciated in England. "They make wine better than any in Spain," an Englishman asserted in 1564; "des meilleures d'Europe," French geographer Duval d'Abbeville concurred.[24] The *vino de islas* (wine of islands), as it was known in the Spanish Atlantic, posed

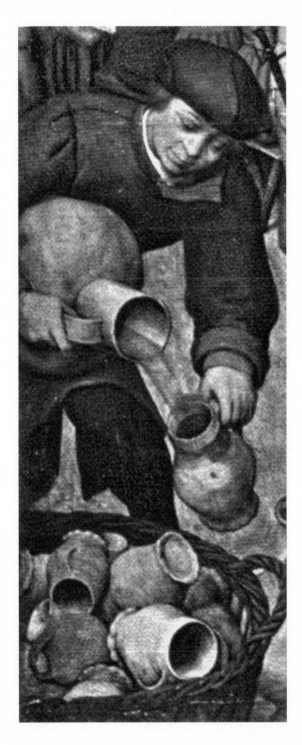

Wine consumption
in sixteenth-century
Europe. Pieter Bruegel,
The Wedding Banquet
(ca. 1568), detail.

serious competition to wineries in Andalusia and elsewhere on the peninsula. In an effort to curb this competition, the merchants of Seville repeatedly requested the crown to prohibit the so-called *navíos sueltos*, independent ships that sailed from the Canaries to the Americas outside the fleets.[25]

The complaints of Seville's merchants were not groundless. Controls over merchandise and people were considerably laxer in the Canaries than on the margins of Spain's Guadalquivir River, and the islands were a notorious trading link between northern Europe and the New World. As always with contraband, the evidence of this traffic is all anecdotal, but the persistent rumors and denunciations undoubtedly contained more than a kernel of truth. In 1608, for instance, the king inquired whether it was true that every year between fifteen and twenty ships from the Canaries called on Havana "loaded with wines, linen, and other merchandise of contraband bought from Flemish and other foreigners" and worth from 100,000 to 150,000 ducados (1.1 million to 1.65 million reales). Local authorities, of course, denied the charges, although they admitted that they had heard "rumors" about large numbers of "Flemish hulks" coming to Havana and its environs in the past. The rumors were not without foundation. In 1595 royal authorities reported that several vessels from the Canaries were stationed illegally in Matanzas Bay, an excellent and isolated port east of Havana that was frequently used to conduct illegal exchanges.[26]

Another way to circumvent legal limits and prohibitions was to falsify cargo registries. The ship *Nuestra Señora de la Candelaria*, which arrived in Havana from La Palma in March 1606 as a courier, illustrates this form of contraband. Courier ships were used to dispatch urgent news and messages across the Atlantic. They represented a vital link in the imperial system of communications and trade, for it was through these couriers that merchants on both sides of the Atlantic learned about market conditions and the composition and movement of the fleets. In the case of the *Nuestra Señora de la Candelaria*, it had been dispatched by the town council of La Palma to alert authorities in Havana about a Dutch armada that was to sail to the New World. These ships were allowed to carry twenty-five pipes of wine to offset expenses. According to a customs official in Havana, however, the ship arrived with 135 pipes of wine, in addition to thirty boxes of tar, plus several barrels of biscuit, cheese, and almonds. The problem, this royal official declared, was that the *regidores* of La Palma, who were supposed to protect the interests of the crown, were the actual owners of the cargo and had correspondence with several merchants in Havana.[27]

Wine came also from the peninsula, although its relative importance in Seville's total exports to Havana was much lower than it was among products from the Canary Islands, whose exports showed a marked concentration on wine

(76 percent, to be precise). Wine topped Seville's exports in terms of tonnage but was a distant second to fabrics and other textiles in terms of value. A few pieces of cloth could easily surpass the value of a ton of wine. Most of the wine imported into Havana from Seville as "wine of Castile" seems to have been produced in Andalusia, particularly in the famous vineyards of Jerez de la Frontera, which in the 1560s produced sixty thousand pipes of wine annually, some of which was exported to the English and Flemish markets. Wines from Cazalla, also in Andalusia, are mentioned in the documents, but in a lower proportion.[28]

Unlike wines, which were all produced in Spanish territories, fabrics and textiles in general illustrate, better than any other product, the importance of European producers in provisioning colonial markets. These textiles came from all major manufacturing centers in Europe, from France and the Low Countries to England and Italy. The production of fabrics was the most important industrial activity in Europe at the time, employing the largest number of workers outside agriculture. In the sixteenth century the opening of New World markets represented a significant stimulus to cloth producers, who had been competing in restricted European markets, characterized by low income levels and the relative autarky of peasant families.[29]

A surprising variety of cloths were imported into Havana between 1579 and 1610: 182 different types are mentioned in the notarial records. Yet a few fabrics took the lion's share of the market. The *ruanes*, the popular linens exported through France's leading Atlantic port of Rouen, headed the list. Owing to a combination of factors, the trade in these linens expanded significantly in the last quarter of the sixteenth century. Production expanded by tapping into cheaper labor in the rural hinterland of Rouen and grew in tandem with the difficulties of Flanders and Brabant, where linen production declined temporarily after the revolt of the Netherlands. This conflict also contributed to the prosperity of Rouen's linen trade in another way: it forced numerous Spanish merchants out of Antwerp, the great European entrepôt of the early sixteenth century. Many of the displaced merchants resettled in Rouen, contributing to the organization of the city's trade with Spain and, most important, its colonies. The New World, in turn, generated significant demand for Rouen's light linens. Colonial markets became so important to the city that according to a scholar "Rouen's economy became intimately tied to the rhythms of the carrera de Indias." Rouen's city council acknowledged the importance of these links: "Linen fabrics are the true gold and silver mines of this realm because they are shipped to the lands from which gold and silver are brought to us."[30]

From Normandy and neighboring Brittany also came large amounts of cheap, popular linen cloths such as generic canvas or lighter canvases such as *vitres*

(vitry canvas) and *brins*. A durable cloth, canvas was widely used for sails and
clothing. Although similar cloths were produced elsewhere in Europe, including
England and the Low Countries, most of the canvas imported into Spain and its
colonies seems to have been produced in northern France. Indeed, Spain grew
dependent enough on the supply of French sailcloth for a seventeenth-century
French author to exclaim: "They may have the ships, but we have their wings."
Small quantities of the higher-quality linen cloths of the region, such as the
bretañas or "brittanies" and the *batistas* or *baptistes* from Cambrai were also sold
in Havana.[31]

Contrary to what some historians believe, however, the bulk of French cloths
imported into Havana were intended for the lower and medium segments of the
market.[32] Higher-quality, pricier linen cloths came from the Low Countries, particularly Holland, which specialized in the production of linens for the Spanish
and Portuguese markets. "In the land of Holland," geographer Martín Fernández de Enciso asserted in the early 1500s, "they make the best and finest linens in
all of Europe, which are called holanda after the name of the land." Most of the
fabrics sold in Havana as *holandas* were probably produced in Haarlem, where
Flemish migrant artisans established their linen industry. Yet Haarlem was also
the center of the Dutch bleaching industry, and it is likely that some of the
fabrics finished in Haarlem and other Dutch textile cities had been produced
elsewhere, from northern France to Silesia. Like other European fabrics, a piece
of linen sold in Havana as holanda was in fact an international commodity with
inputs as varied as Baltic hemp or flax; German, French, or Dutch labor; and
coloring agents from the New World or India, not to mention transportation to
southern Spain and the Americas.[33]

It is more difficult to establish the origin of some of the other fabrics listed in
Havana. Among these were the "nouvelle draperies" or "new draperies," which
were produced in several places in sixteenth-century Europe. Cheaper, coarser,
and lighter than the old fine, thick woolens, these fabrics were represented in
Havana by the *says* and, to a smaller degree, by the *bays* (or baize) as well. The English kerseys, which were quite successful in the European and Mediterranean
markets during the second half of the sixteenth century, made little headway
in Havana, where they appear only in small quantities. However, in order to circumvent trade obstacles, some English kerseys were either finished in Flanders
and France or sold in Spain as continental fabrics, and thus some additional
quantities may have reached Havana under different names.[34]

Following the diaspora of Flemish artisans, the says and bays sold in Havana
could have been produced in a number of European locations. Among these
places was, of course, Leiden, which with the help of artisans from southern

Flanders had become a leader of say production in continental Europe. Large amounts of says and bays were also produced in England, particularly in the Norfolk region, and exported to the continent. In the 1560s bay makers from Ypres migrated to Norwich and developed production there. Ypres, however, continued to be a significant producer of Flemish bays into the late sixteenth century, despite the decline of its well-known textile industry. The notarial records of Havana mention woolens identified specifically as made in Ypres, although others are referred to more generally as "from Flanders." It is likely that fabrics from all these locations entered the trade routes of the Atlantic and were sold in Havana and other colonial markets in the late sixteenth century and beyond.[35]

Spanish fabrics, represented by woolens, silks, and other fabrics, were among the most expensive in Havana. The production of woolens in Castile grew in the sixteenth century under the stimulus of colonial demand, but by the late 1500s foreign fabrics had captured the lion's share of the market. Some of the most important textile centers of Castile, such as Segovia, Toledo, and Cuenca, continued to produce high-quality woolen cloths, but production was in decline, a feature that many contemporaries and modern historians have ascribed to the competition of foreign fabrics. Spain was also a leading exporter of wool to France, Flanders, and Italy, so many of the woolens produced in those areas may have been made at least partially with Spanish raw wool.[36]

Spain was also a large producer of raw silk and of silk fabrics of various kinds, from silk cloths properly to silk-based fabrics such as taffetas, velvets, and damasks. Andalusia, Valencia, and other areas with a strong Muslim influence enjoyed a long and entrenched tradition of silk production that allowed them to respond to growing demand in the sixteenth century. The records of Havana contain references to silk fabrics from Granada – the leading producer in sixteenth-century Spain – as well as Seville, Toledo, and Valencia. Although Granada enjoyed a monopoly in silk exports to the colonies up to 1591, in practice fabrics from other Spanish locations found their way across the Atlantic. Notable among these were fabrics produced in Seville. The existence of a silk industry in the city has generated some debate among historians. On the one hand, scholars of Spanish textiles have always mentioned Seville as one of the centers of silk production on the peninsula. On the other hand, one of the best studies about the Spanish-American trade during the 1550–1600 period found no trace of Sevillian silk among exports to the colonies, thus concluding that no silk was produced in the city during this period.[37] The Havana records suggest that silk was in fact produced in Seville, although there is always the possibility that silk fabrics described as *seda de Sevilla* had been produced elsewhere. As with wool, Spain also exported raw silk to be processed in other textile centers in Europe. Chief among these were Lyon, where silk production expanded dramatically during the 1500s, and several cities in northern Italy.[38]

Silk fabrics were produced in other European locations, including London and Amsterdam, but the records of Havana make concrete reference to the silks of only another European producer, Italy, which is well represented with its taffetas. Still the acknowledged masters of the arts of weaving and dyeing exquisite silk fabrics and of producing silk-based clothes and garments, the Italians continued to reign in the luxury market. Although the Italian silk industry would decline later, in the sixteenth century it continued to flourish in Florence, Bologna, Genoa, Venice, Milan, and Naples. In Venice alone there were more than two thousand looms at the end of the sixteenth century. Milan enjoyed a reputation as a producer of gold threads and textured silks. Its silk artisans, reported an English visitor, were "esteemed so good that they are not inferior to any of the Christian world." Some five hundred workshops produced silk and gold cloth in the late 1500s in the city. In Genoa, three thousand silk weavers were active in 1608, when production had already begun to decline.[39]

As with many other European textiles, a piece of "Italian" silk sold in Havana was in many ways an international commodity, a prime example of how trade had begun to link producers and consumers from various parts of the globe. The Italian silk artisans utilized inputs from northern Africa, the Middle East, the Americas, and Asia. They used raw silks from Persia, Syria, Palestine, Greece, Albania and the Balkans, the Iberian Peninsula, and Italy itself. They colored their silks with top-quality dyes produced in the Mediterranean, the New World, and India. And since these artisans spread all over Europe, they took the secrets of their trade with them. Indeed, it is not unlikely that some of the silk entering Havana without a designated origin had been produced by Italian artisans in other European locations. It was migrating Italian artisans who in the fifteenth and early sixteenth centuries developed silk production in southern Spain, Brugge, and later Antwerp. Their descendants would later flee the troubled Flemish cities along with other textile artisans and contribute to the prosperity of new textile centers in England and Holland. They also retained a prominent role in the commercialization of silk. Well into the 1500s, Genoese and other Italian merchants continued to control the Mediterranean silk commerce, which included the trade in Ottoman and Spanish raw silks.[40]

The fiercest competition to the Spanish pricey silk fabrics in Havana did not come from other European producers, however. It came literally from the other side of the Atlantic. In the case of Havana this competition came from Mexico, in the form of silk fabrics produced in New Spain or of Chinese silks imported into Mexico on board the Manila galleons.

Sericulture and the production of silk began in New Spain as early as the 1520s, and it was probably Hernando Cortés who first introduced the silkworms into Mexico. There is concrete evidence that by 1531 silk fabrics were being produced in the colony and that by midcentury silk growing and production had expanded to Cuernavaca, Puebla de los Angeles, and Oaxaca. By 1543 there were more than forty active looms in Mexico City alone just for the production of velvets. Five years later silk weavers were granted royal authorization to set their own looms in Puebla, and from there production quickly moved to Oaxaca as well.[41] As Franciscan friar Toribio de Benavente Motolinía, who witnessed this growth, explained, it seemed as if New Spain was destined to grow "so much silk" that the region would be "one of the richest in the world and the principal place of the silk industry. . . . More silk will be grown in New Spain than in the entire Chrisian world."[42]

The friar's optimism proved exaggerated, as silk growing in New Spain declined significantly after the 1570s. According to Woodrow Borah, the output of raw silk in the Mixteca declined from 20,000 pounds per year in the 1580s to 1,500 pounds in 1605. Historians have debated the causes of this decline, but they agree that a major factor was the importation, after 1573, of large quantities of cheap Chinese raw silk and silk fabrics. By the late 1500s, weavers and other textile artisans in Mexico were producing satins, damasks, velvets, and other silk fabrics using Chinese raw materials.[43]

Along with other Asian commodities, Chinese silk fabrics enjoyed a reputation for quality. Having been fascinated by Asia and its riches since the Middle Ages, sixteenth-century Europeans identified Chinese products with exotic luxury.[44] Although the Portuguese Carreira da India had begun to break the isolation that had historically separated the Europeans from the Asians, "Oriental" commodities remained out of reach for all but a handful of wealthy consumers. The trade in Asian products expanded after the Portuguese reached China in the 1540s and established a permanent commercial presence in Macao in the 1550s, but it was in 1571, with the Spanish foundation of Manila and the creation of a stable Sino-Spanish commercial link, that Chinese and other Asian products became available in the New World. Financed by American silver and propelled by what seems to have been an inexhaustible demand for Asian spices, drugs, silk, and other luxury items, the trade in Chinese imports through Manila grew at an astonishing rate. Efforts by the crown to limit this traffic and to control the distribution of Chinese commodities within the New World were largely ineffective.[45]

On top of their excellent reputation, Chinese silk fabrics – particularly the damasks – enjoyed a clear competitive advantage in Havana, where they were traded at lower prices than those from Spain and Mexico. In fact, price disparities led contemporaries to explain the decline of the Spanish traditional silk industries of Granada and Toledo in terms of the Philippines trade and the importation of cheaper Chinese textiles.[46] In Mexico the effects were complex. Although the trade with Manila hurt Mexican sericulture, silk weavers in New Spain benefited from the growing supply of Asian silk threads. It is quite likely that some of the Mexican silk fabrics imported into Havana in the late sixteenth century had been made using Chinese raw materials.

Mexican textiles were also able to compete with Spanish quality woolen cloths. As a historian has put it, the woolen cloths produced in Mexico were protected by what may have been the most effective tariff of all: the "tariff of distance."[47] In Havana, the fine cloths from Segovia cost on average 44 reales per yard, almost double the price of similar Mexican fabrics. The prices of fine London woolen cloths, which enjoyed an impeccable reputation for their quality, were even higher than the prices of those made in Spain.[48] Wool cloths were produced in Mexico City and Puebla since at least the 1530s, and by the last quarter of the century production had grown considerably. In 1573 it was reported that the Mexican *obrajes*, manufacturing units that employed dozens of workers, produced 50,000 pieces of wool cloth per year, in addition to 20,000 pieces of says. In 1595 there were forty obrajes in Puebla de los Angeles alone, each with more than fifty workers on average. By 1604 colonial authorities estimated that there were more than one hundred obrajes in operation in New Spain as a whole devoted to the production of wool fabrics of various qualities and prices.[49]

New Spain was also a prime producer of cotton fabrics, many of which were imported into Havana during these years. Common among these were the *mantas de tributo* (tribute blankets or bedding cloths), pieces of cotton cloth woven by the indigenous communities to pay tributes. These mantas were the most important item in the tributary system of the Maya in Yucatán, a region that soon became known as the main center of production for these fabrics. "The main tribute and production of this land is cotton, and cotton fabrics," asserted a colonial official in 1552. In the markets of central Mexico, Guatemala, and Havana, these fabrics were sometimes sold as mantas or *paños* of Campeche, in reference to the port of embarkation. Demand for them seems to have been strong: in the 1560s Yucatán sent about sixty thousand mantas to colonial markets every year.[50]

In terms of prices the cotton mantas from Yucatán shared the very bottom of the market with a similar fabric that was described in Havana as coming from China. These cheap Asian cotton fabrics could have been produced in Ming China – where textile production experienced a significant growth in response to the silver-backed demand of the New World – but they also could have reached

Manila from the great cotton-producing areas of India (and, given their Asian origin, be described as from China). Large amounts of cheap Indian cotton fabrics were reaching Europe at the time through the Portuguese Carreira da India, and there is evidence that Indian textiles, spices, and other products reached Spanish America by the Manila galleon. To begin with, there are records of ships from India in the port of Manila in the early 1600s. Yet most Indian merchandise probably reached the Philippines not through direct trade but through the dense commercial network established by the Portuguese and by New Christian merchants in Asia, which covered an area from the Arabian Sea to the Pacific. Cotton fabrics and other products from India are well represented in the records of merchants living in Manila in the 1590s. Coming from as far as Gujarat, Cochin, and Goa, these goods reached Manila through Melaka – a major trading post with connections to ports in the Indian Ocean – and Macao, where an influential community of New Christian merchants was well established in the late sixteenth century.[51]

The same multiplicity of origins is observed when it comes to clothes and accessories. In many cases the contracts make no reference to the place of origin, probably a sign that such information bore no influence on the price and was not culturally meaningful to the people involved in the transaction. In other cases, the available information is ambiguous. It is difficult to establish, for instance, whether the "camisas de ruan" were shirts made in Rouen, or made with ruan linen, or both. The same is true concerning the shirts and neck garments of holanda, which could have been made in the Netherlands but also elsewhere with the valuable Holland linen. But there are many cases in which the items are described in terms that clearly refer to a place of origin, an indication that these nomenclatures were used to signify different levels of quality and desirability. There was a hierarchy of quality related to origin that was reflected in market prices. Italian stockings from Milan, for instance, were priced 18 percent higher than those made in Toledo and more than triple the price of those produced in Brussels or England. Likewise, hats produced in the textile centers of Castile commanded prices that were on average 10 percent higher than the price of those made in Lyon and more than double the price of hats coming out of the obrajes of Mexico City, although in this case lower transportation costs accounted for at least part of the difference.

Other textile products well represented in sixteenth-century Havana were narrow wares such as ribbons, galloons, trimmings, laces, and decorative accessories including cuffs, ruffs, buttons, and so on. At a time when the richness of clothing was a primary marker of social status, these accessories were central to establishing a person's social station.[52] Again, some producers and regions were identified with specific laces and accessories. From Saxony came the laces of "tedesco." Other laces were produced in Córdoba, Spain, and Brussels. Threads of various qualities were identified as made in Flanders, France, Italy, Portugal, and Spain (Seville and Jaén in Andalusia). The luxurious *passements* – decorative trimmings typically made of expensive materials – were produced in a handful of highly specialized textile centers. By far the largest quantity came from the city-states of Italy, whose reputation for the production of high-quality fabrics and accessories remained uncontested in the late sixteenth century. In making the costly Italian passements, only precious raw materials, such as silver and gold threads, silk, and velvets, were used.[53] Other producers included Seville, "Castile," and China.

Table 2.4 captures the hierarchy of fabrics traded in Havana during the late 1500s. At the top, of course, was silk, without question "the aristocrat" of textiles, as a scholar has stated.[54] Unlike the other fabrics, silks were not usually measured but weighed. They commanded such high prices that, along with precious drugs and spices, they were frequently sold in ounces. Scarce and pricey, silks represented only 1 percent of the total supply of fabrics (in terms of length), with prices that were fifteen times higher than those for fabrics at the bottom of the market. The social significance of this fabric was clear. As a sixteenth-century Italian author put it, "Gentlemen are the ones who wear silk."[55]

If silks were to be worn by gentlemen, commoners used cheap cotton fabrics such as mantas and *crea*, says, and coarse but durable canvases such as vitre and *cañamazo*. Canvas was frequently used to clothe slaves, although garments made with heavier fabrics such as sackcloth were also used for the winter months. These popular fabrics, with average prices under 6 reales per yard, represented about a third of the market in terms of volume but only half of that share when it comes to value. A sort of middle group of fabrics, represented above all by Rouen and other French linens, accounted for about 40 percent of the total fabrics market. These figures support the claim, made by historians of the Spanish Atlantic, that quality products dominated colonial supplies.[56]

The fabrics imported into Havana reflect as well the importance of seafaring in the life of the port town. Several of these fabrics, particularly the French canvases, were used to produce sails to supply local shipyards, transient vessels, and the fleets. Other fabrics, such as the vitre canvas and the much heavier *jergueta*, were used for packing and to protect cargoes.

Sailcloths were only a portion of the naval goods imported into Havana. Ships and naval supplies were, after wines and textiles, the most important items in the inventory of European imports. Ships were bought and sold in Havana to settle accounts, share risks before a voyage, and raise capital to pay for merchan-

Table 2.4. Fabrics Imported, 1578–1610: Quantity, Average Prices,
and Places of Origin

Fabric	Price (per Yard)	Number of Yards	Percentage of Total	
			Yards	Value
Seda (silk)	47.4	1,234	1	2
China	44.5	74		
Castile	46.7	146		
New Spain	52.5	161		
Paño (wool cloth)	22.1	2,431	1	5
England	46.3	99		
Castile	44.0	50		
New Spain	28.6	997		
Damasco (damask)	10.4	722	0	1
China	13.3	435		
Castile	59.5	110		
Holanda (Holland linen)	19.4	2,907	2	2
Tafetan (taffeta)	14.7	6,236	4	6
Castile	14.5	807		
Italy	16.0	337		
China	8.3	307		
New Spain	16.7	1,005		
Jergueta (sackcloth)	13.6	19,753	12	10
Bayeta (bay)	12.5	953	1	1
Ruan (linen, Normandy, France)	9.0	36,587	22	17
Brin (linen, canvas)	7.1	3,345	2	1
Humaina	7.2	2,552	2	1
Naval (sailcloth, canvas)	6.8	7,630	5	3
Crea (undyed cotton fabric)	5.9	8,232	5	6
Cañamazo (canvas)	5.4	11,680	7	4
Vitre (canvas, Brittany, France)	5.3	13,404	8	3
Sayal (say)	4.8	3,464	2	2
Manta (cotton blanket)	3.1	13,976	8	2
China	4.0	8,592		
Yucatán	3.1	372		

Source: ANC, PNH, ER, 1578–1610.

dise and repairs. Most of these ships, of course, did not stay in the city for long. In fact many (about a third) were not acquired by city residents but were transferred by transient merchants and masters among themselves.

The sale contracts tell us little about the origin of these vessels. Only occasionally do they mention the shipyard where they were built. When they do, it is to refer to the esteemed shipbuilding centers of the Cantabrian coast. These references are hardly surprising, as most vessels in the Spanish Atlantic during this period had been built in this region.[57] Among those traded in Havana were some of the most common ships in the waters of the Atlantic. Eighteen out of the 34 ships bought in Havana from Sevillian merchants and sea masters were *naos* or *navíos*. Naval historians have debated the precise meaning of these labels. According to Phillips, "navío" was used "as a general term for a large ship" with either merchant or military purposes. "Naos," in turn, were oceangoing vessels defined primarily as cargo carriers. The balance was made up of smaller ships – caravels, fragatas, and *pataches* – characterized by their speed and maneuverability. Despite their prominence in the transatlantic fleets of the late sixteenth century, no galleons are recorded in the notarial records of Havana as being ever sold in the city, although, as will be seen below, some were built there.[58]

Equally important to Havana's seafaring activities were the naval stores imported from Seville. In contrast to the Canary Islands, whose shipping supplies consisted largely of tar, those from Seville covered a multitude of items, from anchors, cables, cordage, chains, and nails to masts, tallow, pitch, tar, sails, and water pumps. Some of these supplies were produced in Spain. Cables and rigging were produced in Andalusia and Aragon. Nails, spikes, and other iron materials were produced in the foundries of Vizcaya. Masts were typically imported, but various types of ship timbers were produced along the northern coast of Spain. Yet most of these shipping materials had probably been produced in northern Europe and ferried to southern Spain in Baltic hulks. As the organization of the armada in 1588 made clear, Hanseatic supplies were crucial to Spanish shipping activities in the late 1500s. Most sails, in turn, were imported from northern France.[59]

Ironware and weapons followed in importance among transoceanic imports. The former included building materials such as nails, wire, iron bars, locks, keys, and pins. Also imported were tools and utensils of various kinds such as axes, scissors, hoes, machetes, cauldrons, and pots. Many of these goods came from the iron manufactures of Vizcaya and other towns in the Basque region, which had been designated by Philip II as the only area legally authorized to export iron products to the colonies. But as with many other products, there is a significant gap between reality and the monopolistic intentions of the crown, which was unable to prevent other European producers from participating in the Atlantic trade. From France came cutlery and scissors. Most of the steel exported to the New World had been produced in Milan. And some of the nails, locks, and cauldrons were of Flemish origin.[60]

The same was true concerning weapons. Spanish producers of arms, firearms, and ordnance also faced European competition. Italian high-quality knives and daggers competed with Toledan swords and knives. Iron-cast guns from Germany were sold along with those produced in the royal foundries in Málaga,

Seville, and Lisbon. At least some of the harquebuses sold in Havana had been produced in Holland. Of the muskets, some were referred to as German. Indeed, a Spanish author lamented his country's dependence on foreign producers for its military needs and the lack of specialized production centers like Milan, Brescia, Augsburg, Ulm, and Frankfurt.[61] Weapons imported from Seville also included pikes and half pikes, protective weaponry such as chain mails, and supplies such as powder.

A myriad of other manufactured items completed the cargoes of the Spanish ships that called to Havana every year. These items covered a wide spectrum of products, from personal items such as soap, to household wares and furniture, to cultural items such as books, paintings, religious images, and musical instruments. The town had to be supplied with virtually everything through long-distance trade.

Prominent among transatlantic imports were African slaves. Given the destruction of a native settler society, workers had to be imported. Most slaves were imported directly from Africa or through colonial distribution centers such as Cartagena de Indias, but some reached Havana from Seville as well. After wine and textiles, slaves represented the most valuable import item in Havana. This trade had its own peculiarities and routes and deserves separate consideration.

The Atlantic Slave Trade

The trade involving enslaved Africans was a well-established economic activity by the mid-sixteenth century. The Portuguese explorations of the African coast and the establishment of trading factories during the previous century had opened new exchange opportunities and trading routes on the continent. The production of tropical commodities such as sugar in the first Atlantic islands (São Tomé, Canary Islands, Madeira) had in turn created a growing demand for workers that African slave traders were quick to fill. Iberian exchanges with Africa had visible consequences. By the time the Spaniards reached the Americas, Seville and Lisbon had the largest enslaved populations in all of *western* Europe.[62]

The slave trade underwent important modifications in the 1500s, however. During most of the sixteenth century this trade was organized around the system of "licenses," special permits sold or granted by the crown to introduce a given number of slaves into the New World. The king granted free licenses to compensate for services rendered to the crown, as a charity to religious institutions, or to support public works of various kinds. Typically, however, they were sold. The price of these licenses spiraled during the century, from 2 ducados in 1510 to 30 ducados in the 1560s. By then, as several scholars have noted, the slave trade had become an important source of revenue for the royal treasury, which also collected export taxes on each slave.[63]

After 1595, the crown began to rent out the administration of the slave trade to a private merchant in what came to be known as the system of the *asientos*. The *asentista* paid an annual fee to the royal treasury and agreed to introduce a set number of slaves into the New World. For the crown, the system had two perceived advantages: predictability of royal income and control over the number of slaves transferred to the Americas. The asentista, in turn, obtained significant concessions as well, so vast that they undermined in practice the commercial monopoly of Seville. He monopolized the licenses required to transport slaves to the New World, which he could sell to third parties, and was authorized to sell the slaves at market prices in the colonies. The asentista could appoint factors and representatives in the colonial ports and in the African trading factories. He was authorized to ship slaves from Seville, Lisbon, the Canary Islands, or straight from the African coast. Slave ships could travel outside the fleets and could have either Spanish or Portuguese crews. No wonder the slave trade became a major route of contraband.[64]

The crown attempted to regulate not only the organization of the trade and the number of slaves entering the New World but also their "quality," which was linked to certain cultural traits. Throughout the sixteenth century the Spanish monarchs prohibited the importation of slaves deemed undesirable owing to religious or other cultural reasons. For instance, several royal cedulas (1526, 1531, and 1543) prohibited the introduction into the New World of the so-called *ladino* slaves. This term referred to slaves who had become familiar with Iberian cultures, particularly with the Portuguese or Castilian languages. According to these laws, any slave who had lived in Portugal or Spain for a whole year could be considered a ladino. Following the same logic, the entry of "mulato" slaves was also prohibited. The importation of ladinos and mulattoes was deemed counterproductive, for they were allegedly prone to revolt and the source of "other inconveniences."[65]

The crown thus favored the importation of *bozales* – African slaves who had not been exposed to European culture and who, authorities believed, would be easier to control as a result. But some bozales were also deemed undesirable for reasons similar to those mentioned above. Among these were the "white slaves," Berbers and "Moors" from northern Africa who might "publicize the sect of Mahomet" in the colonies. Following the same principle, the king forbade in 1550 the acquisition of slaves from the eastern Mediterranean, even if they were of "Guinea caste," under the suspicion that these slaves may have been influenced by Islam.[66] The other African slaves supposedly barred from entering the New World were those identified with the ethnonym Jolofo (Wolofs). These slaves from the Senegal Valley were described as "arrogant and disobedient" and charged with participating in several "revolts of blacks and deaths of Christians." The Spaniards knew the Wolofs firsthand, as some of them lived in sixteenth-century Iberia, and believed them to be at least partially Islamicized.[67]

As we shall see, however, these prohibitions were only partially effective. A limited number of ladino and "white" slaves came to the island from Seville and Lisbon as the personal servants of Spanish travelers and officials. Some of these slaves stayed in the city. As for the Wolofs, they were introduced into Havana along with many other slaves from the region described by geographers at the time as "Upper Guinea" (the region extending from the Senegal River to modern Liberia), one of the main slave-provisioning areas of the Portuguese in the late sixteenth century.

The system of asientos was beneficial to Havana's economy, as slave imports in the city grew significantly in the late sixteenth century. Cuban residents had frequently complained about the lack of workers on the island and petitioned the crown for authorization to introduce slaves from Africa.[68] Up to the 1590s, however, slave imports remained rather modest. According to the available evidence, the king assigned slave licenses to the island in 1551 (to introduce 300), 1566 (500), 1571 (300), 1579 (100), and 1590 (300).[69] These numbers amount to a total of only 1,500 licenses for the island as a whole in the 1550–90 period. Although other slaves entered Cuba during these years, legally and illegally, it seems clear that they did so in limited numbers.

Huguette and Pierre Chaunu list thirteen slave ships registered in Seville for Havana between 1580 and 1606.[70] These registries, however, are of limited value for studying the slave trade in the colonial world. Many ships changed their destination after making the declaration to authorities in Seville. In addition, it was common to exchange the registered ship for a larger one, so it becomes nearly impossible to determine the link between the original vessel and the ship actually sailing from Africa to America with a name, a captain, a master, and a tonnage that do not coincide with those filed with the royal authorities in Seville.

The Sevillian registries have another problem: they are of course useless when it comes to the vigorous intercolonial slave trade. Contrary to what some historians have claimed, this trade was of prime importance to the Spanish Antilles.[71] During the period of the Portuguese asientos (1595–1640), many slave merchants used Cartagena de Indias as a commercial entrepôt from which slaves were re-exported later to other colonial territories. The importance of these regional distribution centers increased further in the early 1600s, for in 1604 the crown ordered all slaves to be transported to Cartagena and Veracruz in a vain attempt to minimize fraud.[72] Yet these prohibitions also invigorated the contraband slave trade in the Caribbean, and thus Havana imported slaves from such improbable places as La Española, Puerto Rico, and Jamaica.

Despite their many problems, the tendency suggested by the Sevillian registries is correct. In the 1590s the number of slaves imported into Havana increased significantly when compared with the previous decades. The baptism records of adult slaves, which exist for the 1590–1600 years, give us a first indication of the possible number of imported slaves. These figures have to be considered with caution, however. Although it was customary to baptize incoming slaves, masters were not compelled to do so, and some contemporaries entertained doubts as to whether it was appropriate to baptize slaves who were "bozales and with no understanding" of the Christian doctrine.[73]

Between 1590 and 1600, 546 adult African slaves were baptized in Havana, a modest annual average of some 49 slaves.[74] We have found only one major shipment of slaves prior to 1596, when the first slaves of the Reinel asiento reached Havana. This ship entered Havana in 1591. Yet we know from other sources that small numbers of slaves were entering the city. As mentioned above, in 1590 the king granted a license to import three hundred slaves. In 1593 several Havana residents owed money to Hernando de Porras, who was in charge of the administration of slave licenses in Seville. Two years later Luis Lorenzo, a merchant from Tenerife and one of the most active slave traders in Havana during this period, paid 1,500 ducados to the city's royal treasury for sixty licenses that one of his associates had purchased in Seville.[75] Some slaves reached the city through the intercolonial slave trade as well.

Between 1596 and 1600 four slave ships from Africa arrived in Havana. A fifth one, the *Nuestra Señora de la Candelaria*, master Pablo de Monteverde, never made it to a safe port, as it was attacked in late 1596 by an "English pirate" and sunk at Cabo de San Antonio in western Cuba. According to the master, this ship had left Luanda with 175 slaves, 19 of whom had died during the trip. The crew managed to land with the remaining 156 slaves, but apparently many died or escaped, for the master claimed that only 76 had survived and some of them were very ill.[76] As for the four ships entering Havana, two – the *Santiago*, master Antonio Correa, and the *San Antonio*, master Gonzalo Prieto – were *de arribada*. This meant that the ships had been originally dispatched to another point but had called at Havana under alleged duress. By taking their cargoes to places where they were in demand, the illegal arribadas allowed merchants and shipmasters to respond promptly to market conditions in the colonial world.[77] The other two ships had been originally dispatched to Havana from Cape Verde and from "Guinea," a term that, as Philip Curtin explains, "has always been an unstable concept." In the late sixteenth century it was common to use this term to designate the region known to sixteenth-century geographers and slave traders as the "Rivers of Guinea" (the area between the Senegal River and Sierra Leone; modern-day Guinea Bissau) or (more rarely) the "Rivers of Cape Verde." Several descriptions referred to Guinea as a big "country" or "land" that began in Cape Verde and that in some cases extended to the Portuguese fort of São Jorge da Mina on the Gold Coast.[78] But geographers and slave traders also used the term "Guinea" more loosely to refer to the western coast of Africa. The captain of a ship loaded with slaves "of Angola nation" that entered Havana in 1600 described them as "just arrived from Guinea." This meaning persisted in geographic descriptions and accounts well into the eighteenth century.[79]

In all, these ships introduced about 854 slaves into Havana. During the same period (1596–1600) only 368 adult slaves were baptized in the city; therefore more than half of them did not receive (or perhaps refused to receive) the Christian sacrament. Assuming that this proportion remained constant during the previous years (1590–95), when 178 adult slaves were baptized in the Parroquial Mayor (Havana's only church at the time), then some 414 slaves were imported into Havana from Africa between 1590 and 1595. To these we must add another 49 slaves imported from Seville as the domestic servants or companions of immigrants and royal bureaucrats. Many of these slaves were proficient in the cultures of their Iberian host communities and were imported precisely because of their abilities. Despite legislation against the importation of ladinos, personal servants were typically exempted from such prohibitions, and a relatively large number of them came to the New World.[80]

Last, but certainly not least, slaves also came into Havana through the intercolonial slave trade. Tracing this movement is fraught with difficulties. Because no taxes were paid for the importation of these slaves, their existence is not noted in the abundant fiscal documentation. They typically arrived in small groups, not in large cargoes, and are therefore more difficult to spot in the records. And some came from territories where contraband was widely practiced (La Española, Jamaica), so there was a powerful incentive to camouflage the origin of the slaves as much as possible. Despite these problems, we have located about 150–200 slaves who entered the city in small cargoes, mostly from Cartagena de Indias, during the 1590s. To this one would need to add two or three dozen additional individual slaves brought to the city from other colonies by their masters and sold there.

In light of these figures, it seems reasonable to estimate that between 1,300 and 1,500 slaves entered Havana during the 1590s. As low as these numbers may seem, they represented a colossal jump for the town. This influx of African workers was not without consequences, as the proportion of blacks and slaves in the total population clearly increased abruptly. This influx created serious problems for local authorities, who suddenly faced the formidable task of policing a larger slave population (see chapter 6). Official slave entries seem to have declined in the first decade of the seventeenth century, but there are references to three slave ships calling to port in Havana from Africa. Furthermore, in the early 1600s contraband on the island became so widespread that it is plausible, even likely, that large numbers of slaves reached Havana illegally during these years.

Contraband was, of course, not new on the island, and, given their high prices, slaves had always been a preferred commodity for illegal transactions. Because of their strong presence along the African coast, Portuguese sailors and merchants probably enjoyed easier access to the sources of supply than did ships from other countries. The fact is that Portuguese traders figure prominently in court denunciations and judicial processes concerning contraband. In 1565, for instance, a Portuguese caravel illegally entered the Bay of Matanzas, to the east of Havana, with a slave cargo valued at 6,000 ducados. For Havana this was an enormous cargo, of 200 to 300 slaves. Local residents bartered at least some of these slaves for hides, but we do not know how many actually stayed on the island. Another Portuguese ship, the navío *Corpo Santo*, master Alfonso Gonzalez, from Lisbon, also reached Cuba illegally in 1585. According to the master, the ship had been dispatched for Brazil but had been "forced" to arrive in Cuba owing to the lack of water and propitious winds.[81]

Merchants and ships of other nations increased their participation in this lucrative trade by the late sixteenth century. In part, this increased participation was a function of their growing access to Africa, where French, English, and Dutch ships began to break the commercial monopoly of the Portuguese. But it was also an expression of the growing inability of the Spanish crown to insulate the Atlantic and to prevent its subjects from trading with enemies and outsiders. There is evidence that by the 1580s French merchants were introducing slaves illegally into the island, probably using Jamaica as an entrepôt. In 1584 a special judge charged seventeen individuals in Havana with buying around fifty slaves from the French. One of the accused, a native of the Canary Islands, was a permanent resident of Jamaica. This trade apparently grew, for years later the king inquired whether it was true that eight slave ships had illegally sailed to Cuba from Jamaica. By then, in addition to the French and the Portuguese, Dutch slaves ships were visiting the island regularly.[82]

These slaves came from the main export areas of Africa, which in the last

Table 2.5. Origin of Imported African Slaves,
Percentage Distribution, 1570s–1610

Origin	1570–94 (N = 448)	1595–1610 (N = 1,794)
Cape Verde, Senegambia, "Rivers of Guinea"	57	31
Gold Coast and Gulf of Guinea	2	3
Congo, Angola	40	65
Mozambique	1	1

Sources: Inventario mayorazgo de Antón Recio, 1570 and 1575, in ANC, PNH, Escribanía Galleti, 1774–75, fol. 134v; ANC, PNH, ER, 1578–1610; ASCH, Libro Barajas de Matrimonios de Españoles, 1584–1622; Libro Barajas de Bautismos, 1589–1600.

quarter of the sixteenth century already stretched from Senegal and Gambia in the north to Angola in the south. Following the work of previous scholars, and to facilitate comparisons, we have grouped slaves into four main areas according to the exporting region in Africa. The first region was Upper Guinea, which included the region known as the "Rivers of Guinea", where many slave shipments originated. A second area stretched from Ivory Coast on the west to modern Cameroon. In the old European geography of the African continent, this region went from the coasts of Malaguetta and Kwakwa to the Slave Coast and the Calabar rivers. A third area, south of modern Cameroon, was heavily influenced by the Bantu cultures. Included in this region were the kingdoms of Loango and Kongo, as well as the Portuguese colony of Angola, established in the 1570s. Finally, and in contrast to the previous three, the fourth region refers to the Mozambique coast, in southeast Africa. The Portuguese had established a military and commercial presence in this area, in coastal towns such as Sofala, Mozambique, and Kilwa, as early as 1506.[83]

Our figures question some of the estimates that scholars have made concerning the regional structure of the African slave trade. Up to the mid-1590s, Senegambia and the Rivers of Guinea were the leading suppliers of Havana's slave market (see table 2.5).[84] The Portuguese were well positioned in this region, thanks particularly to their colonial settlement in the Cape Verde Islands, which became a major slave entrepôt in the sixteenth century. Traders of Portuguese descent lived also along the coast with the approval of African rulers, and the Portuguese established a few fortified trading factories in the region, such as the factory at Cacheu. But in the late sixteenth century other European powers, particularly the French and the English, began to compete with the Portuguese for control of this region. The French managed to displace the Portuguese from the estuaries of the Senegal and Gambia rivers and confined them to the Cape

Verde Islands and to their bases in the area of the southern rivers. The islands of
Cape Verde, in turn, were themselves attacked by the English and the Dutch in
1578, 1585, and 1596.[85]

Thus after the mid-1590s, particularly after the establishment of the first
asiento with the Portuguese merchant Pedro Gomez Reinel, the supply of African slaves in Havana (and probably in all of Spanish America) moved south to
the region of Angola. This is not a coincidence. As Spanish historian Enriqueta
Vila Vilar has demonstrated, between 1593 and 1623 the asentistas had a personal
stake in the Angolan slave trade, over which they enjoyed monopoly rights. The
second asentista, Juan Rodriguez Coutino, was the governor of Angola, and the
contract was transferred to his brother Gonzalo Vaez Coutino after his death in
1603. Between 1595 and 1610 two-thirds of the slaves entering Havana from Africa
came from this region, which also included the kingdom of Kongo.[86]

Of much less importance was the second region, which includes the Gulf of
Guinea. Although the Portuguese had commercial establishments of import in
this area, such as the famed factory of São Jorge da Mina, founded in 1482, as well
as their colony in São Tomé, this region was well behind Angola or Upper Guinea
in terms of the supply of slaves. Part of the explanation has to do, again, with
European competition. As early as 1556 the Portuguese agent at Mina complained
about the ruinous competition posed by the French and the English, who offered
better and cheaper products to local tradesmen. By the late sixteenth century the
factory, which the Portuguese had founded mainly as a gold-trading post, had
decayed to the point that the crown could not find parties interested in renting
it. European sources at this time described it not as a commercially relevant
point but as a military stronghold whose main purpose was to keep the Portuguese trading routes open. A few decades later it was captured by the Dutch, who
turned it into a major slave-trading factory. The Dutch also attacked São Tomé
in 1600, disrupting the slave traffic in the area. By then, however, the island of
Luanda, which the Europeans claimed had the best port in all those lands, had
become the dominant slave entrepôt not only of Angola but also of Congo.[87]

The region of Mozambique did not escape these conflicts either. Determined
to reach the East and to participate in the profitable commerce of the Indian
Ocean, the English and the Dutch had begun to intrude into this area by the
late 1500s, and by 1607 a Dutch fleet set the town of Mozambique under siege.
This region was of limited importance to Havana's slave market, however. Only
a handful of slaves from this region reached the city, and it is possible that some
of them came to the Americas not via the Atlantic but rather by way of Manila.
This indirect route to Havana would explain the existence in the city of slaves

from the "Yndia of Portugal," a vague denomination that referred to the vast region between eastern Africa and the Spice Islands in the Far East.[88]

The slave trade made a singular contribution to the creation of the Atlantic port city of Havana. Through the slave trade the residents of Havana got closer to Africa and to the various peoples who lived on the continent. Slaves became a permanent presence in the life of the port city, a precondition and function of its growth, and a reminder that there was no Atlantic economy without Africa and its peoples. Slaves were also a major item of trade, not only within the transoceanic trade circuit but also in commercial relations between Havana and other colonial territories.

Intercolonial Trade

As mentioned earlier, Havana maintained an active trade with other territories in the Spanish circum-Caribbean region. In contrast to the transatlantic exchanges, dominated by exports, imports clearly predominated in Havana's commerce with other colonies. Both trade circuits were clearly complementary, for to a large extent intercolonial exchanges were organized either to serve the needs of Havana's service economy or to take advantage of the town's unusual role within the imperial system of trade. These intra-Caribbean relations must be seen as an integral part of the Atlantic economy, a regional network of distribution of commodities and cultural exchanges whose importance has not been fully realized to date. It is worth noting that in those colonial ports for which we have detailed shipping information, the number of ships coming from other colonies was invariably larger than that of ships coming from the other side of the Atlantic.[89]

The connections between these two commercial circuits are particularly evident when one considers the commodities exchanged in each of them. Havana's primary transatlantic export (bullion and specie) was its most important colonial import. In contrast, textiles and wine, the leading European products in Havana, figure prominently among its intercolonial exports (see table 2.3). These statistics corroborate the role of the port city as a regional commercial center that collected colonial products to be reexported to Europe and that, at least to some extent, distributed European goods within the Caribbean. When, for instance, a Sevillian merchant commissioned his partner in Havana, merchant Antonio Hernández Farías, to sell a cargo of wine there or in other "parts of the Indies, in the provinces of Campeche, Honduras, or New Spain," he was making use of Havana's central location to redistribute European goods in the circum-Caribbean region. Conversely, when Havana-based merchants Francisco de

Licona and Alonso Vivas established a partnership with a resident of La Yaguana, in La Española, to import colonial commodities from there, they were taking advantage of Havana's capacity to reexport colonial goods to Europe.[90]

Most of Havana's intercolonial exchanges can be explained in terms of the city's transoceanic connections, but some commodities were traded within the colonial world. Foodstuffs clearly fit this category. Food products were a major item in intercolonial trade, second only to bullion and specie among both imports and exports. The city imported food not only for its own consumption and to provision the fleets but also to supply weaker markets in the region. These exchanges, in turn, were financed with another colonial commodity: silver. The importance of bullion and specie in regional transactions clearly demonstrates that part of the silver stayed in the New World and served to finance various economic activities within the region. The settlements in the Spanish Caribbean reacted to their displacement from the official routes of commerce not only by turning to contraband, as many historians have noted, but also by establishing trade links with those areas that had direct access to the fleets. Along with Cartagena, Nombre de Dios–Portobelo, and Veracruz, Havana was one of those areas.[91]

In terms of value and naval movement, Mexico was by far the most important point in Havana's intercolonial exchanges. In fact, the trade with Mexico was second only to that with Seville. Within Mexico, however, it is possible to distinguish two different regions with which Havana maintained regular contacts. One had its financial center in Mexico City and was connected to the Caribbean via Veracruz and San Juan de Ulúa. The other region was the Yucatan Peninsula and its main ports of Sisal and Campeche.

Each region maintained an active trade with Havana, but the goods traded were different, and Veracruz's share of the total trade was much higher than Yucatan's. Bullion represented the main item of trade between Veracruz and Havana; Yucatan's leading exports were food products and the dyewood palo de campeche, a colonial commodity that was reexported to Europe. Most of Yucatan's products were locally produced, whereas merchandise from Veracruz included some European products, leftovers from its commercial fairs, and sizable amounts of Asian products imported from Manila. Among these were not just the silk and cotton fabrics discussed above but also spices, exotic drugs, and luxury goods such as fans. Prominent among these products were also some Ming blue and white porcelain wares. Chinese porcelains were much appreciated at the time, although those reaching Havana were mostly what a contemporary Chinese author described as "round wares," ordinary pieces made for popular consumption. Thousands of these inexpensive pieces reached the New World every year, frequently as ballast. The first two galleons that sailed from Manila to Acapulco in 1573 carried twenty-two thousand pieces of Ming porcelain.[92]

Despite differences in the composition of their export products, Veracruz and Yucatan shared a major role in supplying Havana with food. Veracruz's main food exports were wheat and corn flour, biscuits, chickpeas, lentils, cheese, and ham. Those of Yucatan included corn, corn flour, honey, and poultry. As previous historians have noted, Havana depended on Mexican imports to provision the fleets, feed the transient population that overtook the city when the fleets were in town, and supply frontier garrisons such as those in Florida. Food products were also imported from Jamaica, which supplied Havana with cassava bread, salted meat, biscuits, and corn flour. It is noteworthy that many of these products were basic staples in the typical diet of ship crews.[93]

In all, more than 90 percent of Havana's food imports (excluding oils and spices) came from other colonial territories. Some of these were reexported to other areas of the Caribbean, particularly Puerto Rico and, above all, Florida, a frontier territory in the Spanish imperial geography that was tightly linked to Havana institutionally, commercially, and militarily. Early on, Havana had served as a military base to spy on, harass, and ultimately prevent French attempts to settle on the peninsula. The institutional links between Havana and Florida were formalized in the 1560s, when Pedro Menéndez de Avilés, then *adelantado* (military chief) of Florida, was also appointed governor of Cuba. The reason for the dual appointment was explicit enough: "Florida has to be provided for with many necessary things from Cuba."[94]

Indeed, in the 1560s Havana became the provisioning base of the Florida garrisons. When in 1577 Baltasar del Castillo Ahedo, a vecino of Havana, made a "visit" to the Florida garrisons on commission by the king, the soldiers at St. Augustine asked him to return immediately to the town so that he could guarantee the prompt delivery of food and other supplies.[95] The crown repeatedly asked Cuban royal officials to supply the Florida garrison properly. As a result, and despite its small population – it was a military outpost of three hundred in the 1580s – Florida became a significant market for Havana, second only to Mexico in the colonial world.

As early as 1566–70 Havana exported merchandise to Florida worth half a million reales. The detailed reports of the royal officials provide good indications about the composition of this trade. Ninety-four percent of these supplies consisted of food, live animals, and wine, including more than 13,000 pounds of biscuits, 1,135 pounds of pork meat and beef, 200,000 pounds of salted beef, 98,400 pounds of cassava, 91 pipes of corn flour (72,800 pounds), and 89 pipes of wine. The cargoes also included salt, corn, honey, bacon, pumpkins, and oil.

Among the live animals were pigs, hens, horses, cows, and goats. The balance of Havana's exports included manufactured products such as textiles and shoes. The proportion of manufactured goods in the Havana-Florida trade increased with time, but food remained the leading export of the city in the 1579–1610 period. Together with oils and wine, food represented almost half of the supplies, followed by reexports such as weapons (21 percent) and textiles (7 percent).

Florida lacked local products of commercial value to exchange for these supplies, although the region began to export small amounts of sassafras toward the latter part of the sixteenth century. The bark and roots of sassafras, a tree of the laurel family, were valued for medicinal purposes. They were used to make infusions believed to cure "all sorts of diseases," from fever or lack of appetite to syphilis and rheum.[96] But the commercial importance of this commodity was still negligible. Florida did not pay for its supplies with local products or services but rather with the silver situado that, since 1570, the crown allocated to cover the expenses of its forts and garrisons. According to Paul Hoffman, the situado amounted to a yearly average of 302,000 reales in the 1560s. As mentioned above, between 1566 and 1570 Havana sent supplies to Florida worth some 500,000 reales, so about a third of the Florida situado was spent to purchase supplies in the port town. This proportion declined in later years, but in 1579–1610 about 20 percent of the Florida situado was still spent in Havana. Thus it should come as no surprise that silver made up 96 percent of the region's "exports" to Havana. In fact, in many cases the situado allocated for Florida never made it there but stayed in Havana, where it was used by the royal officials of St. Augustine to pay for goods and services previously acquired in the local market.[97]

Havana's exchanges with other colonies were highly concentrated on a few products. The important trade with Honduras was centered on añil that was later reexported to Seville in the fleets. The commerce with Cartagena de Indias and La Española was equally concentrated. Slaves represented between half and three-fourths of Havana imports from these two areas. Imports from Cartagena are easy to explain: the South American port city was the main slave entrepôt of the Americas at the time. Slave imports from Santo Domingo are harder to explain. On the one hand, by the late sixteenth century the northwest of the island had become a major center of illegal trade – so much so that the crown would soon order permanent "depopulation" of the area. Slaves certainly figured among the merchandise introduced by European illegal traders in the area. On the other hand, these slave exports to Havana could be also a function of the dissimilar rates of growth of the various economies in the region. Whereas La Española witnessed the development of the first slave-based sugar plantation economy in the New World, sugar production was in decline by the late sixteenth century, precisely at the time that it was being introduced in Cuba. La Española settlers turned increasingly to the cattle economy, which had minimal labor force requirements. Slave exports may thus have been a strategy to relocate the labor force to the most profitable areas within the Caribbean.

Insular Trade

The making of Havana into an Atlantic port city and a regional center of commerce had profound consequences for Cuba's long-term evolution. Increasingly, the history of Havana became distinguished from that of the island's "interior." Pierre Chaunu was correct in noting, years ago, that Cuba's history during the sixteenth century, initially centered around Santiago de Cuba and the island's southeast, became progressively identified with Havana and the northwest of the colony. Closer to Mexico and to the official sea lanes of the Spanish Atlantic, Havana became intimately linked to the empire and its resources. Excluded from the legal routes of exchange, the rest of the island prospered frequently in open defiance of Spanish colonialism. This is what the eminent Cuban historian and demographer Juan Pérez de la Riva referred to as Cuba A and Cuba B. Historians have given less attention, however, to the connections between these "two Cubas."[98]

Yet these connections were significant. Since the sixteenth century an active commerce developed between Havana and the settlements of central and eastern Cuba, which used the port city to participate in the legal transatlantic trade and as a market for their products. By far the most important export product reaching Havana from the "interior" was hides, which were at times used as currency in sixteenth-century Cuba. Small amounts of precious woods, particularly ebony, were also exported through Havana. The relative value of food supplies was much lower (only 3 percent of total Havana imports from the region), but their composition was peculiar. Live animals (pigs and cattle) represented the overwhelming majority of these supplies. Tallow, a critical input for the production of soap and candles, was also important. In return, Havana reexported to these villages and towns European and colonial products such as textiles, wines, foods (mostly Spanish olives, nuts, cheeses, and raisins), and a variety of manufactures, from ironware and shoes to books and candles (see table 2.3).

These exchanges varied by town, depending on the town's distance from Havana, the size of its population, and its local products. Towns closer to Havana, such as Remedios and Trinidad in central Cuba, supplied live animals that were transported through the "royal road" that traversed the island.[99] Initially known as La Sabana of Vasco Porcayo, or simply as La Sabana, Remedios was founded on the northern coast of central Cuba by prominent conquistador Vasco Porcayo de Figueroa. In 1544 it was described as a "sea port visited by many ships."[100] Remedios appears to have been a dependency of Havana's service economy and a transient point in the coastal trade of the island. Bishop Juan del Castillo, who visited the village in 1570, described Remedios as a place that "supplied Havana" and served as a refreshment station for the ships that sailed between Havana and Puerto Príncipe. The small size of the village, which in 1570 was reported to have only twenty vecinos, half of them indigenous people, clearly limited the volume of exchanges between Havana and Remedios. Some sixteenth-century descriptions do not even include La Sabana as one of the populated towns on the island.[101]

Like Remedios, Trinidad supplied Havana with animals and food and sent hides to be reexported to Europe in the fleets. The organization of this trade is illustrated by the activities of Juan Domínguez, master and owner of a ship, and by his partner, sailor Felipe Merelos, a Genoese who had stayed illegally in the New World after crossing the Atlantic. In 1565 Domínguez and Merelos took a cargo of fabrics, clothing, and knives to Trinidad, where they sold them "to the Indians and the Spanish in exchange for hides and reales." These they took back to Havana, where they probably used them to finance a new commercial venture.[102] As with Remedios, however, there was a clear limit on how many products the merchants of Havana could sell or even barter in a place like Trinidad. Founded on the southern coast, the town suffered a demographic collapse after the conquests of Mexico and Peru, to the point that authorities considered fusing the town with neighboring Sancti Spíritus. In the second half of the sixteenth century Trinidad was described as an "Indian" settlement depopulated by the Spaniards. Cosmographer Juan López de Velasco asserted in 1570 that the town existed only nominally, although some fifty indigenous families resided in it. In the early seventeenth century Trinidad began to recover demographically and became a relatively important center of contraband.[103]

Sancti Spíritus better endured the demographic exodus provoked by the expeditions of conquest. Mining in the area survived until the mid-sixteenth century, and it is likely that the remaining European settlers of Trinidad moved to Sancti Spíritus in the 1530s. "It is a good land, healthy, and with many metals," reported the bishop in 1570. Havana's trade with this town was larger than that with the other villages of central Cuba, perhaps a function of a larger (although still very small in absolute terms) population of European descent. Sancti Spíritus's main commodity of trade with Havana was hides, which represented, excluding bullion and money, about half of the town's exports.[104]

The two towns of Puerto Príncipe and Bayamo accounted for about 70 percent of Havana's insular trade. This is not surprising, as Bayamo and Puerto Príncipe were the largest settlements on the island besides Havana: the only other towns of "consideration" in the colony, in the words of a contemporary. Whereas the villages of central Cuba barely had a combined population of 100 vecinos in 1608, more than 300 vecinos lived in Puerto Príncipe and Bayamo. Puerto Príncipe was described as "a place of rich people" with many *hatos* (cattle ranches). These ranches produced the hides and tallow that were exported to Havana. Bayamo was frequently referred to as "the best town" on the island. In the 1570s it was Cuba's largest settlement, larger even than Havana. During this period, many religious and secular authorities spent large periods of time in the town, a clear indication of its importance. As with Puerto Príncipe, Bayamo's prosperity was based on ranching, but the town also benefited from a particularly favorable location. Established in a fertile valley by the Cauto River, the town had access to the sea, thus facilitating commerce, yet it was removed far enough from the coast so as to be protected from hostile outsiders.[105]

This location allowed Bayamo to participate in what seems to have been a very active illegal commerce in the late sixteenth and early seventeenth centuries, a feature shared by Puerto Príncipe as well. Contemporary observers invariably agreed that Bayamo and Puerto Príncipe were the most important and active centers of smuggling on the island. When in 1606 a judge appointed by the Audiencia of Santo Domingo produced a list of 171 culprits engaged in contraband, 75 percent of them were vecinos of Bayamo and Puerto Príncipe. According to the governor, several large hulks from Flanders, Holland, France, and "other enemy nations" visited Bayamo and Puerto Príncipe each year loaded with silks, linen fabrics, wines, and slaves.[106] Although the residents of these towns obtained direct access to European products through these illegal exchanges, contraband was obviously unable to cover all their commercial needs. Otherwise it would be difficult to explain their active trade with Havana, which they used precisely to place some of their local products in the transatlantic trade circuit. Nor would it be easy to account for the exports of Havana to the region, in which European products, undoubtedly more expensive than those that could be obtained through contraband, figured prominently.

The very causes of Bayamo's economic and demographic growth would ultimately undermine its prosperity, however. In response to the illegal trade practiced in eastern Cuba, the crown created a second governorship on the island in 1607, based in Santiago de Cuba, the old capital of the colony. Although Santiago had lost most of its once large population and had been eclipsed by Bayamo as the regional center of trade, its designation as the seat of the eastern governor-

ship channeled some royal resources to the area. In the early 1600s the city began
to recover economically and demographically, eventually displacing Bayamo as
the main urban center of eastern Cuba.

But up to 1610 the city remained well behind Bayamo demographically and
economically. From the 1550s on Santiago was consistently described by visitors
as a "poor and miserable" land, barely a "village" (*aldea*) in the opinion of many
observers.[107] Its small population probably accounts for its limited exchanges
with Havana. Only 2 percent of Havana's insular imports came from Santiago,
which channeled most of its trade through Cartagena de Indias.[108] The only
other Cuban town with which Havana maintained a similarly low level of commerce was Baracoa, the easternmost and smallest of all Cuban towns. In contrast
to Santiago, whose evolution becomes at times indistinguishable from that of
Bayamo, Baracoa seems to have existed in almost total isolation from the other
Cuban towns. It faced Santo Domingo, and most of its economic life and trade
revolved around the northwest of La Española, at the time a major center of
contraband in the Caribbean. It is worth noting that the crown considered de-
populating Baracoa in order to prevent contraband in the area. Baracoa produced
significant amounts of ebony and other precious woods, some of which were
reexported to Spain via Havana.[109]

The making of Havana as a shipping, commercial, and military center of the
Spanish Atlantic had a profound impact on the rest of the island. Although most
of the towns of central and eastern Cuba benefited to some degree from Havana's
direct access to the Atlantic, depending on their location and the size of their
markets, such access was not without a price. The merchants and residents of
Havana were in a privileged position when dealing with the producers and consumers of *tierra adentro*, as the settlements in the Cuban "interior" were referred
to. Local products such as hides were frequently bartered for European products,
with Havana merchants making a profit on both. It is precisely during the period
covered here that Havana began to distinguish itself, economically and demographically, from the rest of the island. Havana prospered thanks to its intimate
maritime and commercial links to the empire. The towns of the Cuban interior
survived despite the commercial limitations of Spanish mercantilism. Havana
became the center not just of the island but also of peripheral colonial areas such
as Florida. This process had enormous consequences for the port city and its inhabitants, whose lives and livelihood depended on the port and its movement.

CHAPTER THREE

The Fleets and
the Service Economy

Although many of the ships and convoys returning to Seville from Mexico and Tierra Firme since the 1530s and 1540s used Havana as a stopover, it was with the organization of the fleet system in the 1560s that the port town was permanently identified as the only point in the Americas where both fleets would gather before crossing the Atlantic. As a political act designed to fulfill the needs of the crown of Castile, the organization of the Carrera de Indias had little to do with the residents of Havana. Rather, it reflected the monopolistic dreams of the crown and its growing dependency on the resources of the New World, which financed Emperor Charles's costly policies in Europe. Yet this policy (or, more accurate, policies) had profound consequences for Havana, at the time a very minor coastal settlement in a relatively remote corner of the Atlantic. The royal cédulas regulating the system were signed by the king in Valladolid, Madrid, or El Pardo in the 1560s, 1570s, and 1580s, but their effects were felt on the other side of the "Ocean Sea."[1]

These effects covered a wide range of economic and social activities and were not always predictable. In addition to the shipping and trading movements described in the previous chapter, the fleets stimulated various economic activities, gave local life a distinct seasonal flavor, and contributed significantly to the shaping of Havana's urban landscape. This chapter studies the fleets' most immediate effect: the creation of a service economy to provision the ships and their crews and passengers. Prominent among these services was protection. In order to safeguard the flow of silver and other precious commodities, the crown invested heavily in the defense of the town and assigned a permanent garrison to protect it. In turn, the ships, particularly those riding the Gulf Stream to sail across the Atlantic, required last-minute repairs, provisions, and sailors. While in town, the crews and passengers needed lodging, food, entertainment, and other services. Some employed notaries to organize their earthly affairs before sailing through an ocean populated by unknown beasts and by well-known pirates, all of them enemies of His Catholic Majesty. Their wills listed family members, loved ones, and dependents. They hastened to include last-minute efforts to gain heaven through generous donations to the church, by giving freedom to a slave, or through other pious acts.

For the residents of Havana, the dozens of ships that came through town each year represented many opportunities to conduct business transactions; learn about market conditions in other colonies, the African coast, or Europe; or renew social and family links with distant acquaintances and relatives. The delay of the fleets augured particularly good years, for they were forced to stay in town until the worst of the winter was over, thus extending the shipping season artificially. By August the fleets were supposed to be sailing through the Bahamas channel, but a 1573 regulation prescribed that if the fleets were unable to leave Havana before October, they should "winter" there until the worst of the season was over.[2]

It seems clear that the residents of the little seashore enclave understood early on that their lives – and more to the point, their livelihoods – would depend on the bay and its traffic. In 1559, when they still lacked the resources, financial and human, to service the fleets and their people, the residents of Havana sought to obtain immediate financial gains from the port by charging an anchorage tax to every ship, according to its tonnage. Although approved by the crown, this tax was collected for only a few years, until 1562. By then even the residents of Havana were opposed to it. They had come to realize that, rather than extracting taxes from the incoming vessels, they were better off attracting as many ships as possible and developing the capacities to service them. As usual, the crown was supportive and eliminated the tax as requested.[3]

More important in the long term, however, was the elimination in 1581 of one of the few surviving loopholes in the fleet system. Until then, La Española had maintained the right to dispatch independent ships to Seville, thus competing with Havana as a regional center of trade and communications with Spain. After 1581, however, the ships from Santo Domingo would have to join the returning convoys in Havana. Fleet admirals were ordered to take them under their protection.[4] With just a few exceptions, all the return maritime movement was now concentrated in Havana.

The Local Market

The large number of vessels that, thanks to the Carrera, began to come regularly through Havana since the mid-sixteenth century generated a significant demand for provisions of various sorts. The 1573 instructions to the admirals of the fleets were explicit in this respect: "Having arrived to Havana, take on water, firewood, and meat . . . and supply all ships properly, so that they do not suffer shortages during the trip."[5]

Among these supplies, foodstuffs represented one of the most important items, for ships had to complete their food provisions in town, and passengers and crews had to be fed during their stay, which could be lengthy. Since, at least through the 1590s, the population of Havana was not large enough to produce the necessary food supplies, they had to be bought from producers in other Cuban towns or imported from other colonial territories. As mentioned above, food products were the largest intercolonial import in Havana, after bullion and specie. As for the island, live animals figured prominently among the goods brought to the city from other Cuban settlements, particularly those closer to Havana.

For the growing population of Havana, the production of food supplies represented one of the main economic activities. This was true during the whole period studied here but was particularly the case during the early decades of the Carrera, when Havana was a small town that did not offer many economic alternatives. The importance of this activity for the local economy is recognized in numerous testimonies prior to the 1580s. "The vecinos of this town have no other gain but what they make when the ships are in this port," the cabildo's (town council) petitioner asserted in 1562. "They raise a large number of pigs whose meat, cut in little pieces and dried under the sun, is used to provision the ships that go to Spain," reported Englishman John Chilton in 1571. Speaking of the need to enlarge the slave population of Havana in 1572, the University of Seafarers of Seville justified it in terms of the production of food supplies for the ships coming through Havana.[6]

The fleets easily outstripped Havana's production capacity and, particularly during the early decades of the Carrera de Indias, created frequent crises of supply. In 1556 the admiral of a fleet asserted that, although it was winter, "necessity had forced him to depart from Havana because it was not possible to find supplies to sustain so many people." The situation improved in later years, but periodic crises could still occur, particularly in those years in which the fleets wintered at Havana. In one of those years, the governor informed the crown that "there was some need for food" despite local efforts to meet the demand: "The

Table 3.1. Issues Discussed by the *Cabildo*, Percentage Distribution, 1550–1610

Issue	1550–70 (N = 422)	1571–90 (N = 440)	1591–1610 (N = 915)
Provisioning, local market	27	22	16
Fleets and trade	4	2	1
Cabildo's activities	4	4	2
Trades, occupations	10	7	18
Urbanization	9	12	19
Aqueduct	3	5	8
Festivities, celebrations	3	3	7
Defense	12	5	2
Slavery	9	2	5
Local taxes	2	7	5
Justice	1	3	10
Other	19	28	7

Source: ACAH, 1550–1610.

people of the land do their best for their own benefit," he reported, but this level of food production still was not enough.[7] "Neither corn nor wine grows on the said island; that which is consumed comes from New Spain, so that sometimes they are very dear," visitor Samuel de Champlain reported, somehow inaccurately, in 1602.[8]

Supplying the local market and the transient fleets with basic staples, such as meat, cassava, and "bread" (either "cassava bread" or wheat bread), became one of the central concerns of Havana's cabildo. During the early decades of the Carrera, between 1550 and 1570, about a third of all the issues discussed and regulated by the town council were related to provisioning the local market and the fleets (see table 3.1). This proportion declined during the following decades but was still very significant in the early seventeenth century, when Havana was a much larger city and was better prepared to meet the provision requirements of the fleets.

The challenges that this growing maritime movement posed to local authorities may have been new, but they responded by adopting procedures and solutions imported from the urban cultures of the Mediterranean. Typically, these regulations dealt with two related problems: guaranteeing a proper level of supplies, and doing so at *just* prices. For instance, when in 1554 authorities were waiting for the arrival of both fleets, they sought to prevent the "scarcity of meat" by contracting the provisioning of the butchery with two *señores de hato* (cattle farm lords) who pledged to maintain it supplied and to do so at the prices set by the cabildo. Similar arrangements were made concerning cassava or cassava bread, a product that required considerable preparation and could therefore create "significant delay" for the transient fleets. In 1554 the members of the cabildo estimated that 800 cargas (50 pounds each) of cassava would be required by August for the fleets, so they "distributed" its preparation among several vecinos (heads of households).[9]

The town council also regulated the local market by setting "fair" maximum prices for certain key products. The presence of the fleets created such a gap between the demand for food and services and the ability of local residents to supply them that prices skyrocketed. A typical fleet in the 1570s and 1580s was formed by twenty to forty vessels, each of which had an average crew of some forty-three mariners. Thus each fleet brought 1,000–2,000 seamen to town. The average number of sailors was even higher in the warships, so the armadas or military convoys that also called on Havana's port added significantly to the numbers just mentioned. In years such as 1594, when both fleets coincided in Havana with the armada of General Francisco de Coloma, the total number of seamen was as high as 5,000. To this number one must add the passengers, which in 1594 were believed to be around 2,000, for a total transient population of about 7,000. These people came to a town that in 1570 reportedly had sixty vecinos and an indeterminate number of slaves and indigenous people (surely no more than just a few hundred).[10]

Food prices increased significantly during the summer months, in the midst of the shipping season, when the numbers of consumers peaked. Although it is difficult to reconstruct seasonal variations in consumption, there is ample evidence that demand increased along with the shipping movement. A local tax collected on three key products – meat, wine, and soap – allows us to trace some of the consumption patterns for the late sixteenth century. As figure 3.1 shows, collection of this tax almost tripled between February and August. It was at this time, the cabildo complained, that sellers attempted to maximize their profits by raising prices beyond reasonable and moral limits. The cabildo criticized residents who took advantage of the "scarcity of cassava in this port due to the many fleets and armadas" to double the usual price. As local authorities stated in May 1556, there was great "disorder" in the prices of meat and bread when the fleets were in town because many "sold them for more than is just," and the cabildo reiterated that it was not proper to sell those staples "at prices higher than the usual among vecinos."[11]

As part of its efforts to guarantee supplies at just prices, the town council devoted significant attention to the metrological units in which those prices were expressed – that is, the type of currency involved, as well as the units of measurement used (of weight, length, capacity) depending on the product. In

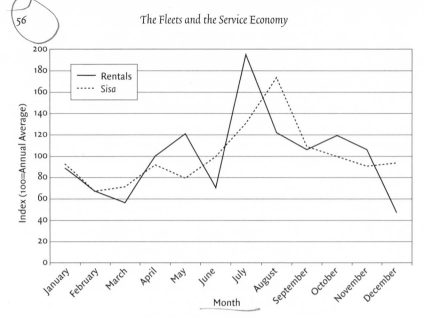

Figure 3.1. Monthly House Rentals (1579–1610) and Collection
of Local Taxes (*Sisa*) on Meat, Wine, and Soap (1566–1610)
Source: ANC, PNH, ER, 1579–1610; AGI, Contaduría, legs. 1089, 1101.

many cases, when the cabildo established a just price for a product, its attention
was not centered necessarily on its nominal price but on the actual quantities
that a given amount of money was able to purchase. Giving the multiplicity of
moneys and measurement units used in local transactions – themselves a function of the confluence of consumers and merchants from various areas of the
Atlantic – bringing predictability and order into the local market was not an easy
task.

Local authorities understood, however, that the development of Havana's
mercantile economy required clear metrological rules and predictability in the
area of currency exchanges. It is certainly not a coincidence that metrological
questions began to get the town council's attention in the late 1560s, when the
fleet system had become organized in a more or less permanent fashion and
Havana was becoming a regional center of trade. Nor is it coincidental that wine,
meat, and cassava, major staples in the local diet, figured prominently in these
early regulations. As economic historian Witold Kula has noted, measurements
were typically unified and regulated first for those products that were most intensely traded.[12]

A discussion by the members of the town council in 1569 shows how street
sellers manipulated the weight of their product to violate the legal prices of
cassava. Although the legal price of a carga (load) of cassava flour (50 pounds)

was 16 reales, they sold cassava torts of a quarter pound for half a real. This was the equivalent of 100 reales per carga, six times the legal price approved by the cabildo. Local authorities understood that there should be a price differential between cassava flour and a ready-to-eat product such as cassava torts, but these margins were deemed unacceptable by them, who described such torts as "too thin." Thus their solution was to fix the weight of the torts at 1 pound, while prescribing that they had to be sold "by weight." Sellers could charge half a real for a 1-pound tort, so they would be able to obtain 25 reales per carga, a profit well below what they were getting at the time.[13]

Local authorities followed well-established practices in order to rein in the metrological chaos in the city. Following medieval customs, the town council appointed monthly deputies among its members to look after the uniformity of weights and measures. These officials performed rounds of the slaughter-house, taverns, inns, shops, and other establishments where food was retailed and fined those who "weigh with false weights."[14] To determine the accuracy of the weights and lengths used by individual vendors, the cabildo asked those who sold "wine, and foods and other things that must be sold by weight or size" to bring their measurements to the town council, where they would be compared with the town's "standards." In 1571 the cabildo's deputy was instructed to collect "all the measures and weights and yards" to have them checked and to punish sellers who falsified them.[15]

The first reference to these metrological standards in Havana corresponds to January 1569, but it is not clear when they were acquired, which units of weight, length, and volume they covered, or what their regional origin was. In 1577 one of the most prominent members of the emerging local elite, Antón Recio, imported from Spain several "measures" of length, weight, and volume "according to the measurement of Avila" (Castile). They were related to some of the most heavily traded items in Havana, such as fabrics, wines, grains, and dry goods of various sorts. These measures were subsequently purchased by the cabildo, which ordered that all the measures used in town should conform to those. Twenty years later, in 1597, local authorities purchased in Mexico "some measures of copper, weights . . . , and a balance of metal" with similar purposes.[16]

The other area that local authorities regulated to bring predictability to market transactions concerned currency values and rates of exchange. Given the multiplicity of currencies circulating in sixteenth-century Havana, setting their relative value was crucial to avoid confusion, speculation, and usury. In addition to coins minted in Spain, Mexico, and Peru, transactions took place using money of account such as the maravedí and the ducado, plus of course gold and silver in various forms, such as bars, "pieces," and, in the case of gold, dust. This multiplicity of coins and currency is exemplified in a denunciation against Governor Pérez de Angulo in 1556, who was said to be fond of gambling: "On their desk there were *tostones* [silver coins minted in Mexico, each worth 4 reales] and bars of silver and pieces of gold."[17]

One of the main problems that local authorities faced at midcentury was the lack of fragmentary currency. In 1528 the petitioners of various Cuban towns reported to the crown that it was necessary to send currency worth 2 million maravedís to the island in coins of one real and in quarters. Owing to the lack of currency, it was necessary to cut gold bars, which of course made it difficult to finance daily retail operations.[18] The shortage of fragmentary currency seems to have been alleviated in Havana only toward the end of the sixteenth century, when the crown's costly military construction, plus a growing population and a more active local market, attracted currency to the city. "Currently there is a shortage of reales in this town," the cabildo asserted in 1569.[19]

Indeed, as late as 1585 local merchants and consumers struggled over transactions not because of disagreements over prices but over the means of payment. Many merchants were reluctant to accept payments in silver bars or pieces, which circulated widely in Havana. Although according to royal regulations an ounce of silver equaled 8 reales (or 272 maravedís), fragmenting the silver into pieces to effect payments implied inevitable losses. Thus merchants charged a premium if buyers paid with silver instead of currency. For instance, a 5 percent premium was added to a sale of provisions for the Florida garrisons in 1590. The increase was due to a payment in silver, for "it had been agreed that such things would be paid for in reales." The cabildo recognized these realities and in 1569 noted that many sellers refused to accept payments in silver unless a premium was involved.[20]

This devaluation of silver was particularly harmful to laborers such as soldiers, sailors, and others who were paid, at least occasionally, in silver. For instance, although the situados (royal funds allocated by the crown to pay for military and other expenses in Havana) were supposed to be paid in currency, they were at times paid in silver bars, which was frequently prejudicial to the soldiers. In 1581, when the royal officials paid the soldiers of La Fuerza, still Havana's only fortress, with silver, they applied a rate of 10 reales per peso or ounce, rather than the usual rate of 8 reales per peso. In real terms it was a salary decrease of 25 percent that had been misappropriated by the royal officials. As a result, the soldiers were described as "malcontents" who did their duties "halfheartedly."[21]

Table 3.2 shows that the monetary unit most widely used in mercantile operations in Havana from the late 1570s through 1610 was the real. One reason that the real appears to have been used so widely is the nature of the sources: the

Table 3.2. Currency Used, Percentage Distribution, 1578–1610

Currency	1578–89 (N = 1,815)	1590–99 (N = 3,707)	1600–1610 (N = 5,301)
Reales (34 maravedís)	67.6	61.1	62.0
Maravedís	0.2	3.8	1.6
Pesos (8 reales)	3.0	9.0	13.8
Pesos plata (10 reales)	0.3	0.1	—
Pesos de Tepuzque	0.4	0.1	—
Pesos oro (450 maravedís)	0.4	0.1	—
Tostones (4 reales)	0.3	0.2	—
Ducados (11 reales)	27.6	25.5	22.5
Doblas	0.1	—	0.1
Patacón (8 reales)	0.1	—	—
Reis	—	0.1	0.1
Escudos (10 reales)	—	0.1	—
Unknown	0.1	0.1	—

Source: ANC, PNH, ER, 1578–1610.

notarial records do not reflect daily retail transactions involving food and other basic staples, in which smaller currencies (half reales, quarters) or monetary units (such as maravedís) could be used. Rather, the notarial records contain market transactions that were large enough to incur the added cost, and also the guarantee, of being registered before a notary.

Yet the prevalence of reales as monetary units was also a function of the price levels of colonial markets. The smallest money of account, the maravedí, was widely used in Castile during the sixteenth century but seldom used in Havana for local transactions. Although this monetary unit was invoked in several mercantile operations in the city (see table 3.2), it was mostly used to refer to the "prices of Castile," that is, the price of origin of various products in Seville. By the time these products had made it to the New World, they were priced in reales. In the case of valuable merchandise, such as wine or slaves, prices were set using a much larger unit, the ducado, another money of account, worth 11 reales (of 34 maravedís each).[22]

Given the importance of the real, changes in its valuation could greatly impact the local market. Although the Catholic Monarchs had set the value of the real at 34 maravedís in 1497, it was not until 1552 that this rate was applied consistently in Havana. Up to then, the real was quoted at 44 maravedís, 10 more than in Castile. When in 1551 local authorities discussed a royal provision of 1549 that set the value of the real in Cuba to agree with that in Castile, some argued that the royal provision should be ignored because a devaluation of the real to

34 maravedís would increase the prices of basic staples and supplies. They also argued that as long as the real was quoted at 44 maravedís in other colonial ports, such as Santo Domingo or Cartagena, it was not advisable to change its value in Havana. Otherwise the little currency available would leave town and move to more propitious markets.[23]

Maintaining the valuation at 44 maravedís had some advantages for local merchants or for merchants conducting business in Havana, who in effect paid lower taxes for their operations. "There is a fair amount of silver reales here," the royal officials declared in 1539, "which they do not use for anything but to pay for export taxes [*almojarifazgo*], because they are worth 44 maravedís here." In practice, this meant a 23 percent tax reduction. The overvaluation of the real was also advantageous to merchants speculating in gold and silver, who bought cheap bullion on the island to resell later in Spain. Barely a few months after the cabildo's decision to maintain the valuation of the real at 44 maravedís, local authorities faced this problem, noting that ship passengers were buying all the gold and silver and taking them outside the land. Although the town council established serious fines for those who engaged in this trade, the effectiveness of these sanctions is doubtful at best. In any case, by May 1552 a new royal provision ratified the value of the real at 34 maravedís and was acknowledged and applied by authorities in Havana.[24]

Once the value of the real stabilized across the Spanish empire, from Castile to the colonies, prices became easier to interpret, thus facilitating commerce. Regardless of the type of currency used in an exchange, the actual value of the operation was made intelligible by referring to the content in reales of the money in use. Thus, a price set using a Spanish currency such as the escudo could be easily interpreted by noting that escudos were worth 10 reales each. The same was true concerning the various "pesos" from New Spain and Tierra Firme (Peru) that circulated in Havana during the last quarter of the sixteenth century (see table 3.2).[25]

Exchanges were also facilitated by the progressive uniformity of monetary units. By 1578, the first year for which notarial records exist in Havana, the multiplicity of currencies in the local market had already declined. The silver and silver coins of Peru, which had circulated widely around midcentury, had been gradually replaced by those of New Spain.[26] Our data points to the growing relative importance of the famed Mexican silver peso or "piece of eight" (worth 8 reales) in local transactions, along with a slow decline in the use of moneys of account such as the ducado. These trends point not only to the importance of Havana's economic links with Mexico but also to the growing monetization of the local market.

The situation was probably different in other regional markets in Cuba's "interior," where transactions frequently adopted the form of barters, with hides and other products of the land functioning as means of exchange. The mercantile lexicon in the 1560s was graphic enough, as many products were sent from Havana to the interior "in exchange for hides and reales." When in a 1567 legal suit one of the parties was asked "how many hides" he owed, the response was that "he owe[d] the freightage of 25 hanegas of salt and for this he owe[d] him two hides."[27] People who accused Governor Diego de Mazariegos of using his office for personal gain claimed that he had gone to the interior not to perform visits and administer justice but "for hides."[28]

Bartering played a small role in Havana's market between 1578 and 1610, when it accounted for only 1.6 percent of the values traded (including slaves, but excluding real estate). The importance of these operations, however, was larger in the exchanges with other Cuban communities, accounting for 3.3 percent of total trade between them and Havana. The percentage was highest in the case of Havana exports (or, more accurate, reexports) to these communities. Five percent of these exports were paid for with products of the land such as hides, meat, or tallow. A "company" set up by Bartolomé de Morales, a vecino of Havana, and Juan López de Villalpando, a vecino of Puerto Príncipe, in 1578 exemplifies these exchanges. López de Villalpando would take with him "220 ducados in clothing, wine, and other products that are listed, to sell them or to barter them for hides that would be sold in Havana, dividing the profits by half."[29]

The cabildo's efforts to regulate the local market concentrated on a selected number of staple foods. Out of 143 price regulations between 1550 and 1610, 27 percent were devoted to meat, 20 percent to bread (made out of wheat or cassava), 11 percent to wine, 6 percent to cassava, and 5 percent to fish.[30] A tariff approved in 1556 to regulate sales in city taverns and inns referred to cassava bread, salted and unsalted pork meat, beef, and wine, plus pineapples and bananas.[31] Many other products were occasionally regulated, but their proportions were much smaller compared with those of the products previously listed.

Building on medieval notions of just prices, these regulations sought to protect consumers from excessive market prices while allowing merchants a moderate or reasonable profit. "The just price of a thing," a sixteenth-century treatise declared, "is that which is commonly used in the place and at the time of the contract, paid in cash, considering the particular circumstances of selling and buying and the abundance of products, the abundance of money, the number of buyers and sellers."[32] The "needs of the republic" qualified doctrinally as a justification for price increases without charge of conscience, and the legal prices established by the town council seem to have honored this principle to some degree.[33] For instance, in the 1550s and 1560s the legal prices of beef increased by 30 percent in the summer months. In 1590, a year in which the fleets wintered in Havana, the legal prices of wheat bread grew by 60–70 percent, depending on its quality, between April and August. Wine prices increased 50 percent between June and August in 1567.[34]

Not only did the town council recognize the need to adjust seasonally the prices of some key products, but its own regulatory activities were very much in tune with the rhythms of maritime activity. Price regulations for fleet supplies were adopted mostly before the arrival of the fleets and the summer shipping season, in the April–June trimester. Thirty-eight percent of all regulations dealing with fleet provisions were adopted during these months. Conversely, almost none (less than 3 percent) were adopted in July, when the fleets were actually in town. The number of regulations increased again in the August–October trimester (32 percent), reflecting cabildo activity in years that the fleets were forced to stay in Havana beyond the summer months.

Local authorities were much less active when it came to lodging prices and practices. The 1556 tariff for taverns and inns established a price for hammocks, and the cabildo had previously ordered that people who operated inns should clearly mark them by placing a wood sign on the door "so it becomes known that guests are taken in the house for money." But no systematic effort was made to regulate these prices, despite the importance of this activity for the local economy. On this, again, the town council followed well-established practices, for fair prices were to be set on "merchandise necessary to human life."[35] Lodging was obviously not included. A 1562 document makes reference to the importance of this activity: "The residents in this village have no gain other than what they make with their houses and a few supplies for the ships that go there."[36] It is noteworthy that, according to local authorities, in 1574 fifty taverns were open in town, almost as many as the number of Spanish households established in it.[37]

Like food prices, rental and lodging prices were sensitive to the fleets and to their movement in and out of the port. For instance, in 1601 a prominent vecino and alcalde in the town council, Juan Recio, rented out a "shop" to a shoemaker for 9 ducados (99 reales) per month, but the contract made special provisions for the visit of the fleets: "If the fleet and armada that are expected this year from New Spain and Tierra Firme stay in this port for one month, he must pay 12 ducados per month and this price he must pay for every month that the said fleet and armada stay in this port." In this case, the fleet premium amounted to a third of the price. In other cases, it was even higher. Thus the renter of a lot in the city who paid 4 ducados per month in 1596 agreed to pay 9 for as long as the fleet stayed in town.[38]

Table 3.3. The Fleets and Mercantile Activity, 1556–1610

| Year | Average Stay of the Fleets | | Total Mercantile Activity | Mercantile Activity by Sector, Percentage Distribution | | | |
	New Spain (Days)	Tierra Firme (Days)	Annual Average (Reales)	Local	Insular	Inter-colonial	Trans-atlantic
1556–70	57	40	—				
1571–80	26	19	901,425	77	8	4	11
1581–90	24	20	1,412,605	32	12	30	26
1591–95	130	111	2,598,634	32	4	20	44
1596–1600	18	5	2,197,672	52	3	12	33
1601–5	7	NA	2,035,486	49	4	20	27
1606–10	8	16	1,208,417	66	2	11	21

Sources: Chaunu and Chaunu, *Séville et L'Atlantique*, 6(1):280, 296; ANC, PNH, ER, 1578–1610.
Note: For mercantile activity, 1571–80 includes December 1578 and 1579; 1581–90 includes 1585–90. Annual averages were calculated by dividing the totals by the number of months for which information is available in each period.

There was, however, an important distinction between food and rental prices. Whereas crews and passengers could hardly avoid the former, it was possible for them to stay on board to avoid the steep prices of accommodations on land. "We must winter in this port of Havana with great discomfort for all passengers and myself," an inquisitor from Peru commented in 1594. This discomfort was, of course, related to Havana's high prices: "I do not know with what I will sustain myself here," he asserted. A royal official living in Havana concurred with this assessment: "I can only sustain myself by eating cassava and meat," he reported in 1580, "due to the high cost of housing."[39]

The volume of room and house rentals also responded to the shipping movement, contributing to the marked seasonality of the local economy. Not only were the summer months the most expensive in terms of lodging, but they were also the most active in terms of business transactions. The total value of contracts of house and room rentals almost quadrupled between March and July, by far the peak month in terms of values (see figure 3.1). This peak reflected both the increase in demand and the high price levels typical of the shipping season.

The shipping movement affected all local mercantile activity, in terms of both total values and seasonal fluctuations. This is to be expected, for as table 3.3 shows, trading (insular, intercolonial, transatlantic) represented a significant portion of the town's total mercantile activity. Havana's total mercantile activity closely reflected the movement in its port. Peak values correspond to those periods when the number of ships also reached the highest point, as in the 1590s (see table 2.1 for a reference). These figures reflect the maritime and commercial bonanza that Havana experienced during the last decade of the sixteenth century. In addition to high shipping volumes, during these years the fleets wintered several times in Havana, thus increasing significantly the demand for local goods and services. One or both fleets wintered in Havana in 1590, 1591, 1594, and 1595. Thus during these years each fleet spent an average of four months in town on its way back to Europe.

In one of the most extreme examples, the fall and winter of 1594–95, more than a hundred ships were docked in Havana for several months. In late July the Armada de la Guardia de la Carrera de las Indias, Captain General Francisco de Coloma; the armadilla (a small armada) of six frigates under the command of Rodrigo de Soto; and the fleet of Tierra Firme, Captain General Sancho Pardo Osorio, all from Nombre de Dios, arrived in Havana to wait for the fleet of New Spain. Commanded by Captain General Marcos de Aramburu, the fleet of New Spain left San Juan de Ulúa, Veracruz, on 14 July and was greeted in the waters of western Cuba, thirty hours away from Havana, by six vessels under the command of Admiral Luis Fajardo, of the armada of Coloma. The fleet entered Havana on 14 August, too late to complete provisions before the season of inclement weather began. The next day, 15 August, the admirals and captains general of the armada and fleets, together with the governor of Cuba, decided to winter in Havana. Most but not all of these ships returned to Spain on 11 March, 1595. By then they had been joined by other vessels: ten from Seville and Tenerife that had sailed to Havana between August and December 1594; seven galleons dispatched for Havana from Seville with supplies for the fleets and armada; and a small group of galleons from Tierra Firme that called to port in the early months of 1595. In the early summer another fleet from New Spain, under the command of Luis Alfonso de Flores, was on its way to Havana.[40]

The wintering fleets not only brought customers and a large influx of money into the local market but also created opportunities for regional and long-distance commerce. Provisioning the fleets was a truly Atlantic enterprise, with supplies being carried from various points of the Spanish empire. In late 1594, for instance, Governor Juan Maldonado Barnuevo sent for flour and other food supplies from New Spain, "the surrounding islands," and Cuba's interior. On 1 December, a ship from Veracruz imported 3,500 quintales (350,000 pounds) of biscuits, a major staple in the diet of seamen. A navío from the Canary Islands carrying 300 quintales of tar, indispensable for coating and protecting the ship hulls, called to port the same day.[41] Both the high levels of total mercantile activity during the five-year period 1591–95 and the large proportion of of it represented by transatlantic transactions are clearly related not just to the vigorous shipping movement of these years but also to the long stays of the fleets in Havana (see table 3.3).

These relationships help explain as well why the value of total mercantile activity declined after 1606. During the period 1606–10, no fleet winters are reported, and the time spent by the fleets in Havana decreased considerably. However, it should be noted that a good portion of this decline in mercantile activity is concentrated in the trading sector, not in local transactions. In comparison with the previous five-year period, the value of activity in the local mercantile sector declined 20 percent, well below the decline experienced by the transoceanic (53 percent) and intercolonial (67 percent) sectors. Indeed, table 3.3 suggests that, despite the fundamental importance of shipping and the fleets to the economy of Havana, about half of all notarized mercantile operations were of a local nature. And our figures underestimate the importance of the local sector, for many daily exchanges never made it to the notarial records.

As mentioned above, the shipping movement in general, and the fleets in particular, contributed to give life in Havana a marked seasonal character. Neither harvest cycles nor climatic changes determined the local calendar, although maritime rhythms were largely based on perceptions of climate and hurricanes. It seems that production was organized to fit the port movement since early on. When Jacques de Sorés disembarked in Havana in 1555, the town was largely deserted because there were no ships in town and the residents had gone to work on their farms. Thirty years later the governor referred to the same process when he reported that many residents had not participated in a military parade because most made a living by "bringing supplies to the armada and fleet" and were out of town.[42] The traditional Christian calendar was an important point of reference for commercial transactions and shaped local life in various ways, but the rhythms of the port exercised an overbearing influence on the town and its inhabitants.

The town's mercantile movement reflected the maritime cycles in several ways. In addition to the price premiums charged during the stay of the fleets, many financial obligations were made with reference to the fleets or to the arrival of the situado, the money assigned by the crown to pay for its garrison and other expenses in the city. Since the situado arrived via the fleet of New Spain, these obligations reinforced the centrality of the fleets to local mercantile life. An expression that was coined during this time – that debts were subject "to the term of the fleet" – reflected this situation. Not surprising, a large proportion of the yearly total mercantile value was exchanged during the summer months, between July and September.[43]

Yet the image conveyed by some historians of a dead city during the interfleet period seems exaggerated, or at least oversimplified.[44] The town's mercantile movement peaked during the summer months, but at least in terms of local exchanges Havana was far from dead for the rest of the year. In fact, the seasonal distribution of local exchanges was much more even than that of exchanges linked to the various commercial circuits. Commercial exchanges (insular, intercolonial, and transoceanic) were heavily concentrated (48 percent) in the trimester July–September and in February, a month in which a large number of ships departed for Seville after spending winter in Havana. These months were important for local exchanges (38 percent), but they were more important for commercial operations. Furthermore, some of the months with the highest levels of local mercantile activity, such as October and January, did not fit the port's movement neatly.

Besides, in a sense, it was when the fleets were in town that Havana was dead, and not the opposite. Although the shipping season clearly stimulated commercial exchanges and infused life into the local service economy, other activities were placed on hold during this time. For instance, as figure 3.2 shows, petitions to the town council for land declined significantly during the summer months, particularly in June and July. They peaked in January and October, when commercial exchanges were at some of their lowest points in the year.

The decline of petitions during the shipping and commercial season probably indicates that many, if not most, vecinos were busy at this time conducting businesses related to the fleets. But it was also a function of the inactivity of the town council, whose members were themselves fully engaged with Havana's mercantile life. As they explained in August 1587, they had not met in June or July because they had been "occupied with the dispatch, provisioning, and arming of the armadas and fleets that were at the port, for which reason they had been unable to occupy themselves with the cabildo and because there were no matters to resolve concerning this republic."[45]

This was not an isolated instance. There were "no matters to resolve" in June and July of 1588, 1601, 1605, and 1609, either. Along with December, July was the month in which the cabildo adopted the lowest number of resolutions in the years between 1550 and 1610. It was also the month when fewer land petitions were made to the town council. In 1600 local authorities acknowledged the fleets' paralyzing effect when they complained that when the fleets were stationed in Havana the vecinos failed to fulfill their civic duties.[46]

Principal among these duties was defense. Although the fleet system provided the residents of Havana with juicy commercial and economic opportunities, it also placed a heavy burden on them: the defense of the convoys and of their pre-

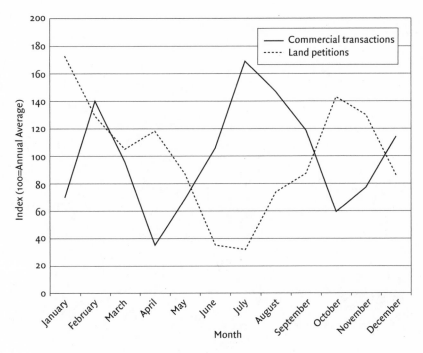

Figure 3.2. Monthly Volume of Commercial Transactions (1579–1610)
and Land Petitions (1550–1610)
Source: ANC, PNH, ER, 1579–1610; ACAH, 1550–1610.

cious cargoes of gold, silver, cochineal, pearls, hides, and other commodities. The designation of Havana as the rendezvous port for the fleets had clear advantages in terms of the organization of trade and the collection of taxes. It had, however, the great disadvantage of turning Havana into a clear military target, one whose capture could disrupt the main commercial routes of the Spanish Atlantic.

Defense and the Local Economy

The strategic importance of Havana in the early modern Atlantic became a well-known fact in the second half of the sixteenth century. Travelers, seamen, cosmographers, and geographers began to produce an image of Havana that, although frequently distorted, emphasized its mercantile possibilities and its central role in the Spanish maritime network. "Havana," an English visitor reported in 1571, "is the principal and most important port of all the King of Spain has in the Indies: because all the ships coming from Peru, Honduras, Puerto Rico, Santo Domingo, Jamaica, and other parts of the Indies, touch there upon their

This distorted view of Havana as a major port city was inspired by the drawings of Baptista Boazio about Francis Drake's expedition to America. "Die Grosse Insel Cuba mit der umbligen der lantschaft" (The Great Island of Cuba and Neighboring Territories), Augsburg (ca. 1580s); courtesy of Biblioteca Nacional "José Martí," Havana.

return to Spain, being this the port in which they take food and water, as well as the largest part of their cargo." John Hawkins was aware of the maritime functions of the town and referred to it in 1564 as "a harbor whereunto all the fleets of the Spaniards come, and do their tary to have one the company of another." So was Francis Drake, who considered attacking the town in 1586 and tried later to capture the fleets that were wintering in Havana in 1594-95.[47]

As these testimonies show, the English, with whom Spain was more or less permanently at war during much of the 1580s and 1590s, knew about Havana and its important maritime functions. Richard Hakluyt's *Voyages, Navigations, Traffiques, and Discoveries of the English Nation* contained several references to Havana. A 1590 letter reproduced in the third volume referred to Havana as the "best harbor and the surest in the world." The same volume also contained a 1585 report by Admiral Alvaro de Bazán, reproduced in Spanish, that warned that should Havana fall into the hands of the English, they would be able to disrupt Spain's commerce and seize the fleets. Additional information about Havana in

English became available in 1598 with the first English edition of Jan Huygen van Linschoten's popular *Discours of Voyages*, originally published in Amsterdam (in Dutch) in 1596; it was also translated into Latin and French in the 1590s and in the early 1600s, respectively. Linschoten was a Dutchman who lived and worked with the Portuguese in Goa, India, during the 1580s. Based on secondhand accounts, his description of Havana concurred with the descriptions in Hakluyt's volumes: "Havana is the chiefest town of merchandise and where all their ships are made," he reported.[48]

Geographic treatises and travel accounts published across Europe painted a similar picture. Some of the earliest references in Italian appeared in the geographic works of Calabrese cosmographer and theologian Gian Lorenzo Anania, who as early as 1573 mentioned Havana as the point of reunion of the fleets, and in the *Relationi universali* of Piedmontese writer and politician Giovanni Botero (1591). Botero's description was clearly laudatory: "The key, not only to this island, but of the whole new world, is the fortress of Havana, with an excellent port . . . which commands all the fleets of Peru and Mexico." A postal itinerary published in Venice in 1611 referred to the city as "metropolis and port . . . excellent and very comfortable."[49]

Many of these accounts were based on previously printed descriptions and on the testimonies and impressions of travelers and seamen returning to Europe. Among these was French traveler Samuel de Champlain, who visited Havana in 1602 and produced a written account that emphasized the wonders of the port: "The said port of Havana is one of the finest that I have seen in all the Indies," he said. "The town is very good and mercantile." Some of the best cosmographies and geographic treatises produced in French in the early seventeenth century contributed to creating an image of Havana that basically reproduced Champlain's two main points: the magnificence of the port and the city's commercial possibilities. "A place of trade," asserted the frequently reedited *Atlas* of Flemish cartographer Gerardus Mercator, published in Latin and French in Amsterdam in 1595. "It surpasses . . . almost all other cities in America, be it on the grandeur and security of its port, or in its wealth and commerce," Jean Laet stated in his influential 1625 *Histoire* of the New World, which was frequently copied later.[50]

The Spanish themselves contributed to creating and disseminating the image of a commercial and maritime metropolis in the tropics, interested as they were in lauding their conquests and in magnifying the grandeur of their possessions. As mentioned already, Martín Fernández de Enciso listed the port of Havana among the world's greatest cities in the 1546 edition of his geography. A world "repertoire" published in Madrid in the 1580s described Havana as one of "the most principal places in the West Indies." "A famous port . . . the best in the world," asserted a Spanish traveler who visited the city a decade earlier.[51] It is, of course, not a coincidence that Havana is prominently featured in all route manuals of the period, regardless of language.[52]

Thus by the late sixteenth century the image of Havana as a wealthy maritime and commercial metropolis was fairly prevalent in the printed materials of Atlantic Europe, from the Iberian Peninsula to the Low Countries, England, or the Italian kingdoms and city-states. Interested in breaking Spanish ascendancy in the north Atlantic and its successful fleet system, the enemies of Spain realized the strategic importance of Havana and its larger Atlantic functions. An English colonial officer neatly summarized this reality a few decades later: "Had we the port and city of Havana . . . this once effected would utterly ruin the Spaniards . . . they much dread an old prophecy among them, viz. *That within a short time the English will as freely walk the streets of Havana as the Spaniards now do.* . . . I esteem . . . the port and harbor of Havana in the West Indies, equivalent . . . to Tanger [sic] in the Straights [sic] of Gibraltar; and if we were at once masters of both, it would without doubt so straiten the Spaniards, as absolutely to admit us a free trade into their ports of America."[53]

The need to protect its port grew along with the fame of Havana. As the attack of Jacques de Sorés showed, such fame was not without consequences. Indeed, the French corsair had decided to attack Havana based on a rumor linked to the maritime functions of the town: that a treasury recovered from a recent shipwreck was being kept in its fort. The rumor turned out to be false, but Havana's maritime roles made it believable.

Havana's first fortress, destroyed by Sorés in 1555, had already been built to protect the port—"for the defense of the ships that go and come from the Indies," as the royal cédula ordering its construction stipulated. When the king ordered in 1556 that a new and better fortress be built, the growing importance of Havana's port was readily acknowledged: "that port of the village of Havana is the main stopover of the Indies, where the ships that come . . . either from Nombre de Dios or from New Spain and other parts call in, and it is necessary that such port always be protected and with great defense, so if the armada of France went to those parts it could not seize such port."[54]

Fortifying Havana, which by the early seventeenth century had become one of the best-fortified port cities in the world, was an Atlantic enterprise. Decisions came from Spain, but virtually everything else came from other areas of the Atlantic. The silver that financed the military works and paid for the garrison came from Mexico. Most workers came from Africa, although skilled artisans from Spain and other parts of Europe also worked in the construction of the forts. Given Spain's own dependency on foreign imports, many of the military supplies brought to Havana from Seville had been produced in various other places in Europe. Military knowledge was also imported, as the engineer who designed Havana's most important forts in the 1590s, Juan Bautista (or Battista) Antonelli, was from Italy.

Last, but certainly not least, the dangers besieging Havana were of an Atlantic nature. As the royal cédula that ordered the construction of La Fuerza in 1556 implied, Spain's defensive efforts were a reaction against the imperial and commercial ambitions of its European rivals. The Spanish labeled "pirate" any foreign ship conducting illegal business in the Caribbean waters, although many of those ships were in fact privateers operating with licenses from their governments or simply interlopers conducting contraband trade. The impact of piracy on sixteenth-century Spanish commerce was significant, for according to one estimate some 250 ships were lost to pirates in the Caribbean between 1536 and 1585.[55]

The northwestern coast of Cuba was a favored area for pirates to operate. Its inlets and bays allowed for protection as they waited for the ships sailing to Havana to pass by. According to Kenneth Andrews, it was customary for English vessels to sail for the Caribbean in March in order to be in the Cuban northwest before Havana's shipping season began. To mention but one example, in 1591 English pirates operating west of Havana captured eight ships coming from Santo Domingo loaded with hides, sugar, ginger, and other commodities. The English privateers alone launched around two hundred expeditions to the Caribbean between 1585 and 1603. And they were not alone. In 1583 the governor of Cuba reported that cabotage trade had been interrupted because the French seized all the ships that ventured into the waters surrounding the island. According to another colonial officer, the following year several French ships stationed around Cape San Antonio, Cuba's westernmost point, "robbed many ships" on their way to Havana. It looked as if "all the Frenchmen" in the world had "come to this island," as the governor graphically asserted.[56]

The residents of Havana were used to living with enemy ships nearby, and the issue was clearly a major concern for local authorities, particularly in the 1550s and 1560s, when Havana was still very poorly defended. In those early decades the defense of the town and its port depended mainly on the limited number of residents, who were forced to "do watch" day and night at El Morro, a promontory at the entrance of the bay from where it was possible to detect any approaching sails. Local residents also had to bear the costs of any works to fortify the area. For instance, in 1553, in the midst of hostilities with France, the cabildo ordered the reinforcement of a bastion that had been built at the beach and ordered fifty residents to contribute a slave with their tools or a real per day for the works.

Some humble residents, obviously unable to satisfy these conditions, were instructed to provide their labor. The cabildo also ordered the nightly watches doubled and bought some artillery to place at El Morro.[57]

Renewed hostilities with France in 1569 were immediately felt in Havana. The king reported that a large "armada of Lutherans from France" was sailing for the New World and instructed the governor in Havana, at the time the seasoned seaman from Asturias Pedro Menéndez de Avilés, to have Havana ready for possible attack. The town council called for a military review to "see if the people [were] ready with their arms" and appointed four notable vecinos as the leaders of an equal number of squadrons. As was customary in these cases, the watches at El Morro were reinforced and the indigenous inhabitants of the nearby village of Guanabacoa ordered to participate. Having learned from experience, the cabildo closed the road that Sorés had used in his attack on the town in 1555.[58]

The largest military threat to Havana did not come from France, however. It came from across the English Channel. In 1585 the most formidable naval squadron ever sent by an enemy of Spain to American waters, twenty-two ships strong, sailed from Plymouth under the command of Sir Francis Drake. Backed by Queen Elizabeth, this operation was a full-scale military expedition against Spain's most precious possessions in the New World. Drake sacked Santo Domingo and captured Cartagena de Indias, one of the most important port cities of the Spaniards in the Caribbean, a stopover for the fleet of Tierra Firme and the main distribution center of the Atlantic slave trade in the Americas. In addition to the ships and slaves taken, ransom in these two places amounted to 132,000 ducados (1,452,000 reales).[59]

Havana was the next logical target, or at least that is what the Council of the Indies feared. "Havana is in danger, for although it has a fort, it is small and weak and if they land artillery they can take it easily," warned Admiral Alvaro de Bazán. The news of the sacking of Santo Domingo reached Havana in February 1586, a few days before Drake sailed to Cartagena. The key to the Indies had to be protected, and a regional scheme was immediately activated for its defense. Two frigates were dispatched to Veracruz and St. Augustine to inform them about the presence of "English corsairs" in Caribbean waters. Reinforcements were requested from Cuban towns and from New Spain. They arrived from both. By late April, when the English squadron was about to sail from Cartagena, about 200 men from Cuba's interior had made it to Havana, and two companies, 300 men strong, had arrived from Mexico. Including Havana's own residents and its small garrison – 50 soldiers at the time – the force gathered to defend the port town was about 1,000 men strong. Sentinels were placed along the northwestern coast, from San Antonio to Matanzas. The roads to Havana were blocked, as was customary in these cases. A chain was made to block the bay's entrance. Several houses close to La Fuerza, Havana's only fortress, were demolished to facilitate its defense. In the event that all these measures did not suffice, two ships were readied in case it became necessary to dispatch the news that Havana had fallen "to the enemies of God and His Majesty."[60]

Preparations included guaranteeing the provisions needed to sustain the men in arms. Local authorities barely dealt with any other issue between February and May 1586. Drake's imminent attack and Havana's defense were the only order of business. Given the lack of local funds to finance the expenses of defense, the cabildo borrowed from "four or six rich merchants of this place" the money needed to purchase 10,000 pounds of biscuits. Additional flour to sustain the soldiers was imported from Mexico and sold to bread makers in Havana at prices set by the cabildo. Several rental houses were taken to house the soldiers and paid for with money from the *sisa*, the local tax on meat and wine.[61]

Drake's squadron reached Havana's waters on 29 May, but it did not attack the town. Tropical diseases had caused heavy losses among his men, disputes threatened the expedition, and Drake was surely aware of the military readiness of Havana. During a brief landing in Cabo de San Antonio, west of Havana, Drake had called his captains to inform them that unless they could do it without risk, they would not attack Havana.[62] His presence in the Caribbean and in Cuban waters had long-term consequences, however. Although Drake was labeled a pirate by Spanish official sources, his expedition was tantamount to a state-backed, full-scale European military operation in the New World. As such, it required a decisive Spanish response, one that showed Spain's ability and determination to protect the integrity of its empire and of the Atlantic sea lanes that made that empire possible.

Phillip II's answer to this challenge was the Italian military engineer Antonelli, who arrived in the Caribbean in 1587 to launch a massive project of fortifications in Santo Domingo, Cartagena, San Juan, Veracruz, St. Augustine, and, of course, Havana. "In the case of Havana, because it is such an important port," the engineer was to design and supervise the construction of two new forts: Tres Reyes on El Morro, and San Salvador on the opposite side of the bay, at the place known as La Punta. As for Havana's only fortress, La Fuerza, the royal order did not introduce any changes: "It will remain as it is at the present time, without fortifying it or dismantling it."[63]

The locations chosen to build the new forts had been used for military purposes since the establishment of a permanent village in Havana. The residents of Havana had been performing watches at El Morro since at least the 1550s, and it was the guard posted there who warned about an incoming vessel when Sorés attacked the town in 1555. As early as 1538 the king inquired whether it was convenient to fortify El Morro, and the royal cédula that ordered the construction of La Fuerza in 1556 instructed as well that "el morro which is at the entrance of such port" be fortified.[64]

It was perhaps following this royal command that Governor Diego de Mazariegos, Cuba's first military governor (1556–65), ordered in 1563 the construction of a watchtower of limestone, six stories high, "and very white," which served both to guide vessels approaching the port city and to "spot corsairs." This is surely the white tower mentioned in some sixteenth-century navigation manuals as a reference for pilots sailing to Havana. "On top of the morro there is a white little tower that looks like a sail from the high seas," one of these manuals stated. In 1571, a visitor made reference to this tower as well, noting that there was always a sentinel in it to warn residents about "sails that appear in the horizon."[65]

The same was true about La Punta (literally, "the point") on the other side of the bay. The strategic importance of the area had been made obvious by Sorés and his forces, who approached the town precisely from that side. Consequently, since 1556 La Punta was constantly mentioned as a place that needed to be safeguarded in case of an attack. Some modest construction and perhaps even some fortifying took place. A trench was dug in the 1560s, and there are intermittent references to it through the 1580s. In 1582 the governor of La Fuerza proposed the construction of a small tower at La Punta and recommended placing artillery in it. It is not certain whether such a tower was actually built, but there are several references to a "fort" with eight small pieces of ordnance in the area when Drake approached Havana.[66]

Thus by the time Antonelli arrived to build the new forts, Havana's defensive geography was well known. The defensive plans for the port and its town were complemented with an element of great practical and symbolic importance: an iron chain locking the mouth of the bay between El Morro and La Punta, as not just the areas but the forts themselves became known. There were precedents for this chain in Havana's short history: the use of a chain had been proposed since the 1570s, and one had been actually deployed as part of the preparations to repel Drake. In November 1597 the installation of the chain was deemed completed. "From one fort to the other there is an iron chain, which traverses the entry of the port," reported a visitor in 1602.[67]

Contrary to what some historians have argued, preparations for the construction of the forts at El Morro and La Punta began almost immediately after Antonelli's visit to Havana, which in turn took place only a few months after Drake's expedition.[68] Antonelli visited Havana in the summer of 1587, reported back to

This drawing of the entrance to the Havana harbor shows plans to fortify La Punta and close the harbor with a chain. The old watchtower, or *atalaya*, is depicted as well. The drawing has been dated erroneously by some authors as 1567 and by others as 1603. Cuban historian Leandro Romero studied the plan and concluded that it was produced in the early 1580s, an assessment that we share. "Plano de la Habana" (ca. 1580), detail, AGI, Mapas y Planos, Santo Domingo, 4.

the crown in early 1588, and was back on the island in 1589 to supervise construction. The instructions given to the new governor, Juan de Tejeda, in November 1588 commanded him to initiate the works and allocated 25,000 ducados from the royal treasury in Mexico to cover the initial expenses. The importance given to Havana within this vast military plan in the region is demonstrated by the

The port city of Havana in the early seventeenth century. A. entrance to the harbor;
B. El Morro; C. La Punta; D. La Fuerza; E. Guanabacoa. Cardona, "Descripciones," fol. 49;
courtesy of Laboratorio Fotográfico, Biblioteca Nacional de España, Madrid.

fact that the engineer was ordered to report there first. Only after organizing
construction in Havana was he to proceed to Cartagena de Indias. The actual
construction began in 1589, and Antonelli reported that the "first stones" had
been placed in December. Having initiated construction, he went to visit San
Juan de Ulúa, in Veracruz. Antonelli returned to Havana in 1591 and stayed there
until 1594. His nephew, Cristóbal de Roda, continued the works, which were not
finished until well into the seventeenth century. Yet as early as 1594 engineer
Antonelli reported that El Morro, although still unfinished, "was in defense,"
and in 1590 the royal treasury began to cover the expenses of soldiers stationed
in the forts under construction.[69]

The two new forts were complemented by La Fuerza, Havana's only fortress
up to the 1590s. Built between 1558 and 1579, La Fuerza was described "by great
captains and soldiers as one of the best forts that one could find." The three forts
together configured an impressive defensive complex that made Havana one of
the best-fortified cities in the late sixteenth-century Atlantic. "So strongly situ-
ated and fortified both by nature and art, that it seems impregnable," asserted
a seventeenth-century English author. "Deemed by many to be impregnable,"

concurred a French geographer. As early as 1590 a visitor to the town concluded that the new forts made Havana "impossible to take." Their assessments were accurate, as it was not until 1762 that the English managed to enter and occupy Havana.[70]

Needless to say, building and manning these forts represented a significant injection of money, technical personnel, and workers into Havana. Between 1572 and 1610, according to the treasury accounts of Havana, more than 21 million reales were received in the city to pay for various military expenses: fortifications (construction materials, salaries, and slaves), garrison salaries, military supplies, and others. This represented an annual average of 676,993 reales, somewhere between 10 and 25 percent of Havana's total mercantile activity, depending on the year.[71] Military expenses increased in the late 1580s, when the first allocations to initiate the construction of El Morro and La Punta were disbursed. They reached their highest point in 1594, when a large number of soldiers were stationed temporarily in the city and the fleets and armada wintering in Havana required substantial additional expenses covered by the Mexican treasury. Expenses increased slightly again in 1602, owing to the expropriation of 24,000 ducados by the governor to cover delayed payments to workers constructing the forts.[72]

Prior military expenditures had taken place at a much more modest level. Between 1558 and 1577, 546,000 reales was spent in the construction of La Fuerza (an annual average of less than 29,000 reales), and the crown sustained a garrison of fifty to man it. In the 1570s and 1580s, to cover the soldiers' salaries and rations, 63,000 reales per year was required. The number of soldiers grew considerably after the 1580s, and with them the expenses associated with Havana's military complex. In late 1590 the king ordered an increase in the number of soldiers to three hundred. To reduce costs, he also ordered the elimination of the soldiers' rations, which in practice meant lowering their salaries by almost 20 percent, from 105 to 88 reales per month. Gunners, of which there were twelve positions, made 110 reales monthly, the same as squadron officers and drummers. Higher officers earned according to their rank. Including salaries and other military expenses, including powder, munitions, medicines, and an allowance for the repair of the forts, the total estimated annual cost of the garrison was set at 35,912 ducados (395,032 reales). This figure, of course, did not include the expenses incurred in the actual construction of the forts, which were set at 20,000 ducados (220,000 reales) per year in the 1590s.[73]

The number of soldiers increased further in the 1590s, but the king did not allow the reinstatement of the soldiers' old salaries despite repeated complaints by the authorities in Havana.[74] In 1593-94, again owing to hostilities with the English in the wake of the defeat of the Invincible Armada (1588), there were more than six hundred soldiers in Havana. The incoming governor, Maldonado Barnuevo, arrived in Havana in 1593 with two companies, which together accounted for three hundred soldiers. Another company from Puerto Rico joined them in 1594.[75]

The king inquired in 1594 whether "so many people" were needed to defend Havana, "given that the conservation and security of such port matters so much." In consultation with the captain general of the armada, Francisco de Coloma, Governor Maldonado replied that Havana's garrison should consist of 450 men, including soldiers, gunners, musketeers, and officers. The crown accepted this figure, allocating 150 men to La Fuerza and 300 for El Morro and La Punta. The actual number of soldiers serving in the city after the mid-1590s was very close to this total. In the early 1600s, a period for which we have detailed and precise figures concerning the number of soldiers in the city, there were between 141 and 176 soldiers at La Fuerza, depending on the year; around 190 in El Morro; and between 70 and 100 at La Punta.[76]

The establishment of a sizable and permanent garrison in Havana in the 1590s had several important effects. First, it added a pool of consumers to the city, thus contributing to the local service economy. The soldiers required food, entertainment, and many other services. Their buying capacity was limited by low salaries and irregular pay, but as a group the garrison represented an annual injection of more than half a million reales from the Mexican treasury. Some of Havana's most humble residents, frequently black women, made a living cooking for them, laundering their clothing, and selling sexual services. As a black freedwoman declared in 1600, she was owed money by the royal treasury "for the time that I gave to eat to certain soldiers from the relief companies that came." Using almost identical language, black freedwoman Francisca de Miranda asserted in 1585 that she was owed money by "His Majesty ... in his royal treasury in this village" for "the soldiers who I give to eat." Residents also rented their houses to the treasury when soldiers from out of town had to be lodged, as happened in 1586 because of Drake's proximity. Local merchants, in turn, provided clothing, shoes, and many other items the soldiers required, frequently on credit. Supplying the soldiers was typically controlled by merchants appointed by the governor, a practice that led to abuses and denunciations.[77]

Second, the presence of the soldiers had a significant impact on local life, for it alleviated considerably the military obligations of local residents. Although they were still called on to participate in military parades and demonstrations, or to seize arms in case of attacks, their duties in the area of defense declined considerably after the 1580s. The number of cabildo instructions and agreements related to this theme declined in the late 1500s and early 1600s, particularly in comparison with the 1550s–1580s period, when Havana's defense was largely contingent on its own demographic resources. The importance of defense in cabildo deliberations declined from 12 percent in the years 1550–70 to just 2 percent between 1591 and 1610 (see table 3.1).

Havana's defenses were improved in yet another way in the 1590s, after the crucial Drake expedition of 1586. Phillip II dispatched two galleys to Havana in 1587 to help protect its port and the coasts of the Cuban northwest, an area favored by corsairs to attack ships sailing to Havana. Galleys had been central to Mediterranean navigation for centuries, but by the late 1500s their former nautical grandeur was decidedly in decline. They had certain advantages over other vessels, however, that made them appealing for military purposes. Foremost among these was propulsion: galleys were driven mainly by oars, although typically they also boasted two masts with lateen sails. This combination allowed them to navigate in a calm sea and to take advantage of winds as well. The result was a capable warship: a light, speedy, and highly maneuverable ship that could be equipped with artillery and whose oarsmen, when necessary, could be turned into combatants. The initial cost for the galleys was estimated at 441,176 reales, and allocations for their expenses are registered in Havana's treasury between 1589 and 1597 for a total of close to 4 million reales.[78]

The galleys seem to have gone out of commission in 1597, when the treasury stopped making allocations for their expenses, although later accounts continued to make reference to the existence of armed vessels in the city.[79] These accounts helped promote the notion of Havana's military readiness and impregnability, even though it is certain that by the early 1600s the galleys were no longer operative. In 1602 Governor Pedro de Valdés informed the crown that the only way to eliminate contraband and combat pirates was to create a small armada that would patrol the waters north of La Española, a preferred refuge for enemy ships, and Cuba's southern waters, constantly visited by smugglers. Valdés asserted that such an armada, which would consist of two galleons and two pataches (small boats), could be built in the shipyards of Havana and gunned with artillery produced in the island. Although this initiative was not approved, several small armadas were organized ad hoc in the early 1600s, with at least some success. The royal officials in Havana estimated in 1608 that these "armadillas" had seized goods valued at more than 100,000 ducados, although figures reported to the royal treasury for tax purposes were considerably lower, amounting to 32,293 ducados.[80]

The complex and multifaceted defense effort launched by Philip II in Havana after Drake's 1586 expedition had other important local effects, some of which are discussed later. To fortify the town, labor was imported. This included, first and foremost, African slaves who worked in the construction of the forts but also European artisans whose skill and knowledge were indispensable. Defense efforts resulted in new economic activities or greatly stimulated old ones. Among the former was copper production in eastern Cuba and the establishment of Havana's first major foundry. Among the latter was shipbuilding, which, although not new, grew considerably thanks to the orders generated by the crown for defense purposes.

The most important by-product, however, was security. That the treasuries of the New World could sometimes be deposited in the forts of Havana for several months was a testament to the military strength of the town, to its aura of impregnability. These were not trivial amounts but millions of reales in silver and other precious commodities, such as cochineal, which stayed behind when both fleets could not sail back together.[81] Security had not come cheap, as the crown had to invest tens of millions of reales to protect the port of Havana, which was in fact an investment to protect the vulnerable sea lanes of the Spanish Atlantic and the flow of bullion from the Americas to Seville. These investments and the security they created, in turn, paved the way for the transformation of Havana into a fast-growing and increasingly complex city.

CHAPTER FOUR

Urban Growth

Havana's defense rested not only on the strength of its permanent garrison, its forts, the chain locking the bay, and the galleys that tried to keep enemy vessels away. It rested primarily on its population, which, up to the last quarter of the sixteenth century, was quite small. In purely demographic terms, the attack by Jacques de Sorés in 1555 had produced a clear lesson: unless it was endowed with a larger population, the key to the New World could be easily seized by Spain's enemies.

Mid-sixteenth-century documents convey a sense of urgency concerning the need to enlarge the population of Havana. But endowing the port with inhabitants was not an easy task. A garrison helped, of course, and soldiers were permanently stationed in town since the 1560s. Military constructions made a contribution as well, as free and enslaved workers were imported to build the forts. Furthermore, the crown attempted to implement policies that were clearly conducive to the growth of the port town through various concessions and grants.

Combined with the economic and commercial opportunities created by the fleets and the maritime movement they generated, these factors produced dramatic results. By the early seventeenth century the old ghost of depopulation had been forgotten, and Havana's population growth was the fastest in the Americas. This growth had far-reaching urban and economic consequences. Construction boomed. New services — educational, religious, and medical — became available. Recognizing these transformations, the crown granted Havana the official title of "city" in 1592. The gradual transformation of Havana into a more complex and multifunctional urban space, in turn, attracted new inhabitants. It was a complex web of interactions in which, as Fernand Braudel would put it, the number of people was at the same time cause and consequence.[1]

Population

To begin, a note on terminology. Sixteenth-century documents never refer to the total number of people residing in town but use other categories with juridical, racial, and gender implications. The term most commonly used was "vecino," a category roughly equivalent to household head, which indicated that a person was domiciled in a given town, paid whatever taxes or tributes its residents owed, and, depending on race and gender, had the right to participate in its civic rituals.[2]

This category had strong racial and sexual undertones, but it was not applied exclusively to males of European origin. People deemed to be of mixed racial ancestry, free blacks, and even freed African people could become vecinos. Widows heading their own households were sometimes included in this category as well. Although the medieval laws of Castile defined "vecino" in gendered terms, to the exclusion of women, as an individual who settled in a place "with his wife, children and family and most of its movable goods," in practice and later in law it was possible for women to become vecinos and to enjoy some of the privileges attached to this condition, such as the right to petition the town council for land. Philip II's Population Ordinances of 1573 provided a legal foundation for this inclusion, for they established that the children of the conquistadores, male and female, were to be considered vecinos, subject to certain conditions.[3]

The problem, of course, is that in order to calculate a population total, it is necessary to apply a multiplier to the number of vecinos. Calculating this multiplier has been the subject of intense controversy among demographic historians. One issue is whether the "total" should include only the free resident population (in the sense of usual residence) or also the transient population, which in the case of port cities such as Havana could be quite sizable. The multiplier also changes if it is to include the nonfamily members of the household, usually dependents of the household head who could be legally free or enslaved.[4]

But if one is interested in establishing temporal changes or the relative importance of a given settlement in the colonial world, then it is possible to use the numbers of vecinos directly, without further extrapolation. However, it should be understood that this category may not have been used consistently in all colonial sources, and that these figures are at best educated estimates made by colonial officials and travelers.

Enough estimates exist for us to attempt a general characterization of the demographic evolution of Havana. The first available figure corresponds to 1538 and was produced by Fidalgo de Elvas, a Portuguese nobleman who accompanied Hernando de Soto on his expedition to Florida. Elvas traveled across the island and reported on the size of all the settlements created by the Spanish in Cuba during the early 1500s. According to his testimony, Havana had about 70 "houses" at the time, a number only slightly lower than that in Santiago de Cuba, the capital of the colony and its main center of gold production and commerce. Compared with almost any other figures from the mid-sixteenth century, however, those of Elvas are extremely high and need to be treated with caution. Indeed, only a few years later Bishop Diego Sarmiento reported that there were 40 vecinos in town, a number that is in line with the figures in other registries from the same period. One plausible explanation – in addition to the tentative nature of these figures – is that the expedition of de Soto contributed significantly to the demographic depletion of Havana and other Cuban towns, as contemporaries indeed asserted.[5]

In any case, there is little doubt that Havana's resident European population remained at best stationary in the 1540s and 1550s. According to the cabildo, in 1553 there were only 30 vecinos living there permanently. Governor Angulo managed to gather some 35 Spaniards during the attack by Sorés in 1555. A list of residents prepared by local authorities afterward enumerated 38 vecinos. When analyzed in terms of vecinos, all available accounts suggest that Havana reached its demographic nadir in the 1550s.[6]

The gradual transformation of the town into a stopover for the returning vessels and into the point of reunion of the fleets after the 1560s had noticeable demographic effects. Initial population growth was quite slow, however: a 1570 pastoral visit reported the existence of 60 vecinos in the town, almost double figure in the mid-sixteenth-century registry but still a very small number in absolute terms. Moreover, Havana continued to be a relatively small settlement even within the Cuban context. The main population center was Bayamo, "the best town in the island, very healthy and with many haciendas," according to the bishop. Bayamo's population figure was somewhat inflated because it included 70 vecinos and 80 "married Indians," whereas in Havana the indigenous people had been grouped – in fact, segregated – into a nearby town, Guanabacoa, where 60 "married Indians" lived. But the bishop treated both categories as equivalent, and, more to the point, later accounts do not distinguish the indigenous population from the vecinos. Instead, later population counts refer to the indigenous people as "hispanicized" or as "already mixed with the Spaniards." In any case, Havana's population was smaller than Bayamo's even if one adds to it the indigenous population of Guanabacoa.[7]

It was during this initial period of slow growth, when the importance of Havana's port and the insufficient size of its population were painfully obvious, that the crown implemented policies that sought to augment the population of the port town. These policies had been actively sought by the residents of Havana and by their allies in Seville, for whom protecting the port town was a matter of financial self-preservation. "We have received reports from the Island of Cuba that such island and its vecinos are very poor and that if we do not give them grants it will depopulate," the king noted in 1566. The University of Seafarers of Seville wrote to the king a few years later to stress the same point: "It is convenient that Your Majesty orders to have a great population there, which can be done by giving immunities and favors and prerogatives to the people who go to populate and to reside in Havana." The Seville merchants even proposed that married men who had committed "excesses" in other colonial territories may be exiled in Havana in order to increase the population.[8]

The crown acquiesced, extending significant benefits to people already living in Havana or going to settle there. In contrast to other areas of the empire, the cabildos of Havana and the other Cuban towns retained the ability to distribute lands until the early eighteenth century.[9] The residents of the port town obtained fiscal concessions as well. Export taxes on some of the main products of the island, such as hides, were cut in 1556 by 50 percent during the next eight years. The residents requested the renewal of this benefit in the 1570s and 1580s and even managed to get a total fiscal exemption for their exports in 1586. At the same time, in 1569 all products imported by Havana residents or by new immigrants to furnish and supply their households became exempt from all taxes for six years. The importance of the population argument was acknowledged in many of these regulations. As a 1576 royal cedula granting a 50 percent tax reduction on exports asserted, without such benefits the island would become "depopulated."[10]

The residents of Havana also obtained important concessions concerning imports from Europe. Whereas taxes on merchandise exported from Seville or the Canary Islands to the colonies increased from 7.5 to 10 percent in the 1570s, exports to Cuba were taxed at a 2.5 percent rate. This benefit was granted by the crown in the late 1570s for just six years, but Havana authorities managed to extend it through the 1590s. Whenever some of these concessions were about to expire, the cabildo instructed its petitioner in court, as it did in 1588, to ask the king for "a prorogation of the grants that this village and island have, of import duties as well as export duties."[11]

These measures, which maximized the commercial advantages of Havana, produced the desired results. Population grew at such a fast rate that by the late sixteenth century local authorities, instead of asking for a renewal of tax exemptions, began to request instead that taxes be raised and their proceeds used to finance the construction of public buildings in the city.[12] It was no longer nec-

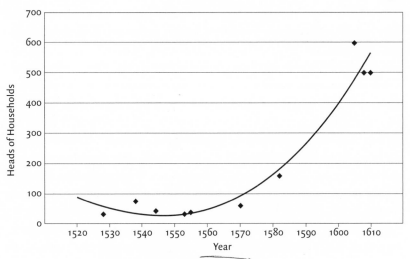

Figure 4.1. Estimated Free Population, 1520–1610
Source: De la Fuente, "Población y crecimiento."

essary, as a royal cedula of 1566 had stated, to induce merchants to go to Havana through exemptions and favors.[13] By then merchants were flocking to the port city attracted by its commercial opportunities and by the security of its well-guarded port.

The old depopulation argument had lost its ability to affect colonial policy because after the 1580s it was impossible to make such a case. After the slow initial recovery of the 1560s, precisely at the time Havana was consolidating as an important colonial port town, demographic growth accelerated. The number of vecinos more than doubled from 1570 (60) to 1582, when some 143 are listed. The next figures available correspond to the first decade of the seventeenth century. By then the number of vecinos had jumped to 500 or 600, depending on the source. Between 1580 and 1610 the resident free population of the city quadrupled. There is even one contemporary estimate, doubtlessly exaggerated, that refers to the existence of 1,500 vecinos in Havana in 1602 (see figure 4.1).[14]

The information available in Havana's parish registries corroborates the existence of a significant demographic growth during these years. Unfortunately, baptism records do not start until 1590 and do not reflect the dramatic changes that occurred during the previous decade or so. Despite this limitation, the trend after 1590 points clearly to significant growth, as the number of baptisms of free children in the city increased from about 20 per year in 1591–92 to about 70 or 80 in the first decade of the seventeenth century – a more than threefold increase.

This demographic growth, however, was not due to natural growth alone.

Immigration played a significant role, although estimating its importance in Havana during this period is nearly impossible. According to the lists of passengers departing from Seville, the number of immigrants to Cuba increased significantly in the late sixteenth century, from 32 in 1540–59 to 209 in 1580–1600.[15] However, many of the people who settled in the city did not come directly from Spain. They are registered in the Seville lists (if at all) as going somewhere else. Many of the new settlers reached Havana after traveling to other areas in the vast colonial world or simply chose the city as the place to defect from the armadas and fleets before sailing back to Spain. Scholars have noted that enlisting as soldiers or seamen in the convoys and deserting later in the Indies was one of the most common and economic ways to emigrate to the New World. Absenteeism of soldiers and seamen could reach high proportions, and many stayed behind in port cities such as Havana, which often represented the last opportunity to remain in the Americas. The same was true for passengers, who chose to stay even when they had permission to remain in the colonies only for a limited period of time.[16]

Local authorities frequently referred to the desertion of soldiers and seamen from the armadas and fleets in Havana. In 1576 the king ordered that "fugitive soldiers from the galleons" be apprehended, punished by whipping, and sent imprisoned to Spain to do forced labor in the galleys for four years. A military officer reported that ships came loaded with passengers and mariners from France, England, Flanders, Germany, Italy, Greece, Venice, Genoa, and Sicily and that many stayed behind in Havana. Desertions were by definition covert, but references to them do exist. For instance, in 1607 authorities captured six soldiers, five apprentice seamen, and twenty-four "youngsters" who had escaped from the armada of General Francisco del Corral. In 1601, when the fleets wintered in Havana, fourteen out of ninety soldiers in the admiral's galleon of the fleet of Tierra Firme disappeared between September 1601 and February 1602. This rate of absenteeism was not unique, for the proportion of soldiers and seamen abandoning their ships could be as high as 20 percent.[17]

As one would expect, most of the free permanent residents of Havana, a category that does not include soldiers or the city's transient population, came from the Iberian Peninsula (see table 4.1). Four-fifths of all immigrants came from Spain, although of course this denomination included peoples from many "nations" whose political unification was still recent and incomplete. As late as the 1520s or 1530s, chronicler Gonzalo Fernández de Oviedo noted that "many different sorts of people" had gone to the New World and that although they were "vassals of the Kings of Spain" differences between them were significant.

Table 4.1. Origin of Immigrants,
Percentage Distribution, 1585–1610

Origin	1585–1610 (N = 379)	1589–1610 (N = 111)
Spain	77.0	74.8
Andalusia	41.8	43.4
Aragon	1.7	—
Asturias	1.7	4.8
Castile	14.4	19.3
Catalonia	2.1	—
Extremadura	3.8	3.6
Galicia	5.5	2.4
León	2.4	7.2
Murcia	0.3	—
Valencia	0.3	1.2
Vascongadas	2.4	3.6
Canary Islands	23.6	14.5
Portugal	8.4	10.5
Azores	2.1	—
Madeira	0.3	—
Italy	2.1	0.9
England	0.3	—
France	0.3	—
Flanders	0.8	—
Germany	—	0.9
Ragusa	—	0.9
Other Spanish colonies	8.7	12.0

Sources: 1585–1610: ASCH, Libro Barajas de Matrimonios, 1584–
1622; 1589–1610: ANC, PNH, ER, 1589–1610.

"Who will concert the Biscayne with the Catalonian, who are from such different provinces and languages?" he asked. How, wondered Oviedo, would people from Andalusia, Aragon, Valencia, Guipúzcoa, Galicia, and Castile get along in the New World? Writing not long before Oviedo, chronicler Pedro Mártir de Anglería referred to the same problem, marveling that the military campaign against the Muslims in the late fifteenth century had brought together people as different as the "proud Asturians" and the "rude inhabitants of the Pyrenees" who had mixed with Castilians and Andalusians "like members of one family."[18]

As in the New World as a whole, by far the largest group of Spanish immigrants in Havana came from Andalusia. Many had been born in Seville and its agriculturally rich hinterland. Others came from cities such as Cádiz, Granada,

Jaén, Córdoba, and Málaga. Living close to the Sevillian gateway had clear advantages, as travel times and expenses were proportionally reduced. Whereas walking from Córdoba could be done in four days, traveling on foot from León, Galicia, the Basque provinces, or Asturias required between fifty and eighty days minimum. As is frequently the case with emigration, there was a cumulative effect as well. The prevalence of Andalusia in the early waves of migration guaranteed its continuing importance later on in the century, as relatives and people from the same towns and cities created networks that facilitated the movement of more emigrants from the same areas. As historian Ida Altman has stated, "Emigrants followed their relatives to the same destinations, where they could hope for assistance in establishing themselves."[19]

Immigrants maintained active ties with their hometown. Doing so with Seville or other Andalusian towns was particularly easy from Havana, given the active correspondence and regular communications that existed between Havana and Seville since the mid-sixteenth century. Some of the immigrants from Andalusia used the opportunities that Havana provided to bring family members or conduct family businesses from afar. A recently established vecino, Francisco de Carrera, for instance, sent with a fleet passenger the money required to cover the travel expenses of his daughter Francisca Carrera and her husband, Baltasar de los Reyes, vecinos of Seville. They were to join him in Havana, where he was established with a house, wife, and children. Likewise, Simón de Padilla gave power of attorney to Captain Pedro de las Muñecas, who was on his way to Seville, so that he could arrange for the trip of his wife and son to Havana.[20]

A somewhat different case is that of Captain Juan de la Vega, a vecino of Havana born in Cádiz. In 1604 de la Vega and his son Miguel de la Vega gave power of attorney to a resident of Cádiz so that Juan de la Vega, Miguel's brother, who also lived in Cádiz, could sell a house in their name. The house, which belonged to Miguel, was being put up for sale because apparently Miguel was going to stay in Havana permanently. Immigration was frequently a family affair in which different members participated and helped in various ways.[21]

The second most important group of immigrants, larger perhaps than that from Castile, originated in the Canary Islands. Emigration from the Canaries to the Americas during the sixteenth century remains somewhat of a puzzle. Scholars of Spanish migration have found little or no evidence of Canarians moving to the colonies, although their migration was legally authorized since the 1520s. Some authors have explained that their absence in the list of passengers does not mean that they did not migrate but rather that they did so without registering with the Casa de la Contratación, as all emigrants were required to do. Others, however, have argued that the low proportion of individuals from the Canaries is not a function of these sources; otherwise they would appear in the colonial documentation.[22]

There is evidence that Canarians moved to the Americas in numbers larger than what the passenger lists suggest. There is also evidence that the islands were used as a boarding station by unauthorized emigrants. The trip of Girolamo Benzoni to the New World in 1541 illustrates this phenomenon. Benzoni traveled by land from Milan to Medina del Campo and from there to Seville. In Seville he took a boat down the Guadalquivir to San Lúcar de Barrameda – Seville's gateway to the Atlantic – where he boarded a vessel for Gran Canaria. After a two-month wait, Benzoni boarded a caravel at La Palma loaded with wines that was going to the New World. His case is surely not unique, although emigrating via the Canaries required resources beyond the means of most commoners. In 1566 the king ordered the justices in the Canaries to strictly prohibit the departure for the colonies of any person without royal license, a clear indication that emigration from the islands was far from exceptional.[23]

The settling of Canarian immigrants in Havana seems to have occurred in large numbers only in the 1590s. A 1582 report of the town's population mentioned that although there were "islanders" in Havana, they left "once they [made] their haciendas and [sold] their wines." Growing maritime and commercial links between the Canary Islands and Havana in the late sixteenth century clearly facilitated the emigration of Canarians to the port city. Like wines, most immigrants came from La Palma and Tenerife, the two islands that maintained a more active commercial relationship with Havana. Many of these individuals probably emigrated illegally. In 1606, for instance, Governor Valdés reported that he had initiated a legal process against Juan Yañez, owner of a vessel from the Canary Islands, because it had brought four passengers without the required royal license.[24]

Canarian migration was distinctive in its gender composition. Men represented the majority of Spanish emigrants to the New World in the sixteenth century, and the records from Havana corroborate this assertion, with masculinity rates (number of men per 100 women) as high as 217. The Canarians were a different story, for they represented the only case in which women were the majority: 61 percent. The sexually balanced composition of emigrants from the Canaries suggests that emigration from these islands was family-based and, perhaps, that laxer controls in the islands allowed for the emigration of single women, which was legally forbidden.[25] Contemporaries themselves associated Canarians with family migration. When the contractor of the copper mines in Santiago de Cuba spoke of the need to bring settlers to the area, he requested royal authorization to bring fifty "married vecinos" from the Canary Islands with their wives and children. Family emigration continued to characterize Canarian migration to Cuba during the seventeenth century, with women still representing a slight majority.[26]

Local records allow us to explore the activities of what seems to have been a small but dense network of Canarian merchants in Havana. Clearly the commercial opportunities and the maritime traffic of the port city attracted large numbers of merchants from the Canary Islands, but not all moved with their families to the city. Among those who established an early commercial presence in Havana was Francisco Díaz Pimienta, a merchant from La Palma. During the quarter century for which Díaz Pimienta's activities are registered in the local records (they begin in 1586), he was involved in mercantile operations worth 1.8 million reales.[27] He specialized in the importation of wine and other products from the islands, but his activities covered many other items, including merchandise from competitors of Canarian producers. In 1599, for instance, Díaz Pimienta received 270 pipes of Canarian wine in two separate shipments from La Palma. He also received a shipment from Seville that included 50 pipes of the so-called wine of Castile. Business was worse in 1600, as two shipments from Seville were partially lost. Díaz Pimienta owned at least one ship that was built in Havana in 1588 and participated in the slave trade as well. In 1591 he imported slaves and sugar from Santo Domingo worth 45,000 reales and, along with several investors from La Palma, financed the voyage of the slave ship *San Antonio*, master Gonzalo Prieto, to Angola in 1600.

Díaz Pimienta never settled in Havana, although he obviously spent long periods of time there conducting his business. His commercial interests in the city were served by his son-in-law, Captain Alonso de Ferrera, also from La Palma, who apparently came first to Havana in 1599. Like his father-in-law's business, Ferrera's commercial ventures covered a large variety of products, although, as always with merchants from the Canaries, wine and naval stores figured prominently among them. His commercial operations between 1603 and 1604 exemplify his diverse interests and ventures. During this period Ferrera bought an armed ship, the *San Luis*, with a capacity of 200 tons. The whole operation was conducted by Canarians. The seller, merchant Rafael Pérez from Tenerife, was acting on behalf of a vecino from La Palma. Ferrera, in turn, bought the ship with his associate Luis Lorenzo, a merchant from Tenerife who, as we shall see, was fairly active in the Caribbean during these years. Also in association with Lorenzo, Ferrera received two hundred pipes of wine from the islands in 1604. On behalf of several investors from La Palma with whom he was associated, his father-in-law, Díaz Pimienta, among them, he collected 40,000 reales for merchandise dispatched to Puerto Rico. In all, Ferrera's notarized transactions in Havana amount to more than 1.2 million reales.

Unlike Díaz Pimienta, Ferrera eventually settled permanently in Havana. He rented a house in 1601 and bought a tile-roof house in 1609. He also built a new house that, according to the governor, was "the best" in the city. In 1610 he brought his wife, Juana Díaz Pimienta, to live with him and "do marital life."[28]

Like Ferrera, merchant Rafael Pérez from Tenerife ended up settling in Havana. Pérez appears in the notarial records for the first time in 1592 selling a slave. In his case the labels describing his status in local society tell part of the story. He is referred to as a "transient" (*estante*) until 1602, as a "resident" (*residente*) between 1602 and 1604, and as a "vecino" after 1605. In 1606 he consolidated his place in local society through a marriage with doña Lorenza Giraldo, daughter of prominent vecino Captain Pedro de Carvajal and of doña María de Rosales. Carvajal, who is described as a merchant in 1598, occupied several important positions in the local structures of power. He was named treasurer of the Santa Cruzada in 1598, served as steward of the cabildo between 1599 and 1602, was appointed alcalde of the Santa Hermandad, the local rural police, in 1602, and finally elected alcalde of the cabildo in 1610. By this time he was also a captain in the local militias. Pérez's marriage thus brought him into the family of a merchant who had become a member of the local elite. He continued his commercial ventures. In 1608 Pérez entered a company with several vecinos of Tenerife to transport and sell three hundred pipes of wine in Havana and Veracruz. By 1609 he owned three houses in Havana, and at least one of them was centrally located in the city's square and described as a "good" house. The same source referred to Pérez as "a rich man from this place."[29]

Another prominent member of this group of Canarian merchants was Luis Lorenzo, from Tenerife. Lorenzo was particularly active in Havana during 1595–1603, when he seems to have resided more or less permanently in the city. He rented a house in 1595 and a warehouse in 1597. Lorenzo imported large quantities of wine, tar, and other products from the Canary Islands and from Seville. But he seems to have specialized in the distribution of these products through the Caribbean, a trade he conducted at least in part in his own vessels. We know that in 1597 he owned the navío *La Veracruz* together with a fellow merchant from Isla de Fierro, in the Canaries. In 1602 his frigate *Nuestra Señora del Rosario* sunk, but two years later he bough another vessel in association with merchant Alonso Ferrera.

Lorenzo also specialized in trading with slaves, whom he imported mostly from the great slave depot of Cartagena de Indias and also via Puerto Rico. His connections to the slave trade predated the first asiento of Portuguese merchant Pedro Gómez Reinel and continued afterward. In 1595 Lorenzo paid 1,500 ducados to the royal treasury for the price of sixty licenses that a vecino of Seville had bought to import slaves into Havana. Years later he was a business partner of merchant Francisco López de Piedra, agent of the asentistas Juan Rodriguez Coutino and Gonzalo Vaez Coutino in the city. In all, the value of Lorenzo's activities amounted to 630,000 reales, a third of which was related to the sale of slaves.

Lorenzo seems to have left Havana permanently after 1603, but he did not interrupt his business activities in the city. In 1607, when a Dutch armada managed to keep the fleet of New Spain anchored in San Lúcar, he obtained royal authorization to dispatch to Havana several ships loaded with merchandise.[30] After 1603 he began to operate from the Canary Islands through agents. Prominent among these was Diego Díaz Ferrera, from Tenerife, who first appeared in Havana in 1599 as the master of the frigate *San Antonio*, which arrived to the city from Garachico, Tenerife, loaded with wines. Díaz Ferrera began to reside more or less permanently in Havana after 1604, when he rented a house for two years. In 1606 he was still in the city, for he issued a power of attorney for his father, Melchor Díaz Ferrera, to arrange his marriage with María Borges de la Cruz, a resident of Tenerife. Two years later he was party to a legal dispute in Havana as representative of Luis Lorenzo. By 1609 he had probably settled permanently in the city, for he was referred to as "vecino."

Although, owing to the very nature of their activities, it is easier to trace the movements of individuals involved in trading, most immigrants from the Canaries or elsewhere did not have the capital, the networks, or the skills required to participate in the Atlantic trade. Many worked the land. Others went to Havana to partake of the city's economic prosperity, as investors or skilled workers. Pedro Gonzalez Cordero, from La Palma, was among the former. He seems to have gone to Havana around 1601. His first recorded activities have him selling hides, which suggests that he was linked to the cattle business. In 1603 he invested 10,000 reales for the construction of a sugar mill on a piece of land that he had previously purchased. By 1605 Gonzalez Cordero was firmly settled in the city, where he married into a wealthy local family. As for workers who came to the city to offer their skills, some of the first sugar masters who worked in Cuba probably came from the Canary Islands. Technical knowledge about sugar production had been transferred from older to newer production areas since medieval times, and the process continued in the Atlantic. In the early 1600s some of the first sugar mill owners in Havana sent to hire sugar masters in the Canary Islands. It is impossible to know how many of these skilled workers actually went to the city to set up sugar manufacturing there, but it is plausible that a few did.

All the sugar masters working in Havana in the early seventeenth century were white salaried workers.[31]

The migration patterns of the Portuguese resemble those of the Canarians in several ways. Although Portuguese migrants are not absent from early sixteenth-century records, their numbers were fairly small. For instance, among those who accompanied Cortés and other conquistadores to Mexico (1519–21), most of whom were recruited in Cuba, the Portuguese represented a modest 3 percent of the total. Although in strict legal terms only "naturals" from the kingdoms of Castile, Leon, Aragon, Valencia, Catalonia, and Navarra were allowed to migrate and to trade in the colonies, there were numerous exceptions to the general rule. A royal cedula of 1531 authorized the emigration of Portuguese individuals to Cuba for six years. Emperor Charles authorized the subjects of his dominions to settle in the New World and even to participate in the trade with the colonies.[32]

By the time Phillip II obtained the crown of Portugal in 1580, the Portuguese community in Havana, although very small in absolute numbers, was not negligible in relative terms. According to a military census conducted by the governor of La Fuerza in 1582, about 11 percent of the town's permanent residents (between 140 and 150 vecinos) and 6 percent of the "transients" were of Portuguese origin. They spanned the whole socioeconomic spectrum within the free sector of the population, from the principal vecinos who were "trustworthy," in the words of the officer who conducted the census, to those he described as "vecinos who work for a living." Among the latter were representatives of various trades, such as carpentry and turnery, fishermen, cowmen, agricultural laborers, and a few individuals without a known occupation.[33]

Some of these working vecinos used their trades and skills to create a comfortable economic situation for themselves and their families. Tracing their activities is of course harder than for members of the commercial elite or the bureaucracy but not impossible. Take the case of mason Gregorio Lopez, who seems to have stayed in the city for the rest of his life. Lopez arrived in Havana in the 1570s and in 1574 petitioned the cabildo for an urban parcel. He probably built two houses on this parcel, which he then sold in 1579. The houses were encumbered by a financial obligation to prominent vecino Juan Recio, a clear indication that it was Recio who had financed their construction.

The same year Lopez borrowed 1,200 ducados (13,200 reales) from another member of the local elite, Gerónimo de Rojas Avellaneda, to buy another urban parcel, three thousand roof tiles, and a slave. Lopez secured the loan with an "estancia," a small farm he already owned, including two slaves who worked on it. He paid Avellaneda an annual rent of 93 ducados – a 7.7 percent interest rate.

Lopez seems to have used this capital wisely. By 1585 he owned at least two houses, one of which he rented for 50 ducados (550 reales) per year. The house, which stood by his own and by the house of Baltasar de Viera, a Portuguese fisherman, contained a kitchen, a shop, a well, and a courtyard.

In the 1590s Lopez moved aggressively into Havana's thriving agricultural service economy. In 1597 he obtained an "estancia" from the cabildo on which to plant sugarcane and a much larger pig farm, the *corral* "El Cuabal," in 1599. The latter was probably to enlarge another farm that he had bought in the same area in 1596. This farm had twenty pigs, two horses, two dogs, plantings of yucca and green vegetables, and a *bohío*, a modest wooden house typically covered with palm tree leaves. Lopez bought two additional pig farms in 1596 and 1598. These units cost him, in all, 1,010 ducados (11,110 reales), a respectable sum at the time.

Again, Lopez seems to have invested wisely, for by 1604 he sold some of these very units at double the price. He turned El Cuabal into a cattle farm, which he sold with ninety cows, two hundred pigs, sixty-two hens, fifteen dogs, and plantings of bananas, yucca, and corn – all major items in the local diet and ship supplies. The farm was worked by a slave, Francisco Angola, who was included in the sale. Along with two other farms and an additional piece of land, this sale brought him 2,275 ducados (25,025 realers), more than double what he had paid for them in the 1590s. Lopez bought still another farm in 1605. In all, the value of his real estate transactions amounted to 68,000 reales. During these years he also bought twelve slaves and sold four, participating in mercantile exchanges worth another 45,000 reales. Two of these slaves he bought in 1600 in partnership with a tile maker, obviously to guarantee a supply for his own construction works.

The union of the crowns of Portugal and Spain in 1580 may have facilitated the emigration of the Portuguese to the island, as some historians have claimed, but it was only in the 1590s, and more precisely after 1596, that they began to arrive in larger numbers in Havana. Although the growing commercial and maritime importance of Havana, magnified by grandiose European accounts, would attract new settlers to the city, this current may have been also part of a larger movement. Emigration from Portugal increased significantly in the late sixteenth century, as many recent Jewish converts fled the country to avoid the Inquisition and tried to start their lives anew in other places, including, notably, Brazil and the Spanish colonies.[34] According to a list of Portuguese vecinos in Havana in 1607, the vast majority of them (89 percent) arrived in Havana after 1596, and more than half had arrived as late as 1601 or later. These figures are somewhat equivocal, however, for they do not include the descendants of the older Portuguese community of Havana. Although these people were considered "naturals" under Spanish legislation, they surely added to the size and viability of the Portuguese "nation" in the city. Out of 49 individuals listed in 1607, only 2 – mason Gregorio Lopez mentioned above and his neighbor, Baltasar de Viera – appear in the military census of 1582.[35]

This community, which again represented about 10 percent of Havana's permanent free population, was heavily oriented toward trade. A full 40 percent of the people with known occupations were described as "merchants," "wine sellers" and, in one case, a shop attendant. Since his arrival in Cuba, Governor Pedro de Valdés reported that more than two-thirds of the city's inhabitants were "from different nations, most of them Portuguese," who, he claimed, had correspondence with France, England, and other enemies of the Spanish crown. He recommended the expulsion of all foreigners and particularly the Portuguese, whom he described as the wealthiest group. Three years later, Valdés insisted that a large number of Portuguese had settled in Havana and other towns with their families. He claimed that many "have shops and trade publicly and have partners of their same nation in Seville. To their hands go all the money, gold, and silver that are sent from here."[36]

Valdés's description of the Portuguese "nation" in Havana was only partially accurate. Some of these merchants were indeed among the wealthiest residents of Havana. They were immersed in large-scale, long-distance transatlantic trade, moving high volumes of European merchandise in the circum-Caribbean area and sending colonial products to their associates in Spain. Many had also managed to acquire real estate in Havana, both in the city and in the surrounding countryside. A few owned sugar mills. But many, indeed most, Portuguese residents in the city did not belong in this category. The majority, 69 percent, did not even own a house in the city or have slaves (87 percent) or possess their own shop (78 percent). Some of the people linked to trade were modest retailers and wine sellers who operated taverns and worked in Havana's service economy. About a third of the Portuguese made a living as tradesmen, working as carpenters, caulkers, shoemakers, and tailors. Another 15 percent worked in sea-related jobs, as mariners and pilots. A few worked in the countryside, one of them as a "sugar master."[37]

Enrique Mendes de Noronha (or Mendez de Noroña in Spanish documents) was among the wealthiest members of the Portuguese nation in the city. He first visited Havana in 1591 and was probably forced to winter with the fleets until early 1592. According to his declaration, Mendes de Noronha became a vecino of Havana in 1596 or 1597 with his brother Diego Lopes de Noronha, although Governor Valdés lists him as a permanent resident of Havana only since 1601.[38] Dates mattered, for Spanish law allowed foreigners to remain in the New World only if they had lived there as "vecinos" for a number of years. The governor's information seems to have been correct in this case, for prior to 1602 Mendes de Noronha is always listed in the notarial records as a resident or as a transient merchant.

Beyond legal technicalities, however, it is clear that Mendes de Noronha decided to settle in Havana in the late 1590s. As was frequently the case, his emigration was part of a carefully crafted family strategy to establish a permanent presence in Havana's thriving commercial enclave. He was married to Isabel Enriquez (or Anriquez), a daughter of wealthy Portuguese merchant Jorge Rodríguez Tavares, who had settled in Seville in 1580, and of Maria Enriques, the daughter of another Portuguese migrant. From Seville, Jorge Rodríguez Tavares had maintained active business relationships with merchants in Havana since the late 1570s. In what seems to have been a decision to move a whole cluster of family members across the Atlantic to Havana, he and his wife joined Mendes de Noronha, their daughter Isabel, and their 2-year-old granddaughter Ana in the city in 1605. By then a brother of Rodríguez Tavares, Antonio Manuel Tavares, also a merchant, had moved to Havana as well. They all joined yet another brother, Hernán Rodríguez Tavares, who had lived in the city for many years and was designated as "vecino" since the late 1580s. By the early 1600s Hernán Rodríguez Tavares was a fairly prominent member of society, lord of the sugar mill San Andrés, and owner of houses and slaves. He was married to Inés Nizarda, with whom he had eight surviving children, some of whom had married into local landowning families of Castilian origin. Hernán Rodríguez Tavares's dealings with many members of his extended family reflect the importance of family links in commercial transactions. Among many others, in 1606 he owed money to Antonio Manuel Tavares and to the latter's nephew-in-law, Enrique Mendes de Noronha, who by then headed his own household and had become fairly prosperous. When interrogated in a 1609 naturalization process, Mendes de Noronha described himself as "married in this city for several years and settled with a large hacienda [estate], including houses and livestock farms, and being as I am a lord and owner of a sugar mill." In addition, he declared that he possessed large amounts of movable goods, merchandise, credit, and "a public shop." He also stated that both he and his brother Diego, although children of Portuguese parents, had been born in Seville. He was in his early thirties.[39]

Another member of this family, Simón Fernandez Leyton, arrived in Havana in 1600 to learn the merchant business. Born in the town of Castel Novo, in the Beira Baixa region, in a family that he described as "old Christians from all sides, without race of Moors and Jews," Fernandez Leyton first served in the shop of his cousin-in-law Mendes de Noronha and then worked at the shop of his uncle Antonio Manuel Tavares.[40] Again, the evidence points to a tight web of family and business relations. In 1608 Fernandez Leyton was importing merchandise from Seville that had been sent by yet another cousin, Jorge Rodríguez Tavares, who resided there.

Fernandez Leyton had a long and successful career in Havana, although his Portuguese origin caused him troubles more than once. In 1606 he married into a local family from Castile that settled in Havana in the 1590s. But in 1608 Fernandez Leyton, along with many other Portuguese residents, faced justice and was accused of having settled in the New World in violation of law. According to several regulations issued in the sixteenth century, married foreigners who lived in the New World for ten consecutive years with a known house and other goods should have been deemed "naturals" for all purposes. But a royal cedula in 1608 made things considerably harder, ordering that to trade in the New World foreigners had to have lived there for twenty years. Of these, ten had to be as a married individual with real estate and other goods.[41]

Most members of the Portuguese nation in Havana did not fulfill these requirements, for, as mentioned above, they had settled permanently in the city only after the mid-1590s. The new governor, Gaspar Ruiz de Pereda, who arrived in Havana in 1608, came with explicit orders: "to expel all Portuguese that you find in the city, single and married . . . and leave only those who have been vecinos and married for more than ten years." Doing this would not be easy, however, as the governor soon learned. Using false witnesses and documents, most Portuguese merchants managed to prove that they had been living in the city longer than the ten years mandated by law. Others, Enrique Mendes de Noronha among them, were sentenced by the governor to return to Portugal but won their cases before the Audiencia de Santo Domingo, the highest court of appeals in the Caribbean. Indeed, the governor complained that the judges of this court extended "great protection" to the wealthy members of the Portuguese nation in Havana. Still others managed to prove that they had been born in Castile, even though "their tongue" indicated a different origin. On top of these excuses, local justices interpreted the law in a lax sense, claiming that if someone was married and had lived in the New World for ten years, he should be exempted from the expulsion order. Finally, several Portuguese claimed that the law did not concern them because they had been born in the Algarve, a region of Portugal that enjoyed the same prerogatives and benefits as Castilians.[42]

Ruiz de Pereda managed to send at least a few Portuguese back, although he warned the king that every ship that called to port from other colonies, the Canary Islands, and even Spain came loaded with them. In 1611 he reported that he expelled, or initiated expulsion processes against, ninety-two Portuguese and other foreigners resident in Havana, although custom authorities in Seville asserted that they had not seen any of them and clearly doubted his assertion. Fernandez Leyton was among those expelled, which seem to have been few in fact. Although he attempted to show that he had been a vecino for more than ten years, in his case the governor found the evidence to be blatantly false. Fernandez Leyton was thus forced to litigate his case before the Council of the Indies, which finally authorized him to return to Havana and, after paying a fine, to continue his merchant business there. In the 1620s he became a sugar mill owner and was named warden of the Brotherhood of the Holy Sacrament. In 1631 he was appointed by the town council of Havana as its petitioner before the court. In the following decade he received an honorary military rank, and he then requested permission from the king to have a permanent escort of two black servants with swords, a clear social display of his "quality" and worth. The boy who arrived in 1600 to work in the shop of Mendez de Noronha had become a landowning nobleman, head of a large and respected family in the city.[43]

The Portuguese were targeted not only because of their wealth and prominence but also because there were well-founded suspicions that many of them were recent converts, new Christians who had fled from religious persecution in Spain and Portugal. Among those suspected was the very governor of the fortress of La Punta, Captain Antonio de Guzmán, accused by Governor Valdés of being a Jew from a Portuguese family, "people of low birth who work in the mechanical trades," whose house was a refuge for "all the Portuguese merchants" who traveled to Havana. Guzmán was accused of providing false testimony in favor of another Portuguese in exchange for a substantial amount of money, although it is not certain whether he was found guilty of perjury.[44] His case was not unique. Blas Ramallo and his wife, Maria de Ribera, both Portuguese, were accused of "escaping" from Spain. Ramallo enlisted as a gunner to go to the New World, and he paid in Peru for a "composition" to legalize his situation. Ribera embarked in the same fleet as a domestic servant for the wife of a colonial official. Both then left Peru, settling in Havana around 1603, where they had a shop. Another Portuguese merchant, Francisco Gomes de León, was imprisoned by the Inquisition for being a Jew and for his illegal involvement in the African slave trade in Havana and Cartagena de Indias.[45]

Some of the members of the Portuguese nation in Havana were in fact people from the various territories of the Portuguese empire. One of the wealthiest vecinos of Havana, Sebastián Fernández Pacheco, described by Valdés as the owner of "the largest hacienda in this city, movable property and real estate," came from Vila Franca do Campo, on the island of São Miguel, one of the Azores. His parents died there in the mid-1590s, and he still had a brother and other relatives in Vila Franca. Another Portuguese included in Valdés's list, Antonio Matos da Gama, a sugar master who "introduced the works of the sugar mills," had been born in Madeira.

Others, like Cristobal Mayorga, a business associate of Alonso Ferrera, the Canarian merchant, were born in Portugal but had traveled throughout the Portuguese world. Born in Portimão, in the Algarve region, Mayorga was described as a "prieto" (black, dark) of "the Portuguese nation" and as a merchant who resided most of the time in Santiago de Cuba. He seems to have been one of those "Atlantic creoles" who, as Ira Berlin points out, were proficient in the Atlantic's various languages and cultures. He arrived in Cuba aboard a slave ship and identified himself as "a pilot of the Angola trade." Black seamen were not rare in Portuguese ships, particularly in those devoted to the African trade, although probably just a few rose to the prestigious position of pilot. Once in Santiago, Mayorga began to ship hides to Ferrera in Havana and other products to Honduras.[46]

Given the importance of family links and networks, women were key to the reproduction of the Portuguese nation in Havana and indeed across the globe. Some of the Portuguese settlers in Havana immigrated with their wives, who frequently were themselves Portuguese or, as in the cases of Isabel Enriquez and Maria Enriquez, daughter and wife of Jorge Rodríguez Tavares, respectively, were the children of Portuguese emigrants, born in Seville or other Spanish territories. Among the Portuguese vecinos listed in Havana in 1607, about half were married, 37 percent of them to women of their own nation (counting only those whose origin can be ascertained). At least some of the spouses born in Spain (32 percent) and Cuba (31 percent), however, were probably the offspring of other Portuguese families, similar to the examples mentioned above.

Because of their more limited public presence, women left fewer documentary traces with which to reconstruct their activities and social trajectories. An interesting case is María Rodriguez, a Portuguese woman resident in Havana since the early 1600s whose husband, Rafael Pérez, departed for Seville around 1602. María Rodriguez managed to stay in Havana using various pretexts, despite all the provisions that ordered married women to follow their husbands. There were rumors of her being adulterous with another Portuguese immigrant, Pedro Francisco, whom she had taken into her house under the pretense that he was her nephew. Francisco was a bookseller who, owing to the little work available in his trade, made a living working on a farm. There is evidence that these allegations were not groundless, for María Rodriguez named Francisco universal heir to all her goods, which were not many, in her 1610 will. The notary even made a revealing mistake: he wrote *mi marido* ("my husband") by Francisco's name, crossing it out later.[47]

Of course the Portuguese were not the only Europeans who resided in Havana without all the legal requirements. Individuals of many other nations found their way to the New World despite the prohibitions issued by the crown since the early sixteenth century to prevent their emigration to the Americas. Many did so by enlisting as soldiers in the royal armies, which were always multinational in composition, or by signing as sailors, of whom there was a chronic shortage. Others used temporary legal loopholes, such as the authorization granted by Emperor Charles in 1525 to all the subjects of his kingdoms, which included territories in Italy, Germany, and the Netherlands, to settle and trade in the New World. And some simply falsified their papers to purchase a legal license or traveled to the Americas aboard enemy ships, staying in the colonies for various reasons.[48]

Their numbers were never large, but their presence was nevertheless conspicuous, owing to their language, customs, and the state of constant warfare that characterized Spanish relations with other Europeans during the sixteenth century. The earliest reports about Havana make reference to these foreigners, sometimes to highlight the danger they posed in the event of an attack. Jacques de Sorés, for one, was assisted by a Portuguese pilot and communicated with the vecinos through a French resident in Havana. Given the rather limited population of Havana in the mid-sixteenth century, no significant effort was made to expel these foreigners, however. In the 1550s and 1560s numerous vecinos testified that many foreign merchants opened shops in town, where they traded with wine, cheese, and merchandise from Spain and the Canary Islands. Among these merchants were a Frenchman, two brothers from Florence, and a ship owner from Armenia who claimed to be a medical doctor. Many of these merchants stayed in town only temporarily but added to the multinational character of sixteenth-century Havana. Others settled permanently. The Frenchman who communicated with Sorés in 1555 still lived in Havana ten years later, where he was accused of not making confession. In the early seventeenth century, colonial officials reported that there were small communities of French, Italians, Flemish, and Germans in the city, but they were described as "poor people" who made a living as fishermen, artisans, or other manual laborers. Adding to the population of other nations in Havana were the prisoners sentenced to hard labor at the forts, many of whom were French and Flemish.[49]

Soldiers contributed significantly to the multinational character of Havana's population. This situation was neither unique nor unprecedented. Since the early sixteenth century, Charles V's imperial armies had been staffed with soldiers from his vast dominions, with Germans and Italians, in addition to Spaniards.[50] Indeed, when the Portuguese were persecuted in Havana in the early 1600s, some of them protested that foreigners made up a significant portion of the king's troops in the city. Their claims were somewhat exaggerated but not totally baseless. Foreign soldiers, from Portugal, the Azores, France, and the Italian states, represented 9 percent of the garrison of La Fuerza and 11 percent of the garrison of El Morro in 1604. Of course, Spaniards represented the bulk of the king's troops in his Havana forts.[51]

Adding to the complexity and diversity of the population of Havana were settlers born in other colonial territories, including New Spain, La Española, Puerto Rico, Jamaica, and others. Their numbers were limited, constituting perhaps one-tenth of the nonslave immigrants living in Havana in the early seventeenth century. The descendants of earlier European emigrants to the New World, many of these individuals were probably mestizos, although they are not identified as such in the sources. In any case, their presence contributed to the growing importance of the creole (American-born) element in the population.

Havana's demographic growth, tightly linked to its port functions, was also caused by the forced immigration of thousands of Africans. As mentioned in chapter 2, during the 1590s the importation of slaves, directly from Africa or through regional entrepôts such as Cartagena de Indias, increased abruptly. That this growth took place precisely at the time that the free population was increasing and relatively large numbers of Europeans were moving to the city is of course not a coincidence. Slave imports increased along with the number of potential buyers and with the needs of the increasingly complex local economy, which required larger numbers of manual workers.

The indigenous population had filled most of the labor needs during the first half of the sixteenth century, but the encomienda was belatedly abolished in 1553. Most of the surviving "Indians" in the region were "resettled" in the neighboring town of Guanabacoa, where there were 40 to 60 households in the 1570s. Although these indigenous people were incorporated into Havana's service economy, they were too few to fulfill the growing need for labor. Besides, they were legally free. The ability of local authorities and vecinos to compel them to work in specific activities was limited and frequently met with official resistance.[52]

African slaves presented none of these problems. In principle their numbers could be increased at will – although supply was always tight – and they could be exploited in virtually any form imaginable. Not that African slaves were trouble-free. They were expensive, rebellious, and vulnerable to diseases and accidents. But, with the exception of convicts, they were the only source of hard labor, as the fortification of Havana clearly illustrated. Whereas the layout for

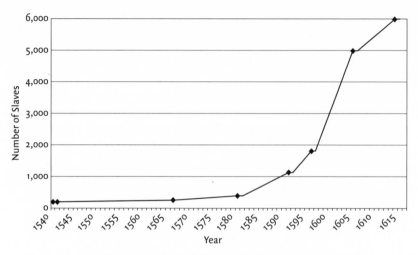

Figure 4.2. Estimated Slave Population, 1540–1615
Source: De la Fuente, "Matrimonios."

the forts was done by European engineers and their construction accomplished with American materials and financial resources, most of the actual work was done by African slaves.

Indeed, Havana's military needs played a significant role in the importation of slaves, particularly in the years prior to the mid-1590s. Since the beginning of the construction of La Fuerza, in the late 1550s, authorities made it clear that slaves were indispensable for the works and sought to obtain them through any means possible. Governor Mazariegos, for instance, ordered the vecinos to rent their own slaves to the crown for the construction works in 1559. He also confiscated every illegal slave he could lay his hands on for such purposes. In 1563 there were 30 slaves working on the fort, including 10 women, and 48 more arrived from Cartagena de Indias the same year. A shipment of 193 slaves was received directly from the Rivers of Guinea region in July 1572. By 1575, close to the completion of La Fuerza, 200 slaves worked there.[53]

The number of slaves working on Havana's military constructions remained at that level during the following decades, and more than once authorities complained that more were needed. In 1605 the crown reportedly had 190 slaves employed in the construction of the forts and another 50 or 60, described as "old" and "useless," who worked on a farm to provide for the others. In addition to these, royal officials employed as well dozens of convicts as forced laborers in the forts. In 1596 there were about 104 of them, including 45 Moor and Turk slaves.[54]

By the early 1600s, however, the relative demographic importance of the royal slaves in Havana's population, either slave or free, had declined considerably. As figure 4.2 shows, the number of slaves increased exponentially after 1590, from a few hundred in the mid-1580s, to close to 2,000 in 1600, to more than double that number by 1610.[55] This increase in size coincided with significant changes in the origins of slaves, for after 1595 the region of Angola became the most important African source of slave exports to Spanish America.

Since the Europeans identified slaves with various "nations," it is possible to determine their regions of origin. These identifications are of course approximations, for they reflect the Europeans' understanding of the labels used by the slaves to identify themselves, as well as the name of geographic points or regions and slave factories.[56] Thus slaves of the Cacheu or Mina "nations" were in fact slaves exported through the Portuguese forts of Cacheu and São Jorge da Mina. The slaves of the Quaqua "nation" came from what old geographers called the Kwakwa coast. Most of the Cape Verde slaves had been previously imported from the nearby continent, although a few could have been born in the islands.

Up to the mid-1590s most slaves in the city came from what geographers at the time described as Upper Guinea, which stretched from the Senegal River to modern Liberia (see table 4.2). "From this coast," a geographic tract asserted in the mid-sixteenth century, "they bring the black slaves to Spain."[57] Many of these slaves came from the Rivers of Guinea, a great slave-exporting region that in the late sixteenth century referred to the area between the Senegal River and Sierra Leone. From this region came the Biafara, Balanta, Bañon, Berbesí, Bioho, Nalu, Cazanga, and Bran. Sometimes the documents made reference to both the "nation" and the location, as in the sale of a slave "of the Bran nation from the Rivers."[58] Although the Europeans considered them to belong to different "nations," these groups lived in close proximity, shared similar languages, and maintained contacts with one another. For instance, from the area between the Casamance and Santo Domingo rivers, described by geographer Luis de Mármol in 1599 as heavily inhabited by "great peoples," came the Balanta, Bañon, and Cazanga. To these were added the Folupo in the early 1600s. The Biafara and Nalu shared the delta of Río Grande with the Bioho, who inhabited the Bissagos islands facing the river.[59]

North of this region, in the Senegal Valley, were located the Mandinga and Jolofo (Wolof), two groups that contemporaries frequently characterized as being at least partially Islamicized. Alonso de Sandoval, who knew the slaves firsthand and worked with them upon their arrival at Cartagena de Indias, asserted that both groups followed the "sect of Mohammed," and he blamed the Mandinga for its diffusion throughout the coast of Guinea. Writing in 1606, a Jesuit referred

Table 4.2. Ethnonyms Applied to African Slaves,
Percentage Distribution, 1570–1610

Area	Ethnonym	1570–94 (N = 460)	1595–1610 (N = 1,804)
Cape Verde, Senegambia, "Rivers of Guinea"	Balanta	0.4	0.1
	Bañon	4.6	4.4
	Berbesi	0.4	0.3
	Biafara	14.1	6.6
	Bioho	3.0	0.8
	Bran	17.4	9.4
	Cabo Verde	0.4	0.2
	Casanga	1.3	0.4
	Folupo	—	0.1
	Fulo	—	0.1
	Jolofo	2.2	1.8
	Mandinga	2.2	1.9
	Nalu	1.5	1.6
	Zape	7.8	2.8
	Zoso	0.2	—
Gold Coast, Gulf of Guinea	Arara	—	1.2
	Arda	—	0.2
	Carabalí	0.2	0.4
	Lucumí	0.2	0.3
	Sao Tome	—	0.4
	Terranova	1.3	0.5
	Zemba	0.4	—
Congo, Angola	Angola	28.0	53.5
	Congo	8.3	9.2
	Enchico	1.7	2.1
	Manicongo	0.7	—
	Mosanga	—	0.2
	Motembo	—	0.1
Mozambique	Mozambique	0.9	0.9
Unknown/other		2.4	0.5

Sources: Inventario mayorazgo de Antón Recio, 1570 and 1575, in ANC, PNH, Escribanía Galleti, 1774-75, fol. 134v; ANC, PNH, ER, 1578-1610; ASCH, Libro Barajas de Matrimonios de Españoles, 1584-1622; Libro Barajas de Bautismos, 1589-1600.

to the Mandinga in similar terms. In addition, both groups were deemed to be fiery and hard to control. The royal officials of Cuba reported in 1561 that the Mandinga were disobedient and lazy, a belief that was shared in other Caribbean colonies. The same was said about the Wolof, whom many contemporaries described as warriors who did not make good and obedient slaves. Although the crown attempted to limit or even prohibit the importation of these groups, par-

ticularly the Wolof, their presence in Havana and other colonies was not negligible. Prohibitions notwithstanding, the wars that resulted in the disintegration
of the Wolof confederation in the mid-sixteenth century made slaves available
for exportation to Iberia and the New World.[60] In the early seventeenth century
members of another group from this area, the Fulo or Fula, reached Havana
as well. According to most contemporaries, the Fulo, who were also considered
Muslims, were neighbors of the Mandinga.[61]

The population of Sierra Leone was represented in Havana by the Zape (or
Sape) and by the Zozo (or Zoso). Quite numerous through the end of the sixteenth century, the Zape represented 8 percent of all the slaves identified in
Havana during the period up to 1595. Conversely, the Zozo were quite rare, although their existence has been documented in Mexico, Venezuela, and Santo
Domingo. Their numbers may have been small because – in many, if not most,
cases – the Zozo may have entered the New World under other denominations.
Sandoval, for instance, says that the Zozo were of "Mandinga caste," so they
could have been imported in the Americas under that name.[62]

Although the Upper Guinea region was the main source of African slaves in
Havana, prior to the first Portuguese asientos (1595), about 40 percent of all slaves
had come from much farther south, from the Bantu-speaking areas of Congo and
Angola. By far the most numerous slaves were those designated as Congo and
Angola – two general denominations that probably encompassed peoples from
a wide area who nonetheless shared certain basic linguistic and cultural traits.
From the northern Congo region were the Enchico or Anchica, who, according
to Duarte Lopez and Filippo Pigafetta, lived in the interior, beyond Loango. In
Mexico these slaves were sometimes mixed with the Mosanga, of whom there
was one individual in Havana in 1597. From the Kingdom of Congo were the
Manicongo, a denomination that referred to the ruler of the kingdom and that
the slave traders mistakenly applied to the slaves from the area. Also from Congo
were the Motembo, slaves who came from what geographer Dapper described as
the "lordship" of Motemo, between Congo and Angola.[63]

By far the largest group during the whole period covered here, from the 1570s
through 1610, was composed of the Angola slaves. Although Angola was conquered by the Portuguese in the 1570s, the slaves from Angola do not appear in
Havana until 1585. Their numbers multiplied significantly thereafter, however,
for the asiento administrators had a personal stake in the Angola trade.

As mentioned in chapter 2, the slaves from the Gold Coast and the Gulf of
Guinea were rarely represented in Havana during this period. As John Thornton has noted, the Gold Coast "exported few slaves during its first century and
a half of contact with Europe." From the westernmost section of this region

came the Zemba, the Arara (also known in Cuba as Arada), the Arda, and the Yoruba-speaking Lucumí. Many of these slaves, particularly the Arara and the Arda, were exported from the factories at Ouidah (Whydah) in modern Benin, which gained in importance during the seventeenth century. Also from this area were the slaves Terranova, exported through the Portuguese enclave of Porto Novo, east of Whydah. From farther east came the Carabalí (Kalabari), who were to become the preferred slaves in Cuba during the nineteenth century. The São Tomé slaves were not necessarily from the island but from one of the exporting regions in the mainland linked to it.[64]

A few additional slaves, about 1 percent of the total, came from Mozambique, and at least one was described as a slave from the "Yndia of Portugal," a vague denomination that could refer to almost any of the Portuguese-dominated territories in Asia, from Sofala to the Java and the Spice Islands. There were also a few North African slaves despite royal prohibitions to the contrary. In 1593, when a Juan de la Cruz was baptized, he was described as a "newly converted, natural . . . of the Africa in Barbary." Among the royal slaves, assigned to the forts and other tasks, there were also several who were described as "Moors." One of these was Mustafa Anatolia, a Turkish slave who was baptized in 1595. By then it was stated that the king had "more Moors than those needed" in the city, and as late as the mid-seventeenth century the local authorities in Havana ordered all owners to declare the number of Moors in their possession.[65]

Adding to the diversity of the slave population in Havana was a growing number of non-African slaves. Most of these were *criollos* born on the island (about 8 percent of the slaves sold in the local market between 1578 and 1610), whose numbers began to grow in the 1590s.[66] Between 1590 and 1599, 236 newly born slaves were baptized in Havana. Creole slaves also came from other colonial territories, including Mexico, Puerto Rico, Jamaica, Cartagena, Honduras, Panama, Guatemala, and even more remote places such as Perú and Bolivia. Almost 2 percent of the total came from Santo Domingo, where the sugar economy was in full decay by the late sixteenth century. A few descendants of Africans came also from the Iberian Peninsula and from Portuguese possessions such as Madeira and the Azores.

The demographic growth of Havana and the multiple origins of its diverse population were expressions of the city's functions and possibilities within the Atlantic. At the same time, however, prevailing notions of social worth and hierarchy imposed a certain degree of simplicity on this Atlantic settlement. Despite the increasing complexity of local society, or perhaps because of it, the population was fragmented into large groups separated by boundaries of status (the free and the unfree) and race and origin (white old Christians versus new converts and gentiles). A brutal homogeneity determined by perceptions of race, class, and origin lay behind the facade of diversity. These lines were, of course, permanently contested and subject to constant negotiation, but they also became increasingly rigid and codified, as an emerging local elite attempted to solidify its newly acquired preeminence and wealth.

By then the old depopulation ghost, so frequently invoked by local residents to exact benefits and concessions from the crown, had lost all its power. On the contrary, late sixteenth-century and early seventeenth-century testimonials coincide in depicting a booming commercial city that had no difficulties in attracting population. As early as 1575 one of the town's alcaldes reported that Havana was "much grown" in terms of population and that each year the fleets brought many more people to it. In 1602 the town council not only reported that the city had experienced "very rapid growth" during the previous eight years but confidently asserted that it was going to grow even more in the near future.[67]

Their prediction proved correct. Although it is nearly impossible to establish with precision the total population of Havana during the early years of the seventeenth century, it is likely that by 1610 between 7,000 and 10,000 people lived in the city and its enormous hinterland. According to several testimonies, there were 500 to 800 vecinos in the city around 1608–10. Their average family size was 5.26, which means a permanent resident population of 2,600 to 4,000 people.[68] To these one must add the garrison (about 450) and a nonspecified number of "residents" who had not become vecinos in the city for whatever reason. Using data compiled from the notarial records, Cuban historian Leandro Romero has estimated that in the 1580s there were roughly 5 vecinos per "resident."[69] If we apply the same proportion to the 1600s, it is possible to estimate an additional 500 to 800 free people living in the city more or less permanently. This means a total free resident population of 4,000 or 5,000 individuals. A similar number of slaves lived in the city as well, according to local authorities. In this case the discrepancies are minimal. In 1609 the town council reported that there were 5,000 slaves living in Havana. A few years later the bishop reported the existence of more than 4,000, and in a memorial sent to the crown in 1618 there is mention of 6,000.[70]

Thus African slaves and their descendants represented nearly half of Havana's total population, a fact that seventeenth-century observers did not dispute.[71] As part of this process of transformation, the Atlantic port city had become a collection of African and European "nations" living by the sea. Needless to say, this growth was not just demographic. The changes experienced by Havana since the 1550s had transformed the physical layout of the city itself.

Urbanization

The town that Jacques de Sorés attacked in 1555 was a modest settlement that was urban only in the sense that within it were concentrated a few basic administrative, economic, and cultural functions. Its main buildings were the old fortress, a hospital, and a stone church. A few dozen houses, inhabited by a small number of Europeans, natives, and Africans, constituted the town. These were very modest constructions, wooden huts covered with palm tree leaves that borrowed freely from the housing designs of the natives. The house of old vecino Juan de Rojas, which Sorés turned into his quarters during the occupation of Havana, stood out as one of the few European-looking stone houses in town. It was also one of the few edifices left standing after Sorés burned the town, although with the roof destroyed.

The process of reconstruction that followed allows us to trace the expansion of the town, the creation of infrastructure, and the construction of new buildings. It also gives us a sense of the priorities of the various actors involved in the process of building the port town (which would soon become a port city). It is hardly a coincidence that, whereas the restoration of the town's only church did not begin until 1570, the vecinos promoted the construction of an aqueduct in 1562, while the crown financed the construction of a new fortress, La Fuerza, which began in 1558. Religion mattered, as the construction of several new religious buildings demonstrates, but provisioning the ships with fresh water and protecting the town mattered more. In this contested corner of the Atlantic God would have to wait. As Manuel Moreno Fraginals has argued, a seafaring, military, and commercial culture avoids abstractions and is reflected in concrete and utilitarian projects. In contrast to some of the administrative and religious centers of the empire, Havana's grandeur was not to be displayed in the magnificence of its temples but in the weight of its ordnance, the size of its garrison, and the capacity of its shipyards. The town lacked a convent but had dozens of taverns and lodging inns where crews and travelers could ease their thirst, gamble, buy sexual pleasure, and find some rest.[72]

The chronology of the works undertaken in Havana during the second half of the sixteenth century suggests that they were driven by concrete economic and military needs. During the initial years, roughly between 1556 and 1570, some of the structures destroyed by Sorés were rebuilt, and a major project, necessary to Havana's maritime functions, was launched. For obvious reasons the construction of La Fuerza received priority. Protection was indispensable for Havana to perform the functions of a maritime station. Second in order was the construction of la zanja, Havana's aqueduct. One of the grave limitations of the

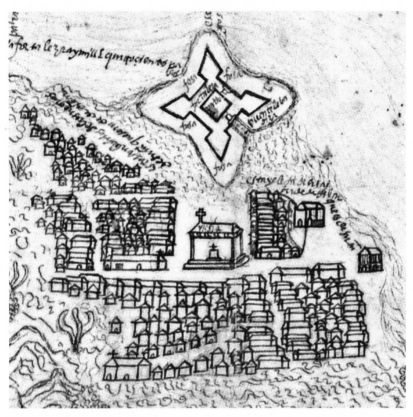

This drawing of the urban area of Havana around 1580 shows the centrality
of La Fuerza and the Parroquial Mayor. "Plano de la Habana" (ca. 1580),
detail, AGI, Mapas y Planos, Santo Domingo, 4.

town's port was that it did not have potable water, which had to be brought in
with great cost and difficulties. This problem was evident as early as 1545: "In this
village there is great need to bring water for the many ships that come here,"
reported the governor. "It is very important that water be brought to the village for the good dispatch of the ships that call to its port," concurred the town
council's petitioner in 1559.[73] In 1562 the crown, responding favorably to local
requests, approved the creation of a special tax on three key products consumed
locally – wine, soap, and meat – to raise money to build the aqueduct. It was initially understood that this tax was temporary and that it would be applied only
until local authorities collected 8,000 ducados (88,000 reales). They also estimated
that the tax, or sisa, would produce 480 ducados per year, so from these figures it
appears that construction of the aqueduct was expected to last about seventeen

years. All these estimates turned out to be grossly inadequate. The aqueduct, which channeled water from the Río de la Chorrera (currently Almendarez) to "El Chorro," a fountain in Havana's central area, in the vicinity of La Fuerza, took twenty-six years to build and was not finished until 1592. Its cost exceeded the original estimates by several times. In 1577 Governor Francisco de Carreño estimated that 12,000 ducados had already been spent and yet it had been impossible to "bring the water." A few years later, in 1583, the new governor reported that another 10,000 ducados was required, and even this new calculation proved conservative, for the new contractor for the works, prominent vecino Hernán Manrique de Rojas, required 30,000 ducados to complete it. Thus the total cost of building the aqueduct amounted to some 45,000 ducados, five to six times the cost estimated by local authorities in the 1560s. In the city, the governor reported in 1592, water was distributed to provision the fleets and armadas, to supply washers and animals, and to cover the needs of the forts. Appropriately, water had reached Havana the same year it was officially designated a "city."[74]

Although the collection of the sisa should have stopped once water was successfully brought to the city, local authorities continued to press for its renewal. These resources, they claimed, were necessary to maintain the aqueduct, which had to be cleaned regularly, and to pay for other expenses for which there was no income in the local treasury. Among these expenses were the payment of a physician, the construction of several public buildings such as a fish market and a jail, and the repair of others. As usual, the crown consented to the requests of the vecinos from Havana. In 1596 and 1607 it granted extensions on the collection of this tax, which continued to fund various public works. Between 1569 and 1610 authorities in Havana collected 912,000 reales under this tax, almost double the amount actually spent on the construction of the aqueduct.[75]

Along with the construction of the aqueduct, the vecinos of Havana rebuilt the hospital, which Sorés had partially destroyed. According to a colonial official, the hospital had been built in the mid-1540s. Its need was linked directly to Havana's port functions "because of the ships that come" as well as the poor who required service. The hospital was enlarged in the early 1550s, only to be set on fire by Sorés. Its reconstruction seems to have taken place fairly soon, for it was in operation when Bishop Castillo visited the town in 1570. It was still, however, a modest construction with just two rooms and a chapel that remained "collapsed." Its only resources were the rents generated by a few donations made by the most prominent vecinos and half of the fines collected by local justices, a charity given for six years by the crown in 1569 and renewed endlessly afterward.[76]

Havana's growth after the 1580s and its consolidation as the return station for the fleets clearly outstripped the limited capacity of its rudimentary hospital. Besides, the old hospital was placed in a very central location, near the town's church and the fortress of La Fuerza. In 1596 the king ordered a new hospital built with the proceeds of the sale of some of his properties in the city. For this purpose, the town council seized a Latin school that was under construction in the outskirts of the city, a place convenient because it was "removed" from the urban center and because it had "all the water it may need" inside. Although it was still unfinished, by 1600 the new hospital, San Felipe y Santiago, was taking patients, and in 1603 the running of the hospital was transferred to the Order of San Juan de Dios. Given its central location, the building of the old hospital was divided into shops and houses, their rents used to pay for the expenses of the new facility. As we shall see, its church was sold to a confraternity of free blacks.[77]

Whereas the hospital was quickly rebuilt after the attack of Sorés, the reconstruction of Havana's only church waited until 1570. Perhaps the most important building of the old village, this stone church had been constructed in the early 1550s with local resources. Between 1550 and 1554 the town council devoted significant attention to this topic and in 1554 asked the king for 1,000 pesos in charity to finish the church and to buy ornaments, which of course had to be imported.[78] Its reconstruction was again undertaken by local initiative and financed by the vecinos. In 1560 authorities reported that the town was "without church," and Bishop Castillo in 1570 asserted that the building lacked a roof. One of the most prominent vecinos of the town, Juan de Rojas, offered to have the church covered at his own expense, a promise carried out by his nephew, Gerónimo de Rojas Avellaneda after the death of the former in 1570. By 1574 the works were concluded, and the town again had a church, of brick and tile. Not even this building was deemed independent from the town's maritime functions: "It is placed in this port," reported the governor, "where it is seen by so many people who pass through with the fleets."[79]

The same argument was used to justify the establishment of monasteries by the Franciscans and Dominicans in the 1570s. As the town council explained in 1574, such institutions were needed to lodge the friars of those orders who traveled through Havana, who otherwise were forced to stay in taverns, inns, and other "indecent" places not appropriate to their vows and religion. The first house of the Franciscans was a modest construction of mud walls with a thatched roof; it could accommodate six to eight friars. In 1577 they requested royal support to finish the construction of a stone building, arguing that when the fleets were in town it was necessary to house fifteen to twenty people. The order also raised about 3,000 ducados locally but in 1580 decided to buy a better parcel, closer to the sea and to the central area of Havana, near La Fuerza. The new monastery received royal favor, and by 1584 it was at least partially built. Two years later the town council, when discussing matters pertaining to the town's urban layout, mentioned the monastery as a well-known point of reference.[80]

This monastery was joined by one founded by the Dominicans during the same years. It was a modest construction, described in 1579 as a "house and thatched church." According to local reports, it had not improved much by the late 1580s, but it was remodeled and improved afterward. Other religious establishments followed suit. In 1609 the Order of Saint Augustine began to build its own monastery, which was initially staffed by a small group of friars coming from Mexico. By then the vecinos were also pressing for the establishment of a convent for nuns in the city, arguing that the population had grown considerably and that many vecinos did not have the means to marry their daughters in accordance with their social worth and quality. Actual construction, however, did not start until the 1630s, so the daughters of wealthy vecinos who remained unmarried were frequently sent to convents in New Spain, particularly one located in Mérida, Yucatán.[81]

A few additional public buildings were added to the town's increasingly complex landscape after the 1570s, when Havana's growth accelerated. Between 1577 and 1581 a customhouse was built. Unlike other constructions, this one was paid for with royal moneys, for the king ordered the customhouse to be built "no matter the cost" in 1577. Located at the entrance of the bay, the two-story house had a spacious warehouse and an office on the ground floor and living quarters for two royal officials on the upper floor. It had its own docks, where ships could unload their cargoes, which were then moved into the warehouse.[82]

The town council also got a house for itself. In the 1580s and 1590s the municipal council frequently deliberated over the need to build a proper house for the local government, as well as buildings for other services such as a municipal jail, a slaughterhouse, and a fish market. A house for the cabildo was finished sometime in the late 1590s, along with several "fountains and other public works" that reportedly were "among the best in the Indies." As usual, the governor requested additional favors and tax concessions from the crown to build a new jail and slaughterhouse, using the customary argument that such works were urgent because Havana was the place "where all the commerce" of the New World came together. Meanwhile, the town council rented a house to use as a municipal jail. Financed largely with local resources, particularly with the sisa, a new slaughterhouse was completed in 1601, and the construction of a new jail and a fish market began.[83]

Needless to say, the urban growth of Havana was not exclusively, or even

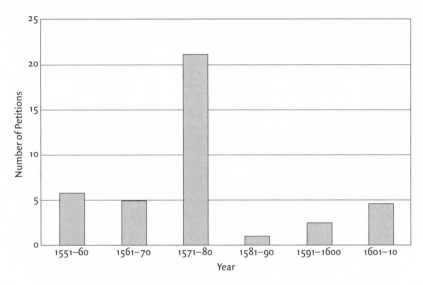

Figure 4.3. Average Annual Number of Petitions for Urban Lots, 1551–1610
Source: ACAH, 1551–1610.

primarily, fueled by the construction of new public buildings. Although these were critically important symbols of the growing complexity of the town and of the sense of worth of its inhabitants, the settlers themselves transformed the village into a colonial city. This process began fairly early, even before the number of immigrants began to increase. In the 1570s, when Havana's total population doubled but remained fairly small (about 100 vecinos toward the end of the decade), petitions to the town council for lots multiplied fourfold compared with the previous decade. There were more petitions for lots in just this decade than there were vecinos in the port town (see figure 4.3).[84]

Given that demographic pressures do not explain this boom in the allocation of lots, one must consider the possibility of speculation. It seems that as early as the 1550s the residents of the port town realized that urban spaces were going to become valuable and scarce and began to accumulate as many of them as possible. By the 1570s, when Havana legally became the stopover for the fleets, the new fortress of La Fuerza was declared "in defense," and the transoceanic maritime movement increased briskly, petitions exploded. At issue was probably not just obtaining enough parcels to build houses for the petitioner or even for business purposes but also excluding future immigrants from access to them, so they would be forced to pay.

There is evidence that petitions outpaced the capacity of the vecinos to build.

Table 4.3. Average Prices (in Reales) of Real Estate, 1578–1610

Type of Unit	N	1578–95	1596–1610
Urban lots	122	987.8	1,489.4
Thatched-roof houses, clay or mud walls	91	8,992.5	5,154.1
Thatched-roof houses, wood walls	50	4,144.7	2,576.7
Tile-roof houses	38	8,951.3	12,978.0
Stone houses	18	10,780.0	33,860.7

Source: ANC, PNH, ER, 1578–1610.

As early as 1555 the town council ordered people who had obtained or bought plots to build houses. The municipal ordinances approved by Alonso de Cáceres, a judge of the Audiencia of Santo Domingo who visited the island in 1573, referred to this problem as well. The ordinances were approved in the midst of the petition boom of the 1570s and clearly sought to put limits on land speculation. "When a plot is given, it should be on condition that it gets populated in six months." Otherwise, its sale or transfer in any other way became prohibited. The problem persisted, however, for in 1608 the town council created a registry of owners who had not built on their plots as they were legally required. By then petitions were again in upswing, but so was construction. The governor asserted in 1612 that the city continued to grow and that in the previous four years more than two hundred houses had been built.[85]

Combined with rapid demographic growth after the 1590s, the vecinos' speculation in urban lots contributed to significant price increases. The value of urban lots, which continued to be sold despite legal prohibitions, grew by 50 percent between the periods of 1578–95 and 1596–1610 (see table 4.3).

However, prices did not increase for all properties. The available evidence suggests that the urban growth experienced by the port city was accompanied by a differentiation in the quality of housing that mirrored parallel processes of social fragmentation. In the first period, up to the mid-1590s, the most humble constructions, thatched-roof houses with wood (bohíos) or mud and clay (tapia) walls represented about two-thirds of all houses sold in the city (64 percent). This proportion declined after 1595, although these houses still represented about half of those sold in the local market (53 percent). There was, however, a noticeable decline in the proportion of bohíos among the houses for sale. These modest buildings represented 42 percent of all sold houses in the years 1578–95, compared with 12 percent between 1596 and 1610. Among lower-priced houses, the mud- or clay-walled houses gradually replaced the wood bohíos. Furthermore, the relative importance of the more expensive construction types, such as tile-

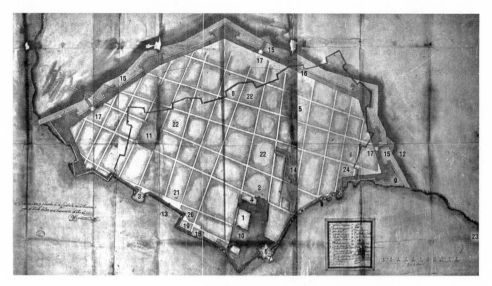

This 1603 diagram of Havana by engineer Cristóbal de Roda shows the most
important buildings and a wall to be built around the city. The wall was not built
until the second half of the seventeenth century. 1. Iglesia Mayor; 2. Monastery of Santo
Domingo; 3. Monastery of San Francisco; 4. Old hospital; 5. New hospital; 6. La Fuerza;
7. Platform; 8. Old fence; 9. New fence to be built; 10. Plaza de Armas; 11. Plaza Nueva;
12. Countryside; 13. Port; 14. Swamp; 15. Moat; 16. Terreplein; 17. City doors;
18. Customhouse; 19. Jailhouse; 20. Slaughterhouse; 21. House of the governor;
22. Housing areas; 23. Port mouth; 24. Foundry. "Descripción y planta de la ciudad
de la Habana, 1603," AGI, Mapas y Planos, Santo Domingo, 21.

roof houses and flat-roof houses typically built with bricks or stone, expanded
after the 1590s. The proportion of tile-roofed houses increased from 24 percent to
31 percent and that of brick or stone houses from 12 percent to 17 percent. These
transformations reflected the growing affluence of the port city and the wealth
accumulated by a group of vecinos. In turn, these changes were reflected in dissimilar price patterns. Whereas the average price of the poorer houses declined
by some 40 percent, those of the best houses increased. Indeed, the average price
of the flat-roofed houses, the most expensive private constructions in the city,
multiplied threefold during these years. Such houses embodied the wealth of
what was fast becoming a successful local elite.

The growing stratification of the urban settlement also had a spatial dimension. Between 1550 and 1610 a central urban area became gradually defined as
the most desirable and exclusive in the town. This area surrounded the town's
plaza adjacent to the fortress of La Fuerza, the town's only church, and the busy

waterfront, with its shipyards, its foundry and arsenal, its forges, and its ware-
houses. Houses around the Plaza de Armas, as this square was known, were consistently described as "the most principal" in town, this location as "the best"
in the whole city.[86]

At the same time, other areas were gradually defined as spaces for the urban
poor. The neighborhood of Campeche, an outlying section southwest of the center of the town, was one such area. This section owed its name to the *campe-
chanos*, natives from the Yucatán Peninsula who were imported into Cuba as
slaves in the early decades of the sixteenth century.[87] The vecinos of Havana
developed a good sense of this neighborhood in both spatial and social terms –
two categories that were of course related. When in 1569 there was discussion
about where to establish a Jesuit school for "Indians," the designated plot stood
"by the place where the Indians of Campeche have their houses." Years later,
the town council planned to build a slaughterhouse in the same vicinity – the
"barrio of Campeche." With time, other poor members of society obtained their
lots there. In 1577 a white resident who described himself as a "poor vecino"
petitioned the town council for a "piece of plot" in Campeche, arguing that rents
were so expensive that "poor men" could not afford them. His plot adjoined that
of freedman Francisco Angola, who was not the only free black residing in the
area. Indeed, between 1578 and 1610, free blacks bought 21 percent of the plots
sold in the area and registered in the notarial records. Campeche thus became
a popular neighborhood where individuals of various racial groups lived. This
situation was not just a matter of choice. There is evidence that the town council
consciously sought to restrict the access of nonwhites to the best areas of the
town and relegated them to neighborhoods such as Campeche. When the free
black woman Beatriz Nizardo requested a plot in one of the better areas in town
in 1561, the cabildo refused, instructing her to "request it in another place, close
to the area where the other free blacks are."[88]

This was only one of the many ways in which local authorities shaped the
configuration of the emerging port town. From their insistence on keeping the
streets clean – by which they meant free of garbage and bushes – to the prohibition of building thatched-roof houses, which caught fire too easily, to the construction of public buildings, urbanization questions captured a sizable share
of the town council's attention. The proportion of agreements and regulations
devoted to these issues grew along with the number of inhabitants and the complexity of Havana (see table 3.1).

This growth was sustained by an increasingly diverse economic structure.
Many of the urban economic activities that proliferated after the mid-sixteenth
century were ancillary to Havana's maritime, trading, and military functions. At

the same time, the growth of the port city was not confined to the urban area but spilled into what was eventually defined as countryside. Although linked to the service needs generated by the shipping movement, the agricultural sector began to produce export commodities that were not always compatible with the town's service functions as defined by imperial policy. In contrast to many port cities, which prospered while serving the needs of their surrounding productive areas, in the case of Havana it was the port town that made an agriculturally rich hinterland.

CHAPTER FIVE

Production

It was in the second half of the sixteenth century, with the consolidation of Havana as an urban center with increasingly complex commercial, military, and administrative functions, that the port city created a hinterland to serve its needs. This hinterland came to be known as *tierra adentro*, a construct that of course placed Havana and its port at the very entrance of the island. The agriculturally rich region that developed around the town during this period responded in various ways to the opportunities and challenges posed by the growing movement of ships and consumers. Some farms specialized in the production of foodstuff to meet local demand, which oscillated cyclically, along with the number of vessels. Others produced commodities for export, taking advantage of the returning ships' excess freight.

Other economic activities further connected the port town with the hinterland. Tile works opened in response to the demand generated by urban construction and the growing resident population. The production of lumber on a relatively large scale provided an export product and supplied local needs. Local demand for wood was fueled by the expansion of Havana and by the growing activity of the various shipyards that operated in the city and its surroundings. Wood was also a military resource. The forests that surrounded the town were part of its defenses and had to be protected from intruders, particularly from humble laborers who produced firewood to make a living. Firewood and copper, the latter from mines in the distant eastern end of the island, were brought to town to be processed in a foundry established by the king to supply the military needs of the fortified Atlantic port town.

Havana's commercial and economic expansion allowed some of its vecinos to accumulate the wealth needed to promote the production of sugar. More than any other, sugar represented an archetypical Atlantic commodity: a cash crop produced in the tropics by African slaves, financed and consumed by Europeans.

Yet there was much of the Mediterranean in the organization of sugar production and other economic activities. What is frequently referred to as a "new industry" was in fact anything but new.[1] The first mills replicated the technologies
used in Cyprus, Sicily, and Valencia for centuries. The technical know-how of
sugar production continued to be learned empirically and reproduced by experienced sugar masters who carefully guarded the secrets of their trade. The
almost total reliance on African slave labor was an Atlantic innovation, first tried
on some of the islands of the eastern Atlantic, but the use of slave labor on the
plantations was certainly not new. Furthermore, in Havana some of the sugarcane was grown by smallholders, reproducing productive arrangements that had
been in use in the Mediterranean since the Middle Ages.

As usual, the vecinos of Havana benefited from the privileged location of the
port city and obtained significant official support to promote some of these economic activities. Royal moneys financed the establishment of a foundry in the
early 1600s and the development of copper mining in eastern Cuba. Several orders
placed by the crown stimulated the activities of the shipyards and contributed
to their growth and sophistication, to the point that Havana became one of the
most important shipbuilding centers in the Spanish Atlantic. A royal loan of
40,000 ducados provided capital to build mills and purchase slaves. Several fiscal
exemptions and privileges – for instance, sugar mills could not be confiscated to
cover debts – further facilitated the expansion of sugar manufacturing.

The king supported sugar production even though its development could
come into conflict with the needs of Havana's service economy. All the economic activities described above were compatible with the functions reserved
for Havana within the Spanish empire. Sugar was the exception. The production
of tropical commodities such as sugar took lands, capital, and workers away
from the cultivation of crops to supply the local market and the fleets. Other
economic activities adjusted their rhythms of production to the movement and
the needs of the port. Sugar imposed its own rhythms, which fit poorly with
those of the returning vessels. Whereas the other economic activities were largely
a function of Havana's port, sugar required the port to be at its service. With
sugar, the hinterland that the port had created attempted to assert its primacy
and hinted at the possibility of a different future, one of plantation slavery and
monoculture. Such a future would come only two hundred years later.

Agriculture

By the time Jacques de Sorés occupied Havana, most of the lands in the western
third of the island remained unoccupied by the Europeans and uncultivated.

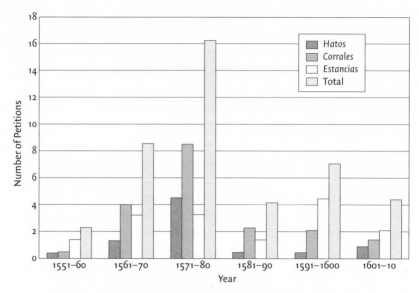

Figure 5.1. Average Annual Number of Petitions for Rural Land, 1551–1610
Source: ACAH, 1551–1610.

Abundant livestock roamed wild in the forests. The lack of predators allowed cattle to reproduce prodigiously, and since the 1530s livestock had gradually occupied the lands that humans could not effectively exploit. In the absence of demographic pressures and opportunities for profit, the few residents of the village lacked incentives and means to exploit the endless space that surrounded them.

This changed during the second half of the sixteenth century. With the consolidation of Havana's role as the return station for the fleets, the residents moved to parcel out the town's vast "interior" and to accumulate as much land as possible. As with the urban parcels, the process of land allocation cannot be explained by population pressures. The number of petitions increased significantly in the 1560s and peaked in the 1570s, when the total number of vecinos was still extremely small. The town had only some 60 vecinos in 1570, but the cabildo received 85 petitions for land in the 1560s and 140 in the 1570s (it should be noted, however, that we lack data for 1579 and 1580). The annual average number of petitions jumped from 3 in the 1550s to 8 in the 1560s, to 19 in the 1570s (see figure 5.1). Around 60 percent of the petitions for land received by the town council of Havana between 1551 and 1610 took place prior to 1580. The residents of the early town were doing their best to hoard as much land as possible.[2]

Most of these holdings were classified in three different categories, although some terminological confusion persisted into the late sixteenth century. Those devoted to the cultivation of provisions for the local market and the fleets were referred to as *estancias* or *sitios de labor*. These farms were smaller than cattle ranches and were traditionally identified with the caballería, an agrarian unit of measure that in Cuba was roughly equivalent to 33 acres.[3] Until the late 1500s, however, the size of the estancias was frequently expressed in "montones de yuca," a unit created by the Spaniards to keep account of the Arawaks' most important agricultural product: cassava. In the second half of the sixteenth century the Cuban caballería was roughly equivalent to 36,000 montones de yuca. That of La Española was five or six times bigger.[4] The association between the productive unit (estancia) and its metrological expression (caballería) was already evident in the mid-sixteenth century. In 1551 a resident addressed the town council saying that he had begun to cultivate "an estancia" and requested "like the other vecinos to be given one caballería of land in the said place."[5]

In the early years of colonization, the term "estancia" referred to a productive unit that combined cultivation and ranching. Traces of this earlier terminology remained in the records of the town council after the 1550s, where one finds references to "pig estancias."[6] Most frequently, however, people petitioning for lands to raise livestock used a different terminology. Pigs were raised in *sitios de corrales de puercos*, whereas cattle farms were referred to as *hatos de vacas* and developed in the *sabanas*, the endless plains of the island that provided pasture in abundance. These units, particularly the hatos, were much larger than the estancias. They were conceived as circular units with a radius of about 1 league for the pig farms and 2 leagues for the hatos. In other words, these units were large enough to accommodate hundreds of estancias: the hatos comprised more than 1,600 caballerias, the corrales more than 400. Judge Cáceres recognized these differences in his 1574 municipal ordinances. He referred to the estancias as units that required "little land," so little in comparison with the cattle farms, in fact, that they could be placed by the town council within the limits of those properties.[7]

By the time Cáceres visited the island, another problem was becoming evident. The initial process of land distribution had been done with little attention to the size and the precise delimitation of the units. The seemingly inexhaustible space allowed town councillors to allocate lands with little regard to their actual limits. After the 1570s, however, the issue began to concern municipal authorities, who had been distributing lands prodigally since the mid-1560s. Cáceres noted that many hatos lacked landmarks and issued orders to mark them out. Three years later the governor called on the cabildo to appoint a surveyor, claiming that with the growth of the town there were many lawsuits about the location of the units. The pig farms, particularly, had become quite profitable because of the demand for meat created by the fleets.[8]

Although the town council appointed a councilman to survey the rural units, the conflicts over the units and their limits probably increased further after the 1570s, along with the town's growing population. In 1585 the town council threatened to fine the landowners who had not demarcated their properties. In 1596 it noted "the great disorder in the distribution of estancias," arguing that some people had managed to accumulate so much land that it was enough to develop "ten estancias." In order to rein in this metrological chaos, the cabildo ordered the creation of a "measure" that could be used thereafter "for the lands that are sold among the vecinos." The problem, Governor Juan Maldonado argued, was that the city council until that moment had lacked a measure that was "certain." Consequently the first official effort was made to create equivalents to the main agrarian unit of measurement used on the island, the caballería.[9]

Although it was still possible to obtain lands from the town council in the first decade of the seventeenth century, it seems clear that by then the best lands, those closest to the Havana urban market, had been distributed. People who wanted to get access to these lands would have to buy them from the privileged vecinos who had obtained them from the local organ of power in the previous decades. Take the case of Cristobal Sánchez. He received a concession for a cattle ranch from the cabildo in 1577. Two years later he sold the property without making any significant changes to it. Gregorio Lopez obtained the hato "El Cuabal" in July 1599 and sold it for a handsome profit in September 1604.[10] These hatos were at least "populated" – they included some livestock. In many other cases, municipal authorities complained, the landlords speculated with the lands without making any investments or improvements to their properties.[11]

As population pressures increased and lands became scarcer, particularly for farms that could be profitable only if they were close enough to Havana, the number of mercantile transactions over land intensified. The average annual number of land-related transactions in the notarial records increased from 15 in the 1580s and 1590s to 23 in the first decade of the seventeenth century.[12]

The growing demand affected prices as well, which rose about 25 percent between the periods 1585–95 and 1596–1610. This aggregate figure hides more than it reveals, however, as price increases differed significantly by unit (see table 5.1). On one end were the hatos. These were by far the largest rural farms, and until the appearance of the sugar mills in the late 1590s, they commanded the largest price per unit of all farms. In part because of this, the hatos were sold less frequently than were other farms. They also experienced the smallest price increase during these years, only 13 percent.

Table 5.1. Average Prices (in Reales)
of Rural Units, 1578–1610

Type of Unit	N	1578–95	1596–1610
Hatos	40	15,107	17,107
Corrales	73	5,455	9,729
Estancias	148	1,925	3,375

Source: ANC, PNH, ER, 1578–1610.

All these elements point to the lack of dynamism of the hatos and to their
slow adaptation to the market conjuncture. Although beef, fresh and salted, was
a key supply for the local market and the fleets, the large hatos were not exploited intensely by their owners. The livestock roamed freely until it was herded
to be conducted to the city's slaughterhouse or sacrificed for hides and tallow,
which was subsequently used in the production of soap and candles. Of the forty
hatos sold during these years and for which we have more detailed information,
only one lists crops of any kind. Fourteen of the units do not list any livestock
at all. Of those that do, only four specify the size of the herds; the other units
simply mention the presence of livestock without further precision. This lack
of detail suggests that most owners had limited knowledge of their units and
that the main object of the transactions was the land. Adding to the impression
that these units were not intensely exploited is the fact that only three of them
were sold with cowboy slaves residing in them. Some hato owners, however,
developed tanneries in their units, mostly to supply local shoemakers and other
artisans.[13]

Smaller and more efficiently exploited, the corrales better reflect the transformation of the port city. Their average price increased significantly, 78 percent
between 1578–95 and 1596–1610 (see table 5.1). Whereas in the earlier period the
hatos were valued three times as high as corrales, the extraordinary valuation of
the latter by the early 1600s reduced this gap considerably. The available evidence
points to a more efficient exploitation of these units: the sale contracts are more
detailed and contain better information about the units, their animals, and their
crops. Out of 73 contract sales, 19 list crops – most frequently cassava, maize, and
bananas – and 50 contain references to the animals in the unit. Forty-three list
more than one type of animal, and many go on to list several. In addition to pigs,
which of course were mentioned in nearly all the contracts that make reference
to animals, horses and mares were mentioned in 23 cases, mules in 6, domestic
fowl in 20, and dogs in 29. Slaves, all of them male, were listed in 11 of the sale
contracts and included as part of the corral.

Even more important from the point of view of Havana's supplies were the estancias. These small farms formed a sort of agricultural belt around the urban center and blended with the outlying areas of the city. They represented the other end of the agrarian spectrum. Their size and price per unit were the lowest, the frequency of their sales the highest. This frequency was not a function of the patterns of land distribution set by the town council. As figure 5.1 shows, between 1550 and 1610 petitions to establish cattle and pig ranches exceeded those to create estancias, which represented only 30 percent of the total. Yet the latter were by far the units most actively traded: 58 percent of rural sales concerned estancias.

The relative intensity with which the estancias were traded and their rising prices reflected the consolidation of a local market in Havana and its growing demand for food. The main purpose of the estancias, as Judge Cáceres succinctly put it, was the "cultivation of bread," that is, the cultivation of yucca and the production of cassava flour. It is for this reason that the town council took a special interest in the estancias, "so that there is no lack of supplies, both to provision this city or the fleets that come to it."[14] As with the corrales, the sale contracts of the estancias make reference to the productive assets of the unit much more frequently than in the case of the hatos. Two-thirds of the 148 sale contracts mention at least one crop, 87 mention two, 55 mention three. A similar number (52) registers at least one type of animal in the units as well. Some contracts even refer to the size of the unit, something that the records on hatos or corrales never do. The average size of the estancias was 2.5 caballerías (82 acres).

Although Atlantic agriculture is always identified with plantation slavery and with the production of commercial crops, the estancias were in many ways archetypical agricultural units of the early Atlantic. They supplied the port city's growing market through a combination of indigenous crops and cultivation techniques, European produce and domestic animals, and African, European, and indigenous labor and agricultural knowledge. They produced an unusual variety of crops. Nearly all cultivated yucca (74 percent) and bananas (73 percent), key staples in the local diet. One-third cultivated maize and various fruits, also important elements in local food. Some also produced rice (6 percent), beans (2 percent), and vegetables such as cabbages, turnips, radishes, and pumpkins. Finally, because of their location and commercial dynamism, the estancias were also the sites where some of the first commercial staples of Cuban agriculture developed. Among theses crops were sugar (listed in 21 percent of all estancias), which quickly became one the island's most important export products, and tobacco (3 percent), still used mostly to satisfy the demand of the growing number of consumers that the sea brought to town each year.

Most of the estancias were worked by their owners and their families, although 14 percent of them employed slaves as well. Although slavery was more common on these farms than on the hatos or corrales, it seems clear that agriculture was not, as would be the case later, mostly a slave activity. On the contrary, the workforce employed on the farms seems to have been mostly of European descent (66 percent), with a significant participation of natives (22 percent) and a smaller number of free blacks and mulattoes (12 percent).[15]

In order to exploit their farms more effectively, the owners entered into what was described at the time as "contracts of company" or "contracts of service," arrangements that frequently included the application of additional labor, either free or slave, to the units. In the "companies" the owner got a partner who was required to manage the farm and work on it in exchange for a portion of production. In one such contract in 1579, vecino Juan de Aceituno entered a company with Pedro Flores, described as a transient, to exploit his estancia for two years. The estancia included the usual crops of cassava, maize, and bananas, a horse, eight hens and one rooster, three ducks, and three turkeys. Two slaves, Miguel and Anton, worked on it. Flores brought to the company "his person" and two more slaves to grow additional crops. Excluded from the company was a *conuco*, or small provision ground, where Aceituno had already grown some cassava and maize.[16]

The "contracts of service" produced similar results: a manager or laborer was hired to work at the farm and compensated with a portion of production—which is why these arrangements were also known as *contratos de partido*. Landowner and vecino Juan de la Fuente signed one of these contracts in 1606, when he "gave in partido" a piece of land to resident Francisco Luis "to harvest tobacco." In addition to the land, the owner offered three men to work at the unit—whether enslaved or not is not clear—whereas Luis brought "his person" to the deal. Luis would receive one-third of production as payment. A similar deal was made between Alonso Suárez de Toledo, a prominent landowner, and vecino Tomas Martín in 1579. In what was described as a contract of service, Martín was "to serve" Suárez de Toledo by visiting his corrales of Yumurí and Corral Nuevo, his hato Canímar, and his estancia "de Matanzas" and by "commanding the people, blacks, and servants" that worked on them. The contract was to last four years, and Martín was to be compensated with one-sixth of all production, which included "hides, meat and tallow and lard, corn, cassava, pigs and cows and fowl and honey."[17]

Although these productive arrangements would suggest that the rural economy was barely monetized, in fact numerous units employed salaried workers, whose payment was at least partially in specie. Workers in about 60 percent of

all labor contracts related to agriculture were paid a salary "in reales or silver."
In 1579, for instance, free black Beatriz Nizardo hired Diego de Toribio, described
as "Indian," to work in her corral for six months for 25 ducados, which he was to
receive "as he was serving." In 1590 landowner and vecino Bartolomé López hired
Pedro Gonzalez, also a vecino, to work on his corral Arcos de Canasí for a whole
year at a salary of 65 ducados. The typical length of the labor contract was one
year (70 percent of the total number of contracts), although a few were for longer
periods of time, up to five or even six years.[18]

According to these labor contracts, about a third of the nonslave agricultural
laborers were compensated through a mixture of specie and goods. This practice
helps explain the wide variations in payment. The salaries for one-year contracts
oscillated between 10 and 80 ducados. Laborers earning lower salaries typically
received additional goods and services for their work, such as food, housing, and
a portion of the products. Juan de la Torre hired Domingo García in 1600 to work
on his estancia for one year. He would pay him 50 ducados (550 reales), half of
the fowl that he raised, and "food according to the custom of the land." Rodrigo
Carreño hired Miguel de Rojas in 1579 to work on his farms for a year for a salary
of 30 ducados plus 3 yards of canvas fabric. Francisco Gutiérrez agreed to work
for a year on a farm for 10 ducados and some clothing. The royal accountant,
Pedro de Arana, hired vecino Antonio de Solís in 1585 to live and work at his
estancia for a year and to command four additional workers and a female slave
whom Arana was to place in the unit. In addition to a salary of 30 ducados, Solís
would receive half of all the crops produced on the estancia: cabbages, turnips,
radishes, onions, chickpeas, sweet potatoes, rice, sugarcane, pumpkins, beans,
and melons.[19]

Payments were also affected by the social position of the laborer, and there is
evidence that workers identified as indigenous (22 percent in the labor contracts)
received lower salaries than those of European descent. The average earnings
of the latter amounted to 6.5 ducados per month, double the wages obtained
by workers described as "Indians" (2.7 ducados). Blacks were somewhere in the
middle (3.4 ducados), although closer to the natives than to Europeans. The subordinate social position of indigenous laborers is illustrated by the agreement
between landowner Francisco Nuñez and Manuel Díaz, "protector of the Indians," to hire two "Indian youngsters," Francisco and his sister Luisa, to work on
his properties. The contract stipulated that Francisco would serve for three years
and Luisa for six. Francisco would be paid 30 ducados for the whole time, plus
food and two sets of clothing per year. Luisa's compensation was even lower, for
in addition to food and clothing she would receive the same amount after the
six years "to help her to marry." The same day, however, Nuñez signed another

labor contract with a resident of European descent: his yearly salary was 50 ducados. Although the "protector" was to represent the interests of the natives, he was frequently instrumental in their exploitation. Bishop Castillo requested the elimination of this office in 1582, arguing that "to assign a protector [to the indigenous people] was to give them an *encomendero* [holder of an encomienda]." The bishop also offered a clue as to the participation of the natives in Havana's mercantile economy: the Spaniards had taken all the lands surrounding the village of Guanabacoa, where the natives lived, so the latter had lost the ability to produce their own crops.[20]

Most of these rural workers labored in agriculture and ranching, but some performed other activities that were linked directly to the urban expansion of Havana and to its maritime functions. Among these activities was the production of tiles. The town council forbade in 1603 the construction of thatched-roof houses and ordered that residences be covered with tiles. Additional demand came from the sugar mills, which after the late 1590s required a yearly supply of pottery forms to purge sugar. In response to these needs, several pottery works were established around the city. At least five of them were in operation between 1589 and 1601, and in the early 1600s several more were established to supply the sugar mills. They produced roof tiles, bricks, earthen pots and vats of various sizes, and, after the late 1590s, sugar forms.[21]

The constructive needs of the town and the shipyards stimulated the production of lumber as well. The growing demand for timber, for local uses and for export, prompted some landowners to establish sawmills in their units and turned forests into valuable commodities. It is noteworthy that some landowners began to sell the woods on their lands rather than the lands per se. It is also significant that the cabildo attempted repeatedly to place limits on the commercial exploitation of the forests, particularly those in the immediate vicinity of the city. Initial regulations were concerned with defense and with construction needs. By the early 1600s the main concern of the town council was to protect a new and increasingly important economic activity: shipbuilding. In 1602 the town council prohibited the production of timber within several leagues around the city, claiming that these woods should be reserved for "the building of ships."[22]

Shipbuilding

In the late sixteenth century Havana became the most important shipyard in the New World and one of the largest shipbuilding centers of the early Atlantic. Descriptions of the city frequently noted the importance of its shipyards: "It is a port of sea," explained the author of a 1629 geographic tract, where "there is a shipyard where they build navios and very strong galleons for the Carrera de las Indias." Linschoten's popular book (1596) mentioned that Havana was a place "where . . . ships are made." Other seventeenth-century books disseminated the same notion: "C'est là où se fabriquent les navires du Roy d'Espagne" (It is there that the ships of the Spanish king are made), noted Dassié in 1677.[23]

Various factors facilitated the construction of vessels in the port city. The passing ships, particularly those making the transatlantic voyage, were in constant need for repairs. The rich forests surrounding Havana provided what seemed like an endless supply of hardwoods, ideal for shipbuilding. Regular and intense contacts with European suppliers via Seville and the Canary Islands allowed for the importation of critical inputs such as tar, pitch, sails, cordage, and hardware. These contacts facilitated as well the settlement of skilled artisans in the city and the occasional visit of well-known European shipwrights. Among the latter was Tomé Cano, a native of the Canary Islands and author of a treatise about shipbuilding, *Arte para fabricar, fortificar y aparejar naos de guerra merchante*, published in Seville in 1611. The royal officials of Havana spoke of Cano in 1605 as a "vecino of this city, a person of satisfaction and trust" who was an "expert" in maritime issues.[24] According to a 1607 commission of shipbuilders from Seville, Havana was an ideal place to repair ships precisely because of the availability of numerous carpenters, caulkers, and blacksmiths, plus the abundance of hardwoods and European naval supplies in the city.[25]

It is quite likely that small vessels were produced in Cuba since the early decades of colonial rule. Three separate royal cedulas of 1516 and 1518 authorized the residents of the island to build ships that could be used in the regional trade. As for Havana, there is evidence of shipbuilding activities since 1552, when two transients in the village requested and obtained the cabildo's authorization to produce the lumber necessary to build a boat to sail to Veracruz.[26]

It is difficult to establish a precise chronology concerning the development of shipbuilding in Havana, but production probably expanded along with the consolidation of the town as a gathering point for vessels and a regional center of trade. By the late 1570s local documents make reference to "the shipyard of this village," where small, agile fragatas and perhaps other vessels were being built. In 1577 the governor of Florida complained that provisions for his soldiers became expensive because of excessive freights and proposed the construction of two fragatas in Havana as a solution.[27]

The proliferation of shipbuilding activities can be traced through several indicators. First and foremost, the number of shipyards operating in the city and its vicinity multiplied. According to the labor contracts preserved in the notarial records, in the 1590s and early 1600s ships were being built in eight locations. The most important center of shipbuilding continued to be the city's shipyard, which was centrally located, between the fortress of La Fuerza and the monastery of San Francisco. This shipyard grew in importance thanks to the royal orders, which were always exceptionally large and lucrative. In 1589, after the crushing defeat of the Invincible Armada in English waters, the king ordered up to eighteen fragatas built in this shipyard for the defense of the colonial territories. To build the initial six, more than 800,000 reales entered the treasury of Havana between 1589 and 1591. Twenty years later, in 1608, the king commissioned the construction of five galleons to be part of the Armada de Barlovento, with a total cost of 3 million reales. When this shipyard was not building vessels for His Catholic Majesty, it did so for his vassals. In 1592 merchant Francisco Díaz Pimienta hired master shipwright Francisco Gutiérrez Navarrete to build in four months a nao "in the shipyard where they finished the fragatas of the King which is close to the fortress of this town." Payment was set at 12,650 reales.[28]

Information about the other shipyards is quite fragmentary, limited to passing references in a few shipbuilding contracts. In addition to the city's shipyard, two others operated in the Bay of Havana: one in the neighborhood of Campeche (1588) and the other on the opposite side of the bay, at the "pier Maria Melena," which is mentioned in 1598. The other sites were located west of Havana and took advantage of easy access to the hardwood forests of the area. Ships were built in Puerto de Baracoa in 1589, where the fragata *Santa Ana* was being made for merchant Melchor Rodríguez. Another shipbuilding center developed in the Bay of Mariel. In 1595, a transient in the city, Gaspar Lorenzo, reported having a ship under construction in that area and mentioned as well that his ship *Nuestra Señora de la Encarnación* was being repaired. Farther to the west were shipyards by the Ortigosa River and the Río de Puercos. Shipwright Miguel de Goada built the fragata *Nuestra Señora de los Remedios*, with a capacity of 1,500 hides, at Ortigosa in 1601. Another master, Miguel, worked at Río de Puercos, where he was building the fragata *La Catalina*, with a capacity of 1,000 hides, in 1608. Closer to the western end of the island, by 1585 Francisco Nuñez had developed a shipyard in his hato Guaniguanico. Another shipyard, which has not been located, is mentioned at the farm "El Descanso" of prominent vecino Juan Recio in 1599.[29]

The surge in shipbuilding was made possible by the presence in the port city of a growing number of skilled artisans. Building a ship required the labor of shipwrights, carpenters, caulkers, blacksmiths, sail makers, cord makers, and sawyers. Historian José Veigas identified 6 caulkers and 8 ship carpenters living in Havana between 1550 and 1577. A 1582 military census listed 4 caulkers, 15 carpenters, and 6 blacksmiths in town. These numbers undoubtedly grew thereafter. Between 1578 and 1610 the notarial records register some 48 ship carpenters and caulkers working in Havana, and their number increased significantly when the fleets were in town, for many vessels carried carpenters and caulkers with them. In 1591 Governor Juan de Tejeda reported that he had allocated 42 carpenters from the fleet to work on the fragatas that were being built by order of the king.[30]

The growth of shipbuilding in Havana and its vicinity also resulted in the production of larger ships, a change that mirrored trends in the Spanish Atlantic.[31] Most of the vessels built in the 1580s and 1590s were fragatas of less than 100 tons. Those built for the king by Governor Juan de Tejeda between 1589 and 1591 averaged 80 tons. Some larger naos and navíos were built as well, but the largest vessels rarely exceeded a capacity of 300 tons. One of the largest was the navío Nuestra Señora de la Encarnación, capacity 300 tons, built in Mariel for master Gaspar Lorenzo in 1595. The average tonnage of fifteen Havana-built ships that participated in the fleets between 1590 and 1600 was 185 tons.[32]

By the late 1590s, however, the shipyards of Havana began to build much larger ships. The nao San Salvador, built by order of Governor Valdés and sold in 1607 for 20,500 ducados (225,500 reales), had a capacity of 650 tons. The six galleons built with royal funds between 1608 and 1610 for the armada of Juan de Borja averaged more than 630 tons; the smallest was 600. Between 1600 and 1620, the average tonnage of thirty-one vessels built in Havana and participating in the Carrera de Indias had risen to 407 tons.[33]

Moreover, the ships built in Havana earned a reputation for quality, hardiness, and durability. These advantages were attributed to the quality of Cuban hardwoods, "the best in the world," according to the exaggerated assertion of a royal official, and to the expertise and skill of master shipwright Francisco Gutiérrez Navarrete, also described as "the best in the world" by Governor Tejeda. In 1603 the Council of the Indies advised the king to build vessels in Havana precisely because "wood in Havana is so good and so abundant, and there is a good master." They anticipated these ships to be "sturdier and more durable" than those produced on the peninsula.[34]

Shipbuilding was a truly Atlantic enterprise that combined supplies and factors of production from various continents. To begin with, the ships were produced in Havana, but technical specifications came from the Mediterranean. When Juan de Borja arrived in Havana in 1608, he found that the boards and planks that had been made in the city did not conform to his diagrams. Woods were the most important local supply but not the only one. Three types of wood are mentioned frequently as those preferred for naval construction: mahogany (Swietenia mahagoni), cedar (Cedrela odorata), and oak (Tabebuia calcicola). Pine trees (Pinus caribaea) were used to make ship masts. Other locally produced supplies

LIBRO SEGVN
DO DE LA MAR, Y SVS MOVI
MIENTOS. Y COMO FVE
INVENTADA LA NA
VEGACION .:.

Atlantic ships. From Pedro de Medina, *Arte de navegar* (1545).

included cordage, made from the sturdy fibers of the majagua tree (Hibiscus elatus), and tallow, which was mixed with imported tar to enlarge it. Most naval stores were imported from Europe, however. These included tar from Biscay or the Canary Islands, mainmasts from Norway, rigging from Riga, cables from England and Flanders, French tools, and steel from Milan. The importance of northern European naval stores was such that the contract to supply the shipyard for the construction of the armada in 1608 was given to a merchant from Antwerp.[35]

And then there were the workers, whose origins were equally varied. Skilled workers were mobilized from distant points to work in Havana. Master shipwright Gutiérrez Navarrete came to town in 1589 from Bayamo in eastern Cuba by request of Governor Tejeda, who offered him a yearly salary of 1,000 ducados. Another master shipwright, Fracisco de Beas, was brought to Havana along with other artisans by General Juan de Borja in 1608. They came from Santo Domingo. A multitude of seamen, artisans, peons, and slaves added to the variety of the workforce employed at the shipyards.[36]

These workers were frequently paid with financial resources from outside the local economy. The royal contracts resulted in the injection of millions of additional reales into the city. As usual, this money came from the mines and mints of Mexico. Additional work was commissioned by transient merchants who did business in the city and built ships for regional or transoceanic trade or by shipmasters in need of repairs or parts. The importance of shipbuilding was magnified further by its linkages to other economic activities that employed a variety of laborers.

Some of the activities performed by these unknown workers can be traced through the detailed accounts of the officials who disbursed the money for the royal contracts. To start the construction of the king's fragatas in June 1589, for instance, Governor Tejeda commissioned four carpenters "to search for woods that were appropriate." After twelve days they found them in the area of Río de Puercos, on the northwestern coast of the island. The fragata San Francisco was then dispatched to the area with forty carpenters, sawyers, and woodcutters. Their average salary was between 8 and 9 reales per day, those of the seamen employed on the fragata about 5 reales a day. Additional wood was purchased from the vecinos, some of whom developed sawmills on their properties. In 1589 Sebastián Fernandez Pacheco, Diego de Lara, Diego Hernandez de Luna, Juan de Horta, and Gaspar Hernandez committed to deliver wood to the shipyard for 11,000 reales. They were no strangers to the lumber business. Lara, a merchant born in Antwerp and vecino of Havana, owned at least one slave sawyer, Pedro Zape, whom he had received as part of his wife's dowry in 1586. A year later he hired a rural laborer who, among other functions, had the function of "sawing." Hernandez de Luna, in turn, hired slave Juan Biafara, "sawyer," to work for him in 1586.[37]

The vecinos supplied the shipyards with other materials. Some hired out their slaves. Owners of slaves working on the king's fragatas were paid a generous daily rent of 8 reales – much more than the usual rent for slaves or wages received by free workers. Other vecinos supplied food. The royal treasury paid 6,187 reales to various vecinos for the rations of fifty-four "officials and peons" employed in woodcutting and sawing in the Río de Puercos area between 30 June and 17 August 1589. Another 5,000 reales was paid for wine, which was offered as part of the rations. Local merchants also sold naval stores and tools, and blacksmiths manufactured a variety of items for the ships.

Because the royal accounts do not include (in either 1589 or 1608) the cost of the naval stores shipped directly to Havana on account of the royal treasury, it is impossible to calculate accurately the relative importance of each item in the total expenses of the city's shipyard. But the available figures offer at least a glimpse of the impact of the city's shipyard on the local economy. The royal treasury disbursed 136,871 reales to pay for woods to build the fragatas between 1589 and 1591. Havana producers charged 17,800 additional reales for other locally produced supplies and 27,200 reales for food. Salaried workers, including artisans, peons, seamen, and officials, received 453,000 reales. Among the expenses associated with the construction of the galleons between August 1608 and March 1609 (213,759 reales in all), wood represented a whooping 54 percent, food 10 percent, and salaries 22 percent. Despite the shortcomings of the accounts, it is clear that a substantial proportion of the royal funds destined to pay for the construction of these ships stayed in the local economy and helped to finance local producers and laborers. It is also clear that shipbuilding mobilized a variety of resources and producers.[38]

One of the obstacles faced by shipbuilding in Havana was the lack of abundant iron parts and supplies, most of which – nails, spikes, chains, anchors – had to be imported. In the production of six galleons made for the king in Vizcaya in the 1620s, iron represented 15 percent of the total cost. The scarcity of iron supplies in Havana was so acute that in the late 1580s Governor Tejeda was forced to dismantle some old harquebuses "because of the lack of iron and nails." This limitation was even more notable because most of the ships that the crown made in Havana had military purposes and were required to be properly armed with artillery. Ordnance was also required by the expanding military infrastructure of Havana. The crown was therefore interested in the possibility of building a foundry in the city. Indeed, in the instructions given to Tejeda in 1588 was reference to the existence of "many mines in that island where it would be possible to extract copper in abundance to build artillery." With royal support, as usual, a foundry was established. It began operations in 1600.[39]

The Foundry

The foundry was created owing to the initiative of the vecinos and of local authorities, who insisted on the need to protect the port city while offering to supply ordnance for "all the kingdoms" of His Catholic Majesty. Governor Juan Maldonado Barnuevo, who took an active role in the promotion of Havana's economy and invested in various productive ventures, insisted that if artillery was not being made in Havana, it was only because of the lack of "negros" and technical personnel. Otherwise, Maldonado and other officials concurred, conditions for the production of artillery on the island were ideal, indeed the best in the world.[40]

The king responded favorably to these reports, issuing in 1597 an annual situado of 246,430 reales to cover the expenses associated with the foundry and the development of copper mining in the vicinity of Santiago de Cuba, in eastern Cuba. A captain of artillery, Francisco Sánchez de Moya, was sent from Spain with several technicians to build the foundry and begin production. Among these were highly skilled workers such as master smelter Francisco de Ballesteros and master carpenter Gonzalo de la Rocha, a specialist in the making of gun carriages. The king ordered the purchase of two hundred slaves as well, although as late as 1604 fewer than half had been actually received.[41]

Like the shipyards, the foundry created linkages that were beneficial to the local economy. Between 1598 and 1603, according to the accounts of Governor Pedro de Valdés, the treasury of Havana spent 1,106,051 reales to cover the expenses associated with the foundry. A variety of artisans, workers, and local economic actors took advantage of these monetary injections. Stonecutters, masons, bricklayers, and tile makers built and repaired the furnaces and the foundry house, for which they were paid 21,854 reales (about 2 percent of the total). The owners of the lots and houses where the foundry was built, near the fortress of La Punta, collected 73,906 reales for their properties. Slave owners rented their slaves out to the works and collected 4 reales per day for their labor. According to the master smelter, thirty-three rented slaves worked regularly at the foundry. Free laborers participated as well, hauling construction materials and firewood, carrying the ore, and working in the smelting process. Another 1.4 percent of the expenses were devoted to paying for their services. Individuals employed by the foundry as officials, including a master smelter and two assistants, a master carpenter, several overseers, a physician, an accountant, a treasurer, and the administrator, collected 49,027 reales. Seamen and shipmasters claimed another 15,732 reales for carrying the ore from Santiago to Havana. According to shipment contracts, shipmasters charged about 1,000 reales for each of these trips with their fragatas. Farmers sold animals as beasts of burden and food, to the amount of 12,814 reales. In 1598, for instance, Sánchez de Moya contracted with a vecino of Guanabacoa 100 cargas (5,000 pounds) of cassava, which were to be delivered in tarts, at the rate of 3 cargas or 90 tarts per week, for 3,000 reales. Woodcutters received 1,684 reales for supplying firewood and 6,733 reales for hardwoods for gun carriages. Cordage makers collected 1,581 reales as well.[42]

Havana claimed the lion's share of the copper situado even though the ore was produced in the copper mines of El Prado, in the vicinity of Santiago de Cuba. Less than a third of the situado was used to pay for expenses related to the mines. It was not without justification that several royal officials questioned whether the foundry should be established in Havana at all and complained that the artillery produced there was too expensive. These complaints were not without effect, as two royal cedulas in 1607 ordered the fabrication of ordnance in Havana suspended and the copper sent to Seville. By then, some forty-five pieces of artillery, weighing a total of 2,336 quintals, had been made in Havana.[43]

As with shipbuilding, the injection of this situado added strength to an activity that preceded the establishment of the royal foundry. Although we know little about them, it is certain that small foundries existed in town since at least the 1570s. Domingo de Quejo, a blacksmith described as mulatto, operated a foundry as early as 1573. A second was established just a few months later, in February 1574, by Melchor Pérez Morillo, a gun maker who settled in Havana with his wife and family. A third foundry is mentioned in 1597, owned by blacksmith Francisco Gonzalez Tavares. The military census of 1582 lists 6 blacksmiths, 3 of them as transients. Between 1550 and 1600, local sources register the existence of 11 blacksmiths, 3 sword makers, and 1 gun maker. As mentioned above, when Sánchez de Moya arrived on the island in 1597, he also brought 3 smelters with him.[44]

The foundry was supposed to serve one exclusive purpose: to produce artillery for His Majesty's service. In fact, it catered to the needs of the local economy as well. In 1603 the king inquired whether it was true that master smelter Francisco de Ballesteros devoted himself to "smelt bells and other things" for private parties instead of attending to the production of artillery. In his report, Governor Valdés denied any wrongdoing on Ballesteros's part, although he acknowledged that in his free time he had made a few supplies for a nascent manufacture: the sugar mills.[45]

Sugar

The development of sugar making in Havana in the late sixteenth century replicated the pattern followed by other productive activities, such as shipbuilding
and the ironworks. Local residents identified opportunities, built some infrastructure for production, and began producing on a small scale. Royal funds
and necessities provided much needed investment, facilitated the transfer of
technical knowledge and technical personnel to the city, and created an artificially large market for some of the local products. The initiative was local, but
the orders came from Castile and the silver from Zacatecas.

Sugar differed from naval construction and the production of artillery in one
crucial aspect, however: it did not serve military needs. To elicit the interest of
the king, the vecinos of Havana used their usual arguments, which had worked
repeatedly before. First, the city and its vicinity already had many sugarcane
fields, "the best of the Indies," plus an abundance of water and firewood for
the mills. Second, with the ingenios (sugar mills), tithe payments would increase
and church personnel would be sustained with local resources, instead of royal
funds. Finally, the sugar mills would attract more people to Havana, and a larger
population would likely place the city "in better defense." As a group of vecinos
explained, they were poor because they spent most of their time on guard, protecting the city against His Majesty's many enemies.[46]

The vecinos were at least partially successful. With the support of Governor
Juan Maldonado Barnuevo, who later became a sugar mill owner, they obtained
in 1595 a royal cedula granting Cuban producers the same privileges and immunities given to mill owners in La Española in 1529 and 1534.[47] Basically, this
meant that ingenios were exempted from liquidation because of debts. More
to the point, and also with Maldonado's support, these vecinos obtained a royal
loan of 40,000 ducados (440,000 reales) to build sugar mills. Granted in 1600 as a
lump sum, the loan was actually disbursed in 1602 by Governor Pedro de Valdés among seventeen prominent vecinos of the city. It was to be repaid in eight
years.[48]

Other requests met with less success. In 1604 and 1606 the town council of
Havana instructed its representative in the Spanish court to petition the king
for additional concessions to stimulate the recently established sugar business
on the island.[49] In both cases the requests revolved around one crucial issue:
trading. The councilmen claimed that by the time the fleets returned to Spain
the harvest had not ended, and they asked for the right to export Havana's sugar
outside the fleets, in the so-called navíos sueltos (independent ships). They also
requested the elimination of all export and import duties, which amounted in

all to 10 percent of the product's final value. Equally unsuccessful was another petition for a loan of 80,000 ducados by a group of fourteen vecinos not included among the beneficiaries of the 1602 loan. In their commission to Juan Gutiérrez del Rayo, whom they promised to pay 2,000 ducados if he succeeded in obtaining the loan, the petitioners asserted that many of them had sugarcane fields and were even building some ingenios on their own.[50]

As had been the case with shipbuilding and the ironworks, the royal funds came to stimulate and expand previously existing economic activities. Even before the first mills were constructed, some melado (sugarcane syrup) and low-grade sugars were being manually produced for local consumption. At least since the 1580s, sugarcane fields appear in Havana's notarial records as part of the inventories of the estancias that catered to the city's food market. Some of these fields, the governor asserted in 1597, had been cultivated for decades. In 1593 Havana was already exporting melado "from the island's harvest" to Florida, and by 1597 more than 3,000 arrobas (34 tons) of low-grade sugars had been exported to Spain, Cartagena de Indias, and Campeche, Mexico.[51]

Local residents took advantage of a particularly favorable conjuncture to develop sugar production in the 1590s. The prosperous cattle-raising economy provided food for the slaves, as well as power for the animal-driven mills. The construction of Havana's aqueduct allowed for the irrigation of agricultural lands and the construction of water-powered mills. Several of the initial mills were built by the aqueduct or the Chorrera River. Military constructions attracted not only abundant currency and slaves to the city but also a large number of skilled artisans who had the ability to build sugar mills. Gonzalo de la Rocha, the master carpenter who came to Havana in 1597 to work at the foundry, built two sugar mills in 1598 and 1599.[52] In Santiago, Sánchez de Moya constructed two mills using "the carpenters, laborers, slaves" and even animals owned by the king to operate the mines.[53] As mentioned above, the foundry produced metal parts and supplies to the mills, particularly cauldrons, kettles, and various copper utensils. Indeed, the inventories of some mills included copper utensils made on the island.[54]

In addition to these conditions, which were as "local" as they could be in sixteenth-century Havana, three equally favorable regional and international factors contributed to the establishment of sugar manufacture on the island. First, the concession of the slave-trade monopoly to Portuguese merchant Gomez Reinel in 1595 increased the supply of African slaves. Second, prices were high. According to historian Earl Hamilton, between 1511 and 1599 the price of an arroba of sugar in Andalusia went from 8 reales to 70 reales.[55] Last, but certainly not least, other Atlantic producers had entered a phase of decline and were facing

great difficulties. Displaced from the official trade routes, the sugar produced in
La Española and Puerto Rico had become increasingly expensive. On the eastern
side of the Atlantic, Madeira and the Canary Islands were also in decline.[56] Sugar
manufacturing had expanded into Mexico and Peru, but their production was
destined mainly for local consumption.[57]

The few mills that began to produce sugar in the 1590s around Havana were
rather modest units manufacturing low-grade sugars and melado. When these
mills were sold, they were not designated as either ingenios or trapiches (see
below) but rather as agricultural units that had incorporated some machinery to
process sugarcane. Thus, in 1591 Pedro de Carvajal, a Sevillian resident in the city,
sold half of a unit described as an "estancia with a trapiche," not vice versa. Likewise, Pedro de Oñate owned in 1595 an "estancia with a trapiche where melado
is made."[58] What seems to be a terminological question is, in fact, a reflection
of production realities. These units were not yet defined by the presence of the
processing machinery. For an estancia to become a sugar mill it had to produce
sugar, not only melado. This production required, in addition to the extracting machinery (the mill itself), separate installations to boil the syrup (boiling
house) and purify sugar (purging house). The mill was then designated and sold
as either an ingenio or a trapiche.

These designations have been the source of much confusion among historians. Following the writings of Bartolomé de las Casas and Gonzalo Fernández
de Oviedo, both of whom described sugar production in La Española, Cuban
historians have asserted that water-powered mills were called ingenios, whereas
trapiches were smaller, animal-driven units.[59] Contemporary documents do
refer to ingenios and trapiches as different types of mills. The 1602 loan covered
eight ingenios, six trapiches, and three ingenios-trapiches. In Cuba, however,
the distinction between these units was not based on the type of power source.
We know, for instance, that the "trapiche" Santa Cruz, built by Manrique de
Rojas in La Chorrera, was water-powered and that the "ingenios" Nuestra Señora
del Rosario and Los Tres Reyes, of Antonio de Ribera and Melchor Casas, were
animal-driven.[60]

The difference between ingenios and trapiches was thus based on different
criteria. When Governor Maldonado reported to the crown how he would distribute the royal loan, he suggested that those building ingenios de agua (water-
driven mills) should get 8,000 ducados; those who built ingenios de caballo de rueda
grande voladora (horse-driven mills with a large overshot wheel) should receive
half this amount, whereas those building trapiches pequeños (small mills) should
not get more than 2,000 or 3,000 ducados. Maldonado calls ingenios not only
those mills driven by water but also those driven by by animals.[61]

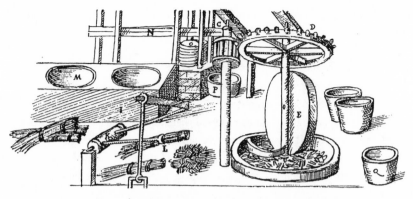

Sugar mill using Mediterranean technology. From Juanelo Turriano,
Veintiún libros de los ingenios y máquinas (ca. 1585).

This information, however, does not elucidate the sort of technological and
productive features that differentiated ingenios from trapiches, beyond the fact
that the latter were smaller, less expensive units. The coexistence of different
technologies and the changing nature of terms further complicate the problem.
In the early years of sugar production in Cuba, it seems that "ingenio" referred to
units using either the old Mediterranean technology of a heavy millstone rolling
over small pieces of cane or the horizontal mill of two rollers, which was also
used at this time in Brazil.[62] Because of their inefficiency, these ingenios always
required a complementary press (*prensa*) to further extract juice from the cane.
In 1603, the ingenio Nuestra Señora del Rosario used a two-roller mill and two
wood presses "full of stone, so they are heavier." When this ingenio was built,
around 1598, its owner described it as a "two-roller mill with its overshot wheel
to mill cane like those of Motril and Salobreña."[63] That is, this mill replicated
the technology used in Mediterranean Spain to manufacture sugar.

Which types of mills were designated as trapiches? One possibility is that
they were smaller traditional mills, without a wheel, powered by the slaves
themselves. Small hand presses had been used to produce sugar in Madeira since
the fifteenth century and were also used in Mexico.[64] In his report to the crown,
Maldonado specified that people building small trapiches would receive money
to help them with "the blacks and the copper for kettles." In contrast to his com-
ments on the ingenios, he makes no reference to any other power source.

The other possibility is that these trapiches referred to the new, three-roller
vertical mills that spread throughout Brazil, the Spanish colonies, and the West
Indies during the seventeenth century. Our problem here is one of chronology.
Reportedly these new mills first appeared in Brazil between 1608 and 1613,

where they were probably introduced by a Spanish priest coming from Peru.[65] Although the available data is not conclusive, it seems that this type of mill was used in Cuba *before* the earliest dates reported for Brazil. As early as 1606, sugar mill owner Hernando de Espinar included in his will "the trapiche San Antonio with three new rollers." Three years later Juana Rodríguez owned an "ingenio with two small rollers and a large one broken."[66] Also noteworthy is that in 1617 the governor of Santiago de Cuba reported that sugar production had prospered in the area because "they have invented small ingenios of three rollers called trapiches."[67] If this technology was first introduced and applied in Brazil, it spread to Cuba remarkably fast. It is, of course, possible that the island received the technology directly from Peru via the passengers of the fleet of Tierra Firme, but the puzzling question is that these vertical mills were frequently referred to as "of new type" (*a la nueva usanza*) or as "of Brazilian type" (*a usanza del Brasil*), an indication that the vertical mill did get into Cuba from the Portuguese colony.[68]

These early mills were transitional in more than a technological sense. The ingenios were changing also in terms of their land extension, the nature of the labor force used, and the sources of their supplies, particularly copper for the boiling kettles and the potter's clay for *hormas*, forms or pots, needed to purge sugar.

Since most of the ingenios were built on estancias, the availability of land for the mills was limited. As mentioned above, the average size of estancias during the 1578–1610 period was about 2.5 caballerías (83 acres). Only part of this land could be used to grow cane, for in most cases significant portions of the ingenios' land had to be reserved for firewood and food production. To buy firewood added greatly to the expenses of the ingenio,[69] especially because Havana's town council attempted to restrict the production of firewood in the area peripheral to the city for defensive purposes and to protect local construction and shipyard activities. Therefore, several *señores de ingenio* added other parcels of land to their properties into the early 1600s, either through cabildo concessions or through purchase. The ingenio San Antonio de Padua, originally established on 3 caballerías of land (100 acres), had incorporated three estancias by 1608, with a total of 10 additional caballerías (333 acres) of land. The Maldonados acquired the "estancia and trapiche" of a Manuel Pérez and added it to their mill in 1603.[70] In 1601 and 1603, Hernando de Espinar and Baltasar de Rojas obtained from the cabildo parcels of land to incorporate into their respective mills. Hernán Rodríguez Tabares did the same in 1608, when he requested a piece of land adjacent to his ingenio "to cut firewood for his mill." In order to cut costs, several señores de ingenio also built sawmills on their units. These mills were then capable of producing their own sugar-packing boxes and various wood parts needed to operate the ingenio. The slaves employed in the sawmill of the ingenio Nuestra Señora del Rosario, for instance, produced boxes, boards for the purging house, and oxcarts in 1603.[71]

Land was also needed to rotate crops and produce food for self-consumption and, if possible, for the local market. Information about the precise amount of land used to grow sugarcane is extremely scarce, and we can advance only very rough estimates about its size. In the second half of the seventeenth century, more than 60 percent of the total sugar mill land was reserved, primarily for the production of firewood. That is, all the mill installations – including notably the *casas de molienda, calderas y purga* (mill, boiling, and purging houses) – the *cañaverales* (sugarcane fields), and the other crops occupied less than 40 percent of the total land, a proportion well below the proportions used by sugar mills in the British West Indies during the same period or in Cuba during the plantation era.[72] In a further step to avoid market uncertainty, most mills included other crops among their products. Corn was grown to feed the animals; large *platanales* (banana fields) supplied one of the main staples in the slave diet – "It is their sustenance instead of bread and they do not get anything else but meat," a sugar mill owner declared in 1603. Additionally, sugar mills grew rice, beans, pumpkins and other vegetables. Despite its limited demand and commercial value, some mills produced tobacco for slave consumption. Cassava was also grown, but at least part of it was destined to produce "bread" for the local market.[73]

Sugar mill owners reacted to these initial limitations of land and sugarcane acreage in yet another way. Some of them milled cane grown by others, a system similar to the Brazilian *lavradores de cana*. Although it is not possible to establish how prevalent this practice was in the early years of sugar manufacturing in Cuba, it is clear that, unlike in Brazil, these sugarcane farmers did not constitute an essential part of the region's sugar economy.[74] In a 1598 report to the crown, individuals planning to build sugar mills asserted that the manufacture would benefit the poor vecinos because they would have the opportunity to grow cane "and take [it] to be milled at the ingenios" of the wealthy vecinos. Sugar mill owner Luis Hernández, for instance, milled cane from the estancia of Jusepe Rodríguez in 1604; likewise, Manuel Baez, a Portuguese, supplied cane to the mill of Juan Pérez de Oporto in 1610. According to sugar mill owner Antonio de Ribera – who explicitly instructed his administrator not to mill outside cane – it was customary for growers to provide some "slave help" during the harvest period and to pay señores de ingenio half the sugar and melado produced.[75] Although this system never disappeared completely, the trend was for mills to grow their own cane and to become self-sufficient units. Furthermore, with the introduction of the three-roller vertical trapiches, sugar technology became significantly cheaper, allowing some of the initial farmers to build their own mills.

The first señores de ingenio also had difficulties in securing a stable supply of labor with the qualifications needed to produce white, purged sugar. The first *maestros de azúcar* (sugar masters) who worked in Cuban mills were white, well-paid artisans usually hired for one or two years. As was usual among Atlantic sugar producers, some of the initial sugar masters came from areas where sugar production had begun to decline. In 1600 sugar mill owner Martín Calvo de la Puerta commissioned a resident of La Palma to hire in the Canary Islands a "sugar master to come to this city to serve the sugar of my mill." Juan Maldonado granted a similar commission in 1602.[76] In 1603 Maldonado and Luis Hernández shared the services of maestro Nicolás Hernández, who became responsible for production in both mills. One of these maestros, Pedro González, ended up co-owning two ingenios in Havana.[77]

As with the land, the señores de ingenio attempted to eliminate this expense and their dependency on hired labor by having their own slaves trained in the trade. The free sugar masters' labor was expensive – more expensive, in fact, than that of a physician in charge of the mill's slaves.[78] The sugar masters' yearly salary averaged about 1,020 reales per year, similar to that of a soldier or a low-ranking officer in the local garrison and 20 percent higher than that of a white rural worker, which, as mentioned above, was about 71 reales per month.[79] Moreover, the masters customarily received also free housing and food. Some mill owners hired maestros de azúcar only on condition that they teach one of their slaves "how to make sugar and purge it, so he can make a living as a sugar master."[80] By the second half of the seventeenth century this task was performed almost exclusively by slaves.

Equally problematic was guaranteeing the supply of copper utensils and purging forms. People promoting the sugar business in the 1590s attempted initially to import these supplies from Portugal, alleging that they were the best available and could not be produced satisfactorily on the island. In 1597 they informed the crown that to initiate production they lacked "two main things: copper kettles and earthenware forms, because they are not available in the island, and no one knows how to make them." In fact, the señores de ingenios were attempting to circumvent Seville's trading monopoly by importing these supplies directly from Portugal "in one or two ships . . . without having to go to Seville to declare" the merchandise. The same year they contracted the acquisition of copper utensils and fifty thousand forms from Aveiro, Portugal, with merchant Juan Rodríguez Quintero, asserting that utensils and forms from Aveiro were widely used by all other Atlantic producers, including those in the Canary Islands, Madeira, São Tomé, and Brazil.[81]

Both needs were soon met through local resources. By the early 1600s sugar mills were using locally produced forms, and new pottery works were being established in the sugar-producing areas. Moreover, in a further move toward self-sufficiency, some ingenios began to produce their own forms and to train slaves in the trade. In 1603, for instance, Antonio de Ribera instructed the administrator of his mill to "contract with an officer who makes forms, because there are many in this city," to build a pottery in his mill capable of producing 1,000 or 2,000 sugar forms per year.[82] When the señores de ingenio rented their potteries to independent masters, they included a yearly supply of free sugar forms as part of the price. Fueled by sugar demand, some of these pottery works had grown by midcentury into units employing as many as eight slaves.[83]

A similar solution was applied to the supply of cauldrons, kettles, and the many other copper utensils required by each mill. The copper mines of Santiago del Prado in eastern Cuba provided abundant raw material. As mentioned above, the foundry established in Havana with royal money processed it, so in practice the crown was supporting the nascent sugar manufactures in still another way. Smaller foundries probably made parts and supplies for the sugar mills as well.

Making the mills self-sufficient in as many ways as possible – including cane, supplies such as forms, firewood and packing boxes, food and labor – represented an effort to minimize their vulnerability to unpredictable market conditions and to maximize protection against the chronic lack of liquid capital that afflicted sugar mill owners. Several of the first mills seem to have run into great financial difficulties in maintaining operations and paying their debts (above all the 1602 loan).[84] Some señores de ingenio mortgaged their units to obtain fresh capital, frequently from the church or local merchants, an early indication of the dominant position enjoyed by commercial capital in the colonial setting. Cuba's sugar history during the whole colonial period is the history of subordination of local producers to merchants and other lenders. As early as 1610 several clergymen and merchants had been able to take control of some of the mills. Antonio de Ribera borrowed 300 ducados (3,300 reales) from the monastery of Santo Domingo in 1601, which he guaranteed with a mortgage on his mill Nuestra Señora del Rosario and for which he paid 21.4 ducados per year (a 7.1 percent interest rate). Gaspar de Salazar, Havana's parish priest, bought half of the mill San Juan from Baltasar de Rojas in 1606; he owned the other half already. Bishop Juan de las Cabezas Altamirano owned a mill by 1607.[85] Merchant Francisco López de Piedra, who had served as guarantor of three señores de ingenio on occasion of the 1602 royal loan, had acquired control of the mill originally owned by Antonio Matos de Gama by

Table 5.2. Sugar Mills, 1601–1615

Owner	Name	Year	Type	Price (Ducados)	Slaves	Horses	Mules	Forms
						Animals		
Melchor Casas	Los Tres Reyes	1601	A	10,000	14	8	8	—
Juan Maldonado	San Diego	1602	W	—	31	—	—	—
Ginés de Orta Yuste	El Rosario	1602	A	—	24	—	—	—
Antonio de Ribera	N. Sra. del Rosario	1603	A	—	14	8	8	700
Hernando de Espinar	San Antonio	1606	A	—	14	7	4	600
Luis Hernández	—	1606	A	—	27	2	9	1,000
P. Suárez de Gamboa	—	1607	A	13,000	16	8	—	1,200
A. Matos da Gama	San Francisco	1607	A	7,000	9	8	5	—
Domingo de Viera	San Antonio	1608	A	3,800	4	7	1	500
Gaspar de Salazar	La Trinidad	1608	A	3,000	3	9	—	—
Juan Mordazo	—	1608	A	—	5	9	—	—
Juan del Poyo	San Antonio	1615	A	9,759	10	16	8	445

Source: ANC, PNH, ER, 1601–15.

Note: Type: A: animal-driven; W: water-driven.

1607. He had also taken control of Melchor Casas's Los Tres Reyes, which he dismantled.[86] Portuguese merchant Enrique Mendes de Noronha bought the mill that had belonged to Lucas de Rojas. Sugar mill owners Domingo de Viera and his wife, Juana Núñez, sold their mill San Antonio de Padua to another merchant, Juan del Poyo Valenzuela, in 1608, who in turn sold it in 1615.[87]

Several sugar mill owners responded to capital scarcity by selling portions of their mills to others, by creating "companies" to build and to administer mills, and by paying debts through participation in the ownership of the ingenio. Martín Calvo de la Puerta sold half of his ingenio Santiago to sugarmaster Pedro González as early as 1598, and the latter also bought one-fourth of Melchor Casas's mill three years later. Hernán Manrique de Rojas and Melchor Casas agreed to build jointly a water-driven sugar mill in 1600, as did Juan Pérez and Pedro González Cordero in 1603.[88] Likewise, the mill San Diego was co-owned by Juan Maldonado and his uncle, former governor Juan Maldonado Barnuevo, even though only the former appeared as beneficiary of the 1602 loan.

The proliferation of these partnerships indicates that the sugar business required a relatively large outlay of capital. The scant information available suggests that the total market value of these initial mills varied widely, from some 3,000 ducados (33,000 reales) to perhaps as much as 20,000 ducados (220,000 reales), depending on the size of the unit, the technology used, and, above all, the number of slaves it possessed (see table 5.2). Each slave added, on average, about 300 ducados to the total value of the unit. The two least valuable mills included in table 5.2, those of Viera and Salazar, had only three or four slaves. Conversely, those with total value of 10,000 ducados or more had three times as many slaves. The ingenio of the Maldonados, with 31 slaves (the largest identified during this period) was probably worth about 20,000 ducados, if not more. The significance of the number of slaves in the total value of the ingenio is exemplified by the mill San Antonio, which was sold for 3,800 ducados in 1608, when it had only four slaves. Seven years later, the same mill—then owned by merchant Juan del Poyo Valenzuela—was sold for an amount that more than doubled the original price. In the process, however, the new owner had added six new slaves to the mill, which alone accounted for one-third of the price increase. Mill owners who were not able to buy slaves rented them during the harvest, but their labor was not cheap, about 6 ducados per month.[89]

Capital shortages, plus the relatively limited supply of African slaves under the asiento system, contributed to check the proliferation of sugar mills and the growth of each unit. There were between twenty and twenty-five mills in Havana around 1610. These were small units, with a capacity of production that rarely exceeded 1,000 arrobas (11.4 tons) per year. Between 1603 and 1610 the city exported legally 57,000 arrobas (648 tons) of sugar to Seville, an annual average of 6,300 arrobas (72 tons). If we assume that about two-thirds of total production was exported to Spain, Havana's output must have amounted to about 10,000 arrobas per year, that is, around 500 annual arrobas per mill. Although this is a comparatively low figure, it is probably close to the real one.[90] The governor of Santiago asserted in 1617 that each animal-powered mill, if it was well supplied, produced a maximum of 800 arrobas per year.[91]

This estimate is corroborated also by the amount of sugar shipped to Seville by some individual producers in the early years of the century. Juan Maldonado, "el mozo," co-owner of the water-powered mill San Diego, for instance, exported an average of 410 arrobas per year between 1606 and 1609. If this figure represented two-thirds of his mill's production, then its total annual output was somewhere around 615 arrobas. Pedro de Oñate, owner of a smaller animal-powered mill, exported an annual average of 320 arrobas between 1604 and 1606 (its total output would have been 480 arrobas per year).[92]

Since slaves were an expensive, indispensable, and difficult-to-replace element of the production process, the señores de ingenio had a vested interest in providing for their basic needs. Those in the mill Nuestra Señora del Rosario received two sets of clothing per year, one made of cañamazo (canvas) and the other made of jerga (sackcloth), which was reputed to be warmer for the winter period. They got also a blanket per year, usually imported from Mexico. As mentioned above, their diet consisted mainly of bananas and meat—pork and turtle—but it is likely that slaves supplemented their diets though their own *conucos*, or provision grounds. Some vecinos took on the production of salted turtle meat for the slaves. Poultry meat was reserved for those who fell ill.[93]

Slaves were strictly prohibited from leaving the mill during the harvest, which began in late December, after Christmas, and extended through July, during the rainy season. Runaway slaves were to be "punished in their body," not only for their own correction but also to serve as "an example for the others." Indeed, as the number of slaves in the city and its surroundings increased, so did the vecinos' fears about their ability to control and police this population group.

CHAPTER SIX

Slavery and the
Making of a Racial Order

On 2 April 1600, the navío *San Antonio* docked at Havana harbor after a two-month-long trip from Luanda. Although it had become increasingly common for ships from the distant African continent to call to port, the arrival of the *San Antonio* was something of an event. After all, it had been more than two years since the arrival of the last slave ship from the African coasts. Smaller groups of slaves were being constantly imported from Cartagena de Indias, Santo Domingo, Puerto Rico, and other points in the Caribbean, but the 195 slaves aboard the *San Antonio* represented a significant number for the local market. Timing was perfect. The expansion of the port city and its regional economy required workers in relatively large numbers. More Africans were needed.[1]

On this point there was little or no debate. By the second half of the sixteenth century, Europeans in general and Iberians in particular were becoming increasingly used to what would eventually be one of the Atlantic's longest-lasting innovations: the association between slavery and Africa, between race and social status. Although there was some discussion among theologians and legal experts about the justness of African slavery and about whether African captives were the products of just wars, the institution itself was seldom attacked and the suitability of the continent as a source of labor rarely doubted. The ownership of slaves posed religious and ethical questions, but these misgivings did not result in a systematic questioning of slavery. The Catholic Church not only condoned the ownership of slaves, even after they were baptized, but was itself a major slave owner. Some thinkers went so far as to claim that slavery was a good thing, for it provided Africans with the opportunity to live among Christians and to be initiated in the mysteries of the Catholic faith.[2]

It is questionable whether by the mid-sixteenth century blackness had already become equated with slavery and degradation, but images of Africans as inferior and bestial, thus naturally predisposed to servitude, were probably widespread enough that the connection was seen as a matter of common sense in some areas of Mediterranean Europe.[3] Many of the European settlers in Havana had been surely socialized in these ideas, for they came precisely from regions where slavery was an entrenched institution. Within Spain, slaves were particularly numerous in Seville, Málaga, and Valencia. They represented about one-tenth of the total population in Lisbon and Evora, Portugal's largest cities. A similar proportion lived in Gran Canaria. Furthermore, in all these places black Africans had replaced Moors and North African Muslims as the largest group of slaves. Therefore we can safely assume that to many, if not most, of the European immigrants in Havana slavery – particularly the enslavement of Africans – was a familiar social practice.[4]

Thus the sale of slaves aboard the *San Antonio* proceeded with normality. As with any other merchandise, slaves were inspected, assessed, and then purchased. Gonzalo Prieto, the shipmaster in charge of the cargo, began by selling the best slaves, those whose perceived age, health, and physical appearance commanded the highest prices. About two-thirds of the slaves aged 15-24 got sold in April, during the ship's first month in Havana, compared with just one-fourth of those 25 and older. By July prices had declined about 20 percent, but by then 85 percent of the cargo had been sold.[5] Almost immediately, Prieto began to settle the accounts related to the voyage. He paid dividends to the Havana associates of his partners in the Canary Islands, the regidores of La Palma Juan de Valle and García de las Muñecas, who had financed the trip. He made additional payments to several other merchants in Havana, including the official factor of the Portuguese asiento, who maintained correspondence and represented the interests of several slave traders in Luanda. The entire process, including the inevitable litigations that followed business ventures involving residents on three continents, subject to different laws and operating with different currencies, took several years. By 1604 Prieto was ready to return to Seville.[6]

The rituals, formulas, and even the language used in the bills of sale were all familiar: they had been in use for centuries. A notary in sixteenth-century Havana would have recognized the constitutive elements of a slave sale contract drawn in imperial Rome, in medieval Genoa, or in fifteenth-century Seville – they all looked the same. Since Roman times sellers were obliged to disclose whether the slaves had any shortcomings – "any disease or defect . . . and whether a given slave is a runaway" – and the contracts typically contained specific information about their health and behavior. Recently imported slaves, however, were frequently sold under general clauses that protected the seller from future claims and litigations. Traditional expressions such *a uso de feria* ("as in fairs"), or *saco de huesos* ("as a sackful of bones"), or *alma en boca, huesos en costal* ("visible bones and soul") continued to be used in sixteenth-century Havana and other colonies. They all meant that the slave was sold "as is," that no knowledge about his or her behavior was known – enslavement sought to obliterate a slave's personal history – and that the buyer assumed all the risks. A similar formula was developed for local sales, in which the slave was transferred "with all his/her faults and defects."[7]

Still, when a slave was known to be ill, had a physical defect, was a thief or runaway, or had other behavioral problems, the seller could not hide behind the general formulas mentioned above. For example, Gonzalo Prieto sold all his slaves without specifying their condition, but in seven cases he made reference to the physical condition of the slaves. Two had a prominent belly button, one lacked four lower teeth, one was deaf, another had scars on his head, and yet another had a heart condition – "too much heart beating." A 25-year-old woman who was referred to as Isabel was in much worse health, with fevers, diarrhea, and *bubas*, a condition so vague that it is almost impossible to determine exactly what condition she had. "The accidents of this disease are . . . many and . . . diverse," Agustín Farfán, a physician resident in Mexico, wrote in 1592. Another physician, Juan de Cárdenas, asserted that there were sixty known varieties of bubas. Given the external symptoms of this condition, which included ulcers, sores, pimples, and swollen ganglions, some considered it to be a venereal disease. Regardless of the precise variety of bubas that Isabel had, a slave like her represented a risky investment, and her price was discounted as much as 45 percent. In all, the average price of infirm slaves in this cargo was 15 percent lower than the price of a healthy one.[8]

It was through these sales, as merchandise or beasts of labor, that African slaves entered local society. Like cattle, they were at least occasionally branded with a red fire to signify that they had been lawfully imported by an authorized dealer. References to this brutal procedure are scarcer for this time than for later years, however, when it became customary to brand slaves with the trademark of the captain or the asiento holder.[9] We lack descriptions of how the local slave market operated, but it is safe to assume that procedures were not very different from those followed in Iberia during the same period. Slaves were sold individually or in lots and could be made available for viewing in various places, from public squares and buildings to private homes and churches. Their bodies were carefully scrutinized to find defects or hidden signs of disease, their mouths examined to assess dentition and figure out age – a key element in price negotiation. They could be forced to perform various movements to demonstrate their youth and agility, "any movements and gestures that somebody who is healthy can do," as a 1579 description of the slave market in Lisbon put it. In order to enhance their physical appearance, sellers had their slaves rubbed with oil.[10]

Most buyers knew these tricks and chose their merchandise carefully. Slaves were sold at high prices and represented a significant economic and social investment. The mean price of slaves imported directly from Africa between 1585 and 1610 was 203 ducados, an important, but far from unreachable, sum for the period.[11] This price was only slightly lower than that of a thatched-roof wood house and equivalent to 185 hides, 140 loads of cassava, or 3 pipes of wine from the Canary Islands. To buy a slave it would take two years of a soldier's salary, eight to ten months of the earnings of a ship carpenter, and seven months of the salary of a mason working in the forts. In this sense Havana was again indistinguishable from the Iberian cities where slavery was common. Slave ownership was widespread enough to be part of the economic and social lives of large sectors of the population, and it was unexceptional for commoners to own a slave.[12]

In addition to sex, age, and physical condition, buyers considered the origin of the slave. They knew that Africans arrived in the New World with skills and abilities that facilitated their integration into colonial economies. Many of the slaves from Upper Guinea, for instance, were experienced at cattle raising and known for their equestrian abilities, which Alonso de Sandoval qualified as "extreme." They grew rice and millet, which were used in the local networks of trade. They also enjoyed a reputation as capable craftsmen. Blacksmiths produced iron tools and weapons, and the excellence of their ivory carving denotes the existence of artisans with very high levels of technical skill. The peoples living between the rivers Casamance and Cacheu were also known for their skills in weaving and dying cotton fabrics, which they sold to traders from the Cape Verde Islands.[13]

Slaves from Congo and Angola had experience with a large variety of economic activities. Coastal dwellers traded in fish and salt. Pottery was widespread and sophisticated. Copper and iron mining were practiced inland. Furthermore, during the second half of the sixteenth century New World crops were introduced, with maize leading the way, an innovation that facilitated the transmission of valuable agricultural knowledge from the African continent back to the New World.[14]

For potential buyers, these skills and abilities were of great value. The Atlantic slave trade generated its own system of knowledge about African peoples, about their physical and moral features, and about their cultures. Whether these ideas were accurate is beside the point. Just as a piece of Italian silk elicited images of luxury and status, buyers associated African slaves from different regions and "nations" with specific personal traits. For the Spanish the slaves from the

Rivers of Guinea were the most beautiful and the best. In Sandoval's words: "They are more loyal than the others, of great reason and capacity, better looking . . . healthy and good for all work. That is why it is well known that these slaves are more valuable than those of other nations."[15]

This was not an isolated opinion. In 1561 the royal officials in Havana requested the importation of slaves from the Guinea region, particularly the Biafara and Bran, whom they deemed to be good workers. Impressions mattered. A royal provision of 1556 regulating the sale of slaves in the colonies stipulated that, because of their "quality," the slaves of the Cape Verde region could be sold at prices 20 ducados higher than the legal limit. The Cape Verde Islands were an entrepôt for the exportation of slaves from the Upper Guinea coast. A veritable expert in the slave trade, Juan Rodríguez Coutino, holder of the asiento and governor of the colony of Angola, asserted in 1601 that slaves from the Rivers of Guinea were sold in Cuba for 250 ducados, whereas those from Angola sold for only 200. He was at least partially correct. Buyers in Havana did pay a premium for the slaves from the Guinea region, but the premium was smaller than that suggested by Coutino. The average price of the Guinea slaves was about 10 percent higher than that of the Angola slaves in early seventeenth-century Havana. The price gap was minimal among the youngest slaves, those around 15 years of age, and grew to more than 20 percent among those 35 and older.[16]

Occupations

Buyers probably used this knowledge when purchasing slaves for specific purposes, although the lack of proper documentation makes it is impossible to establish a direct correlation between the nation of the slaves and their subsequent occupation. Slaves performed a wide range of activities, so wide in fact that every important economic activity benefited from their labor. As in early modern Lisbon or Seville, no occupation seems to have been exclusively associated with slaves, although the development of the first sugar manufactures was in the process of changing this. The association between sugar and African slavery is a distinctly Atlantic process, of which Havana is just another instance.[17] But with the partial and still incipient exception of sugar cultivation and sugar-related work, slaves were found in many of the same occupations performed by poor European immigrants and, of course, by the surviving natives and their descendants.

African slaves built Havana's defenses and the city's urban infrastructure. As mentioned earlier, after the 1570s the crown maintained a contingent of about two hundred slaves to work on the construction and maintenance of its forts. The slaves employed in military constructions "worked very hard," as a public official candidly acknowledged in 1578. In the heat of the tropics they hewed stones, sawed trees, carried construction materials to the building sites, cleared up the construction area, and dug ditches and fosses for the fortifications. The work was intense enough for royal officials to claim that women were "of no service" to them and should be exchanged for males, although there were always women among them. In 1583, out of 126 slaves owned by the king in Havana, 43 were females. Those who survived the rigors of construction work and became "old" and "useless" were assigned to a farm devoted to growing corn, bananas, yucca, and legumes for the sustenance of the royal slaves.[18]

A look into the internal accounting of the military works makes the importance of slave labor evident. In addition to the 150 slaves that the crown owned, in 1604 the royal treasury rented 106 slaves from local residents to help finish the construction of El Morro. These rental slaves represented around 60 percent of the labor force employed in the works (even though in this case the payment was made directly to their owners). As Governor Maldonado Barnuevo asserted in 1597, the forts were built "by force of blacks and rents."[19] These rents referred not just to payments to private owners for their slaves but also to salaries collected by free workers. The latter included managerial personnel, artisans, and "free peons" whose work was similar to that performed by many slaves. These peons were paid a daily salary of 5 reales. Many rental slaves collected a similar rent, though some were paid 4 reales per day.

Although the royal and rental slaves worked on the construction of the forts alongside free laborers and convicts sentenced to hard labor, they tended to perform the jobs that were the hardest and required the least amount of skill. Although no job was exclusively a slave job, the labor division within this important sector was shaped by ideas of race and status, with Africans performing the majority of what were seen as unskilled occupations. This applied to free blacks as well: the "peons" who worked at the lime kilns producing cement from limestone seem to have been all free, but more than half of them were Africans. In turn, the best-remunerated jobs, managerial and technical, were performed by whites. With one exception, all the artisans listed were European: 12 stonemasons, 1 bricklayer, 4 carpenters, 2 blacksmiths, 1 farrier or shoeing smith, and 1 cooper. Barrel making was the only trade in which one slave was listed. His daily salary (8 reales) was below that of the free craftsmen, who earned 9 reales.[20]

The life experiences of royal slaves may have been somehow atypical, given that the crown was by far the largest slave owner in the port city. They were part of an unusually large slave contingent, lived in separate quarters, and were permanently under the care of a "surgeon" charged with their medical attention.

But in many ways the fate of royal slaves was similar to that of other urban slaves. Their nourishment was paid for with public funds, but their diet was probably similar to what other slaves ate: jerked meat, salted beef and pork, fresh meat, turtles, maize, bananas, and, occasionally, biscuits. Like the slaves owned by local residents, they were frequently rented out to other employers whenever the works were interrupted by the lack of funds or because of the personal interests of royal officials.[21] Between 1578 and 1580 royal slaves provided 33,707 workdays to local residents or to various works outside the fortresses. Some were assigned by authorities to public works or to tasks beneficial to the public treasury. In 1580, for instance, numerous royal slaves were used to cut wood (ebony, cedars, mahogany) to be exported for the construction of the monastery of San Lorenzo del Escorial. Others were assigned to the construction of Havana's customhouse or to that of the monastery of San Francisco. The royal officials in charge also used the king's slaves for more menial activities, many of which were probably self-interested: from digging a sepulture to unloading ships or provisioning courier ships (which were frequently used to smuggle goods). In many of these activities they worked along with other urban slaves who were rented out by their owners for various public works such as the construction and maintenance of the town's aqueduct, the construction of bridges, and so on. One gets the impression that royal slaves were fully integrated into the economic life of the city.[22]

The slaves owned by the king were indistinguishable from other urban slaves in at least another sense: they sought ways to increase their personal and financial autonomy as much as possible and bargained to make labor arrangements that were at least partially advantageous to themselves. By the early 1600s, for instance, overseers assigned royal slaves working in the forts daily tasks with the understanding that, once they were concluded, the slaves could perform other activities to their own benefit. Many, the royal officials complained, "took to the forest" to produce firewood to sell in town. Those who worked in the limestone quarries and kilns or sawing wood also used part of the workday for their own purposes. Authorities complained as well that even the privately owned slaves that were assigned to the construction of the forts were not used intensely, for many of them were owned by the overseers themselves or by their friends. Given that owners collected a daily rent regardless of what their slaves actually did, the latter probably found ways to bargain for relatively favorable (even if unstable) working arrangements.[23]

The concerns voiced by authorities about the relative autonomy of the slaves used in the forts echoed similar complaints from private slave owners about their ability to control their slaves effectively. Many of the slaves who were taken to Havana during these years were integrated into the city's service economy in

ways that frequently allowed them to carve out some personal and even financial autonomy. For instance, slaves and free (or freed) blacks nearly monopolized street sales of foods, an activity that allowed them to gain knowledge of
the urban space, build potentially valuable social networks, and establish control over some portion of their labor. Despite numerous attempts to regulate or
prohibit the practice, slaves sold meat in the streets, and many made a living
hunting and selling turtles. Tomas de Avila, a slave described as mulatto, operated the city's slaughterhouse in 1608.[24] Some slaves operated taverns and inns.
"Many black slave women have come to have houses as inns and taverns," the
town council deplored in 1557. Local authorities knew well that opportunities
for financial gain and for establishing social links could be significant in this
trade.[25]

Female slaves also created opportunities for financial gain by providing a wide
range of personal services to the town's growing transient population. Fleet passengers required food, accommodations, laundering, and companionship. So did
soldiers. Female slaves provided these services, and some managed to accumulate significant savings in the process. A surely atypical but nonetheless graphic
case is that of Francisca de Miranda, a 35-year-old Mexican creole slave who in
1585 claimed to be the creditor of "soldiers to whom I provide food." Miranda
had accumulated enough resources to purchase two slaves, a 25-year-old African
woman and a 5-year-old girl born in Havana, whom she used to purchase her
own freedom. Miranda continued to offer these services after becoming free. In
July 1586, Jerónimo Ramírez, a soldier at La Fuerza, declared that he owed her
56 ducados for the food that she cooked daily for him at a rate of 4 ducados per
month.[26]

Juliana, a royal slave, also tended to the needs of the garrison. In 1585 soldier
Francisco Riberos acknowledged in his will that he owed her 20 reales for taking
care of his laundry. In 1589 two soldiers of La Fuerza owed slave Pablo Carreño 245
reales for unspecified services. Juana Peñalosa, a slave of Juan Recio, did laundry
for the soldiers at a rate of 8 ducados per year. These links were intense enough
for a royal cedula to acknowledge in 1583 that soldiers had fathered many children with slaves. Fleet passengers hired slaves as well, who tried to make the
best of their situation. A judge warned passengers that they should recover their
clothes and tools well in advance of the date of departure of their ships, otherwise slaves would hide and keep them.[27]

Many of the slaves who participated in Havana's service economy did so as
ganadores or *ganadoras*, that is, as slaves who hired themselves out in exchange for
a daily rent, or *jornal*, that they paid to their owners. Slaves under this labor system enjoyed considerable autonomy and lived, as Judge Alonso de Cáceres stated,

Black servant in sixteenth-century Portugal. Garcia Fernandes,
The Birth of the Virgin (first half of the sixteenth century), detail.

"like free, working in whatever they want." Many resided in separate houses
and paid their rents weekly or even monthly. According to the town council
petitioner, by 1601 there were more than three hundred female slaves who made
a living as ganadoras.[28]

Slaves who worked under the hiring-out system had privileged access to the
monetary economy – indeed, their status presupposed the capacity to generate

payments for their labor. Many other slaves worked under more rigid arrangements, either because they were exploited directly by their masters or because
they were hired out by their owners to a third party. These were probably the
majority, despite the slave owners' constant talk about the ganadores. It is impossible to estimate the number of slaves dedicated to domestic service, but it
must have been very large. There was a long tradition of using slaves in household work; their ownership was a mark of social status. These slaves could be
sold or transferred temporarily to other households, where they generated income for their masters. Francisca Bañon was placed in this situation when her
owner rented her to Jusepe Rodríguez "for her to nurse a son of his for a year
and two months . . . for the price every day of three reales."[29] Some slaves were
owned for clearly sumptuary purposes. Manuel, Francisco, Gaspar, and Sebastián, all described as Mozambique, were musicians who played the chirimía, a
woodwind instrument shaped like an oboe. Their owners were invariably among
the wealthiest in town: Governors Juan de Tejeda and Juan Maldonado Barnuevo,
and Juan Recio, a prominent member of the local elite. These slaves, who were
always sold with their instruments and music books, may have taught their
skills to others, for in the 1620s there were chirimía players among the slaves
owned by the king in the city.[30]

   In many cases slaves acquired skills while working with master artisans who
employed them directly in their shops. Those who bought slaves more often
were the craftsmen linked to the building trades: carpenters, blacksmiths, stonemasons, and tile makers. But artisans linked to other economic activities acquired slaves as well, including ship carpenters, silversmiths and jewelers, shoemakers, confectioners, turners, and barbers. By doing this, European artisans in
Havana transferred valuable skills and knowledge to Africans, who had in turn
their own skills and craftsmanship. This cultural transfer was further intensified
through the apprenticeship contracts that slaveholders made with master artisans, by which the latter got paid to teach slaves the secrets of a trade. The transfer of valuable technological knowledge is particularly clear in the manufacturing of sugar. The initial group of sugar masters employed in the mills of Havana
were Europeans with experience in the production of sugar in other points of
the Atlantic, such as the Canary Islands and Madeira. Some mill owners hired
them only on condition that they teach one of their slaves "how to make sugar
and purge it, so he can make a living as a sugar master." In time, this cultural
transfer had significant consequences, as the initial generation of slave artisans
developed into a recognizable sector of the population. By the mid-1600s local
authorities acknowledged this development when they complained that slaves

had "public shops as master artisans in tailoring and shoemaking and other crafts."[31]

To maximize control over their valuable labor, the owners frequently rented skilled craftsmen slaves directly to a third party, often along with their tools or even the shop in which they worked. In 1607 Canarian merchant and shipbuilder Alonso Ferrera rented out "four black sawyers with their saws ready" to the city's shipyard for 5 reales per day each. Anton Zape, a 35-year-old blacksmith, was sold as part of the foundry in which he worked in 1579. Slaves skilled in woodcutting, to mention one activity that intensified after the 1570s owing to Havana's growth, were frequently rented out as part of a sawmill. Sawyers Cristobal Biafara, Fabian Biafara, and Fernando Leyton, together with two slaves in charge of the beasts, were involved in this type of arrangement in 1610 when their sawmill was rented for two years. Sugar mill owner Juan Maldonado hired a white sawyer in 1606 to supervise his water-propelled sawmill and the slaves who worked in it.[32]

These slaves were kept under the direct supervision of their owners and over-seers, but, just like the royal slaves, they found ways to participate in the mone-tary economy. Reconstructing this participation is of course nearly impossible, but hints of it do appear in the surviving documents. Local authorities, for in-stance, complained that slaves employed in woodcutting made utensils on their own that they later sold in the local market. Among these utensils were washing trays and other wood vessels that were probably sold to other slaves, who in turn used them to work as launderers and water carriers. An interesting case is that of Diego Hernández, a slave of Sebastián Fernández Pacheco who worked as a ship carpenter and who, with the authorization of his owner, sold half of a fragata in 1604 for 120 ducados. Hernández had somehow achieved a labor arrangement that allowed him to preserve part of the fruits of his labor.[33]

It is impossible to establish the proportion of slaves assigned to urban activi-ties, but it seems to have been fairly high. The available information strongly suggests that farms used a limited number of slaves. Most slaves not employed in urban services lived in the small estancias that surrounded the city. The estan-cias typically employed one or two slaves, who lived in the unit with the owner and his or her family. In order to increase production, estancia owners signed contracts of "company" with administrators who brought their own slaves to work at the unit. According to a 1579 contract, the owner supplied the land, its banana plants, some animals, and two slaves, whereas the administrator brought two additional slaves and his own work to the company. In one extreme case, that of a company established in 1604, the owner and the administrator agreed to apply six male slaves each, plus one woman, to the estancia. But these cases were unusual. In the 1578–1610 period, only 14 percent of all estancias in Havana employed slaves at all.[34]

As mentioned above, ranches were worked by an equally small number of slaves. Out of 178 cattle- and pork-raising farms for which information is available, only 27 list a slave living permanently in the unit.[35] Out of these, only 1 farm employed two slaves permanently. Even relatively large units had only one slave; for example, the hato El Cuabal, southeast of Havana, which in 1604 had 90 cows, 200 pigs, 62 hens, 15 dogs, and crops of cassava, bananas, and corn, employed only one slave, Francisco Angola. Similarly, Sebastián Criollo worked alone in the corral Yumurí east of Havana, which had 3,000 pigs, a mule, a horse, and 4 mares. The main occupation of these slaves was the production of hides and the periodic transportation, particularly during the fleet season, of cattle to be butchered in the city. It is possible that when hides were to be produced the owner would attend to the farm along with additional hired workers, but it seems clear that slaves on these farms spent long periods living on their own.[36]

A growing number of slaves resided in the newly developed sugar mills after the 1590s, but a typical mill in Havana during this period employed permanently only about 15 slaves. The largest mill, the San Diego owned by Juan Maldonado, had 31 slaves in 1602. By 1610, when there were 20 or 25 mills in Havana, the total number of slaves living in these units and working permanently in the manufacturing of sugar must have been between 350 and 400.[37]

The evidence is scant, but it seems that even some rural slaves found ways to participate in the urban mercantile economy as well. To begin with, rural slaves were still spatially close to urban areas. Since the main economic purpose of the estancias was to supply foodstuffs to the local market, easy access to the city was crucial. The same was true of some sugar mills, which were close enough to the urban areas for church authorities to decree as late as 1681 that, unless a church was available on the premises, the slaves employed in them should be brought to town to hear mass every Sunday. In the instructions given by a mill owner to his administrator in 1603, the owner warned him that slaves should go to the city for mill-related jobs only during Easter, an indication that they probably made it to town more frequently.[38] In addition to the slaves' physical closeness to the cities and towns, local authorities complained that slaves' own products were channeled to the local market by slaves and free blacks who made a living touring the estancias and buying goods, which they resold in the city. This was perhaps one of the occupations of Isabel Nuñez, a free black woman who in 1605 declared that she owed 12 ducados to Pedro, a slave of *estanciero* Antonio Hernández, for some 200 pounds of corn that she had received from him.[39]

Some of the activities slaves performed in Havana or the crops they grew may have been specific to the city and its ecology, but the techniques used to exploit these slaves were fairly traditional and had been carried over from Iberia. In organizing production, slave owners reached back to a well-established set of practices about how to make use of slaves profitably and in socially acceptable ways. The custom of letting slaves find their own employment and produce a daily, weekly, or monthly rent, for instance, was fairly widespread in those Mediterranean cities where slaves were common. "A master who was not himself a workingman or tradesman could send his slaves out into the streets, sometimes even to other towns, to sell goods or hire out their services," reports Saunders about sixteenth-century Lisbon. In coastal or port cities such as Ayamonte and Sevilla, some slaves even traveled to the colonies as business agents or signed up as seamen and pilots in one of the vessels that traveled with the fleets. The custom was transferred to the Spanish Atlantic. It was used in the Canary Islands and became widespread in colonial cities. As early as 1528 the justices at the Audiencia de Santo Domingo complained that there were many slaves working under this system and attempted to place limits on this practice.[40]

Other forms of slave usage were equally sanctioned by traditions and customs rooted in Mediterranean forms of slaving. Ideas of gender difference resulted in a division of labor by which certain activities were associated with each sex. Men were preferred for the acquisition of formal skills through the apprenticeship contracts. Construction work was a masculine endeavor. In turn, women almost monopolized certain personal services and retail activities. In addition to laundering, cleaning, cooking, or working as street vendors, a large number of female slaves in all these cities made a living as prostitutes or combined prostitution with some of the activities just listed. Concerns about prostitution indicate not only that slaveholders and urban authorities shared similar religious scruples but also that in practice many masters either condoned or stimulated this activity. The complaints also suggest that under comparable social and economic circumstances female slaves resorted to similar strategies for survival.[41]

Given the centrality of women to the service economy of the urban centers, it is not a coincidence that, in Havana as well as in Mediterranean cities with a substantial service sector such as Seville, Lisbon, or Genoa, young women were priced as high as or higher than men. It is also not a coincidence that in all these urban centers the prime age of women in terms of market values was reached very early, roughly between 15 and 25, when masters deemed them to be at their peak of youth, beauty, sexual desirability, and, of course, capacity for procreation.[42]

Havana replicated the pattern found in other urban markets. First, women represented almost half of all slaves sold in the city between 1578 and 1610 (45

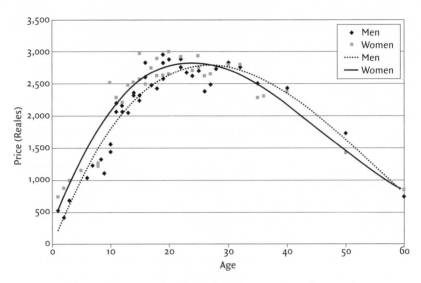

Figure 6.1. Average Prices for Healthy Slaves, 1578–1610 (N = 1,412)
Source: ANC, PNH, ER, 1578–1610.

percent of the total). Second, as figure 6.1 shows, with respect to young slaves up
to their mid-twenties, women were sold at higher prices than men. The gap in
prices was particularly large in the early ages and narrowed slowly afterward.
Between the ages of 25 and 30 slaves of both sexes were sold at similar prices,
although after that point it was men who commanded a price advantage, with
the gap in prices widening after age 40. Even though prices for both men and
women began to decline after age 30 or so, the fact that prices for females were
lower than those for men probably reflected the slaveholders' belief that these
slaves were approaching the limits of their reproductive capacity. However, the
gap disappeared among those few who managed to reach age 60, by which time
they would be considered unproductive, regardless of sex. Sixty years was old
age even for those who had managed to survive the diseases that killed so many
infants and children.[43]

Through their active participation in the urban economy, slaves gained access
to critically important knowledge about market transactions, the workings of
the monetary economy, and the dominant culture more generally. In turn, they
used this knowledge to establish valuable social and family networks, accumulate resources to increase their autonomy and consumption, and perhaps even
to buy their own freedom and that of their relatives. They lived in an oppressive
system and were placed at the bottom of society, but within this system they
created some opportunities for autonomy and improvement, as the daily experi-

ence of many slaves living in town – those operating taverns, hiring themselves out as if they were free, or living on their own – showed all too well.

These opportunities were linked to the peculiarities of Havana's service economy, but the Iberian culture of slaving contributed to their existence as well. The normative system of slavery that the Europeans imported and were in the process of re-creating in places such as Havana had cracks and contradictions. Slaves were supposed to be fed properly and treated humanely, though in practice they weren't. Freedom was the most cherished thing anyone could have, yet many people were enslaved. The church proclaimed that all people were the children of God but was itself a large slaveholder. Baptism was supposed to open the doors of God's inclusive kingdom to the slaves, yet hierarchies and exclusions persisted in it. Slaves' subordination to their masters was total, but there were people in town to whom slaves could appeal in cases of abuse, and there were laws limiting the owners' extensive powers. In short, there were authorities beyond masters.

Slaves learned how to create opportunities for autonomy within this otherwise pervasive normative reality. That they did does not mean that they accepted the social order and became transformed culturally. To begin with, many Africans were familiar with slavery and had their own notions about the sorts of obligations that this status entailed. Furthermore, in many cases slaves used institutions and practices of the dominant culture to re-create some version of their communities and customs. Scholars have debated the extent to which Africans managed to reproduce their cultural practices in the Americas or adopted the religion and customs of the host society.[44] In a sense they did both. Slaves frequently used the institutions and civic and religious rituals of the Europeans while giving them a different content. However, the very use of these institutions exemplifies their selective adoption of the new dominant culture.

Culture and Adaptation

It is not always easy to discern whether some of these cultural practices were imposed on slaves, adopted by them out of self-interest or conviction, or some combination of both. This is the case with baptisms. Slaves' understanding of this sacrament probably varied significantly depending on the circumstances in which it was performed. For the Africans who were baptized en masse, sometimes chained aboard the ships that would transport them to enslavement in the Americas, baptism may have meant little else than an opportunity to get some fresh water on them. According to the testimonies of several missionaries and ship captains compiled by Alonso de Sandoval in the early seventeenth century, it was not unusual to simply sprinkle some water on groups of captives while telling them that they were being baptized, without asking for their consent or without explaining the meaning of the sacrament to them. Indeed, some slaves in Luanda believed that they were being seasoned by the Spaniards to be eaten or that the ceremony was part of a process to turn them into gunpowder. Others simply confessed to having understood nothing of what was done to them.[45]

There was some debate about whether it was appropriate to baptize bozales, slaves who, as opposed to the ladinos, did not understand the language and, at least in the perceptions of the Europeans, had no understanding of their culture. The Council of Trent (1545–63) ordered priests to propagate the Christian doctrine in vernacular languages if necessary in order to reach the uneducated populace. Particular emphasis was placed on the need to explain the efficacy of the sacraments. Yet some priests wondered whether it was appropriate to administer the sacraments to recently arrived Africans. Some of the participants in the synod of the diocese of Santo Domingo celebrated in 1579 reasoned that baptism should not be given to bozales of "so little understanding" that they did not even understand the concept of God, at least not until they learned some doctrinal basics. Most priests, however, disagreed, claiming that with the wait too many slaves would die without the benefits of salvation and that, given their inadequate abilities, slaves' understanding of the faith would be limited anyway. A compromise of sorts prevailed, one that reproduced a canon first approved in 1539: adult African slaves would be baptized without probing their religious knowledge, but only after they had spent thirty days on the island and had been exposed to Christian teachings.[46]

It is impossible to ascertain whether this practice was observed in Cuba. Roughly 35 to 40 percent of the Africans imported into Havana between 1590 and 1600 were baptized in the city, but we know very little about the circumstances under which the sacrament was administered or what prompted some masters to have their slaves baptized. Some (admittedly very incomplete) evidence suggests that some owners waited a significant period of time before having their African slaves baptized.[47] The average interval between the sale and the baptism for a group of twenty-two slaves sold in 1596 was sixteen months. Some owners seem to have had a clear notion of the time required for a slave to be baptized. Juan García bought two slaves, Gaspar and Lucia, in March and July 1596. They were baptized in Havana's Parroquial Mayor exactly two years later, in March and July 1598, respectively. Antonio de Ribera bought four slaves in September 1596; three were baptized ten months later, the fourth waited another five months. Juan de Napoles bought two women, Ines and Maria in August 1596. Ines was baptized in December 1597, Maria in May 1598.

These examples may correspond to a subset of unusually religious owners.

Baptism of Africans. *Book of Hours of Charles V* (ca. 1519), detail.

Although many masters neglected their religious duties – thus leading to the frequent complaint by royal and church authorities that slaves were not taught the Christian doctrine – there is little doubt that some took these obligations seriously and went to great lengths to impose their beliefs on their slaves.[48] After all, the whole ideological justification for slavery rested on the need to bring the gospel to the African pagans. Slave owner and señor de ingenio Antonio de Ribera may have been one of these owners. The detailed instructions he gave to the administrator of his mill in 1603 included several references to religious questions.

First, Ribera commanded that all slaves say their prayers before going to bed and made the administrator responsible for giving them religious instruction. A priest was to be brought to the mill every year during Lent to hear confession and give communion. Three crosses were to be built and placed in the mill: one in the central square, one on top of the master's house, and one in the road leading to the unit.[49]

It is plausible that some slaves were baptized on their own initiative. Having spent some time on the island, they would have realized the potential benefits of belonging formally to the community of believers. This was one of the few spaces in which their humanity was asserted, however ambiguously. The very act of believing implied the consent and cooperation of the slave and the acknowledgment that he or she too possessed a soul. Baptism was not to be imposed through trickery and deceit. God's wish, jurist Juan de Solórzano Pereyra asserted in 1629, was for the sacrament of baptism to be accepted "freely." The principle applied even to those who were not free.[50]

These elements were abstractions, but others were much more concrete. The priests spoke of family. They spoke of brotherhood and the kingdom of God. They explained, as the Council of Trent had ordered, the efficacy and many advantages of baptism. Thanks to the holy water and to Christianity whites had become powerful. Baptism could make these attributes available to blacks. The priests promised that by receiving the sacraments blacks would be "esteemed like whites," would attend the same "temples and houses of God," would socialize and eat with the other Christians, and would be buried in consecrated ground after their death. The name of the baptized was recorded in the same book that contained the records of Spaniards, a rare moment of egalitarianism. Baptism was perceived as such an important social gateway that some owners were uneasy about its compatibility with slavery. As a result, theologians were forced to clarify that baptism did not confer freedom.[51] Salvation may have lain in heaven, but the promised benefits of baptism were very much of this world. And there were others. Slaves could use baptism to establish valuable personal links that went beyond their circle of friends and acquaintances. The priest was a potential mediator in case of conflicts with the master, someone firmly rooted in the dominant sector of society. Godparents became family, at times the only family adult Africans had in the city.

The instrumental use of godparentage is particularly evident in the baptisms of slave children.[52] The choice of godparents reflects the conscious attempt by slave parents, particularly by slave mothers, to provide their children with sponsors of a higher social status (see table 6.1). Forty-one percent of the godparents of slave children born in the city were whites, and another 10 percent were free

Table 6.1. Race and Social Status of Baptism Godparents (1590–1610) and
Marriage Godparents and Witnesses (1584–1622), Percentage Distribution

| Race/Social Status | N | Godparents, Witnesses | | |
		Whites	Free Blacks	Slaves
Baptisms				
Children				
Whites	2,426	99.5	0.3	0.2
Free blacks	76	73.7	13.1	13.2
Slaves	494	41.1	9.5	49.4
Adults				
Slaves	1,058	14.7	7.3	78.0
Marriages				
Whites	2,203	100	–	–
Slaves	539	41	19	40
Blacks and mulattoes – free	79	81	18	1
Blacks and mulattoes – mixed	127	56	17	27
Interracial – free	91	98	2	–
Interracial – mixed	42	95	3	2
Indians	17	100	–	–

Sources: AHCH, Libro Barajas de Bautismos, 1589–1600; Libro Primero de Bautismos, 1600–1610;
Libro Barajas de Matrimonios, 1584–1622.

or freed blacks. In other words, the majority of godparents of slave children were
free. The contrast with the adult slaves, who had free godparents only in 22 percent of all cases, is marked.

A similar case can be made concerning marriages. Almost half of all the godparents and witnesses in marriages between slaves were whites. Their proportion
increased when one of the spouses was free. In mixed marriages, those between
free blacks and slaves, whites were the majority of godparents and witnesses
(56 percent). Among marriages between free blacks, white godparents and witnesses represented the overwhelming majority (81 percent). The designation of
godparents of higher social status allowed slaves to enlarge their family groups
through the establishment of ritual bonds of kinship with whites. And these
bonds mattered: godparentage created a spiritual link sanctioned by custom and
the church that was not to be taken lightly. That is why owners refused to serve
as the godparents of their own slaves in baptisms. The obligations of godparentage were hardly compatible with the absolute authority intrinsic to the ownership of slaves.[53]

In theory slaves could marry even against the will of the master, although in practice this would always imply negotiations, particularly when the spouses belonged to different owners. Given the heavily urban nature of slavery in sixteenth-century Havana and the relatively high proportion of women in the total slave population, slave marriages were frequent. They accounted for 17.5 percent of the total in the years 1584–1622. If one adds those mixed unions in which one of the spouses was enslaved (5.5 percent), then slaves were involved in almost a quarter of all marriages registered in the city during this period. This proportion is lower than the percentage of slaves in the total population, but it is large enough for the practice to have been a regular feature of Havana's social life.

Since matrimony was a church sacrament, slave marriages were protected by custom and by law. The custom was widespread, the law consistent. The European settlers of Havana were surely familiar with both, for in the urban centers of Iberia and the Iberian Atlantic slave marriages were a frequent occurrence.[54] As for the law, it consistently defended two main principles. First was the issue of the free will of the spouses; masters were not to impede the marriage of their slaves or force it upon them. "Marriage has to be free and not compulsory," the king admonished in 1527. Second, marriage did not result in freedom. The thirteenth-century code of Siete Partidas enunciated this clearly, and the point was later reproduced in royal cedulas of 1526, 1527, 1538, and 1541. As with baptisms, the sacrament of marriage created a rare moment in which the humanity of the slave was acknowledged, although this recognition was reconciled with enslavement through the specious distinction of body and soul. However, the very assertion that marriage did not equal freedom suggests the existence of misgivings similar to those provoked by the sacrament of baptism.[55]

An additional element favored slave marriages: they were considered an efficient means of social control. The reasoning, which was thoroughly gendered, was that by having wives and children male slaves would refrain from running away and would serve better. As early as 1514 the king ordered that African women be introduced into La Española so that the slaves already on the island would marry them and become less rebellious. A similar order was given to the royal officials of Cuba in 1526. The purpose was always the same: to keep the blacks "married and secure."[56]

While authorities may have seen marriages as a way to keep slaves content and acquiescent, it is doubtful that slaves accepted this logic or that they fully bought into the Christian vision of these unions. That large numbers of slaves entered into marriages does not imply unconditional acceptance of Christianity; rather, it is a recognition that slaves identified opportunities in law and culture

Table 6.2. Origin of Spouses in Slave Marriages, 1584–1622

	Origin of Female Spouse			
Origin of Male Spouse	"Rivers of Guinea"	Gold Coast	Congo, Angola	*Criollos*
"Rivers of Guinea," Cape Verde, Senegambia	55	6	11	1
Gold Coast and Gulf of Guinea	3	11	3	–
Congo, Angola	6	2	57	–
Criollos	2	–	4	5

Source: AHCH, Libro Barajas de Matrimonios, 1584–1622.

that could be claimed as rights and used to their own advantage. Living in a Christian marriage was a step toward integration into colonial society, but it was a step that slaves took to gain some control over their personal lives and to reconstitute their own cultures of origin. Paradoxically, the Christian sacrament became a door back to African ethnicities, ancestral practices, and cultural continuities.[57] As table 6.2 shows, in most cases slaves chose partners from their same area of origin to formalize a union. Seventy-four percent of the marriages took place with partners from the same region. The proportion increases to 77 percent if we include the criollos born on the island. The tendency toward endogamy can be observed among the slaves from the various areas. Out of the 139 slaves from the Senegambia and the Rivers of Guinea who married a person of known origin, 110 (or 79 percent) married someone from the same area. This preference is evident even when we look at specific ethnic denominations. Fifty-five percent of the Biafara married people of their own denomination. Among the Bran this proportion was 48 percent; among the Zape, 44 percent. The pattern is the same when it comes to slaves from the Gulf Coast, 61 percent of whom entered endogamous marriages. Seventy-eight percent of Arara married other Arara. The rates of endogamy were even higher among slaves from the Congo-Angola region (81 percent), owing in part to its importance in the slave trade after the mid-1590s.

These patterns indicate that the marriages, though Catholic, facilitated the reproduction of African cultural practices on the island and may have reinforced distinctions between the African "nations." Just as the slaves used baptism to seek social alliances advantageous for their children and themselves, they used marriages to rebuild communities and links that had been broken as a result of enslavement and the Middle Passage. The offspring of these unions grew up with African parents who inevitably transmitted elements of their ancestral culture, language, and religion to their children. Yet we should not exaggerate these continuities. After all, most of the criollos who married in Havana up to 1622 did not choose African partners. Out of seventeen criollos identified with partners of known origin, ten married other criollos. Women strongly favored slaves born on the island. The only exception is the case of Ana Rodríguez, a free black born in Río de la Hacha who married slave Francisco Bañon in 1620. All other creole women married criollos. The offspring of these unions could still acquire some knowledge of African culture through their parents and through other members of their extended families, but they lacked what their elders had: firsthand references to Africa. Further evidence of adaptation to the new environment and of attention to the social codes of colonial society comes from creole mulatto women, most of whom were free. Acknowledging the importance of a social hierarchy of color, these women chose lighter partners when possible: 63 percent of them married whites, whereas only 5 percent married a man described as black.

Slaves used other religious institutions to their own advantage and for purposes that were different from those of masters and authorities. The church encouraged the formation of lay brotherhoods and the participation of the faithful in religious festivities and processions such as Corpus Christi. Blacks turned these openings into opportunities to re-create elements of their own social worlds. For instance, the *cofradías*, or brotherhoods, which were always created under the advocacy of a patron saint, were supposed to bring blacks into the church and provide a space for mutual aid and Christian charity. In practice, the cofradías did this and more. They functioned as mutual aid and burial societies. But slaves and free blacks also used these institutions to reconstitute their own forms of social organization and to organize their own festivities under the umbrella of the Christian calendar.

By the time Havana was becoming an Atlantic port city, religious fraternities of blacks had been in existence in Iberia for more than a century. In Seville there were two, one attached to the Hospital Nuestra Señora in the parish of San Bernardo and another in the parish of San Idelfonso. Given the importance of the city's black population, since the fifteenth century the king had appointed an overseer to represent the needs of this group before authorities. In Lisbon the confraternity of Our Lady of the Rosary, founded in the late 1400s by free blacks and slaves, served as a mediator with authorities and as a mutual aid and charitable society. By the early 1600s there were two such confraternities in Havana, one devoted to Our Lady of the Remedies and the other to the Holy Spirit. It is unknown when these fraternities were created; they are first mentioned in 1600. In the 1590s free blacks frequently gave alms in their wills to either all or some of the confraternities in the city, and it is possible that some accepted them as

members. For instance, in 1598 free black Catalina Garay left 8 reales in charity
to each of the cofradías in the city. Freedman Francisco Chan, of Congo origin,
left 4 reales for three confraternities, those of the Holy Sacrament, Soledad, and
Veracruz, in 1587.[58] After 1600, however, the two black confraternities mentioned
above were frequently singled out for charity. Juana Jolofa, a freedwoman who
declared herself to be a member of both societies, left 2 pesos to each and to
no other cofradía in the city. Free blacks Isabel Rodríguez, Fabiana de Miranda,
and Isabel Nuñez also included both confraternities in their wills, and Nuñez
professed to be a member of both. It should be noted, however, that some free
blacks continued to leave money to other confraternities in the city, despite the
fact that they were mostly, if not exclusively, for whites.[59]

The confraternities of Our Lady of the Remedies and the Holy Spirit accepted
negros horros (free blacks) and slaves as members, although, as in Iberian societies,
all officers were free. In 1601 the *mayordomos*, or stewards, of the cofradía of the
Remedies were free blacks Juan de Ygola and Martín Domínguez, who were in
the process of buying retables (painted or carved panels), candles, ornaments,
cloths, and other things for the society's altar. In 1601 they hired artist Juan Camargo, who had painted the retables of Havana's Parroquial Mayor and the monastery of San Francisco, to paint a retable for the confraternity devoted to Our
Lady of the Remedies for 1,800 reales. The stewards of the Holy Spirit, Hernando
Méndez, Francisco Velazquez, and Antonio Gutiérrez, were also all described as
freedmen and vecinos in 1606. This confraternity may have been wealthier than
that of the Remedies. It owned a rental house that produced 100 ducados per year
and bought its own building in 1604, the church of the old hospital, abandoned
after the construction of a new one in the late sixteenth century. This building
was centrally located, facing the city's main church, the Parroquial Mayor. The
confraternity probably gained in importance, for it served as the nucleus of a
new parish and church a few decades later. "Since this city has been growing,"
the bishop reported in 1635, "we will have a new parish because the blacks [*los
morenos*] want to build a temple to the Holy Spirit . . . to have in it their burials;
they are building it, they are many and it will be easy." By the 1640s the church
was finished, and its square served as a social space that "all blacks" used in festivities "to dance and entertain themselves, with the approval of the Bishop and
license from the Governor . . . with this they collect charity for masses, for the
dead, and for the service of the Holy Sacrament."[60]

Although the confraternities served to socialize free and enslaved blacks into
Christianity, they were also used to reproduce African cultural practices. One of
the main functions of these societies was to provide assistance for the Christian
burial of their members, pray for their souls, and accompany their bodies until

they were inhumed. In 1604, for instance, slave Ana Bioho, in an unusual will issued with a license from her master, requested to be "buried in the sepulcher of the brothers of the Confraternity of Our Lady of the Remedies" in the Parroquial Mayor. Sometimes, however, members asked brothers and sisters of the cofradía to bury them in the sepulchers of their own African nation. Thus Juana Jolofa requested to be buried like a Christian in 1600 and asked members of the confraternities of Our Lady of the Remedies and the Holy Spirit to accompany her body. Yet she also asked to be placed "in the Iglesia Mayor of this city in the sepulcher of the Jolofo blacks." Years later, a freedman from Angola likewise requested to be buried in the main church "where they bury the blacks of Angola land as a member of its nation." In these cases the ritual of death was Catholic, but the resting ground was identified with Africa.[61]

In the same way, by participating in public processions and festivities with their dances and parties, blacks created a cultural space in which African practices could be re-created. This was nothing new, of course. The custom in Seville was for slaves to gather during the festivities and dance. Authorities, however, resented any form of entertainment outside their direct control and sought to curb the unauthorized gatherings of blacks. Thus the public petitioner of the town council complained in 1568 that blacks gathered in town to appoint kings and queens and to organize other "reunions and banquets which resulted in scandals." The election of these kings and queens was a common occurrence in urban colonial centers. Girolamo Benzoni mentioned their existence among the Zape, Berebesi, Wolof, and Congo in La Española as early as the 1540s. Perceiving these practices as potential forms of organization that were not properly channeled through the church, religious and secular authorities frequently fought against them. This opposition enhanced the importance of the confraternities. They created a legitimate social space that could be used to camouflage some of these practices while socializing its members into elements of the new dominant culture.[62]

Manumission: The Negros Horros

These forms of socialization were valuable because they could lead to better living and working arrangements and, for a few slaves, even freedom. Opportunities for manumission were always limited, but the possibility of escaping slavery was well entrenched in Iberian slaving practices and in Castilian law. Although masters were not compelled legally or morally to grant freedom to their slaves, manumission was considered a pious act, its legitimacy never questioned. Furthermore, the possibility of purchasing freedom was deemed worthy of legal protection, and slaves were given the right in law to press freedom claims before the justices. Manumission may well have been, as many scholars assert, a mechanism for social control that served to reproduce the system and maintain the social order.[63] For individual slaves, however, it represented a concrete chance to change their lives and those of their relatives or loved ones.

Realizing this possibility was a complex process that involved the slave, the owner, and quite frequently other individuals. Since slaves were rarely able to pay for their freedom in one lump sum, they required third parties to witness that they had in fact paid a given amount to their owners or that there was an agreement concerning price and conditions for freedom. In many cases it was a third party, usually a relative, who paid for the manumission. In many others, slaves had to find guarantors to secure the debt that they almost invariably incurred in order to complete their payment. Masters could cheat their slaves and repudiate their obligations, but there were limits to their ability to do so. Not only was such behavior socially reproachable, but a systematic violation of these agreements would have generated significant distress among slaves and threatened the whole set of assumptions on which manumission was based. Even those cases in which masters granted freedom graciously, either gratis or under certain conditions, implied negotiation. Freedom letters present manumissions as unilateral acts of magnanimity, but this is an illusion. The letters hide previous agreements that are otherwise difficult to detect in the available documentation.

Social networks were therefore crucial. In addition to the capacity to save the amount needed to pay for manumission, access to freedom was often a matter of having the right connections. Many of the slaves who purchased their freedom required help and had to reach out to family and friends to get it. As mentioned above, those who could not pay for the whole manumission price required a guarantor. Masters demanded that these debts be registered properly before a notary and secured by a third party. The procedure was common: 75 percent of the slaves whose freedom was purchased, either by themselves or by someone else, acknowledged owing a portion of the price. On average, these debts amounted to 38 percent of the manumission price. Most of the time it was a freedman or -woman who served as guarantor of these debts, although in about one-third of the cases slaves had the assistance of whites. Either way, such assistance illustrates the slaves' ability to develop valuable networks of support in the city. Some Africans found assistance in members of their own nation, such as Gracia, a 40-year-old Zape who purchased her freedom in 1600 for 300 ducados. Gracia paid 207 ducados; the resulting debt was guaranteed by freedman Anton Zape. Others were helped by relatives, who in many cases paid for the freedom of their loved ones: free black Catalina de Morales bought the freedom of her husband, Juan Galán, for 400 ducados, of which she paid 300 in cash; Carlos de Paz bought the freedom of his wife, Francisca Ortíz, for 240 ducados, of which he paid in fact only half. As for whites, these were people with whom slaves had developed personal relations, of either an affective or financial nature. For instance, soldier Domingo García paid 110 ducados for the freedom of Gracia, a 50-year-old described as "creole from Cabo Verde," and declared himself responsible for the remaining 50 ducados of her price. It is not clear whether García owed this money to Gracia for services previously rendered by her or whether they had an affective relationship, or both.[64]

The importance of these networks is one of the factors that explain the very high proportion of criollos among the slaves manumitted. Criollos born on the island represented only 8 percent of all slaves sold in the local market. Yet 45 percent of the slaves manumitted were criollos. If we assume market proportions to reflect broadly the structure of the slave population at large (there is no guarantee that they did, but there is no question that Africans were a large majority), then manumission rates for criollos were more than ten times higher than those for Africans. Most slaves, however, regardless of origin, had to pay for their freedom. This was true among both Africans (83 percent of all cases) and criollos (70 percent). The important difference was who paid. Most Africans paid themselves (74 percent), whereas only 31 percent of criollos did. Family members paid for the freedom of one-fifth of the criollos manumitted. Africans benefited from family assistance in only 1 percent of the cases.

There was another important difference that worked to the advantage of criollos. Many – 68 percent, to be precise – were freed while they were still children under 10 years of age. These children were born slaves but spent almost all their lives as free. The average age of manumission was only 10 for the criollos, compared with 39 for the Africans. This difference is not surprising: children and youths represented an important proportion of the manumitted in many colonial cities, and there is no evidence that old or infirm slaves were singled out for manumission, as some historians used to claim.[65]

The presence of children raises the possibility that at least some of them were the offspring of their masters or of other white men with whom the slaves maintained, or were forced to maintain, sexual relations. These relationships are very difficult to uncover, needless to say, but the existing documentation does provide interesting clues. First, mulattoes constituted a high proportion of the slaves who were manumitted. Whereas mulattoes were the object of just 3 percent of market transactions, one-fourth of the manumitted were described as mulatto. Second, most of these mulattoes were children, some of them ex-

tremely young. Indeed, 67 percent of these slaves were 5 or younger and the
average age of the group only 6.5 years. Last, but certainly not least, in 28 percent
of these cases the manumission price was paid for by white residents who did
not acknowledge any family link with the slave, even though such links probably existed. This could easily be the case of the 8-year-old mulatto slave Luis
de Sandoval, whose freedom was purchased in 1597 by a white resident of Veracruz, Pedro de Sandoval. It could also be the case of Juanica, a 1-year-old mulatto
whom prominent vecino Hernán Manrique de Rojas manumitted gratis in 1602
and who was the daughter of one of his slaves, Maria "mulata." It was certainly
the case of Maria Manrique, a mulatto slave whose freedom Captain Gómez de
Rojas Manrique purchased in 1604 "for the service of God and because her father
was an honorable man and my friend." It is impossible to know who this "friend"
was; it may well have been a member of his immediate family. Maria had been
born and grown up in the house of his brother Juan de Rojas and had later been
transferred to the household of his other brother Hernán Manrique de Rojas,
whose last name she had been given. Was Manrique de Rojas the father? The
fact that he had just died may have prompted Gómez de Rojas to pay for Maria's
freedom.[66]

Of course African slaves could not benefit from links of this sort. In contrast
to the criollos, they had to reconstitute their families and create new bonds of
kinship after arriving on the island. As a result, not only were they much less
likely than the criollos to obtain freedom, but when they did, it was at a much
older age. Sixty percent of the Africans manumitted were between 30 and 50 years
of age; another 20 percent were even older. The average age at time of importation was just above 15 years, so for those few who managed to obtain freedom it
took two decades to accumulate the resources and acquire the knowledge needed
to become free.

A gendered division of labor resulted in significantly greater opportunities
for freedom for African women than for African men. Whereas the gender composition of the criollos manumitted was even, three-quarters of the Africans
were women. This imbalance was due to at least two factors. First, preferential
access to the urban service economy allowed women to save the money needed
to purchase their freedom, in real terms almost the only road to freedom available to them (82 percent of the total). This participation in the service economy
is probably how Juana Jolofa managed to obtain her freedom. She operated a
tavern that catered to soldiers and seamen, some of whom owed her significant
amounts of money. It also explains why some soldiers intervened on behalf of
African women and either paid for their freedom or served as their guarantors.[67]
Second, work in the domestic sphere as wet nurses, nannies, or caretakers for

the elderly and the infirm facilitated access to freedom as well. The domestic sphere was itself gendered, and this circumstance facilitated contacts between enslaved women and their mistresses. Female slaves probably worked closely with, or under the direct supervision of, female owners, and thus it is not a co-incidence that female owners tended to favor women in manumissions. When it came to Africans, female owners were much more likely to grant freedom to women than to men. As scholars have noted in the past few years, manumission was a gendered process in terms of both the slaves who managed to obtain free-dom and the owners' behavior and preferences.[68]

In turn, the peculiar social and demographic makeup of the manumitted had important implications. The preponderance of fairly young criollos and mulat-toes among the recently freed population facilitated their insertion into the free sector of colonial society, although their social place continued to be marked by ideas of race and ancestry. As for the adults, they were a select group that had mastered the limited but nonetheless meaningful routes to social mobility and improvement that colonial society could offer. The preponderance of women (who represented 65 percent of all slaves manumitted) in turn contributed sig-nificantly to the accelerated growth of the free black community in the port city. Most of these women were still at reproductive age when they became free, which probably led, as was the case in other colonial cities, to higher reproduc-tion rates among the free blacks.[69]

It is impossible to estimate precisely the number of free blacks and mulat-toes at any given time. Limiting the growth of the community was the fact that manumission prices were extremely high, in fact much higher than market prices (see figure 6.2). Slaves paid a premium of about one-third of their market price when they were in their twenties – that is, during their most productive years and when they had already mastered the secrets of a trade or economic ac-tivity. High manumission prices are explained at least in part by skill: this group was likely composed of unusually entrepreneurial and productive slaves. Skill, however, does not explain the price differential among children: for that group we are left with the greed of masters and with the desire of parents and other relatives to buy their children's freedom.

Despite the high prices and other obstacles to gaining freedom, a commu-nity of free blacks and mulattoes existed in the port city very early on, perhaps since the very creation of Havana. Among the 80 or so black individuals gathered by Governor Angulo in 1555 to repel Jacques de Sorés, some surely were free. A few years later local authorities noted that there were "many" freedwomen in town, and by 1565 the size of the community of free blacks and mulattoes was estimated at 40, or about 10 to 15 percent of the town's free population. A 1582

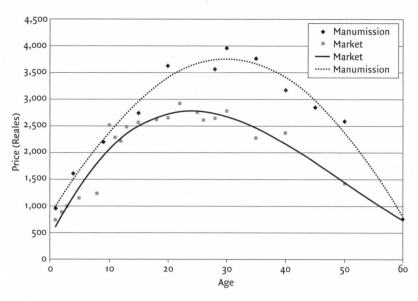

Figure 6.2. Average Manumission Prices and Sale Prices for Women, 1585–1610 (N=942)
Source: ANC, PNH, ER, 1585–1610.

military register offers a similar proportion. It lists 25 freedmen, 155 white men, and 39 "Indians" living permanently in town. Among the free children baptized in the Parroquial Mayor between 1590 and 1600, free blacks represented 7 percent of the total. This proportion seems to have remained stable, despite the significant growth experienced by the white resident population of the city at the end of the sixteenth century and the beginning of the seventeenth. Free blacks also accounted for 7 percent of all free spouses entering marriage in Havana between 1584 and 1622.[70]

References are scarce, but they all point to the existence of a sizable community of free blacks and mulattoes who participated actively in the life of the port city. The Cáceres ordinances of 1574 mentioned that there were "many" freedmen in the town who were "vecinos." As such, they did nightly watches to spot enemy vessels, particularly in times of war. They had their own company in the militias, which was placed under the command of a black officer. They participated in the local economy mostly as salaried workers but also as small owners of land, businesses, and houses. As mentioned above, in the early 1600s the group was wealthy enough to sustain two confraternities, those of Our Lady of the Remedies and the Holy Spirit.[71]

The majority made a living as salaried laborers in the service sector, sea-related jobs, the trades, and agriculture. They did work that in many cases was also done by slaves and poor whites. Three weeks after registering his freedom letter with a notary in 1579, for instance, Hernán López signed a service contract with vecino Luis Boto for a year to work on Boto's properties or in his house for a yearly salary of 35 ducados. Freedman Gregorio worked as a fisherman for a salary of 6 ducados per month in 1592. Juana Hernández was hired as a wet nurse in the household of Captain Alonso Velázquez de Cuellar to feed and care for his daughter for a year. Hernando Horro was hired to work as a laborer on the properties of Gaspar Pérez de Borroto for a year at a salary of 57 ducados in 1585. However, Horro managed to include in the contract a favorable clause that exempted him from work while the fleets were in town "so that he could earn whatever he could."[72]

A few freedmen and -women, however, were able to accumulate small fortunes and to escape poverty altogether. Diego de Rojas was one of them. In 1577 he petitioned the cabildo for the corral Rio Grande, west of town, to establish a pig farm, a petition the town council granted. In 1579 his wife, Beatriz Nizardo, hired an indigenous laborer, Diego de Toribio, to work on the farm for six months for a payment of 25 ducados. Rojas went back twice to the town council to request more land for cultivation in 1588. He also owned urban properties: in 1603, shortly before his death, he sold half of a parcel to another free black, Domingo de Hevia. Rojas's son Antonio de Salazar worked as a sugar master in 1599 and was probably involved later in the service sector as a tavern owner, buying wine in 1601 and 1603. It is noteworthy that neither Salazar nor his son Melchor de Salazar were identified as black in the notarial records. Rojas and Nizardo also had a daughter, Juana Nizarda, of whom little is known.[73]

Another relatively successful small landowner and entrepreneur was free black Carlos de Paz. He first appears in the documents in 1588 as a daily salaried laborer (*mozo de soldada*) working on two estancias of Gómez de Rojas Manrique in exchange for 20 percent of production. In 1596 Paz rented slave Francisca Ortíz from her owner, Juan Benítez, a vecino of Sancti Spíritus in central Cuba. Either Paz and Ortíz already had an affective relationship, or it developed afterward: the fact is that four years later Paz bought the freedom of Ortíz, who was by then referred to as his wife. He owned an estancia that he sold for 108 ducados in 1588 plus a house near the Plaza Real in the city that he used for rentals. He owned yet another house that he sold in 1605 for 300 ducados. By the early 1600s Carlos de Paz had become one of the stewards of the confraternity of the Holy Spirit and was instrumental in obtaining the authorization from the Royal Hospital to occupy its chapel. In exchange, Paz and the other stewards agreed that the cofradía would pay 60 reales in rent annually to the hospital.

Wealthier than either Paz or Rojas was freedwoman Cecilia Velázquez. We know little about her life. She married Sebastián Bravo, a white man, in 1587. By then she already had two children, Mariana de Avalos and Francisco de Rojas. Avalos probably worked as a seamstress: in 1605 she bought, with the financial backing of her stepfather, Bravo, about 70 yards of various fabrics and 50 ducados' worth of clothing. She owned at least one slave and a house. She may have inherited these from her mother, who declared in her will ownership of a house, a pig farm, six slaves, personal goods of various kinds, and more than 1,200 ducados in cash and credits. In all, Velázquez's properties amounted to some 36,000 reales, not a negligible amount. She was probably atypical, but other cases of land- and slave-owning freedwomen exist. Catalina Bran owned one estancia and a slave in 1603. Isabel Rodríguez owned a house in the city, one estancia, and two slaves in 1609. And Isabel Nuñez had an urban lot, one estancia, and one slave in 1605.

We do not know how Cecilia Velázquez or these other women made their small fortunes, but women like them frequently did it by working in Havana's service economy and using their savings carefully and astutely. Freedwoman Catalina Garay did it by renting urban properties. She received an urban lot from the town council in 1559; by 1598 she owned "three pairs" of thatched-roof houses that she rented mostly to other members of the community of free blacks and mulattoes. Freedwoman Inés Suárez made her fortune by selling wine and by speculating with urban properties. Between 1596 and 1604 she sold two houses and one urban lot and was commissioned to sell another house on behalf of a third party. She is referred to in some of these operations as a "vecino," or househead. Selling wine is also how Leonor Hernández managed to first buy her freedom in 1595 at the considerable price of 400 ducados (4,400 reales) and then to accumulate some wealth, which she used to buy a piece of land in 1601 and a slave in 1606. Hernández was married to ship carpenter Diego Hernández, a slave of vecino Sebastian Fernández Pacheco. Obviously, Diego Hernández was not an ordinary slave and was himself active in the city's monetary economy. In 1604 he sold, with his owner's license, half of a vessel that he had built for 120 ducados.

The existence of a group of property owners of color suggests that these individuals managed to create some opportunities for integration and mobility in Havana's sixteenth-century society. The letters of manumission stipulated that, once liberated, the slave would enjoy "total freedom . . . not subject to captivity or enslavement, rather as a free and freed person may go to trial and issue a will and designate inheritors and do all the things that free and freed persons can do."[74] The former slaves could become house heads (vecinos) and petition the town council for lots to build a house or for lands for cultivation. There is even evidence that they participated in some of the civic rituals of the town, including the election of public petitioners.

Yet this freedom was limited in a number of ways. Freedmen and -women could solicit parcels in the town, but authorities insisted that they be in specific areas "where the other blacks are," creating in the process an urban geography of race and status.[75] Blacks represented 5 percent of the petitioners to the cabildo for land between 1550 and 1610, a proportion that, though substantial, was smaller than their percentage in the population. It is noteworthy, however, that half of these petitioners were women (49 percent). Blacks were also underrepresented in the city's total mercantile activity, at least as reflected in the notarial records. In terms of total values, they handled only 0.3 percent of the trade in merchandise, 2.1 percent of the trade in slaves, and 3 percent of the real estate sales.

Traditions legitimized discrimination against this group. The residents of Havana did not need to invent new social idioms to accommodate those who had crossed the divide that separated the enslaved from the free. These conventions were well known to the peoples of the urban Mediterranean, particularly those who had been in contact with slavery. By the sixteenth century there were important communities of freedmen and -women in the major slave centers of Iberia, such as Seville, Valencia, and Lisbon.[76] Although legally free, these men and women became members of societies of deference, in which status was linked not just to wealth and property but also to lineage, purity of blood, and honor. Freed slaves lacked all these attributes: their lineage had been severed by enslavement and the Middle Passage; they could not claim to originate in a family of old Christians, free of mix with Muslims, Jews, and other "bad races." They had become themselves a "bad race." They had been slaves, and enslavement was the most dishonorable status.

The construction of blackness as a key criterion for exclusion and debasement had important precedents on the Iberian Peninsula, but it was in the New World that it became a fundamental feature in the process of social formation. Traditionally, slavery in Iberia and the Mediterranean had been – and to some degree continued to be in the 1500s – a multiethnic phenomenon. As late as the seventeenth and eighteenth centuries, Moors and Berbers from North Africa and Turks were still a sizable portion of the slave populations of Cádiz and other cities in Andalusia.[77] In the Atlantic, however, slavery was identified with blackness. There were slaves from other areas, but sub-Saharan Africans were the overwhelming majority.

Still, the creation of a racial order in the Americas was neither natural nor automatic. As the Europeans attempted to reproduce their own societies of hierarchy and stratification in the colonial world, they made conscious and deliberate efforts to turn race into a major principle of social organization. The need to delineate the contours of social inclusion and exclusion was felt everywhere, but perhaps more urgently in places such as mid-sixteenth-century Havana, where rapid social change and economic circumstances threatened to loosen the structures of a properly ordered society. In response, the emerging local elite attempted to shape local society in ways that kept them atop the social structure and relegated racial others to the bottom or the margins of society. From the 1550s on, they systematically tried to create a racially stratified order, one in which blacks, whether enslaved or "free," were marked as social subordinates.

The Making of a Racial Order

Thus when local authorities regulated various aspects of the economic and social life of the town, they did it in ways that tended to blur distinctions between blackness and slavery. Some of these regulations clearly referred to slaves yet spoke about *negros* ("blacks") in general. Of this sort is an ordinance issued by the cabildo on 28 January 1554. Local authorities complained that "some blacks, men and women" (*negros y negras*) lived in houses "separate from the house of their masters," where suspicious gatherings of blacks "and even Spaniards" took place. Thus they ordered "that no black man or woman could have his own house to live outside the houses of his master." The regulation did not speak of slaves, although the reference to "masters" would suggest that it dealt primarily with them (although, as we shall see, masters were sometimes mentioned with reference to freedmen and -women as well). The same strategy is followed in a 1550 regulation that prohibited "negros" from cutting trees around the town, under penalties of three hundred lashes and ten days in the stocks of the public jail.[78]

Other regulations targeted blacks regardless of social status. "In this town," the town council complained in 1553, "some negras have lodging houses and serve food and sell wine which is of great damage to this town . . . it is convenient to remedy it." In 1561 the council ordered collection of the weapons that "many negros of this town have in their houses and estancias." A 1585 prohibition forbade the sale of wine to blacks "given that there is little wine," and a 1612 regulation prohibited the sale of meat outside the butcher shop to all individuals "of any quality or condition," but it stipulated different penalties for Spaniards and for "*negras y mulatas.*"[79]

Many regulations referred explicitly to enslaved and freed blacks as two separate groups yet established similar prohibitions and penalties for both groups, thus erasing differences between the two and highlighting the primacy of race over freedom as a marker of status. One of these regulations spoke candidly of "those who have been recently manumitted" as "free slaves," making it clear that for authorities the line separating slaves and freed blacks was tenuous. A 1551 ordinance prohibited the sale of crabs and fruits to hiring-out slaves "and to any other negro." One in 1565 banned blacks "slave and freed" from hunting cattle on their own. Another in 1570 forbade black "freedwomen and captives" from selling wine. A 1599 ordinance prohibited "negras captives and freed" from going to the estancias to make a living. One in 1621 stipulated that no black, either "captive or freedman," was allowed to sell meat in the streets under penalty of two hundred lashes. A 1589 regulation stipulated that a person selling corn tortillas at unfair prices "being the person slave or black should be jailed until her master" paid a penalty.[80]

Finally, a few regulations placed limits and prohibitions on the negros horros specifically. One in 1565 prohibited them from hosting slaves in their houses. Another restricted the freedwomen's ability to wear gold and silk, two materials that in the eyes of the elite should be used only by members of their own group. A 1603 ordinance against vagrancy ordered all "mulatto youngsters and freedmen to take on a master in the following month" and settle on farms. It is noteworthy that this regulation placed "freedmen" and "masters" (amos) in the same sentence, another example of the authorities' desire to reduce the social distance between slaves and freed blacks.[81]

Whatever the specific purpose of each individual ordinance, this body of local laws was clearly discriminatory and sought to reduce the autonomy of free blacks (along with that of slaves) as much as possible. They were barred from some economic activities, kept away from some forms of consumption, and given penalties that were in many cases as stiff as those for slaves. For the most part the cabildo lacked the means required to enforce many of its own regulations – hence their repetition – but every new ordinance promulgated in the squares of the port city reinforced the image that blackness was inexorably associated with slavery and inherently dishonorable. Every piece of local legislation contributed to the creation of a racial knowledge that would become one of the central traits of the Atlantic system and a defining element in Cuba's history.

The local elite's vision of a perfectly stratified society of well-defined *castas*, however, was impossible to realize. The very existence of the free blacks and mulattoes complicated the colonial social formation. Furthermore, as we have seen, some former slaves managed to accumulate modest wealth and became property holders, the community kept growing, and by the end of the century it started to develop its own institutional spaces for social life and representation. Indeed, when in 1623 local authorities attempted to force free blacks, and particularly freedwomen, to participate in the processions of Corpus Christi, the community of negros horros of Havana complained directly to the king. In response, the king issued a famous royal cedula ordering that free blacks be well treated, their privileges recognized and protected. For the local elite, evidence of the self-assertion of free blacks was abundant: they were in the militias and had their own officers. They controlled two confraternities. Black women transgressed social conventions and displayed their riches in public. When authorities tried to force free blacks to participate in public festivities, they proudly refused, using the very conventions of gender and honor that local elites claimed to be theirs. And there was more: the governor complained that free blacks and mulattoes participated in the elections of public petitioners, and he warned that one day they could elect "a mulatto or his son" for the position.[82]

Cognizant that the very existence of a community of free blacks and mulattoes complicated their ideal social formation considerably, the emerging local elite attempted the ultimate solution in 1557: to expel all freed people of color from the town. Alleging that their presence was "damaging," the town council sought nothing less than "to throw them out and banish them from this town and Island." The details of the process are unknown, but it is obvious that the community of free blacks resisted with some success. The case was transferred to the Audiencia de Santo Domingo, which found against the cabildo in 1577 and condemned it for the expenses of the trial. Not only were the free blacks vassals, however low, of His Majesty, but the cabildo's proposal took place when royal policy was to populate Havana at almost any cost.[83]

The attempt to banish the freed people of color from the town came at time of rapid change for local society. The attack by Sorés had demonstrated the vulnerability of the town. Population had dwindled. The simplicity of local life and of the local economy tended to reduce social distances, which is precisely why local notables tried desperately to mark social hierarchies and their own preeminence so rigidly. Opportunities to exploit slaves directly were limited. Many enjoyed significant degrees of autonomy and could probably obtain manumission with relative ease. A 1556 town council regulation spoke of those "who have become free recently."[84]

The concerns of the local elite began to change in the 1590s with the influx of larger numbers of slaves. Up to then, the regulatory efforts of the cabildo had concentrated on the relative autonomy that slaves enjoyed as operators of taverns and lodging houses, as workers in the hiring-out system, and as settlers who lived in their own houses, outside the supervision and control of their masters. These topics were also prominent in the municipal ordinances issued by Alonso de Cáceres in 1574. The *ordenanzas* reproduced many of the regulations previously issued by the town council, such as those curbing the autonomy of the urban slaves or prohibiting slaves from carrying weapons. There was little innovation in these regulations: similar rules had been approved by local authorities in Iberia and the colonies for decades, a clear illustration that the members of the Havana cabildo were operating within a culture of slaving that transcended the port town.[85]

As a trained lawyer and a judge in the Audiencia de Santo Domingo, the place that witnessed the creation of the first slave society in the Americas, Cáceres was not only familiar with the legal doctrines of Castile; he had firsthand knowledge of slavery in La Española and of its vast body of local law. His ordinances are a genuine Atlantic cultural product: they incorporate Castilian doctrinal principles along with concerns grown out of slaving practices in the Caribbean. Articles 60 and 61, which deal with the treatment of slaves and with the duties of masters, exemplify these influences. The articles state that many masters treated their slaves "with great cruelty" and did not feed or clothe them properly. These slaves had to steal from farms in order to eat and "rebelled and became fugitives" to escape bad treatment. Justices were to seek out these masters, punish them, and order the sale of the abused slaves.[86]

Although Spanish traditional law granted owners full powers over their slaves, they were supposed to feed them properly and to refrain from severe punishments and physical abuses. Justices were to pursue these cases and order the forced sale of the abused slaves. Cáceres's articles reproduced these principles and combined them with the information he had gathered during his years in Santo Domingo. This information concerned local legal sources as well as local slaving practices. The audiencia had issued ordinances to regulate slavery in La Española in 1528 and 1535: they both contained articles very similar to those included later by Cáceres in his own set of laws. As for slaving experiences, four years before arriving in Havana, Cáceres described the treatment of slaves in Santo Domingo using language that was virtually identical to the text of his 1574 ordinances. Referring to sugar slaves in Santo Domingo, he said that they "were badly treated by their masters, who do not feed or clothe them," forcing the slaves "to steal in the country what they can, and commit other crimes, compelled by the bad treatment of their masters."[87] Historians have treated the ordenanzas as a local legal product; they are in fact anything but local. The ordinances were approved for Havana and the other settlements of the island of Cuba, but they were based on sound Castilian legal doctrines and on the knowledge and experiences concerning slavery that the Spaniards had accumulated in Santo Domingo.[88]

Owing to these influences, the ordinances devote several articles to the repression and control of runaways, a theme that is notably absent from local regulations up to that point. This topic is one that the town council had not deemed worthy of discussion in the previous twenty years. Runaways were mentioned only once, in 1569, apropos of six or seven slaves who had escaped and stayed together as a gang. Despite the cabildo's endless attempts to regulate slavery and bring slaves under control, runaway slaves had not been one of its concerns. It was Cáceres's knowledge of slavery in Santo Domingo, where *cimarrones* (maroons; runaway slaves) had been a serious social problem for decades, that prompted him to include the subject in the ordinances.[89]

Not that fugitive slaves were not part of Havana's life. Runaway slaves had been present in the colony since its very creation, and there are occasional references to them in Havana. For instance, in 1558 the governor reported the presence of three runaway slaves "in the country" who were allegedly heading for the "interior" of the island. As mentioned above, in 1569 there was talk of a group of six or seven runaways. The most frequent form of escaping slavery, however, was practiced by slaves arriving with the fleets who disappeared when they were about to depart, staying in town or trying to reach some of the other urban centers on the island. Gracia Conga ran away "at the time of departure" of the fleets in July 1604; four Angolan slaves aboard a ship coming from Las Palmas ran away as soon as they touched land in 1595. A mariner on the ship *Nuestra Señora del Rosario* from Tenerife also used the stopover in Havana to run away. Beatriz Conga, a slave of fleet passenger Ana de Rojas, disappeared in 1603. The slave of another passenger, a mulatto woman named Lorenza, criolla of Santo Domingo, ran when the fleets were about to depart in 1605. Just as the Europeans used the Havana stopover to jump ship and stay in the New World, slaves saw in Havana, a port city with a large revolving population, an opportunity to disappear and begin a new life as free men and women.[90]

None of these forms of running away, however, had attracted the attention of local authorities. They were individual expressions of resistance that did not represent a threat to the social order – expressions of what historians have called *petit marronnage*.[91] The situation, however, would change, and change drastically, after the 1590s. The importation of what was for Havana a massive number of African slaves strained the ability of local institutions to absorb this population and control it effectively. The local elite responded: the most intense effort at institution building and state construction ever witnessed by the city followed. Between June 1599 and August 1603, the town council discussed the problem of the runaways on thirteen different occasions, approved the first "ordinances for the reduction of the black runaways," created a permanent salaried squadron of slave hunters, and introduced a new local tax to finance their activities.[92]

Unlike Cáceres's ordinances, the Ordenanzas de Cimarrones were the product of a local initiative. But in an Atlantic port city such as Havana, local events were by definition connected to outside influences and realities. Authorities justified the need for the new apparatus of repression based not only on the existence of "large numbers of male and female black runaways" but also on the knowledge that other slaveholding societies had accumulated about the dangers posed by the runaways. "As we have seen in our own times in the provinces of Tierra Firme, Santo Domingo and other places," they explained in 1600, repression had to be swift and effective; otherwise it would be difficult and costly to bring the runaways under control. It is possible, indeed likely given the centrality of Havana in the imperial system of communications and trade, that slave owners in the city had fresh information about efforts to eliminate the runaways elsewhere in the circum-Caribbean area. They surely knew that in Panama the cimarrones had assisted Francis Drake's expeditions, or they had heard about King Miguel and the *palenques* (maroon communities) in Venezuela. They knew for sure that Santo Domingo had been in a state of permanent war against the runaways since the 1520s and that the runaway villages of Baoruco had been reduced only in 1596. They must have heard of the runaway community of Orizaba in Veracruz, which was not seized by the Spaniards until 1609. As the public petitioner in Havana put it, the examples of Mexico, Cartagena, and Santo Domingo were out there for all to see.[93]

The perceived need for swift repression was translated into increasingly draconian measures against the runaways. The Ordenanzas de Cimarrones stipulated that captured maroons were to be taken to the public jail and, if they had been absent for just a few days, given fifty lashes for the first time and two hundred for the second. If they led a gang or were armed, they were to be hanged. That was in July 1600. Two months later the public petitioner complained that these penalties were too "benevolent" and recommended death for those who ran for a second time. The town council responded by ordering two hundred public lashes for the first time and the same plus mutilation of the ears for the second time. The advantage of introducing even harsher penalties was discussed again in 1603 and approved in 1610, when the town council ordered that the nose of all runaways be mutilated for identification purposes and to prevent them from disappearing in the midst of the city's population of free people of color. By 1611 the wave of repression reached the free black community of the city, with the cabildo ordering all its members to register with local authorities and declare their place of residence under penalty of becoming royal slaves.[94]

The fears of local authorities were probably exaggerated, however, and these regulations seem to have had a limited impact on the social life of the port city.

The ordinances were never fully implemented, owing mostly to the lack of co-operation of slave owners, who refused to pay the new tax to fund slave hunters and did not report their own runaway slaves to authorities. In other words, individual slave owners did not feel that maroons were a problem of such magnitude that the owners should transcend their petty interests and fund state repression. The Council of the Indies said as much when it refused to ratify the ordinances: "It is not clear that there is a need to incur these expenses against runaways, rather it seems that this is a tax for town councilmen to have money to use it in other expenses." Even for the cabildo the regulation of slavery and of runaways was never one of the leading themes of discussion (see table 3.1).[95]

The frantic legislative activity against runaways during the first decade of the seventeenth century had as much to do with actual maroons as with the fear that the influx of African slaves would destabilize the precarious racial order that the local elite had attempted to build so laboriously since the 1550s. Protecting this order was crucial to the consolidation of this social group. After all, the making of the local elite was a very recent process, one that, along with the transformation of Havana into an Atlantic port city, had taken place during the previous few decades.

CHAPTER SEVEN

The People of the Land

A law of the Siete Partidas summarized elites' views about social stratification and order in medieval Castile. The main division in *status hominum* was between free and servile, but there were important "graduations" among the free as well, depending on wealth, family, legitimacy of birth, religion, and of course gender. "Men of noble descent are honored and judged, in another way from those of inferior rank, and priests from laymen, and legitimate children from bastards, and Christians from Moors and Jews. Moreover, the condition of a man is superior to that of a woman in many things and in many respects."[1] These notions were part of the values and aspirations that the Iberians brought with them to Havana and other areas in the Americas. As any manual of Latin American history duly notes, the conquistadores and settlers sought to replicate their social organization in the colonies. This structure is usually identified with the medieval society of orders: the nobles, the clergy, and the commoners.

In Havana, the small group of settlers who from the mid-sixteenth century on tried to constitute a local elite used all the conventional Castilian idioms of difference to stake a claim on nobility and preeminence. They referred to their quality and social worth, the sacrifices incurred in the service of the king, and the purity of their blood. They spoke of their lineage of Old Christians, free from bad castes of Moors, Jews, or other social inferiors.

Social preeminence did not rest on just family trees and genealogical dossiers, however much those mattered. The members of this group moved aggressively to accumulate the best lands, seize the most centrally located urban spots, and obtain or buy government positions. Particularly important was the control of the town council, the organ authorized to dispense lands and regulate local life in all its complexity, from supplying the slaughterhouse or collecting local taxes to the organization of festivities and religious processions. A small number of privileged vecinos, many of them relatives or linked through various nexuses of dependency, monopolized the cabildo during the whole period studied here. Smaller, less dramatic acts reinscribed social distinctions in daily life: clothing, the elaborate etiquette in social exchanges, participation in civic and military duties, the seating area in the parochial church, and myriad other elements of self-fashioning – speech, manners, poise – that are difficult to reconstruct from the available documents.

Reproducing the ideal medieval society of orders in the Americas would not be possible, however. Not only was a critical ingredient, a dependent peasantry, missing, but by the mid-sixteenth century the tripartite society of orders was in transition even in Castile. American bullion and wealth were transforming traditional social relations and attitudes on the peninsula.[2] The authors of Spain's literary golden age, the Siglo de Oro, took note of the social effects of money and the erosion of traditional hierarchies and distinctions. Luis de Góngora (1561–1627) referred to money as a great equalizer in a world in which everything was for sale, from the luster of the court to university knowledge. His contemporary (and archenemy) Francisco de Quevedo (1580-1645) used similar language. In a famed *letrilla*, Quevedo claimed that *don dinero* – money – embodied the new nobility. It turned the ugly handsome and made the indigent and the rich equal. When it came to money, all blood was royal.[3]

The erosion of traditional social hierarchies was probably even more acute in port cities, where life revolved around trade, shipping, and the sea, rather than the plow. Port cities experienced a constant demographic turnover and housed large transient populations, elements that did not contribute to the reproduction of traditional links of deference.[4] Havana shared these traits. Furthermore, unlike the mainland viceroyalties, Havana had very few native residents. This virtual lack of a native population had several social and institutional consequences that distinguished the port city from other colonial areas. The European settlers represented a proportion of the total population in Havana that was significantly larger than that in densely populated Mexico or Peru. The limited number of indigenous people meant, as well, that on the island the church was a relatively weak institution, the clergy an important but not crucial element of the colonial elite. There were not enough "Indians" to subjugate.

Further erosion of traditional social boundaries took place through participation in Havana's trading economy. Although rural production increased with the use of slave labor, most income was made through participation in Havana's mercantile activities. Even the highest members of colonial society, including the largest landowners, government officials, and church prelates, engaged in commerce. As the inquisitors from Mexico who had jurisdiction over Havana asserted in 1595, "In the Indies, men persevere little in honorable pursuits, esteeming more highly those that work to their advantage." Colonial governors, new to Havana, complained frequently about what they perceived as a general relaxation of social etiquette and about the lack of deference displayed by the inhabitants of the port city, who treated them as equals. Behind the numerous conflicts that characterized Havana's life – conflicts between colonial officials, military officers, local notables, ship captains, and fleet commanders – were frequently questions of ritual precedence and proper hierarchy. "They all want to command and nobody wants to obey," complained Governor Gabriel de Luján in 1588.[5]

The Landed Elite

By "all," Governor Luján meant, of course, just a few. Most of the inhabitants of Havana, about half of whom were enslaved, obeyed orders all the time, every day. Those who resisted the governor's authority were the members of a small oligarchy that as early as the mid-sixteenth century controlled the municipal government, possessed the few stone houses in the village, and thought of themselves, as Alonso de Rojas put in 1552, as "principal vecinos."[6]

Reconstructing the composition of this group is exceedingly difficult. Because of their prominence the members of this group left a presence in local records, but frequent name changes create nearly insurmountable obstacles to family reconstitution. Children were not forced to keep the last names of their parents, and, even worse, they did not use those last names consistently. Thus Melchora, daughter of Melchor Gómez Buitron and Luisa de Salazar, is sometimes referred to as doña Melchora de Salazar, doña Melchora de Buitron, or simply doña Melchora. Lucía, the daughter of Martín Recio and Catalina Márquez, is named Lucía Recia in the marriage registry, Lucía Márquez in the baptism of her son Antonio in 1596, and Lucía Recio in the baptism of her daughter Maria a year later. The wife of Francisco Pérez de Borroto is registered as Juana de Soto on occasion of the baptism of their son Juan in 1596 and as Juana de Rojas in her marriage, which took place a year earlier. As we shall see below, the Soto (or Sotolongo) and the Rojas were two branches of the same family, and Juana could use any of these last names indiscriminately. An additional difficulty concerns the records of the parish, which do not start in Havana until fairly late, when the town's population had begun to grow, the parochial church had been rebuilt, and the Council of Trent's orders concerning record keeping began to be enforced. When Bishop Juan del Castillo performed his pastoral visit to the island in 1570, he noted that there were no books of baptisms, confirmations, marriages, or burial tariffs.[7] The book of marriages starts in 1584, that of baptisms in 1590, and the one for burials in 1613.

Despite these problems it is possible to establish the contours of this social group and, through multiple record linkages, learn about its family liaisons and business interests. The making of a local landed elite was not a fortuitous process but the result of conscious actions and strategies by the family groups that controlled local life in the mid-1500s and by newcomers who, through either royal service, participation in Atlantic commerce, or both, managed to enter the group, usually through marriage alliances.

Access to and control of the town council were crucial in this process. Since Cuban cabildos retained the authority to distribute lands, a position in the town council as either regidor or alcalde basically guaranteed that the town councillor, plus his relatives and clients, would be favored in the allocation of farms and urban slots. Although in the early 1550s the vecinos participated in the election of alcaldes and regidores, as municipalities in Castile had done traditionally, the cabildo came under the control of a reduced group of individuals. Several factors contributed to this process. First, the number of elected regidores declined, as these posts were sold by the crown to raise funds. By 1571 all five regidores were "perpetual," their posts held for life. The auction of one of these offices raised more than 1,200 ducados in 1607. Elections were still occasionally held, but only in cases of vacancy. Second, after 1568 the alcaldes were elected by the regidores, instead of the vecinos, further restricting the already limited participation of the vecinos in municipal affairs. As a governor complained later, the election of alcaldes had become a farce, for the regidores made arrangements among themselves to appoint each other's relatives and clients. Only the procurator or petitioner was still elected by the vecinos.[8] Other local offices were auctioned as well, which contributed further to the consolidation of a local elite.

Thus a small group of families and individuals exercised significant control over local affairs. Juan de Inestrosa, who was also the royal treasurer, son of former governor Manuel de Rojas, was a member of the cabildo continuously between 1554 and 1571. Rodrigo Carreño, first mentioned as a regidor for life in 1571, was a member of the cabildo until his death in 1606. His son, Nicolás Carreño, obtained the office from the king while his father was alive and remained in the town council after he passed away. He shared the council with Diego de Soto, whose father, also named Diego de Soto, served fifteen times as elected regidor or alcalde between 1551 and 1577, at the time that Carreño father was regidor. Brothers Juan and Lucas de Rojas Sotolongo were also in the cabildo in 1609 and 1610, just like their other brother, Baltasar, had been between 1598 and 1602 and their father, Alonso de Rojas, who was elected eight times between 1564 and 1585. The town council of Havana was a family affair.[9]

Needless to say, the main beneficiaries of this family affair were the families of the councillors, including their dependents and clients. A group of thirty-two councilmen obtained 187 urban lots and farms for themselves and their relatives between 1550 and 1610. Some families obtained the lion's share of these lands. The Rojas obtained 51 concessions; the Soto or Sotolongo, closely related to the Rojas, another 23. The Recios received 29 lots, the Pérez de Borroto 21. More than 100 rural and urban parcels were given to these four families alone.

The preeminence of this oligarchic group was consolidated further through careful marriage alliances, so that by the late sixteenth century all these families had become related. Some vecinos complained about this, arguing that it was impossible to get fair treatment in a place where all members of the town council were relatives, either through blood or through links of godparentage. As royal officials put it concerning one of the members of this elite, treasurer Juan Bautista de Rojas, he was "everybody's nephew and cousin" and therefore "partial to his kin."[10]

The treasurer belonged to one of the largest extended families – and surely the most prominent one – in sixteenth-century Havana. One branch was headed by the brothers Alonso de Rojas and Diego de Soto or Sotolongo, who settled in the village around 1540 with their uncle Juan de Soto (or Juan de Rojas). Each brother came to head a dense network of relatives and kin who played important roles in the life of Havana. Alonso de Rojas represented Havana's town council before the Audiencia de Santo Domingo in the 1550s. He was elected regidor in 1564, 1568, 1570, and 1576. Between 1569 and 1585 he was also elected alcalde four times. In the process, Alonso de Rojas accumulated numerous lands, including the hatos (cattle lands) San Felipe y Santiago, Las Cruces, and San Francisco de las Vegas. In all, he received seven concessions of land from the cabildo between 1559 and 1590. Using his family connections in Madrid, in 1573 he obtained a royal grant to occupy and exploit for ten years what he had described in his petition to the king as "the small" Isla de Pinos, the second largest island of the Cuban archipelago. It is possible that he was given possession of other smaller islands, for seventeenth-century navigation manuals refer to some "keys of Alonso Rojas" in the northwest of Cuba.[11]

Three of his sons with Juana Giménez, Lucas, Juan, and Baltasar, continued this trajectory. They were all appointed to the cabildo at one point or another and managed to get additional land concessions. Baltasar de Rojas was an officer in the prestigious cavalry company of the city and owned the corrales Río Hondo and Espíritu Santo, which he had received from the cabildo in 1578 and 1598. Elected alcalde in 1610, Lucas de Rojas received cattle lands in 1603. As for Juan, he entered the town council in 1598 with the votes of his brother Baltasar and of a second or third cousin. His membership in the council probably helped him get the ranch La Herradura in 1598, plus a farm in the area of the Cojímar River, east of Havana, in 1600. Their brother Pedro, in turn, owned the hato San Francisco de las Vegas.

The family group acquired additional influence through advantageous marriages. Catalina de Rojas, daughter of Alonso de Rojas and Juana Giménez, married Pedro Suárez de Gamboa, a powerful and prosperous landowner, son of Alonso Suárez de Toledo, alcalde and regidor who was described in a 1581 royal cedula as one of the richest men in Havana, and Inés de Gamboa.[12] They owned large estates in the vicinity of Matanzas Bay: the estancia of Matanzas; the corrales Yumurí, Puerto Escondido, and Corral Nuevo; and the hatos Caní-mar and Macurijes. Catalina's sister, María de Rojas, married another prominent local figure, one of the cabildo's regidores for life, Rodrigo Carreño, owner of two corrales in Gibacoa and the hatos Sabana de las Lomas and Sabana de Pavia.

An equally prominent family group descended from Diego de Soto or So-tolongo, the brother of Alonso de Rojas, who married Juana Inés Gonzalez. As mentioned above, Diego de Soto served almost continuously in the cabildo be-tween 1551 and 1577. He was mentioned in a 1567 report as a "very honorable man and one of the richest in this town." A 1575 document referred to him as "an old vecino of this town, who has many children in it, and sons and daughters in law, and grandchildren, and brothers and nephews and brothers in law and other relatives." The family was reportedly very tight and made all important decisions together – "they don't do a thing without conferring all together." This probably explains why Rodrigo Carreño, who had been married to a daughter of Soto's, Isabel de Soto, remarried upon her death her cousin María de Rojas, for which the family had to ask for a papal dispensation.[13]

Just like the descendants of Alonso de Rojas, those of Soto helped enlarge the social standing of the family. His son Diego de Soto married Juana de Ulloa, who claimed to descend from the conquistadores of Mexico and was the beneficiary of certain rents given to her family by the king. Diego's sister María de Sotolongo married Antón Recio, member of one of the most important families in colonial Havana. Historians have frequently referred to the Rojas and the Recios as com-peting clans, but both groups were in fact related through marriage and family links despite the fact, well known to contemporaries, that this family could not claim total purity of blood. One of the founding members of the family, also named Antón Recio (uncle of María de Sotolongo's husband, brother of his father, Martín Recio), did not have children with his wife and passed his fortune to his illegitimate child Juan Recio, "mestizo, son of an Indian," as Governor Gabriel de Luján noted with scorn. Although prejudices concerning purity of blood and lineage made mestizos, as a contemporary writer put it, "people without virtue,"

Juan Recio became a full member of the local elite and the holder of public office. His fortune contributed to this, as he inherited the first entailment known in colonial Cuba, which in 1568 was estimated at 20,000 ducados.[14]

Although these dense family networks tended to reproduce themselves through endogamy, some newcomers were allowed in the group because of their standing in the royal bureaucracy, the king's army, or their wealth. One of these was captain Tomás Bernardo (or Bernaldo) de Quirós, a young man from Asturias who arrived in Havana in the mid-1580s. Quirós served as deputy governor of La Fuerza, although there were persistent accusations that he devoted most of his time to trading. His incorporation into the local elite took place in 1587 through a marriage with María Recio, daughter of Juan Recio, a union that may have been facilitated by Recio's mestizo origin. That same year Quirós was elected to the town council, and in 1602 he was commissioned by his father-in-law to represent his interests in the court.[15]

As in other colonial cities, most newcomers who entered the upper stratum of Havana society were merchants active in the Atlantic trade.[16] Among these were Sebastián Fernández Pacheco and Bartolomé de Morales. Fernández Pacheco was originally from San Miguel, one of the Azores, where some members of his family still lived by the end of the century. Between 1594 and 1602 he established a trading company with Melchor López, a merchant resident in Garachico (Tenerife, Canary Islands) who shipped wine, tar, and other products to him in Havana.[17] His ties with the local landed elite came through the marriage of his daughter, doña María Pacheco, to Gonzalo Mejía, a scion of the important Manrique de Rojas family, son of Hernán Manrique de Rojas and Catalina Mejía. The newly acquired status of Fernández Pacheco was recognized in 1604, when he was elected alcalde of the cabildo of Havana.

Unlike Fernández Pacheco, who entered the upper stratum by marrying his daughter into one of the most prominent local families, Morales married himself into the local elite. Acceptance into this group was not immediate, however. Morales, a merchant from Seville, arrived in Havana sometime in the 1560s: the first time his presence was recorded in the town was in the municipal elections of 1567. Two years later Morales presented the town council with a title of notary of ships and registries issued by the Audiencia de Santo Domingo, his first attempt to hold a public office in the town. The town council, however, refused to honor the title, alleging that the audiencia did not have jurisdiction to appoint officers on the island. Not to be deterred, in January 1570 Morales purchased a notary from fellow merchant Melchor Rodríguez. The cabildo welcomed Morales to the exercise of the office but demanded royal confirmation of the transfer in two years. The merchant persevered. Between 1574 and 1576 Morales was able to

show a confirmation of his appointment as notary of ships and registries, to obtain the important post of chief notary, and to become collector of the Santa Cruzada, the pardons sold by the papacy to raise funds for the crusades. Two years
later, in 1578, Morales purchased a position of regidor for life in the town council
that ten years earlier had been reluctant to accept him as one of their own. His
ascent into the privileged circle of the local elite was validated further through
his marriage in 1589 to Juana de Orellana, daughter of Hernando de Orellana
and Diego de Soto's daughter Juana de Soto. Thus Morales entered the Rojas-
Sotolongo family, the most important kin group in sixteenth-century Havana.
In 1595 he was helping a member of the family, Gómez de Rojas de Manrique,
obtain an appointment from the king.[18]

Another merchant who married into the local elite was Melchor Rodríguez,
whose presence in Havana is registered since 1561. Rodríguez was even more
active than fellow merchant Bartolomé de Morales in the local market, where
the total of his notarized operations amounted to 287,420 reales (compared with
Morales's 170,981). Like Morales, Rodríguez first attempted to hold public office
by buying a notary in 1569. He became a councilman in 1577, when he was first
elected regidor, a position to which he was reelected in 1585 and 1586. He remained in the cabildo for yet another year, this time as alcalde. By this time
he had married Catalina Sánchez, sister of Alonso de Rojas and Diego de Soto.
Rodríguez received significant concessions of land from the cabildo. Between
1566 and 1584 he obtained the hatos Hanabana (1566), Sabanas de Guaniguanico
(1576), and Boca de la Chorrera (1584), plus two corrales and two urban lots. He
had four daughters and a son, Diego Sánchez, who married a member of the
Recio family.[19] The links with the Recios were probably long standing, for in
1569 Rodríguez served as guarantor of Antón Recio when he purchased the office
of *depositario general*, the public trustee who administered the funds overseen by
the courts.[20]

Effecting these advantageous marriages involved careful selection and negotiation. Parents sometimes made arrangements for the marriage of their children well in advance of their age to "take state," as contemporary documents put
it. Catalina Sánchez, the widow of merchant Melchor Rodríguez, for instance,
agreed to marry off her daughter Catalina de Cárdenas even though Catalina was
only 9 years old and thus not of the age required by canon law to enter matrimony. Both the mother and the future husband, Agustín de Pliego, a transient
who was "present" in the city, agreed to wait until she was of age to avoid a
penalty of 2,000 ducados. Five years later they were married.[21]

Arrangements could be made even in the case of widows, as with doña
Mariana Manrique, the daughter of Hernán Manrique de Rojas and Catalina de

Mejía, whose first husband, Gutierre de Miranda, the governor of Florida, died in the 1590s. In 1598 Hernán Manrique issued a power of attorney to a resident of Puerto de Santa María, in Spain, to arrange the details of a marriage between his daughter and García de Avila Villavicencio, a vecino of Jerez de la Frontera. We know little about Avila Villavicencio, but his selection was clearly not fortuitous. In 1599 he paid 500 ducados to a court solicitor who would "request and negotiate one of three governorships which are Florida, Caracas, or Campeche" on his behalf. Although unsuccessful, García de Avila and his new family obviously thought him worthy of such an appointment.[22]

Parents used dowries to select appropriate husbands for their daughters. Women of the upper stratum were typically given a dowry by their parents, who guaranteed in this manner the financial viability of the couple while reaffirming the bride's and the family's position in society. Large dowries allowed parents to negotiate favorable marriage arrangements by imposing their choice not only on their own children but also on their future sons-in-law, who typically lacked financial means and were not independently wealthy. In other words, dowries guaranteed that daughters submitted to parental marriage arrangements, but they also forced male offspring to marry within their own social class women who could bring significant assets to the union.[23]

There are 134 dowries registered in the notarial records of Havana between 1578 and 1610, of which some 23 correspond to families that clearly belong to the local elite. This proportion is much larger than would be expected given the small numbers of families in this group, but such imbalance is not surprising, as dowries represented a statement about a family's worth and social status. Owing to the social profile of these dowries, their composition differs from what historians have found in other colonial areas, where cash and personal items constituted the bulk of the dowry.[24] More than a fourth of the dowries included real estate properties, either houses (30 percent) or rural farms (26 percent). The majority included slaves (56 percent); goods such as household items, linens, clothing, and jewelry (65 percent); and cash, including silver bars or cash receipts (56 percent). The transfer of the real estate was frequently nominal: the daughter received the portion of the house in which her parents lived that belonged to her as inheritance. Doña Inés de Gamboa, for instance, received in her 1602 dowry half of the stone family house, plus half of most (if not all) family properties: a sugar mill, four hatos, four corrales, and one estancia. She also received half of all the slaves, twenty-two in all. These grants were meant to allow the couple participation in the family's economy, not to actually divide these units.[25]

Gamboa's dowry was among the largest in Havana, worth 12,685 ducados (139,535 reales). Hers was one of only three dowries worth more than 100,000

Table 7.1. Elite Dowries, Value and Composition, 1578–1610

Value (Reales)	N	Percentage with					
		House	Farm	Goods	Cash	Slaves	Arras
Under 30,000	13	27	8	62	69	46	38
30,000 to 100,000	7	29	29	57	71	43	57
Over 100,000	3	67	100	33	33	100	33
Total	23	30	26	56	65	56	43

Source: ANC, PNH, ER, 1578–1610.

reales, which were distinguished by the inclusion of real estate property and large numbers of slaves (see table 7.1). In contrast to the smaller dowries, in which goods and cash represented the core of the dowry, most of the value in the richest dowries was represented by farms and slaves. Indeed, two of them do not even bother to list goods of any kind. Such endowments gave parents significant latitude in choosing spouses for their daughters, so that Hernán Manrique de Rojas, who gave his widowed daughter Mariana the largest dowry on record (159,500 reales), could basically import from Spain a convenient husband for her. Manrique allocated a much smaller dowry (2,200 reales) to another daughter of his, María Giménez. Unlike in the case of Mariana Manrique, however, María's mother is not mentioned in the document, which strongly suggests that María was an illegitimate child.[26]

Some grooms contributed to the marriage as well, mostly in the form of *arras*, a financial contribution that by law could not exceed 10 percent of their assets. The arras assumed the form of a donation to honor the woman's "virginity and lineage" and could be claimed by her or her family in case of dissolution of the marriage. About 40 percent of the grooms in these elite marriages offered arras, in amounts that varied between 300 and 1,000 ducados. There are also cases in which parents gave sons parts of their inheritance to "help sustain marriage expenses," but these contributions did not take the form of arras and could not be claimed by the wife's family. For instance, Diego de Soto gave his son Juan 2,000 ducados for his marriage with Melchora de Salazar in 1590. Councilman Juan Recio gave significant assets to his son Antón Recio for his wedding as well, including various rural properties, jewelry, household goods, and ten slaves. One wonders whether behind this unusually generous allocation of assets there was an attempt to compensate for Antón's less than illustrious ancestry. After all, he was marrying María del Corral, a member of one of the oldest families on the island. She was the daughter of Alonso Velázquez de Cuellar, a descendant of conquistador Diego Velázquez de Cuellar, and of Magdalena de

Rojas, daughter of treasurer and regidor Juan de Inestrosa and granddaughter of Manuel de Rojas, governor of the island between 1531 and 1535. Was this an investment in racial purity? We have no evidence that María brought a dowry to her marriage, even though hers was a family of means. Her brother Alonso, for instance, offered 1,000 ducados in arras to his bride, Catalina de Borroto Costilla, daughter of notary and councilman Gaspar Pérez de Borroto and Isabel Suárez Costilla.[27]

It would seem that these arrangements, particularly those made on behalf of very young girls, rendered women powerless to choose partners. As historians Asunción Lavrín and Edith Couturier have noted in their study of colonial marriage practices, "women were still seen more as objects than actors in marriage matches." Particularly in elite marriages, in which control of the dowry gave parents the power to select an appropriate husband for their daughters, the latter's choices were probably quite limited. But there is evidence that, at least occasionally, daughters managed to challenge the arrangements made by their parents. Magdalena Gonzalez was one of these cases. She had been promised in marriage by her mother when she was 18 months old but apparently refused to comply. A legal suit before religious authorities followed. Since the church consistently held that the free will to choose partners was sacred, it was not impossible for children to reject the choices of their parents.[28]

Dowries had another important and intended effect: financial security for women. The dowry did not belong legally to the husband, who was not entitled to dispose of it or even perform transactions with it without the explicit consent of the wife. That is why some notarized transactions were performed by husbands with their wives' "license."[29] When accepting dowries, husbands committed to preserve them and to return them in case of dissolution of the marriage, a promise they frequently fulfilled, as numerous wills make clear. Women could dispose of their dowry by will and distribute those goods among their children.

Only under exceptional circumstances could a man try to gain control of the dowry and deprive a woman of it. One of these was female adultery. As the Partidas stated, a man acquired the dowry "by the offence which a woman commits when she is guilty of adultery." For this to happen the husband had to proceed legally against the adulterous wife and establish her guilt, in which case he could dispose of all dotal goods as his own. As an aggrieved husband explained in his will in 1595, his wife should be "excluded from her dowry and profits and any of my goods because she has lost them all due to adultery." The children of adulterous relationships also suffered significant discrimination in the law.[30]

The dowry represented an instance in which a woman's legal personality was fully recognized, as well as her ability to possess property and perform legal acts. Castilian law placed women in a subordinate social position – the general statement in the Partidas concerning status makes this abundantly clear – but afforded them some degree of legal protection as well. According to the Leyes de Toro, which were promulgated in 1505 and constituted the family code applied to the colonies, women were subordinate either to their father or to their husband. They could not enter into contracts, perform other legal acts, or litigate without marital license. Any such acts were rendered legally invalid. However, the code acknowledged that wives could manage the couple's patrimony under certain circumstances, as in the absence of the husband or if the wife obtained a license from a justice. Moreover, she could receive a general license from her husband, in which case she could perform all sorts of legal acts. If the husband died, the widow could assume full responsibility for the family's patrimony and administer the inheritance of her children.[31]

Regulations allowing women to perform legal acts were not dead letter. Women, including elite women, participated in local life performing mercantile operations, administering the estate of their children, claiming dowries, paying and collecting debts as will executors, making arrangements for their daughters' marriages, and managing all sorts of affairs. Isabel Sotomayor (or Soto), wife of prominent merchant Melchor Casas, who sailed to Seville in 1590, took charge of her husband's many businesses in Havana during his absence. With the assistance of her widowed daughter María de Casas, Isabel collected debts from as far away as Santiago in Cape Verde, imported corn flour from New Spain, and issued payment receipts to local merchants such as Diego de Lara, a trader and silversmith from Antwerp. Two years later she demanded control of her dowry because of the death of her husband.[32]

A woman who was fairly active in the local market after her husband, Captain Alonso Velázquez de Cuellar, passed away was doña Magdalena de Rojas. Between 1598 and 1605 she was involved in notarized operations amounting to 28,410 reales. These included transactions over slaves, real estate, and the purchase in 1599 of a cargo of merchandise from Sevillian merchant Pedro Arias Maldonado that contained fabrics, tools, clothing, and other products. In April 1600 her son Alonso Velázquez de Cuellar married Catalina de Borroto Costilla, a woman of his social group, and five months later doña Magdalena donated half of the corral Gonzalo to her son.[33]

Women in general, and elite women in particular, participated in notarized economic transactions in a proportion well below their population share (1.9 percent in transactions covering general merchandise). Yet it is important to note that female participation increased in those areas that were critical to the

family's patrimony, such as real estate (10.8 percent) and slaves (7.6 percent).
They acquired control of these goods through their dowries, through inheritance – since Castilian law did not discriminate against women when it came to
inheritance – and through their own dealings in local economic life. A few white
women also obtained land concessions directly from the cabildo – white women
made 7.3 percent of all petitions for land made by white residents – and there is
no evidence that they always did so on behalf of male members of their families.
On the contrary, quite a few of the petitioners were widows. This was the case of
Leonor Costilla, who obtained urban lots in 1551, 1559, and again in 1575, when
she justified her petition on the grounds that she was a longtime resident in the
town. Some female members of the elite were able to accumulate significant
amounts of rural lands, such as Inés Gamboa, who obtained the hatos Canímar
and Macurijes in 1573 and the corral Puerto Escondido in 1573. Ursula de Salazar,
daughter of Cristobal de Soto, asked for two urban lots in 1609.[34]

The fact that councilmen justified some of these land concessions on the basis
of the female petitioners' relationship to male family members – "because her
father and husband were conquistadores" – indicates, in addition to the low proportion of female beneficiaries, that land petitioning was thought of as mostly a
male domain. The female members of most elite families in town are markedly
absent from the records, a good indication that this activity was not deemed to
correspond to their station in society.[35]

In turn, most male members of the elite engaged in economic activity of
questionable honorability, notably commerce. Virtually every prominent family
in Havana's upper stratum participated in trading and shipping activities. The
same was true of colonial administrators and royal officials. Despite their vows of
poverty and proclaimed dedication to the king, civilian and religious authorities
participated customarily in trade, frequently in partnerships with local merchants and shipmasters. For instance, Governor Gonzalo Pérez de Angulo always
had "quantities of wine to sell," and his deputy Juan de Rojas conducted business
transactions while carrying the justice staff, a symbol of authority. Treasurer
Juan de Inestrosa had several "public shops" in town; he imported products from
Castile to exchange for hides. Francisco de Zayas, a deputy of the adelantado
of Florida and governor of Cuba Pedro Menéndez de Avilés, reportedly arrived
in town with merchandise worth in excess of 2,000 ducados, which he and his
wife sold through the town crier and "a black who is a broker." Captain Gutierre
de Miranda, who would become governor of Florida and who married Mariana
Manrique of Havana, also brought with him merchandise that he had loaded
illegally in Bilbao. Even Governor Valdés, who distinguished himself for persecuting smugglers, used prisoners illegally to carry wood for his ships and sent

two vessels annually to the Canary Islands loaded with silver and local products. One of his deputies allegedly retailed meat from his house, whereas the bishop dealt in slaves, silver, and sugar. Trading was so widespread among functionaries, a witness complained, that even the royal pardons were for sale: "I understand that at court they will obtain pardon in exchange for money."[36]

Most members of what was becoming a local elite also participated in commerce, including the least honorable ones, such as retailing. Whereas long-range commerce was deemed an honorable activity, retailing was not. Merchants involved in transoceanic trade incurred heavy risks and performed a valuable service to the republic, whereas *regatones* – literally, people who bargain – "never buy merchandise to benefit the republic" but rather hoarded products to make them scarce and sell them at unduly high prices.[37]

Thus the most prominent vecinos of Havana not only welcomed well-to-do merchants into their families but also practiced commerce themselves. Unlike other economic activities, such as cattle raising and farming, trade accrued immediate profits, owing largely to Havana's enviable position in the shipping routes of the early Atlantic. Some of these vecinos even bought or built their own ships to transport their own cargoes. Merchant and notary Bartolomé de Morales built a fragata in 1578 that he devoted to the "commerce of tierra aden-tro [the Cuban interior]." Captain Tomás Bernardo de Quirós commissioned the construction of a ship in 1588 and bought a portion of another vessel the same year. His father-in-law, Juan Recio, bought one-third of a fragata in 1585 and had two vessels built on his own lands in 1598 and 1599. Hernán Manrique de Rojas owned half of the fragata La Candelaria in 1590. It is because of these activities that in some early legal documents the most prominent vecinos of the town are referred to as "merchants."[38]

Colonial administrators referred at times to these vecinos – who held public office fit only for honorable people of clean lineage – with undisguised contempt. Governor Luján spoke of "one Juan Recio, mestizo," the "son of an Indian who is unfit to hold office." Captain Tomás Bernardo de Quirós, a regidor, was not really a soldier but a *tendero*, a shop owner without experience in war matters. The governor described him as "a merchant, who has a shop in his house, who sells all sorts of things, even fish and cassava, which is the bread made here, and this is not from his harvest, he is a public retailer."[39]

Despite their active participation in the mercantile life of the town, the members of this upper stratum saw themselves as honorable men who were entitled, because of their wealth, social position, service to the king, and exercise of arms, to noble status. Many of their lands may have been "depopulated," but lords of estates they were nonetheless. The labels that the members of the group used to refer to themselves and their equals are graphic enough: "the most principal vecinos," "most illustrious sir," "nobleman and soldier," "very honorable man and one of the richest in this town," and so on.[40] They wrote to the king and to the Council of the Indies protesting to be loyal vassals who, as knights, bore arms for His Catholic Majesty and defended his port town against heretics and Lutherans. They staffed the local cavalry company, which the governor described in 1608 as formed by "the most principal and illustrious" people of the city. As loyal vassals they requested favors and offices, for themselves and for members of their families.[41] A few also commissioned detailed reports about their lineage in an effort to prove their noble ancestry and purity of blood, free of Jews, Moors, or other lowly people. To be called "a Jewish dog" or, as a royal official was called in 1550, a *puto judío toledano* (a fucking Jew from Toledo) was one of the worst insults that could be inflicted on a person.[42]

The brothers Hernán Manrique de Rojas and Gómez de Rojas Manrique illustrate how the members of this upper social stratum combined knightly pursuits, typical of noble life, with opportunities for profit. First, a note on their perceived social status. They described their ancestors as "*caballeros hijosdalgos* of illustrious lineage" from the village of Cedillo at the service of the Marquis de Poza. When asked about his occupation in 1575, Gómez de Rojas declared that he had "no trade because he is a caballero who lives off his hacienda." We do not have a similar declaration from brother Hernán, but he was customarily referred to as a "principal man" or an "honorable hidalgo of much courage."[43]

Hernán Manrique de Rojas was one of the most enterprising characters in Havana's sixteenth-century society.[44] He had been in Havana since at least the 1560s and, as a man of arms, performed numerous services to the crown. In 1564, for instance, Governor Diego de Mazariegos named him captain of a twenty-five-man force that went to Santa Helena, Florida, to gather military intelligence about French activities in the region. Upon his return, Hernán Manrique brought with him a marble column bearing the arms of the French royal house, a prisoner, and detailed information about the coast, its harbors, and their location. Twenty years later, in 1586, he played a prominent role in organizing the defense of the city against Francis Drake. Governor Gabriel de Luján referred to him as "a person of experience and a very good soldier."[45] Other royal and honorific positions to which Hernán Manrique was appointed included governor of Jamaica (ca. 1570), "protector" of the "Indians" relocated to the town of Guanabacoa (1577), patron of the Royal Hospital (1575), and alcalde (1603).[46]

His economic activities were equally varied. There is evidence that at least part of his fortune – and certainly that of his brother Gómez de Rojas – originated in contraband and other illegal operations. His years as governor of Jamaica – one of the most active centers of smuggling in the whole Caribbean – had given him the opportunity to profit directly from contraband. According to some testimonies, he had taken "large quantities of money and hides" from the island. Hernán Manrique was accused also in 1565 before the Council of the Indies of trading with Portuguese smugglers in Cuba, from whom he received slaves in exchange for hides. Twenty years later he owed money to the crown, but when royal officials attempted to collect the debt, he left the city and went to the Cuban interior.[47] Equally suggestive of his involvement in contraband is the purchase in 1590 of the hatos of Isla de Pinos – those given originally to Alonso de Rojas – for 5,500 ducados (60,500 reales). Because of its isolation, Isla de Pinos was an ideal place to provision the numerous foreign ships that sailed through the Caribbean as well as to engage in other illegal operations.

But some of his economic enterprises were legal. In 1583 he bought the license to exploit the copper mines of Santiago de Cuba. Using his power and prestige, in the last decade of the century Hernán Manrique obtained from the cabildo the collection and administration of the sisa, the local tax on wine and meat used to pay for the construction of Havana's aqueduct. He also obtained the contract to build the aqueduct, for which he received 10,000 ducados (110,000 reales).[48] In the early 1600s he was among the privileged few who benefited from the royal loan to build sugar mills. By then he owned the water-driven trapiche Santa Cruz.[49]

The career of Gómez de Rojas paralleled that of his older brother Hernán in many respects. Gómez could also claim to have served the king, with his body and sword, in a variety of occasions. He fought the French when he was "a youth of short age." After coming to Havana, probably in the 1550s, he was in charge of the old fortress, fought against indigenous maroons, was captain of the local militia for eight years in the 1560s, and commanded the mission to rescue a lost fleet in 1563. He was also appointed captain in an armada formed in Santo Domingo against French pirates in the 1550s and commanded a force against "English Lutheran corsairs" in Jamaica, probably at the time that his older brother was governor there. In the late 1560s he traveled to Spain, where he fought in the War of Granada (1568–70) against the Moriscos "with two horses and six servants at his expense." Back in Havana he was given temporary command of the fortress of La Fuerza, and Governor Luján made him his deputy in Santiago de Cuba in 1585. Fifteen years later Gómez de Rojas was in charge of organizing the repression against maroons in Havana.[50]

Gómez de Rojas's sense of worth and honor is illustrated in his conflicts with his relatives, the brothers Diego de Soto and Alonso de Rojas. When Governor Gabriel de Montalvo, in Bayamo in 1575, named Diego de Soto his deputy in Havana, the latter appointed Gómez de Rojas as governor of La Fuerza. According to Gómez, however, Soto canceled the commission because his brother Alonso was Gómez's enemy and had shown Gómez "many signs of enmity." Instead of abandoning the fortress, however, Gómez locked himself in La Fuerza, raised the gate, and refused to surrender the fortress until higher authorities declared publicly that he could do so "without harm to his honor and credit." When Governor Montalvo placed Gómez in prison, the latter requested to be released because the town's jail was not "decent according to the quality of his person." The governor agreed but made Gómez pay bail of 6,000 ducados in order to be released. Because of his services, in 1595 he requested an appointment as governor of La Punta or as a royal official.

One of the distinguishing characteristics of Havana's upper stratum was the absence of a sizable clergy among its members. Part of the explanation had to do with the organization of the Catholic Church on the island. The cathedral remained in Santiago de Cuba despite repeated efforts by the vecinos of Havana since at least the late 1590s to have it moved to their town. As a result, the bishops and other functionaries of the church resided in Santiago and Bayamo most of the time. Havana's parochial church was not repaired, after Sorés burned it down, until the mid-1570s. The collection of tithes, which were imposed on agricultural production, remained extremely low until the first decade of the seventeenth century, when it multiplied because of sugar manufacturing and a more effective exploitation of the rural hinterland. The royal treasury of Havana registered only 15,227 reales in tithes between 1570 and 1580. Collection grew to about 7,000 reales in 1599 and, following the favorable economic conjuncture, quadrupled by 1610, when some 30,000 reales was collected. Given the almost total disappearance of the indigenous population and the lack of gold or silver mines on the island, Cuba remained a relatively poor bishopric well into the seventeenth century. In 1626 its annual rents were estimated at some 4,000 pesos, lower than those in Santiago de Chile, Venezuela, or Panamá and only a fraction of those in the silver-producing dioceses of Peru, Bolivia, and Mexico.[51]

The presence that the Catholic Church did have in Havana, however, was largely a function of the support and commitments of its vecinos. Some of the most prominent members of the local elite exhibited their wealth and social worth by devoting significant resources to endow religious institutions. As mentioned in chapter 4, Juan de Rojas, brother of Gómez de Rojas and Hernán Manrique de Rojas, and their nephew Gerónimo de Rojas y Avellaneda paid for the completion of the parochial church. The cabildo acknowledged the importance of this commitment, writing to the king that Rojas Avellaneda had spent 9,000 or 10,000 ducados to complete the church, "a great benefit to the republic and His Majesty." Rojas Avellaneda also left a significant portion of his inheritance to the

Order of San Juan de Dios and the hospital of San Felipe y Santiago.[52] Diego de Soto and his brother Alonso de Rojas, in turn, offered to build the three chapels of the monastery of San Francisco at their own expense in 1579. The chapels would be made of brick and stone and covered with tiles. In exchange, the two families would enjoy the status of patrons of one chapel each, which gave them and their descendants the right of burial. The third chapel was for the monastery to give out to another patron as it wished.[53]

Having two chapels in one of Havana's monasteries as the burial site for a family was of course a sign of great distinction. Just as there were many ways to live, there were many ways to die and spend the afterlife. The members of the local elite purchased space in the parochial church and in the monasteries of the Franciscans and Dominicans to guarantee that their families would enjoy, in death as in life, a privileged place to be and to be seen. In 1596, for instance, some notable vecinos purchased sepulchers in the monastery of Santo Domingo for themselves and their families through contributions that ranged from 25 to 100 ducados. The largest contributions were made by Antón Recio, Rodrigo Carreño, and Captain Juan Tremiño. The resting place of the Carreños was contiguous with that of the Recios, "in the chapel near the Gospel." Close to them was another important family: that of notary Juan Bautista Guilisasti. Vecinos who made smaller contributions received sepulchers that were less centrally located.[54]

Having a privileged burial place was important, but the members of this upper stratum displayed their social worth and religious zeal through other means as well. They made elaborate arrangements for their funerals, commissioned masses for the salvation of their souls, gave alms to the poor and to the brotherhoods of their preference, and in some cases bequeathed significant amounts to priests, who were frequently members of their own family. The burial of María de Urquiaga in 1584, which cost 269 reales, illustrates how the funerals of the affluent were conducted. Accompanied by the priest of the church, by ten candle-holding Franciscan and Dominican friars, and by the bearer of a high cross, her body was conducted from her house to the parochial church, where she was to be buried. They paused thrice along the way and offered prayers while the church's bells rang. Once at the church, the priest offered a sung mass. Another eight masses were offered by the Franciscans and Dominicans.[55]

Some of the most principal vecinos of Havana, as they liked to call themselves, were also linked to religious institutions as syndics and administrators. Juan Recio was appointed "syndic and general administrator" of the monastery of San Francisco. Merchants Diego de Lara from Antwerp and Antonio Hernandez Farias functioned as syndics of the same monastery. Hernán Manrique de Rojas and his nephews Gerónimo de Rojas y Avellaneda and Jorge Manrique served as administrators of the hospital on several occasions. Merchant Francisco López de Piedra performed the same function for the parochial church between 1601 and 1603. These positions carried prestige, for, as Miguel de Cervantes noted, nothing was more honorable than to serve God.[56]

The importance that Havana's elite attributed to religious institutions is illustrated by the town council's requests to transfer the cathedral church from Santiago to Havana. As Bishop Juan de las Cabezas Altamirano asserted in 1603, this would create opportunities for the vecinos to reward their children – that is, it would open new opportunities for mobility to the status-hungry residents. The city's petitioner in court – in fact a delegate of the local elite before the king – argued in 1598 that whereas Santiago lacked population and defenses to protect the church, Havana was not only the most populated place of the island but "the most important of all the Indies and the key to their trade and commerce." Bishop Cabezas Altamirano concurred with this assessment, referring to Havana as "the throat" of the New World with a population, resident and transient, that required the permanent attention of a bishop.[57]

Philip III did not grant this concession to a city that the crown saw primarily, if not exclusively, as a fortified outpost to protect the fleets. It did eventually authorize, however, the Habaneros' request for another religious institution: a convent. The need for a convent was argued by the town council, the governor, and Bishop Cabezas Altamirano. Their arguments were always the same: many "poor honorable vecinos" spent all their assets and time serving the king, protecting his prized port city, and did not have the means to offer their daughters a proper dowry for them to marry. Although a few vecinos had bequeathed sums to endow poor honorable young women to marry, this money was not enough. Despite its importance, the city had no convent, so many vecinos were forced to send their daughters to Mérida, in Yucatán. "Convents," noted the bishop, "are the safeguards of noble people who are poor," and many vassals of the king had nothing but "honor" under their roofs. In order to facilitate the construction of the convent, which was built in the 1630s, the vecinos pledged some 160,000 reales in 1610.[58]

By the early years of the seventeenth century the vecinos and the town council were also insisting on the need to endow Havana with better educational facilities. One of the advantages of moving the cathedral to the city was the fact that its personnel included a preceptor of grammar. Concerns about instruction and literacy seem to have gone beyond the upper stratum. In this, as in many other things, the vecinos of Havana relied on models and values grounded in the European world of their ancestors. Castile was in the midst of a cultural

renaissance since the fifteenth century, and the demands of the growing imperial bureaucracy resulted in the expansion of institutions of learning and in
opportunities for mobility for men of letters. The Spanish writers of the period
captured the trend. Cervantes noted that letters had created more entailments
than arms; Quevedo asserted that noble status required, at least, some ability
to write. Literacy was growing, particularly among urban males, and so was the
commercial availability of printed books. Education had become one of many
requisites for noble status.[59]

Although some vecinos hired instructors to teach their children reading,
writing, and the Christian doctrine, in the 1580s there is a first reference to a
"schoolteacher" among the residents of Havana.[60] By the late 1590s the town
council supported two schoolteachers with annual salaries of 100 ducados each,
and a new school was under construction. By 1603, however, the cabildo complained that the salary was too low and that the city was in urgent need of a
preceptor. Claiming that the vecinos had many children in need of education,
local authorities requested authorization to devote a portion of the sisa or other
local taxes to increase the salary of the teacher to 300 ducados.[61] By 1607 Bishop
Cabezas Altamirano had established a *colegio*, or secondary school, named after
Saint Thomas Aquinas, with "many pupils, children of vecinos, with teachers
that teach them grammar, arts, and other virtues." The school, which was only
for boys, was supported by a group of prominent vecinos who donated beef daily
for the sustenance of the children and the teachers. The opportunities for instruction expanded toward the end of the decade, as the Augustinians began to
offer lessons for the children as well.[62]

Girls had less access to grammar instruction, which resulted in lower rates of
literacy. Some contracts for the education of girls do not even mention reading
or writing among their purposes but rather concentrate on Christian virtues
and on activities such as sewing.[63] We can measure literacy rates, roughly, by
using the ability to sign one's name as an indication of writing abilities. Since
most children were taught how to read before they acquired any writing skills,
the ability to sign can be taken as a reliable indicator of knowledge of the alpha-
bet. Contractual documents usually mentioned when one of the parties did not
know "how to sign." One 1600 contract, however, equated signing with writing
by noting that some of the participants did not sign because "they do not know
how to write."[64] According to this indicator, female literacy in sixteenth-century
Havana was dismal. Of all women doing notarized transactions whose ability to
sign can be clearly established, only 12 percent knew how to sign their names,
compared with 80 percent among males. These figures may appear extreme: they
were not. Gender-based differences in literacy rates in sixteenth-century Castile

were as significant as those found in Havana and in other colonial territories. As historian Susan Socolow states, "Feminine education was not only limited, it was rare. . . . Most women, including elite Spanish women, were illiterate." Our figures are comparable to those found in urban Andalusia (1595–1632), where 70 percent of males and 11 percent of females were considered literate; in the Archdiocese of Toledo (1601–50), where 70 percent of urban males and 12 percent of females knew how to sign; or in the diocese of Cuenca, where literacy rates were at 54 percent for males and 13 percent for females between 1571 and 1590.[65]

Literacy was only one of many areas in which the local elite could be barely distinguished from lower social groups. This upper sector was permeable, not only in the sense that newcomers found ways to enter the group but also in the sense that its social boundaries were never totally clear. Although a small core of families could more or less claim noble lineage, purity of blood (however dubious), and, by the late 1500s, time of residence in the port city, Havana's vibrant mercantile economy created significant opportunities for social ascent, particularly (but not exclusively) for people involved in transoceanic trade. Those at the top liked to distinguish themselves from the "citizens and people of lower station," but social realities were considerably more fluid than these characterizations might suggest.[66] As mentioned in chapter 4, by the early seventeenth century a new group of merchants, many of them of the Portuguese nation or from the Canary Islands, began to arrive in Havana and moved up the social ladder from very inauspicious beginnings. Furthermore, as the population of Havana grew, so did the complexity of local society. Among the people referred to as "citizens" were individuals who, by education and wealth, were barely distinguishable from those of the upper crust.

Commoners

The sugar business exemplifies the possibilities for social mobility that some newcomers were able to create in Havana's mercantile economy. Most in the initial group of señores de ingenio were members of the local elite, either by birth, marriage, or both. Others, however, came from less distinguished social backgrounds. In a military census prepared by the governor of La Fuerza in 1582, two of the initial sugar mill owners do not appear among the vecinos described as "dependable" and "trustworthy" but among those "who live by working." These were Hernán Rodríguez Tavares and Ginés de Orta (or Dorta) Yuste, both of whom benefited from the royal loan of 1602. Listed as a water supplier (aguador), Orta Yuste obtained the cabildo's contract to carry water to the town in 1576. Rodríguez Tavares was named without any specific trade.[67] Wealth and sugar opened the doors of the cabildo to these lower vecinos, although it is noteworthy that neither Orta nor Rodríguez Tavares was ever elected alcalde or regidor, at least until 1610. Orta Yuste was elected alcalde of the Santa Hermandad in 1600, the body in charge of persecuting runaway slaves. Rodríguez Tavares was appointed to this position in 1599 and was also the steward of the town council in 1597 and 1598.

How did these vecinos accumulate the resources required to build sugar mills and the social capital needed to be included among the beneficiaries of the royal loan of 1602? In a few words, by participating in Havana's trade. When the wife of Orta Yuste, Catalina Díez, issued her will in 1579, she declared that at the time of their marriage "we were poor and I did not bring any dotal goods and my husband did not bring any goods either."[68] It is doubtful that water carrying gave Orta Yuste the means needed to invest in sugar production. Rather, there is evidence that he and his wife traded with a variety of items. Orta Yuste was involved in several transactions buying wine and other European merchandise that he retailed locally and for which he paid with commodities such as hides and wood. In 1579 he and his wife bought 585 hides from a local producer for export. Unlike the large transoceanic merchants with whom he operated – Francisco Díaz Pimienta from the Canary Islands or Pedro Arias Maldonado from Seville – Orta Yuste operated in the local market as an intermediary and retailer.

Hernán Rodríguez Tavares occupied a similar place in the networks of trade but was much better connected than Orta Yuste. He was involved in several commercial transactions, importing European merchandise and exporting hides that he had previously bought in Bayamo. In these exchanges he probably acted as a front man for his brother, Portuguese merchant Jorge Rodríguez Tavares, who operated from Seville and who ended up moving to Havana around 1605. Despite his involvement in transoceanic and insular commerce, Hernán Rodríguez was not in the same league as the big merchants operating in Havana. His notarized exchanges amount to 54,205 reales. Although this was not a negligible sum, it pales compared with the volume of operations of the early transatlantic merchants of Havana, such as Melchor Rodríguez (287,420 reales) or Bartolomé de Morales (170,981 reales), and it is only a fraction of the sums handled by the merchants from the Canary Islands and Portugal who began to operate continuously in the city after the 1590s. To put this sum in perspective, the commercial activities of Francisco Díaz Pimienta from La Palma involved more than 1.8 million reales; those of his son-in law, Alonso de Ferrera, 1.2 million reales. Rodríguez Tavares's family connections, however, allowed him to profit enough from long-distance trade that by the early 1600s this man, who was described in 1582 as a commoner who worked for a living, was able to arrange a marriage for his daughter Catalina Rodríguez with a member of the Pérez de Borroto family and to give her a dowry of 1,000 ducados.[69]

Some of the most interesting cases of social ascent in sixteenth-century society involved skilled artisans and workers, some of whom managed to accumulate significant assets and a certain social notoriety. One of these was Antonio Matos da Gama (or de Gama), a maestro de azúcar (sugar master) from Madeira who arrived in Havana around 1590. We know little about his activities. Matos da Gama never received a concession of land from the cabildo and was forced, like most newcomers, to buy a farm in order to settle. The earliest reference to him in the local records is in 1591, when he bought an estancia where he later built his sugar mill San Francisco, which he sold in 1607 to merchant Francisco López de Piedra for 7,000 ducados.[70] Another sugar master, Pedro González, managed to purchase shares of two sugar mills as well: half of the mill Santiago of Martín Calvo de la Puerta in 1598 and one-fourth of Melchor Casas's Los Tres Reyes three years later. He paid the considerable sum of 55,220 reales for these units and raised some of the money through the sale of one estancia that he owned.[71]

The success of these sugar masters illustrates the importance of a middling sector of artisans in sixteenth-century Havana. The urban growth of the port city, the rapid increase of its shipping services, and the development or expansion of new economic activities such as shipbuilding, iron melting, tile making, and sugar production required the skill and labor of an ever growing number of skilled artisans. Some of the constructive activity, in turn, demanded the participation of artistically inclined artisans such as silversmiths, painters, and sculptors. These artists painted the retables for the parochial church, the hospital, and the monasteries, made crosses and chalices, and sculpted saints for their chapels. The initial members of this social group were all immigrants, but they passed on their skill and knowledge through their apprentices, who almost always were boys born on the island or in other colonies or African slaves. The importance of this social group is illustrated by the fact that by the early 1600s many trades had their own confraternities. These brotherhoods paraded together in religious processions and displayed their own theatrical skits and dances. Carpenters were grouped in the confraternity of San Jusepe, tailors in Nuestra Señora de los Reyes, shoemakers in San Crispín, and ironsmiths in San Lorenzo.[72]

The contracts of apprenticeship offer a view into the reproduction of this group and its composition. Individuals who placed either themselves or a minor into one of these contracts hoped that the apprentice would learn the mysteries of the trade from the master and would be able to make a living afterward as an "officer." Typically, the master artisan was to teach the trade "without hiding anything" and to provide lodging, food, and medical care for the apprentice.

Table 7.2. Apprenticeship Contracts by Trade and
Average Learning Time, Percentage Distribution,
1578–1610

Trade	Percentage (N = 85)	Average Time (Months)
Blacksmiths	2	48
Sword makers	2	36
Carpenters	14	41
Carvers/woodworkers	2	30
Tile makers	4	6
Locksmiths	1	42
Shipwrights	8	49
Caulkers	8	35
Shoemakers	13	37
Tailors	26	39
Silk makers	1	36
Silversmiths	5	54
Goldsmiths	4	58
Confectioners	1	24
Barber-surgeon	6	46
Sugar master	1	24

Source: ANC, PNH, ER, 1578–1610.

At the end of the contract, he was also to provide the apprentice with one set of ordinary clothing, plus "tools so that he can work and eat." The apprentice, in turn, was to serve the master in anything he ordered, and if he ran away, he would be returned to the master, to whom he was dependent.[73] The world of the mechanical trades had its own hierarchy, with masters at the top and apprentices at the bottom. Masters were themselves stratified. Those referred to as "master examiners" or "main master" had reached the highest possible level in the trade and were to certify the qualifications of others. Some of these highly skilled artisans existed in Havana: master shipwrights Francisco Gutiérrez Navarrete and Francisco de Beas; master smelter Francisco Ballesteros, in charge of the royal foundry; and master carpenters Gonzalo de la Rocha and Pedro Rojo.

Since learning a trade was basically an empirical process, the apprenticeship typically implied several years of service. Depending on the trade, learning could take from six months in the case of tile makers to five or six years for goldsmiths and silversmiths specialized in the making of religious objects (see table 7.2). At times learning a trade implied following the master around and serving him "in land and sea." This was the case of Antonio Gonzalez, from Lisbon, who signed up as an apprentice with ship caulker Juan Pérez, a resident of San Lúcar de Barrameda in Andalusia, in 1596. Antonio was to learn the trade while working on Pérez's ship, following him to Seville and back to Mexico and Havana. He would not receive any salary for the first ten months and would divide his earnings with Pérez thereafter.[74]

The frequency of contracts was probably a function of which occupations were perceived to be in greater demand and perhaps of the availability of masters and officers to train apprentices. The most numerous contracts involve trades that catered directly to the needs of the city's fast-growing population: tailors, including highly specialized artisans such as a doublet maker or a silk maker; shoemakers; and carpenters. These were followed by occupations in the shipping trades, such as caulkers and shipwrights. The residents in the port city obviously believed that Havana's maritime functions would provide employment opportunities for these apprentices.

One of the trades for which there was some demand was barber-surgeons, an occupation that, Quevedo noted with characteristic humor, made gold out of blood and hair. Since barbers performed operations of minor surgery and bleedings – an effective remedy against most ills, according to the humoral medicine of the time – they were trained and examined by master surgeons. In the absence of university-trained physicians, the practitioners of this "dangerous and delicate" trade, as Tirso de Molina called it, performed a valuable social function.[75]

For long periods of time, practically no doctors resided in town, although some came with the fleets every year.[76] In 1552 the cabildo welcomed Juan Gómez, who had just come to town, as its "barber and surgeon" to exercise his trade in exclusivity. In 1569 the town council agreed to pay a salary to a physician trained at Alcalá de Henares "because this town has great need for a pharmacy and a physician and a surgeon." The *licenciado* committed to cure and bleed the ill "giving them the best remedy for their health," but he apparently did not stay in town long enough to deliver on his promise. There are references to several surgeon-barbers practicing in town after the 1570s, including those who tended to the medical needs of the soldiers, and to a doctor, licenciado Francisco Pelaez, who probably died in the mid-1580s. No other permanent doctor is mentioned until the 1590s, when licenciado Bartolomé de Cárdenas appears in the local records. It is possible that Cárdenas went to Havana as part of the group that Captain Francisco Sánchez de Moya brought with him to work at the foundry and the copper mines. Cárdenas collected a salary as the foundry's physician and tended to the medical needs of soldiers as well.[77] According to Governor Valdés, however, the man was an impostor. His real name was Alonso Vélez; he came from a family of Moors from Baeza, and he did not have a medical title. Rather, he had worked as a servant for the real Cárdenas and appropriated his name and title after the death of the latter. Because of his deception, many patients had been "killed . . . with his poor cures," and the governor wanted him replaced immediately. Maybe there was some truth to Valdés's claims, for Cárdenas left town around 1608. His departure prompted local authorities to ask the king for permission to raise 500 ducados per year to pay for a doctor. Not even the hospital of San Juan de Dios had a physician. It used a surgeon "who does not know much about his art and cures according to his understanding," complained the governor. "There is nobody who can take the pulse of a patient or order a bleeding." In 1610 a new physician came to live in the port city subsidized by the town council.[78]

A relatively large number of apprentices were trained to be silversmiths and goldsmiths. These artisans made ornaments, jewelry, silverware, and other domestic wares. Juan Herrera, for instance, made plates, pots, buttons, bells, boxes, sword ornaments, key holders, saltcellars, and key rings. Some specialized in the making of religious ornaments. The religious institutions, including the Catholic fraternities, hired these artisans to produce artifacts for their chapels and retables. The monastery of San Francisco, for instance, paid 3,600 reales to silversmith Manuel Fernandez, who specialized in the making of religious ornaments, for the construction of a 15-pound silver cross.[79] These institutions also employed wood carvers and painters to decorate their altars and chapels. At the turn of the seventeenth century, painter and retable maker Juan de Camargo, who was described as a "resident" in the city, made, carved, and painted the retable for the main altar of the Parroquial Mayor, the monastery of San Francisco, and the brotherhood of Our Lady of the Remedies, of free and enslaved blacks. The work for the main altar of the parochial church must have been considerable, given its high cost: 2,000 ducados. Furthermore, the town council paid another 400 ducados for the rent of the house where Camargo lived and worked.[80]

Like the sugar masters mentioned above, some of these artisans reached a certain status in local society and accumulated significant wealth. Master carpenter Gonzalo de la Rocha, for instance, thought highly enough of himself to issue a power of attorney to be represented before the king and the Council of the Indies for any petitions or requests that he might have. Some artisans combined their occupation with trade and made small fortunes. This was the case of silversmith Diego de Lara from Antwerp, who appears in the notarial records both as a merchant and as an artisan. Lara was an active and prosperous trader. Although he was occasionally involved in transoceanic trade, importing products from Seville, most of his operations took place in the regional and insular circuits of trade. In fact, he seems to have specialized in the reexportation of European goods to Puerto Príncipe and in the importation of Mexican food products for the local market. In terms of volume, the total amount of his operations (255,751 reales) compared favorably with the amounts of the Havana-based merchants of the 1580s and 1590s such as Morales and Rodríguez, but it was small in relation to the long-distance Atlantic traders from the Canary Islands and Portugal.

Despite his wealth, there is no mistaking this merchant and silversmith for a member of the local elite. Although a prominent vecino, Lara could make no claims of noble status or knighthood. He received only one land concession from the town council and was never elected to the cabildo. He purchased himself a good burial place in the monastery of Santo Domingo and married into a middling local family in 1586, but he did not break into the upper stratum of society, even though his mother-in-law, Antonia Millán, entered into marriage for a second time with one of the Pérez de Borroto.[81]

Nevertheless, Lara surely belonged to the upper sector of his social group, along with other master artisans who managed to accumulate some wealth. Fellow silversmith Gabriel Sánchez de Villarreal, a Castilian from Córdoba by birth, was one of those. Toward the end of his life he owned two houses, six slaves, an 8-pound piece of silver, the tools of his trade, and other personal items. Vecino and carpenter Alvaro Hernández, a native from Portugal, listed in his 1600 will two houses, one estancia, four slaves, his tools, the tools in the estancia, some furniture, and clothing. As was frequently the case, the dowry, which in this case amounted to 4,000 reales, was excluded from this inventory.[82]

What distinguished these relatively wealthy master artisans from the hidalgos of the elite was not necessarily wealth but how that wealth was acquired. Lara and fellow artisans worked with their hands, something that hidalgos abhorred. These social distinctions materialized and were reproduced whenever members of the elite hired master artisans to perform manual labor for them. An illustrative case is that of Gómez de Rojas, who hired master carpenter Juan Alemán to make him his coat of arms. Alemán was a relatively wealthy artisan, the owner of several slaves, but the social distance separating him from Gómez de Rojas was nonetheless significant.[83]

Furthermore, most artisans occupied a lower position in the social hierarchy. As officers in their trade, they worked for the more prosperous masters who owned their own shop. In 1609, for instance, carpenter Juan de Guevara worked in the shop of master carpenter Juan Alemán for a monthly salary of 14 pesos (112 reales). The wills of these artisans are significantly more humble than those of the masters mentioned above. They typically include modest houses, frequently with thatched roofs, the tools of their trade, and personal items such as clothing and furniture. These artisans were not destitute men, but they were certainly not well-to-do either. Guevara's salary was similar to the salaries of soldiers, a group that, most observers concurred, gravitated toward the bottom of the city's free population.[84]

Indeed, the salaries of soldiers were not much higher than those earned by agricultural laborers (see chapter 5). More to the point, the royal treasury was frequently in arrears when it came to their pay, contributing to their lack of discipline and to their destitution as well. The available evidence – and there is plenty – indicates that this group belonged to and interacted with the poor of the city. As mentioned in chapter 6, many of the services the soldiers required, such as laundering and cooking, were performed by black women, free and enslaved. Because their pay did not come regularly, many of these services were provided on credit, so soldiers' wills are full of references to debts to the most humble inhabitants of the city. In 1601, for instance, Antonio Domínguez, a soldier from Galicia, declared that he owed 300 reales to a female slave who had lent him this sum of money while he was sick. Domínguez's goods were quite limited: three sets of clothing, one hat, one sword, and 61 pesos in cash and drafts. A Portuguese soldier declared in 1605 that his only assets were his salary, of which he was owed eighteen months, and "his weapons." Slightly better off was Martín López, from Andalusia, who owned four shirts; four sets of clothing; a bed with its mattress, sheet, and pillow; plus a sword. The assets of some of these soldiers could barely cover their debts and burial expenses. As one soldier put it in 1586, "I am poor and I don't have enough for burial, for I owe more than what I have."[85]

At least some of the soldiers attempted to improve their precarious situation by marrying locally – which was prohibited by law – and by working other occupations on the side. These occupations ranged widely, from fishery to cooking and playing cards. Some had been trained in the mechanical trades and could complement their income working as shoemakers, carpenters, and ironsmiths and in other trades. One managed to acquire a small estancia and worked on it.[86]

The social world of the soldiers was a world of cooks, fishermen, launderers, daily laborers, street sellers, gamblers, and prostitutes. This was the world of Pedro Arias, a humble fisherman from the Canary Islands whose clients included slave Pascual Hernandez and whose only possessions were some clothes that he described as worn out. It was also the world of Sebastián de Esquivel, a cordage maker who also cooked for the soldiers for a living, or that of wine seller Catalina Gómez, from Fuentes de León, Spain, whose only goods were some clothes and a pipe of wine.[87]

This was also the world that seamen inhabited while they waited in Havana to enlist with a new crew to cross the Atlantic or to visit some of the ports of the circum-Caribbean area. Each year the fleets and many other vessels brought hundreds of sailors to town, where shipmasters frequently liquidated their accounts and paid their crews. Havana functioned as a sort of clearinghouse for ships' crews, which allowed them, pretty much as happened with merchandise, to move from one shipping circuit to another. This is what Tomé Andrés, a mariner in the Carrera de Indias, did when he decided to stay on the island and to sign up with one of the fragatas that connected Havana with the towns of the so-called interior. Andrés obviously became proficient in the shipping routes of Cuban waters and in the trading opportunities that the island had to offer. His business dealings covered Remedios, Sancti Spíritus, Puerto Príncipe, Santiago, and Havana. Other sailors used Havana as their primary residence, settled in town, formed families, and bought houses.[88]

Making Havana a primary residence was probably atypical, however. Sailors were by definition transient people, always on the move. They were, in a sense, true inhabitants of the Atlantic, whose personal relationships, business interests, and spiritual concerns spanned several locations and continents. The wills of sailors reflect these idiosyncrasies. They frequently asked to have prayers said for their souls in various locations, regardless of where they died and what happened to their mortal remains, and to settle affairs in a variety of ports. A pilot from the Carrera asked in 1596 for prayers at Havana's parochial church and in Seville, the city of his birth and residence. He left money to a sister in Seville and to an illegitimate child in Cartagena de Indias. Another pilot left donations to religious brotherhoods in Havana and in his native village in the Algarve, Portugal, while settling accounts in Seville and in La Palma. The specificity of this group was best illustrated by a soldier in a 1591 armada, who asked to be buried in Havana or "at the sea" if for whatever reason he did not make it to the city alive. He knew well, of course, that dying on the high seas was not a rare occurrence. The sailors' limited wooden world was one rich in diseases, full of dangers, and of very high mortality. The greed of shipmasters and owners only made matters worse.[89]

The seamen inhabited a hierarchical world, with shipmasters, captains, and pilots at the top and sailors, apprentices (*grumetes*) and pages at the bottom. This hierarchy had stringent financial implications: the average sailors' salary could be only one-fifth or even one-tenth of pilots' salaries (see table 7.3). Pilots capable of navigating on the high seas were highly skilled specialists who had to make complex calculations in order to stay on route. Much knowledge was still acquired empirically, after years of experience at the sea. But in the sixteenth century navigation was becoming increasingly complex. Pilots had to learn how to use the astrolabe, calculate longitude, and read detailed *portolanos* that described how to access a port. Whereas masters were in charge of the administration of the ship and its load, pilots were in charge of nautical matters. The importance

Table 7.3. Average Wages (in Reales) of Seamen by Route and Occupation, 1578–1610

Route	Ship-masters (N = 7)	Pilots (N = 34)	Stewards (N = 9)	Boat-swains (N = 9)	Sailors (N = 131)	Appren-tices (N = 57)	Pages (N = 9)
Seville-Havana-Seville	4,400	4,987	–	–	495	–	–
Seville-Indies-Havana	–	1,716	885	1,312	652	529	292
Canary Islands-Havana	–	1,127	577	578	432	298	138
Havana-Indies-Seville	4,950	3,655	–	1,540	1,027	–	440
Havana-Seville	1,045	1,439	660	942	502	220	98
Indies-Havana	–	550	396	–	138	88	66
Havana-Indies-Havana	–	1,430	–	880	229	134	–

Source: ANC, PNH, ER, 1578–1610.

Note: These salaries do not include the value of daily rations.

of this occupation is best illustrated by the fact that pilots' salaries were the highest among the men of the sea, comparable in fact to those of masters. By the late sixteenth century a pilot hired in Seville to sail to the Indies and back could expect to earn, as Spanish naval historian Pablo Pérez-Mallaína has stated, in the neighborhood of 400 ducados.[90]

Sailing to Seville from Havana with a stop in another colonial port increased significantly the price of labor. Whereas the average salary of a pilot sailing straight to Seville from Havana was about 100 ducados, it more than doubled when the ship was to call into another port in the circum-Caribbean area first, such as Puerto Rico or Santo Domingo. These increases took place across the board, from the masters or pilots down to the lowest workers on the ships, such as the pages. The salaries of sailors doubled; those of boatswains increased by 60 percent. Sailing to another port in the treacherous waters of the Caribbean not only meant additional sailing time but made the trip significantly more danger-ous, as the waters of the Caribbean were infested with enemies. Furthermore, at least some of these vessels were courier ships that traveled alone, instead of going with the fleets, and sailing alone increased their vulnerability.

At the bottom of this hierarchy were the apprentice sailors and the pages, or cabin service boys, who tended to the needs of shipmasters and pilots. En-joying the services of a page was a great privilege, one of the reasons that ship merchants and pilots could aspire to a middling position in society. Sailors, ap-prentices, and pages, in turn, fell easily into the category of the urban poor. The wills of these workers of the sea reveal a world of great destitution, like that of Andrés de Alegría, a sailor from Vizcaya whose only possession was "a box with his clothing," or that of a Greek sailor who listed his salary as his only assets.[91]

Paying sailors before the transatlantic voyage.
From G. Braun, *Civitatis Orbis Terrarum* (1599).

This highly mobile, multinational labor force made important contributions to local culture, although the available sources limit our ability to capture many of their social interactions in their complexity. Seamen were a social and occupational group large enough to establish its own Catholic brotherhood in the city, the Cofradía de San Telmo. The brotherhood had a chapel at the monastery of Santo Domingo and paid 1,200 reales per year to enjoy free religious and burial services. Among these services was a weekly prayer for "the brothers and for the sea men who sail through the waters of the sea."[92]

These men of the sea contributed to the production of valuable nautical knowledge as well. They came to know the waterways of the Caribbean and its coasts, bays, keys, and inlets better than anybody. It was based on this knowledge that European cartographers began to produce detailed navigation manuals about the Caribbean and the Gulf of Mexico in the sixteenth century.[93] Pilot Antón de Alaminos, for instance, discovered the Gulf Stream as he sailed back to Europe through the Florida Straits and the Bahamas; Cabo Cañaverales, on the eastern Florida coast, was explored by Havana-based pilots in 1595.[94]

To secular and religious authorities, however, seamen constituted an unruly social group that was large enough to pollute the religious and moral lives of the community. According to various authorities, seaports such as Havana posed special problems when it came to matters of the faith. The inhabitants of the port city were in constant exchange with sailors, most of whom were foreigners – English, German, French, Irish, Scots – of dubious religious affiliation. These foreigners introduced heretical books and ideas and added a layer of heresy to a community that was already affected by the presence of many proselytizing Jews, wizards, and sorcerers. A good example of this nefarious influence was that of a Michael Juan, a sailor from Sicily who had used three different names and married five times within the Atlantic: in Sicily, Valencia, Seville, Havana, and Mexico.[95] The seamen also patronized the numerous gambling houses that existed in the city, where they fraternized with soldiers and with the low social element that the fleets brought to town – "people of low living who do nothing but gamble."[96]

Rituals and Interactions

To many colonial officials, particularly those who arrived in the port city from Spain, the heterogeneous population of Havana appeared to have little regard for authority and were difficult to control. In their perception, the residents of the port city showed no deference to social superiors and treated them as equals. As Governor Luján complained, it looked like nobody wanted to obey orders. Governor Valdés marveled at the insolence of "the people of the land" who treated him "with equality and without distinction" despite the fact, obvious to Valdés, that his social station and rank entitled him to deferential treatment. The vecinos, in turn, accused him of being despotic and arbitrary. In 1608, for instance, a group of vecinos who described themselves as "honorable people, good Christians who live peacefully in this republic and are important in it," charged that the governor had banished some residents without regard for their condition, even though some were well-known noblemen.[97]

Local residents complained repeatedly about colonial officials' attempts to mark their social superiority and raised all sorts of accusations against them. Since the crown was always jealous of the power of its own bureaucracy, residents were not just allowed but actually encouraged to denounce colonial authorities. The *juicios de residencia* that officials had to endure at the end of their mandate offered plenty of opportunities to channel those complaints. In these legal proceedings, subjects were allowed to voice grievances against colonial officials. Local residents could then slander them at will. To mention but one extreme example, the vecinos of Bayamo, many of whom made a living through smuggling, accused Bishop Díaz de Salcedo of *nefandum peccatum* (sodomy). Disbelieving such temerity, the bishop noted that it was the "style" of the land to mistreat prelates. Other functionaries concurred with his assessment. "When a judge makes justice, it is the quality and habit of the people of the land to raise a thousand testimonies to deprive him of his honor and income," complained a governor. Another official described locals as "gossipy and ill intentioned."[98]

Letter by letter, colonial authorities began to produce a disparaging image of *la gente de la tierra*. The people of the land supposedly knew no boundaries, respected no rank, and refrained from nothing. They were egalitarian, insolent, and prone to sin. Bishop Castillo described them as "the most incorrigible and free from the commandments of the Church that there is in all the Indies, and so there are many public sins and many vecinos who are married two and three times with their wives alive." According to his and other testimonies, many people in the city cohabited outside holy marriage and committed "atrocious sins."[99] Perhaps the most notorious of these sins was sodomy. According to Governor Maldonado Barnuevo, in 1595 more than fifty people had been captured practicing the *nefandum peccatum* and were burned at the stake. A port city such as Havana, noted the governor, was visited by the scum of the world.[100]

Although portrayals of social disorder were probably exaggerated, as much a function of local practices as of the expectations of colonial officials, several factors contributed to subvert traditional social hierarchies in Havana. It was not only that the city was visited by the scum of the earth, as Governor Maldonado put it. For much of the sixteenth century Havana was an Atlantic community in the making: social distances and distinctions were inherently unstable. The relative weakness of religious institutions contributed to this state of affairs and mitigated the Counter-Reformation zeal that affected other parts of the empire.[101] There was not even a commissary of the Holy Inquisition in Havana until the first decade of the seventeenth century despite the fact, noted by religious authorities, that Havana was "the most visited of all the ports in the Indies," where blasphemies, superstitions, and heresies reportedly took place regularly.[102] Whereas historians concur that the impact of the Inquisition on Spanish social life was significant, in Havana its influence was, to say the least, limited. The commissary could prosecute offenses against the faith but had to send the accused to the inquisitorial courts of Mexico or Cartagena de Indias. For this he needed the support of religious and secular authorities who, jealous of their own jurisdiction and power, were notoriously uncooperative. The sparse records of the Inquisition on the island speak volumes about the weakness of the institution.[103]

Precisely because many authorities resented these egalitarian impulses, conflicts over precedence and rank proliferated. Functionaries were extremely jealous of their prerogatives and jurisdictions and fought one another frequently about these issues. In these conflicts, ritual elements could be of the utmost importance. Governor Valdés, for instance, ordered the removal of the velvet cushion and the baton that the governor of the fortress of El Morro brought with him to the parochial church. These, Valdés claimed, were attributes of command that only he could display. By bringing them to church, El Morro's governor implied that "there was no difference" between him and Valdés, something that the latter took as an insult. His explanation was categorical: "There is some difference between my person and his in quality and service."[104]

Questions of ritual precedence and worth were equally important in religious processions and other festivities. These were moments in which the population of the city came together, but these celebrations served to reinscribe differences and reproduce the social order. As historian Alfredo Castillero-Calvo has noted, "The city of the Indies was the great instrument of state by which unity was forged out of multiplicity."[105]

Some of these feasts were calendrical. The Christian year had its own rhythms, and these rhythms were similar in all the areas of the empire, regardless of their location or latitude. The most important feasts, such as Corpus Christi, were celebrated across the Spanish territories, from Madrid or Toledo to Havana, their execution the subject of detailed preparation. In this sense, they were Atlantic events, although with a conspicuous Castilian flavor.[106]

These festivities served several purposes. They helped to create a sense of belonging to the larger community of believers and the kingdom, but participation in them was highly ritualized and frequently mandatory. As historian Teófilo Ruiz has noted, participation in religious processions such as the Corpus Christi represented a "public and political reaffirmation of faith by all social classes." Their religious purpose notwithstanding, these feasts contained elements of carnival and secular diversions such as theater presentations, comedies, dances, and martial games such as the *juegos de cañas*, in which men on horses fought with wooden lances.[107]

These festivities took place across the empire, but their organization of course varied according to locality. The evolution of the Corpus Christi in Havana mirrors the larger changes that took place in the port city. The earliest references to the feast in the 1550s suggest mostly a military parade, in which vecinos on foot or horse were to present themselves armed to display their military readiness. Reference was not even made to the consecrated host, which was supposed to be at the center of the procession. Havana honored Corpus Domini, the Lord's Body, by displaying the strength of its arms, a graphic illustration of how the defense of the faith and of His Majesty's territories had become one and the same thing. Given the political nature of these ritualized celebrations, participation was not voluntary: the vecinos were compelled to attend under stiff financial penalties.[108]

By the 1570s the character of the feast had changed to a popular celebration in which secular diversions had become central. Rather than calling on the vecinos to display their arms, the town council ordered artisans "such as tailors, carpenters, shoemakers, ironsmiths, and caulkers" to display "inventions and games" for the enjoyment of the people who were present. Local authorities also ordered free blacks to become organized and to "help with the feast ... with their invention." As would become customary, a person was designated to supervise preparations. Residents were instructed to clean their properties as well for the procession.[109]

This would be the format of Corpus Christi in subsequent years. As the town grew in size and importance, the cabildo began to subsidize the feast by paying for the staging of theatrical skits, comedies, dances, and masquerades. The growing complexity of the festivities paralleled similar trends elsewhere within the Spanish empire, however, and was also a reflection of the Council of Trent's transformation of Corpus Christi "into the triumphant religious holiday of the Catholic year."[110]

Religious processions were also organized on occasion of epidemics and plagues of various kinds. Some of the ecological challenges that the residents of Havana encountered, such as plagues or hurricanes, may have been new to most of them, but they reacted to these challenges by appealing for protection to a repertoire of saints and formulas of proven efficacy. Thus in 1569 the town council adopted apostle Saint Simon as its advocate against ants, which damaged harvests, and collected alms to say masses in his honor. When this saint failed to deliver, they turned to another. Starting in the 1580s, masses, processions, and feasts were organized to invoke the protection of Saint Martial against ants, worms, and other despicable bugs. In 1607 a bullfight was staged in his honor, and the bishop ordered Saint Martial Day to be observed as one of the Catholic feasts in the city. Prayers and processions were organized to fight epidemics as well.[111]

The population of the city came together to honor not only God but also the king. The birth of a prince, the proclamation of a king, a royal wedding – these were all causes for celebration, whereas the death of the king demanded acts of collective mourning. Here, again, the nature and organization of the festivities changed along with the port city. In July 1557 the cabildo learned officially about the renunciation of Charles V in favor of his son Phillip II. The town councilmen swore loyalty to the new king and ordered residents "to raise flags in his name," but no other celebrations were scheduled. By 1599, when Phillip III ascended to the throne, the town council ordered all vecinos and residents to gather in front of the town council house "in recognition of obedience and happiness" for the new king. They would parade around town, playing music and displaying the royal banners, which would be deposited in La Fuerza. Heading the procession would be the governor, royal Officials, and of course the town councillors, followed by men on horse and those on foot. When a few months later news was received about the king's wedding, the cabildo organized juegos de cañas, bullfights, and other festivities "according to the obligation that they have as loyal vassals."[112]

These civic and religious rituals were complex social and performative affairs. They created opportunities for residents of the port city to celebrate across class and racial boundaries. At the same, however, these events reinscribed social differences. The elaborate order in the processions was meant to evoke an ideal social order in which people were clearly divided according to their social station: town councillors, noble horsemen, commoners on foot, artisans, blacks. In this sense, the parades and processions were an elaborate exercise in social discipline that contained obvious elements of coercion. People were asked to participate under penalties of various kinds. When Phillip II died, the town council ordered all inhabitants in the city to mourn and dress properly. Women were to wear black headdresses, men hats with large crowns. The town councillors provided for their own attire with public funds while imposing a penalty of 10 ducados on those inhabitants who did not observe the mourning. Free blacks, women in particular, were forced to take part in the Corpus Christi processions and were authorized to wear silk and gold only on such occasions. The authorization of silk and gold was not only an attempt to guarantee their participation in the festivities but also an effort to police their social place through clothing, which constituted at the time one of the fundamental languages of difference.[113]

These rituals gained in complexity and importance as Havana grew from town to city. It is not only that residents wanted to display the prosperity of the port city. These rituals of civic and religious communion became more necessary as the population of the city grew in size and complexity. The very growth of the port city threatened its survival. The threat no longer came from without, from a lonely Lutheran pirate such as Jacques de Sorés. The city was basically impregnable to anything but a formidable military force. The problem, rather, lay within: an increasingly diverse population, a growing number of slaves, a mass of transient seamen, and soldiers of dubious religious purity.

Epilogue

The Havana of the early seventeenth century was a very different place than the town that Jacques de Sorés occupied and destroyed in 1555. The city had grown in size, population, and complexity. In 1555 Havana was a coastal town that lacked basic urban functions, from a school or a monastery to a customhouse. Its lack of population and inadequate defenses made it an easy prey for foreign predators, who attacked the town in 1538, 1543, and twice in 1555. Civilian and religious authorities lived elsewhere on the island and stayed away from the town, which had mosquitoes in abundance but no drinkable water. Even the bread of the land, a bishop noted disparagingly, was not bread at all but made out of tubers and known by the indigenous name of *casabi*.[1]

Cassava bread did not go away, although it had to compete with corn and wheat breads. Everything else, however, changed. By 1620 Havana was said to have 1,200 vecinos, twenty times as many as in 1570. By then it was the ninth largest urban Spanish center in the Americas, compared with the seventieth place it occupied in 1570.[2] In the meantime the physical layout of the port city was transformed. Royal moneys paid for the construction of three new forts and financed productive activities such as shipbuilding and the manufacturing of ordnance. New religious institutions were built, including a new parochial church; a hospital; monasteries for the Franciscans, Dominicans, and Augustinians; and a colegio, or secondary school. Using local resources, the town council built a jailhouse, a slaughterhouse, a fish market, and the aqueduct. The construction of stone and brick houses proliferated. Colonial authorities settled in the city. The number of town councillors increased. New institutions were created.

Behind this remarkable transformation was the sea. Havana was not just a place in the Atlantic but an Atlantic place. The sea was the engine of the local economy and a key factor in the organization of the economic, social, and institutional lives of the residents. The movement of shipping shaped productive activities, consumption patterns, and the frequency and content of town council meetings. Port cities are more than human settlements by the sea; they are settlements whose productive and social lives are organized around the sea.

Not all coastal settlements, not even all ports connected to the Carrera de Indias, benefited from the expansion of colonial commerce in the late sixteenth century. Veracruz remained a relatively minor urban settlement despite functioning as virtually the sole transoceanic port for the viceroyalty of New Spain. The town, which was moved in the late sixteenth century to a more convenient location across the fortified island of San Juan de Ulúa, had only 400 vecinos in the 1620s, compared with 350 in 1570.[3] The settlements of the Panamanian isthmus experienced a similar fate. Nombre de Dios, which Chaunu characterizes as "an episodic city" that was populated cyclically to serve the needs of the convoys, was replaced by Portobelo after Francis Drake destroyed it in 1596. Despite its maritime importance and imposing defenses, Portobelo did not become a major urban center. Between 1597 and 1630 its population oscillated between 30 and 40 vecinos. As for the city of Panama, the main Spanish settlement on the isthmus and the seat of the audiencia, its population remained basically unchanged between 1570 (400 vecinos) and 1630 (500 vecinos).[4]

Yet these were, in terms of value, the great port cities of Spanish Atlantic commerce. The Nombre de Dios–Portobelo–Panama compound handled from 55 to 60 percent of the total value of trade between the New World and Spain between 1540 and 1650. Veracruz handled an additional 39 percent of the trade.[5] These were the Atlantic ports of the great viceroyalties, the points where much of the silver, gold, indigo, cochineal, pearls, and other colonial riches were exchanged for European manufactures. Why did they fail to capitalize on the late sixteenth-century cycle of expansion?

Precisely because of their relationship to the viceregal centers of colonial power, several historians argue. Christopher Ward notes, for instance, that Panama lacked significant "commercial activity" besides the fairs of Portobelo, that most of the wealth produced by these transactions was not invested in the region, and that internal transportation costs consumed much of the profits. Likewise, Veracruz was the loading and unloading station for Mexico, a "transit place," another of Chaunu's "episodic cities" whose real social foundation was located inland, in Mexico City.[6]

In contrast to these settlements, which were shipping stations for the wealthy viceroyalties, other port cities such as Havana and Cartagena became nodal points in a complex circum-Caribbean web of commerce, developed connections to expanding agricultural hinterlands, and gained in size and population. Cartagena's population was smaller than Panama's and Veracruz's in 1570, but it was three to four times larger by 1630. Havana was of course a very modest town in 1570, with only sixty vecinos and a single church that was partially destroyed. Of the total number of vecinos resident in the district of the Audiencia de Santo

Domingo in 1570, only 3.5 percent lived in Havana. By 1630, almost one-fourth of district's population lived in Havana, which was on its way to becoming the largest urban center in the circum-Caribbean region.[7]

Havana's relation to the increasingly complex Atlantic system was reflected first and foremost in its role as a center in the Caribbean regional web of distribution and commerce. The Carrera de Indias was surely the prime expression of the organization of the Spanish Atlantic, but other networks of trade were created in the shadow of the fleets and enjoyed some degree of autonomy. As the return station for the fleets, the only point in the Americas where both fleets gathered, Havana had distinctive advantages for the exportation of colonial commodities to Europe and for the distribution of European manufactures in the colonies. As a result, the port town (and later, port city) was able to participate in and to profit from various Atlantic networks of communication and trade. Along with royal funds, these profits helped finance the growth of what John Elliot has aptly characterized as "the emporium of a transatlantic trade" that grew considerably in size and complexity during the second half of the sixteenth century, precisely during the years covered by this study. It was during this period that Havana came into "its own" as an Atlantic port city, to use the expression of Knight and Liss, or "came to age," as Socolow and Johnson put it.[8]

Most historians, however, have missed the vital signs of this growth and continue to see Havana as an imperial military outpost at the service of the fleets. This is surprising, given that contemporaries constructed a laudatory vision of the port city that, if anything, exaggerated its size and commercial importance. The traditional historiography of Cuba described the city as a frontier garrison whose only function was to protect the fleets against intruders. This vision has been reproduced by even the best historiography of the Spanish empire, and for good reasons. From the vantage point of Seville, Havana was nothing but "a protected outport on the periphery" of the mainland mining centers whose "main function" was to serve as a naval base for the Carrera. But as John J. TePaske has argued, these peripheries were integral to the empire as a whole, and some became themselves core regions.[9]

The characterization of Havana as protected outport contains elements of truth, but it conflates lived experience with design. It reduces the history of the port city and its inhabitants to the functions prescribed for them by the centers of imperial power. These prescriptions mattered, of course, but as Richard Morse noted years ago, even if towns were embedded in frameworks of empire, they "were not hermetic enclaves but a locus of tension between local ambition and imperial design."[10] These two elements – local ambitions, imperial design – interacted in complex and sometimes unexpected ways. In the case of Havana, and precisely because of the imperial design of the city as the gathering point for the fleets, local residents managed to obtain significant concessions from the crown. These concessions ranged from tax exemptions, loans, or subsidies to institutional concessions such as the town council's unrestricted ability to distribute land. Local ambitions took advantage of the imperial design.

What has come to be known as the Atlantic history approach should have helped us solve some of these problems, for one of the goals of Atlantic history is precisely to transcend national and imperial boundaries. Even when studying a particular locality, as is the case in the present work, Atlantic history seeks to place it within a larger geographic and historical space in which producers and consumers interacted across political, religious, and ethnic lines.[11] It thus becomes less important to study what empires designed, frequently with limited information about the lands beyond the ocean sea, than to look at the movements, interactions, and activities of various social actors within this space and how those interactions and mutual influences shaped local events.

Atlantic history has been slow in delivering on some of these promises, however. Although, as Alison Games puts it, the Atlantic "tends to look very different when viewed from different vantages," most views of the Atlantic continue to be constructed from Europe and particularly from Great Britain.[12] Furthermore, by concentrating on the British experience, historians tend to privilege certain processes and questions. Thus the Atlantic becomes equated with slavery, especially plantation slavery, and with the production and exportation of colonial commodities. This is particularly the case during the eighteenth century, when the exchanges between European consumers, African slaves, and colonial plantations reached their apogee.[13]

Despite the Atlantic cover, this approach is in fact another attempt to write the history of Europe. The questions and the chronology are those of European capitalism and the industrial revolution in England. What Pieter Emmer has called the second Atlantic becomes "the" Atlantic. The first Atlantic – which was not defined by plantation slavery and commercial agriculture, which reached its commercial apogee in the late decades of the sixteenth century, and which did not result in the industrial takeoff of Spain or Portugal – is largely erased. We need to "Iberianize" the Atlantic, to use Jorge Cañizares-Ezguerra's expression. After all, Iberian peoples played no minor role in the creation of this historical space.[14]

The Eurocentric, British-centered vision described above tends to emphasize as well the novelty of the Atlantic as a space of mass production of tropical commodities for distant markets. The so-called New World looks really new when viewed through this prism. In more than one sense, however, the societies that the Europeans created in the Americas were anything but new. Although local conditions and ecologies dictated what could be achieved and how, the colonists responded to these realities by turning to "a home culture whose formative influence could never be entirely escaped." This culture shaped responses even in the plantation societies of the Caribbean, which are frequently seen as the ultimate European innovation in the tropics.[15]

Finally, a Eurocentric history of the Atlantic that remains prisoner of the national imagination has other limitations. As the story of Havana shows, the Atlantic as a space of commercial and cultural exchanges was not particularly respectful of national or imperial boundaries. The crown's efforts to the contrary notwithstanding, there was much in the Spanish Atlantic that was not Spanish — including human, material, and spiritual elements. In addition to Africa's human and intellectual contributions, there were individuals and even small communities of non-Spanish nations in the colonies. And then there were others who, like Jacques de Sorés, came uninvited to trade, plunder, and disseminate pernicious ideas. As for merchandise, the residents of Havana and other colonial cities consumed products that originated not only in different parts of Europe, from Italy to the Baltic region, but also in Asia. Through the various Atlantic networks of trade, the residents of Havana connected with producers who sometimes lived well beyond the ocean sea, in India or China.

Notes

Abbreviations

ACAH	Actas Capitulares del Ayuntamiento de la Habana
AGI	Archivo General de Indias, Seville
AGN	Archivo General de la Nación, Mexico
AH	Academia de la Historia
AHN	Archivo Histórico Nacional, Madrid
ANC	Archivo Nacional de Cuba, Havana
ASCH	Archivo del Sagrario de la Catedral de la Habana
BL	British Library, Manuscript Section, London
BNM	Biblioteca Nacional de España, Sección de Manuscritos, Madrid
CODOIN I	*Colección de documentos inéditos, relativos al descubrimiento, conquista y organización de las antiguas posesiones españolas de América y Oceanía*, 1st ser., 42 vols. (Madrid: M. B. de Quirós, 1864-84)
CODOIN II	*Colección de documentos inéditos relativos al descubrimiento, conquista y organización de las antiguas posesiones españolas de ultramar*, 2d ser., 25 vols. (Madrid: Establecimiento Tipográfico "Sucesores de Rivadeneyra," 1885-1932)
ER	Escribanía Regueira
PNH	Protocolos Notariales de la Habana
RC	Real cédula
RP	Real provisión
SD	Santo Domingo

Chapter One

1. The description of the attack is based on Relación y estragos que los franceses corsarios hicieron en la villa de la Habana, 1555, CODOIN II, 6:386-427; Relación enviada por Diego de Mazariegos, 1555, CODOIN II, 6:376-86; and García del Pino, "Ataque de la Habana."

2. Mosen Boteller a SM, Santiago de Cuba, 15 January, 1556, CODOIN II, 6:436.

3. RC of 28 February 1515, in CODOIN II, 1:58. Concerning the establishment of the original Havana, see López de Gómara, *Historia*, 1:74-75; García del Pino, "¿Dónde?" and Pichardo Viñals, *Fundación*.

4. On the lack of gold in the area, see Alonso de Parada a SM, 2 July 1527, in Llaverías,

Papeles, 1:120. Concerning economic activities, see the testament of Velázquez, in CODOIN I, 35:524.

5. Bernardino de Quesada a SM, Santiago de Cuba, 1 July 1538, CODOIN II, 6:40.

6. Ibid.

7. Chaunu, *Sevilla*, 69. On the decline of the native population in the New World, see Cook, *Born to Die*; on Cuba, Pérez de la Riva, "Desaparición," 61–84. On gold production, see Marrero, *Cuba*, 2:20.

8. Manuel de Rojas a SM, Santiago de Cuba, 10 November 1534, in Sagra, *Historia*, 2:35. On Santo Domingo's sugar economy, see Rodríguez Morel, "Esclavitud" and "Sugar Economy."

9. Marrero, *Cuba*, 1:173. The colonists had complained about the impossibility of inheriting encomiendas. See Memorial de Fr. Bernardino de Manzanedo, 1518, in Llaverías, *Papeles*, 1:54.

10. Opinión del Consejo contra la libertad de los indios, 20 April 1543, CODOIN II, 6:182.

11. Marrero, *Cuba*, 1:139.

12. RC of 28 September 1532, ANC, AH, leg. 56, no. 638; Los oficiales reales a SM, Santiago de Cuba, 6 May 1532, AGI, SD, leg. 18. Concerning Velázquez's appointment of a lieutenant in Havana, see Capítulos presentados ante la Audiencia de Santo Domingo contra el licenciado Altamirano, October 1525, CODOIN II, 1:221–22.

13. Fernández de Enciso, *Suma* (1546), 442. For other early accounts that refer to the centrality of Havana, see Benzoni, *Historia*, and Anania, *Universal*.

14. RC of 20 May 1538, in Wright, *Historia* (1927), 1:184.

15. El cabildo de la Habana a SM, 25 August 1552 and 20 March 1553, CODOIN II, 6:333, 375.

16. For an example, see the testimony of Benzoni, *Historia*, fol. 174.

17. Hardoy and Aranovich, "Urban Scales."

18. The best studies of early colonial Havana continue to be those of Irene A. Wright. Recent valuable studies include Marrero, *Cuba*, and Macías, *Cuba*. Kuethe's "Havana" and McNeill's *Atlantic Empires* are of great value in the study of the port city in the eighteenth century. This book follows Kuethe's approaches and suggestions more than once. With regard to the growing literature about port cities in general, we have found to be particularly useful the collection edited by Knight and Liss, *Atlantic Port Cities*; Pérotin-Dumon's *Ville aux îles*; the collections edited by Broeze, *Brides of the Sea* and *Gateways of Asia*; and Konvitz's *Cities and the Sea*.

19. Braudel mentioned the "Atlantic economy" in his *Afterthoughts*, in which he advanced some of the notions concerning "world economies" that he discussed more fully in other works.

20. Our ideas about port cities have been greatly influenced by scholars working on Asian port cities, especially those represented in Broeze, *Brides of the Sea* and *Gateways of Asia*.

21. For examples in Cuban historiography, see Lufríu, *Impulso*; Friedländer, *Historia*; Ely, *Economía*; Pino-Santos, *Historia*; Masó y Velásquez, *Historia*.

22. Morse, "Urban Development," 91.

23. Parry, *Spanish Seaborne Empire*, 134; Pérez, *Cuba*, 36; Stein and Stein, *Silver*, 32.

24. Kuethe, "Havana," 13.

25. Putnam, "To Study the Fragments," 618.

26. The quotation is from Champlain, *Narrative*, 44, who visited Havana in 1602.

27. This point is developed by Elliot, *Empires*.

28. Chaunu, *Sevilla*, 222–23, 322; MacCleod, "Spain and America," 370; Lorenzo Sanz, *Comercio*, 2:236–38.

29. *Relación y estragos*, 1555.

Chapter Two

1. The valuable series compiled by Chaunu and Chaunu, *Séville et l'Atlantique*, is very useful, but only for the transoceanic movement.

2. Traslado de provisión de la Audiencia de Santo Domingo, Havana, 26 July 1553, CO-DOIN II, 6:347–55.

3. Many of the vessels devoted to the intercolonial trade were smaller than those used in the Carrera, so this may not be true in terms of tonnage or cargo space. For the figures mentioned here, see Chaunu and Chaunu, *Séville et l'Atlantique*, vol. 6, pt. 2, pp. 638–39.

4. References to these ships appear in nonfiscal local sources such as notarial records.

5. RC of 13 February 1569, ANC, Reales Ordenes y Cédulas, leg. 229, no. 1.

6. Pérez, *Winds of Change*, 8.

7. Fisher, *Economic Aspects*, 64.

8. Sella, "European Industries," 360; Morineau, "Revoir Seville," 283. Colonial exports have been much better studied. For a recent and excellent assessment of this trade, see Phillips, "Growth," 34–101. See also Lorenzo Sanz, *Comercio*, 1:545–626, and Chaunu, *Sevilla*, 315–17.

9. Linschoten, *Discours*, 116; Molá, *Silk Industry*, 130–31; Fragoso, *Discurso*, fol. 38; Nieto-Galán, *Colouring Textiles*, 17; Boyajian, *Portuguese Trade*, 44–45; Lorenzo Sanz, *Comercio*, 1:392–93. On indigo production in Central America, see MacLeod, *Spanish Central America*, 176–78.

10. Lorenzo Sanz, *Comercio*, 1:548, estimates that cochineal represented 42 percent of the value of colonial imports in Seville between 1550 and 1600, compared with 10 percent for indigo.

11. Molá, *Silk Industry*, 120–21; Schneider, "Anthropology," 427; Brunelle, *New World Merchants*, 17; Lorenzo Sanz, *Comercio*, 1:549–85.

12. Molá, *Silk Industry*, 130.

13. Juan Maldonado Barnuevo a SM, 11 June 1600, AGI, SD, leg. 100, ramo 1.

14. Sarsaparilla was frequently mentioned by authors dealing with New World drugs. See Thevet, *Cosmographie*, 2:973; Fragoso, *Discurso*, fol. 104; Anania, *Universal*, bk. 4, fol. 5; Hernandez, *Quatro libros*, fol. 165v; Arias de Benavides, *Secretos*, fol. 15.

15. Hernandez, *Quatro libros*, fol. 39v. Hernandez died in 1587; his remarkable pharmacopoeia was not published until the next century. For ginger and cassia fistula exports,

see Lorenzo Sanz, *Comercio*, 1:606, 609–10. For the medicinal uses of cassia fistula, see also Acosta, *Tractado*, 131, and Fragoso, *Discurso*, fol. 77v.

16. Hernandez, *Quatro libros*, fol. 177v.; Fragoso, *Discurso*, 41. The English reference comes from "Report of a Voyage Undertaken for the West Indies by Christopher Newport," in Hakluyt, *Voyages*, 569.

17. Champlain, *Narrative*, 45. For similar testimonies, probably based on Champlain's firsthand account, see Ordoñez, *Viage*, fol. 240v, and Abbot, *Description*, no page.

18. For comparative export figures, see Lorenzo Sanz, *Comercio*, 1:620–21, who uses and adds to the figures compiled by Chaunu and Chaunu, *Séville et l'Atlantique*. For a discussion of the importance of hides in Cuban exports in the sixteenth century, see Marrero, *Cuba*, 2:176–77. For a discussion of trends in the seventeenth century in comparison with La Española, see de la Fuente, "Población."

19. Rapp, *Industry*, 9. On leather production in other areas of Europe, see Sella, "European Industries," 356–57, and Bottin, "Structures," 977. On prices in Seville, see Chaunu and Chaunu, *Séville et l'Atlantique*, vol. 5, pt. 2, p. 1016.

20. Vicens Vives, *Economic History*, 383; Braudel, *Mediterranean*, 2:834. See also Vázquez de Prada, *Siglos XVI y XVII*, 594–95; Le Flem, *Frustración*, 60–62; Minchinton, "Patterns," 131.

21. In terms of tonnage, wine was the largest European export to the New World, but textiles, particularly fabrics, commanded a higher value. In Havana, textiles were a close second in terms of value. Lorenzo Sanz, *Comercio*, 1:427; Morineau, "Revoir Seville," 283.

22. García de Palacio, *Instrución*, fol. 109; Pérez-Mallaína, *Spain's Men*, 141–42; Minchinton, "Patterns," 123–24; Ruiz, *Spanish Society*, 209–13; Phillips, *Six Galleons*, 170, 241.

23. These figures are based on the registries of Havana's royal treasury, AGI, Contaduría, legs. 1089 and 1101. These pipes are described as containing 17.5 arrobas (262.5 liters) of wine.

24. Hakluyt, *Voyages*, 502; Abbeville, *Abrege*, 89. On Canarian wine's reputation, see also Boemus, *Libro*, fol. 250v; Abbot, *Description*; Stafford, *Geographicall and Anthologicall Description*, 43; and Avity, *Etats*, 205.

25. Lorenzo Sanz, *Comercio*, 1:467.

26. Gaspar Ruiz de Pereda a SM, 18 June 1609, AGI, SD, leg. 100, ramo 4; Oficio contra Francisco Díaz, 1595, AGI, Escribanía de Cámara, leg. 36B. On the Canaries trade with the New World, including contraband, see Peraza de Ayala, *Régimen*.

27. Autos seguidos por Juan de Talabera, Havana, 16 March 1606, AGI, Escribanía de Cámara, leg. 38B, no. 2.

28. Morineau, "Revoir Seville," 283; Vázquez de Prada, *Siglos XVI y XVII*, 391–97. The importance of Jerez among Spanish wine exports is confirmed by García Fuentes, "Viñedo," 31–33.

29. Sella, "European Industries," 355–58; de Vries, *First Modern Economy*, 271; Mazzaoui, *Textiles*, xiii; Braudel, *Mediterranean*, 1:427–33.

30. Benedict, "Rouen's Foreign Trade," 33. The quotation of Rouen's city council is from Sella, "European Industries," 363. See also Bottin, "Structures," 975–95; Brunelle, *New World Merchants*, 10–47; Phillips, *Spain's Golden Fleece*, 246.

31. The quotation is in Braudel, *Mediterranean*, 1:478. See also Woronoff, *Histoire*, 70–71; Gascon, *Grand Commerce*, 1:74; Brunelle, *New World Merchants*, 15; and Montgomery, *Textiles*, 177, 187–88, 372.

32. Mazzaoui, *Textiles*, xxv; Lorenzo Sanz, *Comercio*, 1:458. Scholars have noted, however, that the French produced their best cloths with linens imported from Holland. See Gascon, *Grand Commerce*, 252–53, and Woronoff, *Histoire*, 73.

33. On the production and commercialization of Holland linens, see de Vries, *First Modern Economy*, 290–91; Benedict, "Rouen's Foreign Trade," 55; and Sella, "European Industries," 363. The quotation comes from Fernández de Enciso, *Suma* (1530), fol. 28.

34. Wilson, "Cloth Production," 209–14; Sella, "European Industries," 377–78; Benedict, "Rouen's Foreign Trade," 49; Kerridge, *Textile Manufactures*, 25–27; Rapp, *Industry*, 76.

35. Wilson, "Cloth Production," 213–14; de Vries, *First Modern Economy*, 283; Kerridge, *Textile Manufactures*, 9–10, 89–102; Montgomery, *Textiles*, 159–60, 342–43; Lorenzo Sanz, *Comercio*, 1:458.

36. Phillips, *Spain's Golden Fleece*; García Sanz, "Competitivos," 397–434; Vicens Vives, *Economic History*, 352; Vázquez de Prada, *Siglos XVI y XVII*, 577–94; Le Flem, *Frustración*, 60–65.

37. The questions about silk production in Seville have been raised by Lorenzo Sanz, *Comercio*, 1:432. For the traditional – and it seems correct – assessment, see Vázquez de Prada, *Siglos XVI y XVII*, 590–91, and Mauro, *Europa*, 25.

38. On Lyon's silk production and the use of Spanish raw silk, see Gascon, *Grand Commerce*, 1:65, who estimates that about 15 percent of the silk processed in Lyon was imported from Spain. For a lower estimate, see Woronoff, *Histoire*, 73.

39. The quotation about Milan is from Sella, *Ducato*, 111. See also Molá, *Silk Industry*, 15–18, and Rapp, *Industry*, 7.

40. Molá, *Silk Industry*, 24, 55–75, 110–30; Kerridge, *Textile Manufactures*, 126; Vázquez de Prada, *Siglos XVI y XVII*, 588; Rambert, *Histoire*, 3:472.

41. Borah, *Silk Raising*; María y Campos and Castelló Yturbide, *Historia*, 37–58; Bazant, "Evolution," 59–61; Lorenzo Sanz, *Comercio*, 1:440–41.

42. Motolinía, *Motolinía's History*, 326.

43. Borah, *Silk Raising*, 87–96; Miño Grijalva, *Manufactura*, 57; María y Campos and Castelló Yturbide, *Historia*, 60–66; Bazant, "Evolution," 61.

44. For sixteenth-century descriptions of Chinese commodities, particularly silk, see Münster, *Treatyse*; Linschoten, *Discours*, 38; and Román, *Republicas*, 3, fol. 220v. For a good example of the Europeans' knowledge of China, see González de Mendoza, *Historia*. See also Dor-Ner, *Columbus*, 7–43.

45. On the Portuguese Carreira, see Boyajian, *Portuguese Trade*. On Chinese silk production and the Sino-Spanish trade via the Manila galleon, see Atwell, "Ming China," 376–416, and Chaunu, *Filipinas*. For descriptions of silk production in China see Kuhn, *Textile Technology*, 247–417; Heijdra, "Socio-Economic Development," 502, 512–13; and the remarkable seventeenth-century account of Sung, *T'ien-Kung K'ai-wu*, 35–59.

46. Gómez, *Discursos*, fol. 72.

47. Salvucci, *Textiles*, 39.

48. For a testimony about this reputation, see Fernández de Enciso, *Suma* (1530), fol. 30.

49. The New Spain obrajes have been studied by Salvucci, *Textiles*; Miño Grijalva, *Manufactura*; Viqueira and Urquiola, *Obrajes*; and Bazant, "Evolution."

50. Quezada, "Tributos," 73; Garcia Bernal, *Población*, 379; Borah and Cook, *Price Trends*, 26; Bazant, "Evolution," 66; Miño Grijalva, *Manufactura*, 28.

51. On these commercial networks and the presence of Indian merchandise in the Manila galleon, see Subrahmanyam, *Portuguese Empire*, 116-22; Boyajian, *Portuguese Trade*, 47, 76-81; McPherson, *Indian Ocean*; Chaunu, *Filipinas*, 146-47; and Schurz, *El galeón*, 68-69. On the production of cotton fabrics in Ming China, see Heijdra, "Socio-Economic Development," 496-513; Atwell, "Ming China," 404; and Kuhn, *Textile Technology*, 57-59, 187-98.

52. Minchinton, "Patterns," 132-33; Gascon, *Grand Commerce*, 249; Lester and Oerke, *Illustrated History*, 470-561; Kerridge, *Textile Manufactures*, 24.

53. Sella, *Ducato*, 112; Sella, "Rise and Fall," 106-26.

54. Woronoff, *Histoire*, 71. See also Gascon, *Grand Commerce*, 1:56-58.

55. L. Fiovaranti, *Dello speccio di scientia universale* (1572), quoted by Molá, *Silk Industry*, xiii.

56. Lorenzo Sanz, *Comercio*, 1:428-30; Salvucci, *Textiles*, 39.

57. Despite its importance, shipbuilding in Spain has received little scholarly attention. There is, however, some debate about the state of the Spanish shipbuilding industry in the late sixteenth century. For contrasting points of view concerning the industry, see Vicens Vives, *Economic History*, 353-54; Goodman, *Spanish Naval Power*, 109-37; and Casado Soto, "Atlantic Shipping," 99-101. On Spanish shipbuilding, see Phillips, *Six Galleons*, and Serrano Mangas, *Función*.

58. Phillips, *Six Galleons*, 39; Martin, "Ships." For a good summary of the evolution of European naval technologies, see Chaunu, *L'expansion*, 273-308, and Unger, *Dutch Shipbuilding*, 24-35. On shipbuilding in Havana, see chapter 5.

59. Martin, "Ships," 63-68; Phillips, *Six Galleons*, 78-83; Serrano Mangas, *Función*, 127-59.

60. On Spanish iron production and European competition, see García Fuentes, *Sevilla*, 41-44, 105-45; Fernández Alvarez and Díaz Medina, *Austrias*, 116-19; and Le Flem, *Frustración*, 66-68.

61. The reference is taken from Kamen, *Empire*, 168-169, who analyzes Spain's dependency on military imports.

62. On this initial period of the Atlantic slave trade and the expansion of slavery to the Atlantic islands, see Thornton, *Africa*, 21-42; Blackburn, *Making of New World Slavery*, 97-123; Curtin, *Rise and Fall*, 3-28; Lobo Cabrera, *Esclavitud*; Vieira, "Sugar Islands"; and Phillips, *Slavery*, 131-70. On the importance of slavery in Iberia during this period, see Franco Silva, *Esclavitud*; Saunders, *Social History*, Cortés López, *Esclavitud*; and Pike, *Aristocrats*, 170-92.

63. On the slave trade during the sixteenth century, and particularly the "licenses" system, see Lorenzo Sanz, *Comercio*, 1:511-28, and Garcia Fuentes, "Introducción," 249-74. Despite its legalistic tone, the classic and much quoted work of George Scelle, *La traite*, remains useful.

64. By far the best study of the asientos during the so-called Portuguese period (1595-

1640) continues to be that of Vila Vilar, *Hispanoamérica*. Also useful is Lorenzo Sanz, *Comercio*, 1:528–42. The contract with the first asentista, Pedro Gomez Reynel (or Reinel) appears in Encinas, *Cedulario*, 4:401–10.

65. RC of 11 May 1526, 13 January 1531, and 1 May 1543, in Encinas, *Cedulario*, 4:383–84. A similar principle was endorsed by the ordinances approved by local authorities in La Española in 1528. See Malagón Barceló, *Código*, 135.

66. Concerning Moors and Berbers, see RC of 19 December 1531, 14 August 1543, and 13 November 1550, in Encinas, *Cedulario*, 4:383. On slaves from the eastern Mediterranean, see RC of 16 July 1550, in ibid. See also Ley 19, Título 26, Libro 9, of the *Recopilación*.

67. RC of 28 September 1532, CODOIN II, 10:141; Cortés Alonso, "Procedencia," 127; Alvarez D'Almada, *Tratado*, 9, 26; and Carreira, *Cabo Verde*, 443.

68. Petición de los procuradores de Cuba, 17 March 1540 and 28 April 1542, CODOIN II, 6:95, 173.

69. CODOIN II, 6:317; RC of 29 April 1566, ACAH, 2:63; Contrato con Juan Hernández de Espinosa, 20 October 1571, ACAH, 2:289; Wright, *Historia* (1927), 1:58; Marrero, *Cuba*, 2:356.

70. Chaunu and Chaunu, *Séville et l'Atlantique*, 3:378, 432, 454, 492, 544, 550, 552.

71. For examples see Mellafe, *Breve historia*, 83, and Deive, *Esclavitud*, 1:257.

72. Vila Vilar, *Hispanoamérica*, 14, 158. On the importance of Cartagena as a regional distribution center of slaves, see also Vidal Ortega, *Cartagena*, 117–65.

73. For an example of the doctrinal discussions surrounding the baptism of adult slaves, see the Diocesan Synod of Santo Domingo, 1576, in González, *Marco*, 152. For religious debates concerning enslavement, see Andrés-Gallego and García Añoveros, *Iglesia*, 119–29.

74. These figures were computed from ASCH, Libro Barajas de Bautismos, 1590–1600, and Libro Primero de Bautismos, 1600–1610. Unfortunately the Libro Primero is not the original but a later seventeenth-century copy that does not include slave baptisms beyond 1600.

75. ANC, PNH, ER, 1590, fol. 72v; Vila Vilar, "Asientos," 10; and the deposit made by Luis Lorenzo in the royal treasury of Havana, 24 September 1595, AGI, Contaduria, leg. 1091.

76. Autos seguidos por Pablo de Monteverde y consortes contra Pedro Gomez Reinel, 1597, AGI, Escribanía de Camara, leg. 36B, no. 7.

77. "Provision y ordernanza . . . que se ha de guardar en los puertos de la Carrera de las Indias en impedir que no se hagan arribadas," 17 January 1591, in Encinas, *Cedulario*, 4:166; Solórzano y Pereyra, *Política*, 5:23.

78. Curtin, *Atlantic Slave Trade*, 104. For a concrete example of the rarely used expression "Rivers of Cabo Verde," see the contract between Baltasar Fernandez del Campo (or Ocampo) and Esteban Díaz, in ANC, PNH, ER, 1609, fol. 871. For sixteenth-century descriptions of Guinea that coincide roughly with this view, see "Discurso de un gran capitano di mare francese del luoco di Dieppa sobre le navigationi fatte alla terra nuova dell'Indie occidentali," in Ramusio, *Navigationi*, 3, fol. 429; Boemus, *Libro*, fol. 329; Botero, *Relationi*, 1:154; and Mármol y Carvajal, *Segunda parte*, fol. 21v.

79. ANC, PNH, ER, 1600, fols. 113, 433. For the usage of the term "Guinea" in this sense, see Abbeville, *Abrege*, 53; Leblanc, *World*, 321; and Dapper, *Description*, 251.

80. The slaves from Seville are calculated from García Fuentes, "Introducción," 262.

81. El capitán Juan de la Parra con Hernán Manrique de Rojas, AGI, Justicia, leg. 979, no. 9, ramo 2; Autos hechos en la Habana antes el escribano real Pedro de Herrera, July 1585, AGI, SD, leg. 118, ramo 4. On the importance of contraband concerning the slave trade and the Portuguese participation in it, see Vila Vilar, *Hispanoamérica*, 157–82. On the "arribadas" of ships dispatched to Brazil, see Mellafe, *Breve historia*, 46.

82. ACAH, September 1584, October 1616; Pedro de Valdés a SM, 18 August 1603, AGI, SD, leg. 129.

83. This grouping by area follows closely the export regions (and cultural zones) proposed by Thornton, *Africa*, 117–19, 187–92, with the addition of Mozambique (which is not included in his discussion). Other authors divide the third area into two, one centered around São Tomé and Congo, the other around Luanda and Angola. See Curtin, *Atlantic Slave Trade*, 103–16; Mellafe, *Breve historia*, 73; and Aguirre Beltrán, *Población*, 99–150.

84. These results do not agree with the estimates of Thornton, *Africa*, 118–19, who argues that as early as 1550 half of the slaves exported from Africa came from the Congo-Angola region. Our results are closer to those of Curtin, *Atlantic Slave Trade*, 104–109, who summarizes the figures compiled by Chaunu and Chaunu, *Séville et l'Atlantique*. Curtin estimates that between 1581 and 1595, 47 percent of slaves transported to Spanish America came from the Cape Verde region (including those embarked through the Canaries). In part, however, his figure is lower than ours because he counts all the ships from "Guinea" as coming from the Gulf of Guinea.

85. Carreira, *Cabo Verde*; Barry, "Senegambia," 262–73; Diagne, "African Political, Economic and Social Structures," 40–42; Malowist, "Struggle," 1–12; Aguirre Beltrán, *Población*, 114–29.

86. Vila Vilar, *Hispanoamérica*, 27, 104–11; Vansina, "Kongo," 558–63.

87. Aguirre Beltrán, *Población*, 123–37; Malowist, "Struggle," 2–11; Voisin, *Trois mondes*, fol. 44; Botero, *Relationi*, 1:153.

88. Salim, "East Africa," 756–67; Aguirre Beltrán, *Población*, 142–48; Lopez and Pigafetta, *Relaçao*, 135. For examples of slaves from "Yndia" or "Yndia de Portugal," see ASCH, Libro Barajas de Matrimonios de Españoles, 1584–1622, fol. 131v; ANC, PNH, ER, 1630, fol. 942v.

89. Incoming ships from other colonial territories represented 70 percent in Santo Domingo (1603–31), 75 percent in Cartagena de Indias (1590–95), 40 percent in Puerto Rico (1621–32), 65 percent in Nombre de Dios (1550–79), and 55 percent in Veracruz (1590–95). The same imbalance was evident in Havana until at least 1650. See Gil-Bermejo, *La Española*, 129; Borrego Plá, *Cartagena*, 68; Vila Vilar, *Puerto Rico*, 41; Chaunu and Chaunu, *Séville et l'Atlantique*, vol. 6, pt. 2, pp. 714–94, 814–30; and Macías, *Cuba*, 157. See also Vidal Ortega, *Cartagena*, on the making of a regional market in the Caribbean.

90. ANC, PNH, ER, 1602, fol. 311; 1600, fol. 859.

91. For a discussion of this adjustment to the new commercial realities, see Pérez Herrero, "Estructura," 809–10. On the importance of contraband in the region, see Andrews, *Spanish Caribbean*, 79–80, and Vidal Ortega, *Cartagena*, 100–115.

92. On contemporaries' perceptions about Chinese porcelain, see Román, *Republicas*, 3, fol. 220v, and Linschoten, *Discours*, 38. The contemporary Chinese testimony is that of Sung, *T'ien-Kung K'ai-wu*, 147. On the production of porcelain in Ming China, see also Atwell, "Ming China," 379–80, 391, and McPherson, *Indian Ocean*, 172.

93. Phillips, *Six Galleons*, 169–72; Pérez-Mallaína, *Spain's Men*, 140–45. On Havana's dependence on Mexican food imports, see Pérez Herrero, "Estructura," 788. On Jamaican supplies, see Morales Padrón, *Jamaica*, 308.

94. RC of 24 October 1567, ACAH, June 1568.

95. Baltasar del Castillo Ahedo a SM, 12 February 1577, in Connor, *Colonial Records*, 1:218.

96. Fragoso, *Discurso*, 113; Hernandez, *Quatro libros*, fol. 21v; Hakluyt, *Voyages*, 361.

97. Hoffman, *Spanish Crown*, 215. For later situado figures, see Sluiter, *Florida Situado*. For the use of the situado in Havana, see Autos hechos en la villa de la Habana, 1570, AGI, Justicia, leg. 980, no. 3; Hernán Pérez a SM, St. Augustine, 28 September 1567, AGI, SD, leg. 71, no. 1, fol. 367; and ANC, PNH, ER, 1595, fol. 157.

98. Chaunu, *Sevilla*, 87; Pérez de la Riva, *Barracón*, especially the essay "Una isla con dos historias"; and de la Fuente, "Población."

99. According to Governor Valdés, this road had existed since the times of the conquest. The road was important enough to be noted in seventeenth-century descriptions of the island. Valdés a SM, Havana, 25 September 1604, AGI, SD, leg. 100, ramo 1; Barrozo, "Derrotero," fol. 63v.

100. El Obispo Sarmiento a SM, Santiago de Cuba, 15 July 1544, in CODOIN II, 6:221–32.

101. Testimonio de la visita de Juan del Castillo, Obispo de Cuba, August 1569–April 1570, ANC, Donativos y Remisiones, leg. 209, no. 395; Residencia que fue tomada al doctor Angulo, 1556, AGI, Justicia, leg. 83.

102. El fiscal con Felipe Merelos, 1567, AGI, Justicia, leg. 999, no. 2, ramo 3.

103. Información hecha por el gobernador Manuel de Rojas, 24 September 1534, ANC, AH, leg. 24, no. 33; López de Velasco, *Geografía*, 114; Testimonio de Juan del Castillo; Marrero, *Cuba*, 3:5–6.

104. Testimonio del escribano de cabildo de Sancti Spiritus, 12 December 1531, ANC, AH, leg. 52, no. 450. Testimonio de Juan del Castillo.

105. Testimonio de Juan del Castillo; El cabildo de la Habana a SM, 8 January 1602, ANC, AH, leg. 85, no. 329; Marrero, *Cuba*, 2:191; Macías, *Cuba*, 22.

106. Valdés a SM, 18 July 1603, AGI, SD, leg. 129; ACAH, September 1606, May 1607; Marrero, *Cuba*, 4:134; García del Pino, "Obispo."

107. For examples of these testimonies, see Informativo del canónigo Alvaro de Quesada, 18 February 1563, AGI, SD, leg. 150, ramo 1; Juan Maldonado Barnuevo a SM, 16 March 1600, ibid., leg. 100, ramo 1; and El cabildo de la Habana a SM, 8 January 1602, ANC, AH, leg. 85, no. 329. Some outdated European geographic accounts still referred to Santiago as a major city, however. For examples, see Boemus, *Libro*, fol. 319; Girava, *Dos libros*, 222; and Botero, *Relaciones*, fol. 181v.

108. Vidal Ortega, *Cartagena*, 183–86.

109. Marrero, *Cuba*, 3:5. On Baracoa's reduced population, see Marrero, *Cuba*, 2:324; Juan de las Cabezas Altamirano a SM, 24 June 1606, AGI, SD, leg. 150, ramo 2. On contraband in the northwest of La Espanola and the forced "depopulation" of the area, see Hernández Tapia, "Despoblación," and Gil-Bermejo, *La Española*.

Chapter Three

1. The organization of the Carrera was done gradually. Important regulations were passed in 1561, 1562, 1573, and 1582, establishing two main principles: navigation outside the fleets was prohibited, and the returning vessels were to gather in Havana to sail with the fleets. See Encinas, *Cedulario*, 4:130, 137, and Veitía Linage, *Norte*, 557. On the organization of the fleets, see Haring, *Comercio*, 238, and Chaunu, *Sevilla*, 190–209.

2. Solórzano y Pereyra, *Política*, libro V, cap. XVIII, no. 19; "Provisión e instrucción para los generales de las flotas y armadas," 8 April 1573, in Encinas, *Cedulario*, 4:113.

3. The tax was approved by the RC of 11 March 1559 and revoked by the RC of 3 October 1562, both in AGI, Contaduría, leg. 1101. An RC of 2 December 1563 reestablished the tax temporarily to build a tower at the entrance of the bay. Wright, *Historia* (1927), 1:200.

4. RC of 23 July 1581 and 18 June 1582, in Encinas, *Cedulario*, 4:90. This policy contributed to the decline of the mercantile economy in La Española. See Moya Pons, *Historia*, 99.

5. "Provisión e instrucción para los generales de las flotas y armadas," in Encinas, *Cedulario*, 4:110.

6. ACAH, June 1562; Chilton's 1571 testimony is reproduced in García Icazbalceta, *Relaciones*, 40–42; Exposición de la Universidad de maestres, pilotos y señores de navío de Sevilla a S.M., 1572, ANC, AH, leg. 85, no. 312.

7. Benzoni, *Historia*, fol. 174; Juan Maldonado a SM, Havana, 1 December 1594, AGI, SD, leg. 127.

8. Champlain, *Narrative*, 45. Corn was in fact produced in Cuba, although not in quantities large enough to provision the fleets.

9. ACAH, June 1554.

10. The size of the fleets can be established using the figures compiled by Chaunu and Chaunu, *Séville et l'Atlantique*. For average numbers of mariners in merchant and military vessels, see Pérez-Mallaína, *Spain's Men*, 50–52. For a discussion of the local effects of these fleets in 1594, see Marrero, *Cuba*, 2:154.

11. ACAH, June 1551, May 1556.

12. Kula, *Problemas*, 503.

13. ACAH, July 1569.

14. In the early 1600s the cabildo began to appoint specialized officials for these purposes. See ACAH, June 1602, November 1603, March 1604, April and October 1608. Hevia Bolaños, *Labyrintho*, 121, refers to the importance of these public officials in Spanish cities.

15. ACAH, January 1569, January 1571. See also March and April 1569 for similar regulations.

16. ACAH, January 1569, January 1578; AGI, Contaduria, leg. 1090.

17. Residencia del gobernador Pérez de Angulo, 1556, AGI, Justicia, leg. 83.

18. Marrero, *Cuba*, 2:276.

19. ACAH, April 1569.

20. ACAH, January 1585; ANC, PNH, ER, 1590, fol. 501v; ACAH, April 1569.

21. RC of 5 March 1581, AGI, Contaduría, leg. 1088 (2).

22. For the monetary conversions in the Spanish colonies, see Carrera Stampa, "Evolu-

tion"; Borah and Cook, *Price Trends*, 9–10; Rubio Serano, "Unidades"; and Phillips, *Six Galleons*, 228.

23. ACAH, January 1551; Marrero, *Cuba*, 2:277–78.

24. Marrero, *Cuba*, 2:277; ACAH, May 1551, May 1552.

25. In Spain, by contrast, most monetary conversions were done using the maravedí. See Echagoyan, *Tablas*.

26. There is also evidence of a preference for Mexican silver over Peruvian. In 1566, Mexican silver was quoted at 65 reales per marco (8 ounces), compared with 55 reales per marco for Peruvian, and local residents were reluctant to accept payments in South American silver. See ACAH, August 1566.

27. El fiscal con Diego Merelos sobre haber tratado y contratado en las Indias, 1567, AGI, Justicia, leg. 999, no. 2. Hanega: a dry measure equivalent in Castile to 55.5 liters.

28. Residencia de Diego de Mazariegos, 1566, AGI, Justicia, leg. 89.

29. ANC, PNH, ER, 1578, fol. 55, in Rojas, *Indice*, 1:31. In Rojas citations, the first number is the number of the transaction, rather than page number.

30. All these calculations are based on ACAH, 1550–1610.

31. ACAH, April 1556.

32. Calle, *Instrucción*, fol. 16v–17.

33. A 1517 "opinion" was conclusive in this respect. See González Ferrando, "Dictamen," 291. See also Marrero, *Cuba*, 2:164–70.

34. All these figures are based on ACAH.

35. Hevia Bolaños, *Labyrintho*, 152.

36. ACAH, April 1556, February 1552; RC of 3 October 1562, AGI, Contaduría, leg. 1101

37. ACAH, January 1574.

38. ANC, PNH, ER, 1601, fol. 221v; 1596, fol. 172. See Pérez Herrero, "Estructura," 788.

39. Dr. Juan Ruiz del Prado, Inquisidor del Peru al Consejo de la Santa Inquisición, Havana, 17 August 1594, AHN, Inquisición, leg. 2178, no. 2; Melchor Sardo de Arana a SM, 26 August 1580, in Llaverías, *Papeles*, 1:80.

40. Based on Chaunu and Chaunu, *Séville et l'Atlantique*, 3:504–69, and the almojarifazgo accounts in AGI, Contaduria, leg. 1091. It is nearly impossible to establish the exact number of vessels traveling with each of these fleets, as the configuration of the fleets changed constantly. But roughly, these are the numbers, based on the sources mentioned above: fleet of Osorio, 29; armada of Coloma, 9; armadilla of Soto, 6; fleet of Aramburu, 59; fleet of Flores, 41.

41. Marrero, *Cuba*, 2:162; Chaunu and Chaunu, *Séville et l'Atlantique*, 3:564n11.

42. Gonzalo Pérez de Angulo a SM, Havana, 23 December 1555, AGI, SD, leg. 99, ramo 1; Gabriel de Luján a SM, Havana, 10 July 1587, ANC, AH, leg. 83, no. 175.

43. Forty-five percent of promises of payment were made for the months of June–September, to coincide with the shipping season. About 5 percent of all made explicit reference to the fleets or the situado. Christmas was another date favored in these promises of payment (10 percent). For a concrete example, see ANC, PNH, ER, 1604, fol. 494v.

44. Morse, "Urban Development," 91; Lufríu, *Impulso*; Friedländer, *Historia*.

45. ACAH, August 1587.

46. ACAH, October 1600.

47. García Icazbalceta, *Relaciones*, 40. For Hawkins, see Hakluyt, *Voyages*, 515; on Drake's intentions, Dudley, *Arcano*, vol. 1, bk. 2, p. 5, who reproduces the account of an English pilot who traveled with Drake's expedition in 1594. See also Kelsey, *Drake*, 272–74, 378.

48. Hakluyt, *Voyages*, 515, 531; Linschoten, *Discours*, 222.

49. Anania, *Universal*, bk. 4, fol. 11; Botero, *Relationi*, 1:226; Codogno, *Nuovo Itinerario*, 306–8, 426.

50. Champlain, *Narrative*, 44; Mercator, *Atlas*, fol. 701; Laet, *L'Histoire*, 18; Linda, *Descrittioni*, 106–7.

51. Fernández de Enciso, *Suma* (1546), 442; Hera y de la Barra, *Repertorio*, fol. 43; Ordoñez, *Viage*, fol. 240. It should be noted that the previous edition of Fernández de Enciso's *Suma* (1530) did not include this reference to Havana.

52. Manuel, "Derrotero," fol. 16; Oliva, "Portolano"; "An excellent Ruttier for the Islands of the West Indies, and for Tierra Firma, and Nueva Espanna," in Hakluyt, *Voyages*, 603–13; Figueiredo, *Roteiro*.

53. The quotation is from a letter of Major Smith, governor of the Isle of Providence, 1665, in Ogilby, *America*, 336.

54. RC of 20 May 1538 and RC of 9 February 1556, in Wright, *Historia* (1927), 1:189, 192.

55. The estimate is Hoffman's, *Spanish Crown*; see also Kamen, *Empire*, 258.

56. Andrews, *Elizabethan Privateering*, 166; Andrews, *Trade*, 283. Gabriel de Luján a SM, Havana, 31 April 1583, AGI, SD, leg. 153; Marrero, *Cuba*, 2:192.

57. ACAH, March and April 1553.

58. ACAH, June, September, and October 1569.

59. Drake's life and maritime activities are well known. For a good biography, see Kelsey, *Drake*.

60. "Parecer de Don Alvaro Bazan, marques de Santa Cruz, tocante la Armada de Francisco Draque, estando en las Yslas de Vayona: Hecha en Lisboa a 26 de octubre, estilo de Espanna de 1585," in Hakluyt, *Voyages*, 530–32; Marrero, *Cuba*, 2:211–16; Gabriel de Luján a SM, Havana, 4 May 1586, AGI, SD, leg. 99. The houses that were demolished were paid for with royal funds from New Spain; see AGN, Archivo Histórico de Hacienda, leg. 424, no. 10, 130 and 131.

61. ACAH, March and April 1586.

62. Kelsey, *Drake*, 274.

63. RC of 23 November 1588, in Encinas, *Cedulario*, 4:50. On Antonelli's work around the Caribbean, including Havana, see Angulo Iñiguez, *Antonelli*; Calderón Quijano, *Historia de las Fortificaciones*, 16–25; Ward, *Imperial Panama*, 162–68; Blanes, *Castillo*; Wright, *Historia* (1927); and Weiss, *Arquitectura*, 36–42.

64. ACAH, April 1551, March 1552, April 1553, February 1556, January 1559; RC of 20 May 1538 and RC of 9 February 1556, both in Wright, *Historia* (1927), 1:184, 192.

65. RC of 2 December 1563, in Wright, *Historia* (1927), 1:200; Manuel, "Derrotero," fol. 16; Escalante de Mendoza, "Itinerario," fol. 217; García Icazbalceta, *Relaciones*, 41.

66. ACAH, February 1556, February 1570, October 1571; Juan Bautista de Rojas y Manuel Díaz a SM, Havana, 9 December 1582, in Llaverías, *Papeles*, 2:21; Roig de Leuchsenring, *Monumentos*, 3:51–52; Wright, *Historia* (1927), 1:122–23.

67. Francisco Calvillo a SM, 6 April 1581, and Juan Bautista de Rojas a SM, 20 February 1586, both in Wright, *Historia* (1927), 1:240; 2:31; ACAH, November 1597; Champlain, *Narrative*, 44.

68. See Kamen, *Empire*, 261.

69. Instrucción que S.M. dio a Juan de Tejeda, 23 November 1588, in Encinas, *Cedulario*, 4:50–51; Macías, *Cuba*, 245–62; RC of 21 November 1590, AGI, Contaduría, leg. 1092; Blanes, *Castillo*, 17–24; Antonelli a Juan de Ibarra, Havana, 18 June 1594, in Wright, *Historia* (1927), 2:194.

70. Ordoñez, *Viage*, fol. 240; Heylyn, *Cosmographie*, 1097; Laet, *L'Histoire*, 18; Juan de Porrúa Canavate to López Canavate, Havana, 17 October 1590, in Hakluyt, *Voyages*, 559.

71. We are using as a reference the annual averages included in table 3.3. These averages, however, have been calculated using the records of the only surviving notarial registry (one out of three), so in absolute terms they probably represent about one-third of the real totals. The percentages mentioned here are based on this assumption. Military expenditures were calculated from the royal accounts in AGI, Contaduría, legs. 1088–1101.

72. Ibid., leg. 1093. This payment had been authorized by the RC of 18 December 1600, AGI, SD, leg. 100, ramo 1.

73. On the number of soldiers in La Fuerza, see the testimony of Gómez de Rojas Manrique, captain of the garrison (1575), in AGI, Justicia, leg. 41, no. 4. On salaries, RC of 21 November 1590, AGI, Contaduría, leg. 1092. On costs associated with the forts, see Maldonado Barnuevo a SM, 9 January 1594, in Wright, *Historia* (1927), 2:187, and RC of 18 December 1600, AGI, SD, leg. 100, ramo 1. Governor Maldonado later protested the change in salaries. See Wright, *Historia* (1927), 2:206–11.

74. Maldonado Barnuevo a Juan de Ibarra, 30 November 1594, and Maldonado Barnuevo a SM, 1 December 1594, in Wright, *Historia* (1927), 2:206, 210. As late as 1598 the governors of La Fuerza, La Punta, and El Morro were still trying to raise the soldiers' salaries to their 1580s levels. ANC, PNH, ER, 1600, fol. 411v.

75. Relación de la gente de guerra que hay en las fortalezas de la Habana, 2 September 1593, ANC, AH, leg. 84, no. 248; RC of 23 June 1593, AGI, Contaduría, leg. 1089.

76. RC of 17 January 1594 and Maldonado a Juan Ibarra, 30 November 1594, both in Wright, *Historia* (1927), 2:190, 206. Soldier figures are taken from AGI, Contaduría, leg. 1094, and El gobernador Gaspar Ruiz de Pereda a SM, 6 Janaury 1609, AGI, SD, leg. 100, ramo 4.

77. ANC, PNH, ER, 1600, fol. 731; 1585, fol. 701v, in Rojas, *Indice*, 1:654. On lodging, see ACAH, March 1586, August 1586, and October 1588. On supplies, Gerónimo de Quero a SM, 29 December 1606, AGI, SD, leg. 100, ramo 2.

78. RC of 2 August 1587, in Veitía Linage, *Norte*, 555; AGI, Contaduría, leg. 1089. On the galleys and their maritime use, see Chaunu, *L'expansion*, 274–77, and Balard, "Coastal Shipping," 133–34.

79. Botero, *Relationi*, 1:226 (this information is reproduced in the 1599 Spanish edition, *Relaciones*, fol. 181v); Mercator, *Atlas*, fol. 701.

80. Macías, *Cuba*, 328–35; Los oficiales reales a SM, 19 January 1608, AGI, Escribanía de Cámara, leg. 74A, pieza 8; Ruiz de Pereda a SM, 28 January 1609, AGI, SD, leg. 100, ramo 4.

81. For references, see Tejeda a SM, 29 September 1591, in Wright, *Historia* (1927), 2:180; Maldonado Barnuevo a SM, 11 June 1600, AGI, SD, leg. 100, ramo 1.

Chapter Four

1. Braudel, *Civilization*, 1:8.

2. As Kinsbruner, *Colonial*, 35, notes, the category of "vecino" was not consistently applied in different times and places.

3. Minguijón Adrián, *Historia*; Escriche, *Diccionario*; Ley 2, Título 24, Partida 4. For the ordinances, see Ley 8, Título 5, Libro 4, of the *Recopilación*.

4. For this discussion, see Borah, *Siglo de la depresión*, 21; Cook and Borah, *Ensayos*, 2:87; and Sánchez-Albornoz, *Población*, 90. For Cuba, see Inglis, "Historical Demography," 69; Marrero, *Cuba*, 2:325; Castillo Meléndez, "Emigración," 419; and de la Fuente, "Población," 62–63.

5. Elvas, *Relaçam*, fols. 11–13. Elvas seems to equate "casas" with "vecinos." Visita pastoral del Obispo Sarmiento, 1544, CODOIN II, 6:221-32.

6. El cabildo de la Habana a SM, 20 March 1553, CODOIN II, 6:345; "Relación de los vecinos y moradores que residían en esta villa," 20 December 1555, CODOIN II, 6:429-34.

7. Testimonio de la visita de Juan del Castillo, Obispo de Cuba, August 1569-April 1570, ANC, Donativos y Remisiones, leg. 209, no. 395. For a discussion of the terms used in this document and its implications, see de la Fuente, "Población." Other sources estimated the population of Guanabacoa to be smaller, however. A Franciscan friar reported that "forty Indian vecinos" lived there in 1577. Francisco de la Cruz a SM, 19 January 1577, AGI, SD, leg. 153, ramo 1.

8. RC of 29 April 1566, ACAH, May 1569; Exposición de la Universidad de maestres, pilotos y señores de navío de Sevilla a S.M., 1572, ANC, AH, leg. 85, no. 312.

9. The authority to distribute land in Mexico was centralized under the viceroy and the audiencia as early as 1535. See Altman, "Spanish Society," 418, and Marrero, *Cuba*, 2:58, 63. According to Solórzano y Pereyra, *Política*, libro V, cap. XIII, no. 26, and libro VI, cap. XII, no. 5, the crown took the power to distribute land away from the cabildos, although in practice whether or not they continued to distribute land probably varied from place to place. It is noteworthy that in his careful study of seventeenth-century Popayán, Marzahl, *Town*, 55-73, does not discuss land distribution among the functions of the cabildo.

10. RC of 29 April 1566, ACAH, May 1569. Petitions to renew these grants in ACAH, July 1575, January 1578, July 1585. RC of 30 September 1586, mentioned in Wright, *Santiago*, 93; RC of 3 February 1569, AGI, Justicia, leg. 1002, no. 1, ramo 5. The reference to "depopulation" is in RC of 9 April 1576, AGI, Contratación, leg. 2469.

11. ACAH, July 1585, May 1588. The king lowered export taxes to Havana again in 1592. See AGI, Contaduría, leg. 1091.

12. ACAH, December 1584, March 1597.

13. Mentioned in El fiscal con la isla de Cuba sobre ciertos almojarifazgos, 1572, AGI, Justicia, leg. 1001, no. 3.

14. Representación del Procurador de la Habana Lope de Vallejo, 2 March 1062, AHN, Inquisición, leg. 2178, no. 2.

15. Boyd-Bowman, "Patterns," 602.

16. See in particular Jacobs, "Legal and Illegal Emigration," 59-80.

17. Auto del Gobernador Valdés, 17 November 1607, AGI, SD, leg. 100, ramo 2; Marrero, *Cuba*, 2:154, 346, and 3:6–7; Jacobs, "Legal and Illegal Emigration," 76–77.

18. Fernández de Oviedo y Valdés, *Historia*, 1:54. Anglería's piece was written in 1489, quoted in Kamen, *Empire*, 17.

19. Altman, "New World," 38.

20. ANC, PNH, ER, 1590, fol. 132v; 1606, fol. 380; 1605, fol. 573.

21. Ibid., 1604, fol. 3v; Altman, "New World," 37.

22. Pérez Bustamante, "Regiones," 88; Rodríguez Arzúa, "Regiones," 702; Peraza de Ayala, *Régimen*, 27; Boyd-Bowman, "Patterns," 590.

23. Benzoni, *Historia*, fol. 1; Peraza de Ayala, *Régimen*, 27.

24. Diego Fernández de Quiñones a SM, 12 December 1582, ANC, AH, leg. 82, no. 110; Valdés a SM, 26 November 1606, ibid., leg. 86, no. 347.

25. See RC of 28 February 1575, in Veitía Linage, *Norte*, 309. On the composition of Spanish emigration by gender, see Sánchez-Albornoz, *Población*, 87, and Boyd-Bowman, "Patterns," 599.

26. Sánchez de Moya a SM, Santiago de Cuba, 8 May 1611, AGI, SD, leg. 451. On Canarian migration to Cuba during the late seventeenth century, see Castillo Meléndez, "Emigración," and Guanche Pérez, *Significación*.

27. These partial life histories, reconstructed from our various databases, are based on information from many sources, particularly the notarial records, cabildo records, parish registries, and fiscal documentation from AGI, Contaduría.

28. Ruiz de Pereda a SM, 3 August 1610, AGI, SD, leg. 100, ramo 5.

29. Ruiz de Pereda a SM, 20 September 1608, ibid., ramo 3.

30. RC of 18 October 1607, AGI, Contratación, leg. 2841.

31. ANC, PNH, ER, 1600, fol. 99; 1602, fol. 246.

32. Boyd-Bowman, *Indice*, xli; RC of 4 April 1531, ANC, AH, leg. 55, no. 592; RC of 10 November 1525, ANC, AH, leg. 52, no. 430.

33. Diego Fernández de Quiñones a SM, 12 December 1582, no. 110.

34. For the impact of 1580 on Portuguese emigration, see Magalhaes Godinho, "Portuguese Emigration," 17–19; for Cuba, see Macías, *Cuba*, 30.

35. This list is in Valdés a SM, 22 August 1607, AGI, SD, leg. 100, ramo 2 (also in ANC, AH, leg. 86, no. 355). On the legal condition of immigrants' children, see Veitía Linage, *Norte*, 336.

36. Valdés a SM, 25 September 1602 and 15 October 1605, AGI, SD, leg. 100, ramo 2.

37. This is based on Valdés a SM, 22 August 1607.

38. In addition to the local sources used to reconstruct these life stories, for Mendes de Noronha we also used Demanda de naturaleza de Enrique Mendez y Diego de Noroña, 1608, AGI, Escribanía de Cámara, leg. 74A.

39. Ibid. See also the testament of Hernán Rodríguez Tavares in ANC, PNH, ER, 1604, fol. 76.

40. Some of his personal information comes from Simón Fernandez Leyton, mercander contra Francisco de Angulo, 1608, AGI, Escribanía de Cámara, leg. 74A, no. 12.

41. Earlier regulations are spelled out in the RC of 14 July 1561 and that of 21 February

1562, in Veitía Linage, *Norte*, 331; RC of 2 October 1608, AGI, Escribanía de Cámara, leg. 74A. The RC of 1608 is also mentioned by Veitía.

42. RC of 24 January 1608 to Ruiz de Pereda, AGI, Escribanía de Cámara, leg. 74A; Ruiz de Pereda a SM, 22 September 1608, ANC, AH, leg. 86, no. 365; Ruiz de Pereda a SM, 23 November 1609, AGI, SD, leg. 100, ramo 4.

43. Ruiz de Pereda a SM, 14 April 1610, AGI, SD, leg. 100, ramo 5; Los oficiales de la Casa de Contratación a SM, 26 July 1611, ibid., ramo 6; Fernandez Leyton contra Angulo; Marrero, *Cuba*, 4:165–66.

44. Valdés a SM (no date, but 1610s), BNM, MS 3047, "Papeles varios," fols. 227–28. Macías, *Cuba*, 190, asserts that Valdés had a conflictive relationship with Guzmán.

45. Blas Ramallo con el Sr. Fiscal sobre su naturaleza, 1615, AGI, Escribanía de Cámara, leg. 38C, no. 9; Los Inquisidores de Cartagena al Consejo de Indias, Cartagena de Indias, 6 July 1617, AHN, Inquisición, libro 1008, fol. 418.

46. Pleito de Cristobal de Mayorga contra Alonso Ferrera, Havana, 1615, AGI, Escribanía de Cámara, leg. 38C, no. 5; Berlin, *Many Thousands Gone*, 17–28; Saunders, *Social History*, 11–12.

47. Based on Valdés a SM, 22 August 1607, and on María Rodriguez's testament, ANC, PNH, ER, 1610, fol. 224.

48. For an overview of the regulations prohibiting the emigration of foreigners, see Veitía Linage, *Norte*, 327–37. Charles V's temporal authorization is contained in the RC of 10 November 1525, ANC, AH, leg. 52, no. 430.

49. Some of the early references come from the information gathered in the "juicios de residencia" of governors Gonzalo Pérez de Angulo (1549–56), Diego de Mazariegos (1556–65), and Francisco García Osorio (1565–68), all in AGI, Justicia, legs. 83, 89, and 95. For later references, all in AGI, SD, leg. 100, see Valdés a SM, 15 October 1605, ramo 2; Ruiz de Pereda a SM, 14 April 1610, ramo 5; Gerónimo de Quero a SM, 29 December 1606, ramo 2.

50. Kamen, *Empire*, 56–62.

51. Blas Ramallo con el Sr. Fiscal sobre su naturaleza, 1615. The information on soldiers is taken from Copia de la gente de guerra que sirvió en la Fuerza Vieja de la Habana, 1604, and Relación de los soldados del castillo del Morro, 1604, both in AGI, Contaduría, leg. 1094.

52. The issue figured prominently in the *residencia* trials of Angulo (1556), Mazariegos (1566), and García Osorio (1568), AGI, Justicia, legs. 83, 89, and 95.

53. Wright, *Historia* (1927), 1:39–45; El fiscal con Cristóbal Ambrosio y Juan Rodríguez de Noriega por dos esclavos, 1563, AGI, Justicia, leg. 997, no. 4, ramo 4; Relación de los esclavos de S.M. que llevó Francisco López, 1572, AGI, Contaduría, leg. 1174; Informaciones presentadas por Gómez de Rojas Manrique, 19 May 1575, AGI, Justicia, leg. 41, no. 4.

54. Wright, *Historia* (1927), 1:133–43; RC of 6 June 1605, AGI, Contaduría, leg. 1099; Valdés a SM, 3 January 1604, AGI, SD, leg. 100, ramo 2; Marrero, *Cuba*, 2:345.

55. This summarizes findings from de la Fuente, "Matrimonios," 509–14, in which some of the sources and methods used to calculate these figures are discussed.

56. For recent discussions of this problem, which is not new in the literature, see Thornton, *Africa*, 183–92, and Sweet, *Recreating Africa*, 19–20.

57. Boemus, *Libro*, fol. 329.

58. ANC, PNH, ER, 1628, fol. 423v.

59. Mármol y Carvajal, *Segunda parte*, fol. 30v. For a discussion of the location of these groups, see de la Fuente, "Esclavos africanos," 135–60, and Thornton, *Africa*, xv–xxxvi, 198–99.

60. Sandoval, *Tratado*, 106; de la Fuente, "Esclavos africanos," 140, 142–43; Thornton, *Africa*, 188–89, 293; Sweet, *Recreating Africa*, 87–89, 181; Cortés Alonso, "Procedencia," 127.

61. Mármol y Carvajal, *Segunda parte*, fol. 27v; Sandoval, *Tratado*, 106; Lobo Cabrera, *Esclavitud*, 140; Saunders, *Social History*, 161.

62. De la Fuente, "Esclavos africanos," 145; Aguirre Beltrán, *Población*, 120; Acosta Saignes, *Vida*, 105; Deive, *Esclavitud*, 1:250; Sandoval, *Tratado*, 108.

63. Lopez and Pigafetta, *Relaçao*, 37; Aguirre Beltrán, *Población*, 138; Dapper, *Description*, 341.

64. Thornton, *Africa*, 110, 189–90; Dapper, *Description*, 307; Aguirre Beltrán, *Población*, 132; de la Fuente, "Esclavos africanos," 150–52.

65. ASCH, Libro Barajas de Matrimonios, fol. 131v; ANC, PNH, ER, 1630, fol. 942v; ASCH, Libro I de Bautismos, fol. 4; ANC, PNH, ER, 1595, fol. 1058; ACAH, May 1650, November 1656.

66. Only slave sales are used to avoid the overrepresentation of creoles in the parish registries.

67. Probanza hecha en la Habana, 1575, AGI, SD, leg. 153, ramo 1; El cabildo de la Habana a SM, 8 January 1602, ANC, AH, leg. 85, no. 329.

68. This family size was calculated using the vecinos' own declarations concerning family members and dependents contained in 153 wills in the notarial records between 1579 and 1610. The figures of vecinos come from Obispo Cabezas Altamirano a SM, 22 September 1608, in Wright, *Santiago*, app. 3, 77–83, and Certificación expedida por Gaspar Pérez de Borroto, 9 March 1609, AGI, SD, leg. 116, ramo 3.

69. We thank Leandro Romero for sharing with us these results, which remain unpublished.

70. Certificación expedida por Pérez de Borroto; Almendáriz, "Relación," 188 (Bishop Enríquez de Almendariz visited Havana around 1615); Marrero, *Cuba*, 5:32.

71. Gabriel Fernández de Villalobos, the Marquis of Varinas, who probably visited Havana, asserted in the 1670s that blacks and mulattoes outnumbered Spaniards in Havana in his "Grandezas de Indias," BNM, MS 2933.

72. Moreno Fraginals, "Claves," 4.

73. El gobernador Juanes de Avila a SM, 30 March 1545, CODOIN II, 6:252; RC of 11 March 1559, AGI, Contaduría, leg. 1011.

74. A good summary of the available documentation is presented by Marrero, *Cuba*, 2:410–15.

75. For the renewals of the sisa, see RC of 6 June 1605 and 8 June 1607, AGI, Contaduría, leg. 1011. Calculations on the amounts collected are based on "Cuentas de derecho de anclaje y sisa," 1566–1581, ibid., leg. 1089, and "Cuentas de agua: Impuestas para la conducción del agua de la Chorrera," 1581–1610, ibid., leg. 1011.

76. Wright, *Historia* (1927), 21, 77, 185–87; RC of 15 January 1569 and RC of 18 December

1576, AGI, Contaduría, leg. 1088; El hospital de la Habana pide prorrogación, 1575, AGI, SD, leg. 153, ramo 1; RC of 12 October 1594, AGI, SD, leg. 153, ramo 3.

77. ACAH, April and June 1597, August 1598, September 1603; Maldonado a SM, 18 March 1600, AGI, SD, leg. 100, ramo 1; Weiss, *Arquitectura*, 139–41; Pérez-Beato, *Habana*, 77.

78. ACAH, August–September 1550, July 1551, December 1552, January 1553, April 1554.

79. Wright, *Historia* (1927), 1:20–21, 34; ACAH, April 1570, May 1574; Weiss, *Arquitectura*, 43–45; Fransisco Carreño a SM, 8 July 1578, in Llaverías, *Papeles*, 2:11.

80. ACAH, December 1574; Wright, *Historia* (1927), 1:78–80; Fr. Francisco de la Cruz a SM, 19 January 1577, AGI, SD, leg. 153, ramo 1; RC of 31 March 1583, AGI, SD, leg. 153, ramo 3; ACAH, October 1586.

81. Wright, *Historia* (1927), 1:80–81; Weiss, *Arquitectura*, 47–49. On Santo Domingo, see also Petición de Fr. Diego Baraona, 3 July 1587, AGI, SD, leg. 153, ramo 3; ACAH, February and March 1578, December 1587. On San Agustín, see ACAH, January 1609. On the convent for nuns, ACAH, April 1603, September 1610, and ANC, PNH, ER, 1598, fol. 870.

82. Weiss, *Arquitectura*, 55; Wright, *Historia* (1927), 1:76; Francisco Carreño a SM, 8 July 1578, and Gabriel de Luján a SM, 24 December 1580, both in Llaverías, *Papeles*, 2:8, 32.

83. Maldonado a SM, 20 March 1600, AGI, SD, leg. 100, ramo 1; Valdés a SM, 22 December 1602, ibid.; ACAH, December 1584, November 1590, December 1596, January 1598, January 1601, October–November 1601.

84. Because there are gaps in the town council records, figure 4.3 displays the annual average number of petitions for each decade, which was calculated by dividing the total number of petitions by the number of years (or fractions of years) for which information is available.

85. ACAH, July 1555, March 1608. The ordinances of Cáceres are reproduced in Marrero, *Cuba*, 429–44, see especially articles 67 and 68 (p. 439); Ruiz de Pereda a SM, 10 January 1612, ANC, AH, leg. 87, no. 398.

86. For concrete examples, see ANC, PNH, ER, 1595, fol. 299, and 1599, fol. 299. For a description of the area, see Ruiz de Pereda a SM, 20 September 1608, AGI, SD, leg. 100, ramo 3. On the creation of the Plaza de Armas, see Weiss, *Arquitectura*, 26–27; on the importance of these central squares elsewhere in the Caribbean, see Castillero-Calvo, "City," 224–29.

87. Marrero, *Cuba*, 2:82. On the importation of slaves from Yucatán, see MacLeod, *Spanish Central America*, 50.

88. ACAH, February 1569, July 1602, March 1603, February 1577. Between 1578 and 1610, 63 plots and houses were identified as being sold in the neighborhood of Campeche. Free blacks bought 13 of those. The petition of Nizardo in ACAH, June 1561.

Chapter Five

1. Guerra y Sánchez, *Azúcar*, 65–66.

2. All these figures are calculated using the land petitions to the town council in ACAH, 1550–1610. The total number of surviving petitions is 331. On the process of land appropriation, see the excellent study by Sorhegui, "Surgimiento."

3. As mentioned below, however, the actual size of many estancias was larger than this.

4. Marrero, *Cuba*, 2:54–55; ACAH, October 1596.

5. The petitioner was none other than Governor Gonzalo Pérez de Angulo; ACAH, August 1551.

6. For an example, see ACAH, September 1556. About the older estancias, see Le Riverend, *Problemas*, chap. 2, and Marrero, *Cuba*, 2:56, 111.

7. ACAH, January and March 1558, January 1574, September 1577. Marrero, *Cuba*, 2:70–76, 440.

8. See article 74 of the ordinances in Marrero, *Cuba*, 2:440, and ACAH, September 1577.

9. ACAH, January 1585, October 1596.

10. See Sánchez's concession in ACAH, April 1577, and the sale in ANC, PNH, 1579, in Rojas, *Indice*, 1:392. For López, see ACAH, July 1599, and ANC, PNH, ER, 1604, s/f.

11. ACAH, August 1577, February 1578. See also article 68 of the Cáceres ordinances in Marrero, *Cuba*, 2:439.

12. These calculations are based on the years with actual information in the notarial records. The total number of land-related transactions of various kinds between 1578 and 1610 is 459.

13. ANC, PNH, ER, 1600, fol. 938; ACAH, April 1577.

14. Article 71 of the ordinances in Marrero, *Cuba*, 2:440; ACAH, April 1600. See also ACAH, April 1609.

15. These figures and the discussion that follows are based on fifty-eight labor contracts related to agricultural activities located in the notarial records.

16. ANC, PNH, ER, 1579, in Rojas, *Indice*, 1:366.

17. ANC, PNH, ER, 1606, fol. 557; 1579, in Rojas, *Indice*, 1:346.

18. ANC, PNH, ER, 1579, in Rojas, *Indice*, 1:93; 1590, fol. 195.

19. ANC, PNH, ER, 1600, fol. 487; Rojas, *Indice*, 1:137, 662.

20. ANC, PNH, ER, 1585, in Rojas, *Indice*, 1:599, 600. Bishop Castillo a SM, Merida, 31 December 1582, AGI, SD, leg. 100, ramo 1.

21. ACAH, January 1603; ANC, PNH, ER, 1589, fol. 209; 1599, fols. 224v, 321; 1601, fol. 440; 1604, fol. 394.

22. ACAH, September 1550, July 1551, November 1602. See also Valdés a SM, 3 January 1604, AGI, SD, leg. 100, ramo 2.

23. Calderón de Salcedo, "Tratado," fol. 119; Linschoten, *Discours*, 222; Laet, *L'Histoire*, 18; Dassié, *Description*, 160–61.

24. Cano, *Arte*; Cargo y data de la Habana, 1605, AGI, Contaduría, leg. 2156.

25. Quoted in Ortega Pereyra, *Construcción naval*, 8.

26. RC of 29 December 1516, ANC, AH, leg. 29, no. 215; RC of 7 November 1518, CODOIN II, 1:81; RC of 12 December 1518, ANC, AH, leg. 30, no. 247; ACAH, December 1552.

27. See references to the building of a fragata for vecino Bartolomé de Morales in 1578 in ANC, PNH, ER, 1578, in Rojas, *Indice*, 1:32; Pedro Menéndez Márques a SM, Santa Elena, 31 October 1577, in Connor, *Colonial Records*, 1:274.

28. "Cuentas del cargo de la consignación de la fábrica de fragatas, 1589–91," AGI, Contaduría, leg. 1089 (hereafter cited as "Cuentas, 1589–91); Ruiz de Pereda a SM, 20 September 1608, AGI, SD, leg. 100, ramo 3; ANC, PNH, ER, 1592, fol. 600.

29. ANC, PNH, ER, 1588, fol. 580v; 1589, fol. 839; 1595, fols. 144v, 412; 1601, fol. 513v; 1608, fol. 89; 1585, fol. 683v; 1598, fol. 433; 1599, fol. 464v.

30. Veigas, "Fichero ilustrado: Resumen" and "Fichero ilustrado"; Diego Fernández de Quiñones a SM, 12 December 1582, ANC, AH, leg. 82, no. 110; Tejeda a SM, 29 September 1591, AGI, SD, leg. 99.

31. Casado Soto, "Atlantic Shipping," 107–9.

32. Marrero, *Cuba*, 2:202; ANC, PNH, ER, 1595, fols. 144v, 412.

33. Marrero, *Cuba*, 4:76, 82, 91.

34. Diego de Arana a SM, 19 February 1600, AGI, SD, leg. 119; Tejeda a SM, 29 September 1591, ibid., leg. 99; Marrero, *Cuba*, 4:74.

35. References to specific types of wood and materials used in the construction of ships abound in the accounts of the royal officials in AGI, Contaduría, legs. 1089, 1090, 1098, and 1100. On the contract with merchant Dyonisio Lhermite from Antwerp, see also "De las naos que vinieron de la Habana," 1610, AGI, Contratación, leg. 2128, and Ruiz de Pereda a SM, 13 July 1610, AGI, SD, leg. 100, ramo 5. See also Marrero, *Cuba*, 2:203–4 and 4:80–81.

36. Reference to Gutiérrez Navarrete is in "Cuentas, 1589–91." See also Marrero, *Cuba*, 4:78.

37. The reconstruction of these activities is based on the "Cuentas, 1589–91," and completed with information from the notary records.

38. These figures are based on the "Cuentas, 1589–91," and on Gastos en la fábrica de galeones, 1608–9, AGI, Contaduría, leg. 1098. Compare with those that Phillips, *Six Galleons*, 234, offers about the construction of galleons in Vizcaya in the 1620s.

39. Phillips, *Six Galleons*, 234; Marrero, *Cuba*, 2:204; RC of 23 September 1588 and Instrucción que S.M. dio a Juan de Tejeda, 23 November 1588, both in Encinas, *Cedulario*, 4:50–51.

40. Marrero, *Cuba*, 2:34–36.

41. Francisco de Ballesteros a SM, 1606, BL, Add. MS 13992; Marcos de Valera Arceo a SM, 11 July 1600, AGI, SD, leg. 100, ramo 1; ANC, PNH, ER, 1604, fol. 660.

42. These figures were calculated from the accounts included in Valdés a SM, 18 July 1603, AGI, SD, leg. 100, ramo 1, and from references in the notary records, ANC, PNH, ER, 1607, s/f.; 1598, fol. 85.

43. Francisco de Ballesteros a SM, 1606; RC of 26 March 1607 and RC of 17 December 1607, AGI, SD, leg. 100, ramo 2 and ramo 3; Macías, *Cuba*, 93.

44. ACAH, October 1573, February 1574, June 1597; Diego Fernández de Quiñones a SM, 12 December 1582; Veigas, "Fichero ilustrado: Resumen."

45. RC of 6 September 1603 and Valdés a SM, 12 July 1604, AGI, SD, leg. 100, ramo 1.

46. Juan Maldonado Barnuevo a SM, 12 August 1598, AGI, SD, leg. 116; ANC, PNH, ER, 1602, fol. 46. On the origins of sugar manufacturing in Cuba, see also Marrero, *Cuba*, 2:305–21, 4:1–33, and Macías, *Cuba*, 47–64.

47. RC of 30 December 1595, AGI, SD, leg. 116. The 1529 privileges are reproduced in CODOIN II, 9:400.

48. RC of 24 July 1600, ANC, AH, leg. 85, no. 325; El Rey a los oficiales reales de Mexico, 24 July 1600, AGI. SD, leg. 100, ramo 1.

49. Petición del cabildo de la Habana, 14 February 1604, ANC, AH, leg. 86, no. 334; Instrucciones a Alonso de Guibar, 1 September 1606, ACAH, September 1606.

50. ANC, PNH, ER, 1602, fols. 46, 623; RC of 23 August 1603, ANC, AH, leg. 85, no. 325.

51. AGI, Contaduría, leg. 1089; Juan Maldonado Barnuevo a SM, 12 August 1598.

52. ANC, PNH, ER, 1598, fol. 70v; 1599, fol. 580.

53. Causa seguida a Juan de Eguiluz, 11 February 1634, AGI, SD, leg. 104.

54. For instance, the ingenio Nuestra Señora del Rosario. See ANC, PNH, ER, 1603, fols. 362–68.

55. Quoted by Marrero, Cuba, 2:320.

56. Rodríguez Morel, "Esclavitud," 100–117, and "Sugar Economy," 107–9; Duncan, Atlantic Islands, 31–37; Lobo Cabrera, Esclavitud, 232; Vieira, "Sugar Islands," 72–75.

57. Barret, Sugar Hacienda, 4; Chevalier, Land, 78; Palmer, Slaves, 72; Bowser, African Slave, 88–93.

58. ANC, PNH, ER, 1591, fol. 28; 1595, fol. 1005. The 1591 reference is the first concrete reference we have seen about a sugar-producing unit in Havana.

59. Ortiz, Contrapunteo, 341.

60. ANC, PNH, ER, 1603, fol. 362; 1601, fol. 464v.

61. Juan Maldonado Barnuevo a SM, 12 August 1598.

62. Schwartz, Sugar Plantations, 126. See also the introduction of Gil de Methodio Maranhao to Soares Pereira, A origen, 10–11.

63. ANC, PNH, ER, 1603, fol. 362; 1598, fol. 70v. Phillips, "Sugar in Iberia," 36, shows that in the sixteenth century Motril had the largest number of mills in Spain.

64. Duncan, Atlantic Islands, 10; Chevalier, Land, 79.

65. Schwartz, Sugar Plantations, 127–28; Mauro, Portugal, 230. The great sugar historian Noël Deer, History, 1:536, popularized the idea that these mills had been invented by Pietro Speciale, a prefectum from Sicily, in the fifteen century. His claim was later disproved in detail by Soares Pereira, A origen.

66. ANC, PNH, ER, 1606, fol. 529v; 1609, fol. 806.

67. Relación de las cosas más necesarias, 18 June, 1617, BL, Add. MS 13992, fols. 529–32. The copy of this letter in ANC, AH, leg. 104, no. 13, is dated in 1613.

68. Causa seguida a Juan de Eguiluz, 11 February, 1634, AGI, SD, leg. 104; ANC, PNH, ER, 1652, fol. 853.

69. In 1692 it was estimated that to produce 1,000 forms of sugar 1,500–3,000 cartloads of firewood were required. A free worker could cut up to 12 or 14 cartloads per day and was paid around half a real per cartload, plus food. See Informaciones sumarias y demás diligencias sobre la averiguación de las talas hechas en el monte vedado de Cojímar (1692), AGI, SD, leg. 465, no. 2, fols. 52v, 63, 89.

70. ANC, PNH, ER, 1608, fol. 548; 1603, fol. 434v.

71. Ibid., 1603, fol. 362. Another mill that incorporated a water-driven sawmill was the San Diego, of Juan Maldonado "el mozo" and his uncle, Governor Maldonado Barnuevo. Ibid., 1602, fol. 663.

72. This discussion is based on de la Fuente, "Ingenios," 45, and Bergad, *Cuban Rural Society*, 151–57. Bergad estimates that in Cárdenas (1860–78) cultivated acreage represented from 45 to 56 percent of the mill's total land.

73. This is largely based on the detailed description of the ingenio Nuestra Señora del Rosario (1603), but similar references to other crops appear as well in less detailed inventories. See ANC, PNH, ER, 1603, fol. 362; 1608, fol. 548; 1615, fol. 131.

74. Schwartz, *Sugar Plantations*, 295–312. This system is similar to the *colonato* that became popular in Cuba in the late nineteenth century; see Bergad, *Cuban Rural Society*, 277–84.

75. ANC, PNH, ER, 1604, fol. 82v; 1610, fol. 181v; 1603, fol. 362.

76. Ibid., 1600, fol. 99; 1602, fol. 246.

77. Ibid., 1603, fols. 433, 495v.

78. Juan Maldonado, for instance, paid physician Francisco Salvador 80 ducados (880 reales) per year for "curing . . . the blacks of my mill." Ibid., 1604, fol. 40v.

79. The average salary of the sugar masters was calculated from ten labor contracts in the notary records between 1599 and 1608. Some of the salaries of the garrison are reproduced by Marrero, *Cuba*, 2:300–301.

80. ANC, PNH, ER, 1599, fol. 162; see also 1596, fol. 596.

81. El cabildo de la Habana a SM, 27 November 1597, AGI, Santo Domingo, leg. 116. The contracts with Rodríguez Quintero appear in ANC, PNH, ER, 1597, fols. 225v, 232v, 237.

82. ANC, PNH, ER, 1603, fol. 362. See also 1599, fol. 321.

83. A good example is the contract between sugar mill owner Ambrosio Gatica and Francisco García. The latter rented an estancia with a pottery works from Gatica for five years, for which he paid annually 500 pesos (4,000 reales), plus 300 free forms to make sugar and the training of Gaspar *embuila*, a slave of Gatica, as a tile master. Ibid., Escribanía Ortega, 1653, fol. 622v. A pottery works that had expanded based on its location near several mills was that of Luis Matías de la Cerda, a priest, which had eight slaves, four of them "tile masters." This unit was rented in 1652 for 1,200 pesos (9,600 reales) per year. Ibid., ER, 1652, s/f (contract dated 5 October). For other examples, see ibid., 1630, s/f (contract 15 January), and Escribanía Fornari, 1639, vol. 3, s/f (contract 3 October).

84. About the difficulties collecting the 1602 loan, see Gaspar Ruiz de Pereda a SM, 22 August 1608, ANC, AH, leg. 86, no. 360; La ciudad de la Habana a SM, 7 June 1609, ibid., no. 380; and Ruiz de Pereda a SM, 14 August 1611, ibid., leg. 87, no. 397.

85. ANC, PNH, ER, 1601, s/f; 1606, fol. 468v; 1607, fol. 17.

86. Ibid., 1607, s/f; Relación de los dueños de ingenios, Havana, 1610, AGI, SD, leg. 100.

87. ANC, PNH, ER, 1605, fol. 856v; 1608, fol. 548; 1615, fol. 131.

88. The agreement between Manrique de Rojas and Casas was disputed frequently, even after Manrique's death in 1604. Ibid., 1600, fol. 1036v; 1604, fol. 294v; 1605, fol. 458; 1606, fol. 277v. The company between Pérez and González Cordero in ibid., 1603, fol. 62.

89. For examples, see ibid., 1608, fol. 56v; 1609, fol. 143.

90. Sugar mills' output in Puerto Rico and La Española ranged from 45 to 60 tons, from 30 or 40 tons to as many as 200 in Mexico, and from 40 to 100 tons in Brazil. The Xochimancas, a Jesuits' mill in Mexico, produced about 120 tons per year in the 1660s. These figures

are all rough estimates. Production varied widely from mill to mill and from year to year, depending on climate and many other factors. As Schwartz claims, referring to Brazil, "the average productive capacity" of a sugar mill is "uncertain." See Rodríguez Morel, "Esclavitud," 94; Chevalier, Land, 77–78; Schwartz, Sugar Plantations, 167–68; Mauro, Portugal, 239, 298–99; Berthe, "Xochimancas," 104.

91. Relación de las cosas más necesarias, 1617, BL, Add. MS 13992, fols. 529–32.

92. Certificación de Juan de Eguiluz, Havana, 4 May 1611, AGI, SD, leg. 116.

93. ANC, PNH, ER, 1603, fol. 362. A description of the turtle business and its connection to the ingenios is provided in the "Relación del obispado de Cuba" (ca. 1650), BNM, MS 3000.

Chapter Six

1. We have limited information on the San Antonio. The ship was registered in 1598 to sail to New Spain with 132 slaves. In the notarial records of Havana there are sale contracts for 117 of the 195 that the ship reportedly introduced into the city. See Vila Vilar, Hispanoamérica, app. 2; Chaunu and Chaunu, Séville et l'Atlantique, 4:54.

2. On these debates, see García Añoveros, Pensamiento, 177–95; Saunders, Social History, 38–44; and Franco Silva, Esclavitud, 39–44. On popular misgivings about slave ownership, see Schwartz, "Imperial Crosscurrents: Anti-imperial Dissidents in the Iberian World," paper presented at the colloquium "L'Expérience Coloniale: Dynamiques des Échanges dans les Espaces Atlantiques à l'Époque de l'Esclavage (XVe-XIXe siècles)," Nantes, June 2005.

3. Blackburn, Making of New World Slavery, 62–79; Sweet, "Iberian Roots"; Vaughan and Vaughan, "Before Othello"; Braude, "Sons of Noah."

4. Pike, Aristocrats, 172; Franco Silva, Esclavitud, 131–51; Cortés López, Esclavitud, 200–203; Lobo Cabrera, Esclavitud, 144–49; Saunders, Social History, 55–57; Ramos Tinhorao, Os negros, 78–86; Phillips, Historia, 163–66.

5. All these calculations are based on the sale contracts in the notarial records. All slaves were sold in 1600 except three, who were sold in October 1603. But this later date probably reflects just a notarization of the contract, rather than the actual sale of the slaves. The association between "quality" and sale timing is suggested by Galenson, Traders.

6. ANC, PNH, ER, 1601, fols. 3–6, 44; 1604, fols. 87–88, 434v.

7. Bradley, Slavery, 51–52; Epstein, Speaking, 67, 81–83; Franco Silva, Esclavitud, 105–6; Bowser, African Slave, 84.

8. Farfán, Tractado, fol. 82v.; Cárdenas, Problemas, fol. 197v.

9. For a concrete example, see ANC, PNH, ER, 1595, fol. 24v. This example corresponds to a group of slaves who were exported to Honduras on the nao San Miguel, master Antonio Fernández. On the fiscal purposes of branding, see Mellafe, Breve historia, 76. Branding was also used for identification purposes, particularly in the case of runaway slaves. See Pike, "Sevillian Society," 348; Lobo Cabrera, Esclavitud, 248; and Cortés López, Esclavitud, 121–22.

10. Stella, Histories, 99–101; Franco Silva, Esclavitud, 85–86; Cortés López, Esclavitud, 128–32; Phillips, Historia, 166.

11. Annual price variations were minimal, ranging from 173 ducados for a group of ten slaves imported in 1585 to 217 ducados for the slaves imported on the *San Antonio* in 1600.

12. Cortés López, *Esclavitud*, 64–71; Franco Silva, *Esclavitud*, 275–331; Saunders, *Social History*, 62–63; González Díaz, *Esclavitud*, 105–26.

13. Thornton, *Africa*, 135; Sandoval, *Tratado*, 104, 111–12; Barry, "Senegambia," 266; Wondji, "States and Cultures," 382–84.

14. Vansina, "Kongo," 546–63; Thornton, *Africa*, 222; Sandoval, *Tratado*, 134.

15. Sandoval, *Tratado*, 110, 136.

16. Los oficiales reales a SM, Havana, 1561, AGI, SD, leg. 115; RP of 6 June 1556 in Encinas, *Cedulario*, 4:398. For a discussion of how these prices were calculated, see de la Fuente, "Esclavos africanos," 147–48. The same difference in prices has been noted for Lima by Bowser, *African Slave*, 80.

17. Saunders, *Social History*, 84–85; Cortés López, *Esclavitud*, 104–5; Franco Silva, *Esclavitud*, 193.

18. Cuentas de las cajas de la Habana, 8 April 1578, AGI, Contaduría, leg. 1174; Memoria y lista de los negros de SM, 1583, ibid., leg. 1088; Governor Valdés a SM, Havana, 3 January 1604, AGI, SD, leg. 100, ramo 2; Ruiz de Pereda a SM, Havana, 7 January 1609, ANC, AH, leg. 87, no. 370. The existence of a farm to sustain the royal slaves is mentioned first in 1565. See Wright, *Historia* (1927), 1:48.

19. Maldonado Barnuevo a SM, Havana, 4 November 1597, ANC, AH, leg. 85, no. 307. See also Governor Gaspar Ruiz de Pereda a SM, Havana, 22 August 1608, AGI, SD, leg. 100, ramo 3.

20. These calculations are based on Gastos de Fortaleza, 1604, AGI, Contaduría, leg. 1099.

21. Data de reales pagados por comida de los negros de SM, 1583, ibid., leg. 1088; Data de lo que se ha gastado con los negros y forzados, 1604–1607, ibid., leg. 1099.

22. Relación de los vecinos que han utilizado esclavos de SM, 1578–1580, ibid., leg. 1088 (3). For payments to slaves applied to various public works, see ACAH, March 1603, December 1605, January 1608, November 1610. For an example of a contract renting out a royal slave to a resident, see ANC, PNH, ER, 1579, in Rojas, *Indice* 1:91.

23. Instrucción . . . en el uso de los oficios de sobrestante, herramentero y apuntador de los negros in Valdés a SM, 15 April 1608, AGI, SD, leg. 100, ramo 3.

24. ACAH, June 1551, January 1554, Febraury 1556, January 1557, August 1565, February 1621.

25. ACAH, May 1557, January 1553, January 1609, August 1620.

26. ANC, PNH, ER, 1585 and 1586 in Rojas *Indice*, 1:652–54, 2:193.

27. ANC, PNH, ER, 1585 and 1586 in Rojas, *Indice*, 1:573, 2:193; 1589, fol. 241; RC of 31 March 1583, in Konetzke, *Colección*, 1:547; Ordenanzas de Cáceres, article 54, in Marrero, *Cuba*, 2:437.

28. Ordenanzas de Cáceres, articles 54 and 55, in Marrero, *Cuba*, 2:437; ACAH, February 1601, July 1599, January 1554, November 1589.

29. ANC, PNH, ER, 1600, fol. 876. Contracts like this were very frequent; see an additional example in Rojas, *Indice*, 1:527.

30. ANC, PNH, ER, 1595, fol. 402v. The reference to "Francisco chirimía of His Majesty" appears in his 1628 marriage in ASCH, Libro I de Matrimonios, fol. 48.

31. Artisan participation in the slave market is taken from a database of 2,046 slave sales during the period 1578-1610. We have located 85 apprenticeship contracts, of which 7 correspond to slaves. For the sugar masters, see chapter 5. The complaint by local authorities is from ACAH, June 1650.

32. ANC, PNH, ER, 1607, s/f (contract 23 August); 1579 in Rojas, Indice, 1:78; 1610, fol. 155v; 1606, fol. 126; 1608, fol. 218.

33. ACAH, September 1550; ANC, PNH, ER, 1604, fol. 386v.

34. This figure is based on the analysis of 124 inventories of estancias from ANC, PNH, ER, 1578-1610. For the "companies" to exploit these units, see Rojas, Indice, 1:366, and ANC, PNH, ER, 1604, fol. 376v.

35. These totals are larger than those used in chapter 5 because they include not only sales but also inventories that appear in wills, dowries, and other documents. But the proportion of slaves in the farms remains basically the same: 12 percent according to the sale contracts and 15 percent when the other documents are included.

36. ANC, PNH, ER, 1604, s/f; 1610, fol. 157v. On the labor demands of these units, see Pérez de la Riva, Origen, 109.

37. See chapter 5 for a discussion of sugar manufacturing.

38. See the Lib. 2, Tit. 1, Const. 4, of Diocesan Synod of 1680 in García de Palacios, Sínodo, 46; ANC, PNH, 1603, fol. 367v.

39. ACAH, June 1599, February 1601; ANC, PNH, ER, 1605, fol. 810v.

40. Saunders, Social History, 75; Pike, Aristocrats, 184; Phillips, Historia, 166–67, 174; González Díaz, Esclavitud, 80–82; Lobo Cabrera, Esclavitud, 244–45; Bernand, Negros, 108–13; see article 12 of the Ordinances of 1528, Audiencia de Santo Domingo, in Malagón Barceló, Código, 131.

41. Franco Silva, Esclavitud, 199; Cortés López, Esclavitud, 96–97; Lobo Cabrera, Esclavitud, 245–46; Deive, Esclavitud, 1:310; Bernand, Negros, 40.

42. Cortés López, Esclavitud, 134–36; Franco Silva, Esclavitud, 108; Saunders, Social History, 24–26; González Díaz, Esclavitud, 71–72; Epstein, Speaking, 183–91; Bowser, African Slave, 81, 342–45. Prices for women were higher in the late sixteenth century in the Canary Islands as well according to Lobo Cabrera, Esclavitud, 175–76.

43. Average life expectancy at birth was under 40 in late sixteenth-century England, but this figure is impacted by high infant mortality rates. See Wrigley and Schofield, Population History, 234.

44. Among those who emphasize adaptability to the new culture are Thornton, Africa, 235–71; Saunders, Social History, 165; Pike, Aristocrats, 188–91; and Phillips, Historia, 167–68. For those who emphasize the reproduction of African mores, see Sweet, Recreating Africa, 110–13, and Queirós Mattoso, To be a Slave, 125–27.

45. Sandoval, Tratado, 382–90.

46. Diocesan Synod of 1579 in González, Marco. Similar dispositions are found in other diocesan synods, such as those of San Juan of Puerto Rico (1645) and Lima (1613). See Lobo Guerrero and Arias de Ugarte, Sínodos de Lima, 174, and López de Haro, Sínodo de San Juan, 54.

47. This seems to have been the case in seventeenth- and eighteenth-century Cádiz as well according to Stella, Histories, 52–54.

48. An RC of 3 February 1587 specifically decried that royal slaves in Havana did not hear mass or live like Christians; see Konetzke, Colección, 1:572. For similar complaints, see RC of 25 October 1538 and 21 September 1544, in Encinas, Cedulario, 4:392.

49. ANC, PNH, ER, 1603, fols. 362–68.

50. Quoted in Andrés-Gallego and García Añoveros, Iglesia, 126, who study the debate concerning free will and the forced Christianization of Africans (119–29); see also Bonnassie, From Slavery, 30–31, and García Añoveros, Pensamiento, 88–91.

51. On the priests' messages, see Sandoval, Tratado, 422. The first books of baptisms and marriages in the diocese of Havana, the "libros Barajas," include records of blacks and whites, free and slaves together. This, however, changed in the seventeenth century. On the uneasiness about baptism and its effects, see Epstein, Speaking, 147, 179; Blackburn, Making of New World Slavery, 50, 64; Cortés López, Esclavitud, 142; Lobo Cabrera, Esclavitud, 260–62; Vaughan, "Origins Debate," 43; Saunders, Social History, 40–42; and Morris, Southern Slavery, 393.

52. This expression is borrowed from Schwartz, Sugar Plantations, 408.

53. López de Haro, Sínodo de San Juan, 50; Schwartz, Sugar Plantations, 407; Saunders, Social History, 90. The proportion of whites among marriage godparents and witnesses is similar to that found in Cádiz by Stella, Histories, 144.

54. Cortés López, Esclavitud, 83; Lobo Cabrera, Esclavitud, 219–20; Saunders, Social History, 102–05; Stella, Histories, 142–45.

55. The 1527 quotation is from RP of 28 June, in Konetzke, Colección, 1:99–100; for regulations concerning marriage and freedom, see RP of 11 May 1526, CODOIN II, 9:239–42, and RC of 10 July 1538 and RC of 26 October 1541, in Encinas, Cedulario, 4:386–87. On the belief that Christian marriage implied freedom, see also Epstein, Speaking, 97.

56. Saco, Historia, 4:83; El Rey a los oficiales reales de Cuba, 9 November 1526, ANC, AH, leg. 80, no. 7. See Davidson, "Negro Slave Control," 85, and Phillips, Slavery, 207–9.

57. This is an observation that other scholars have made. See Schwartz, Sugar Plantations, 391–92; Thornton, Africa, 200–201; Sweet, Recreating Africa, 44–48; and Bennett, Africans, 91–104.

58. Pike, "Sevillian Society," 173; Phillips, Historia, 167–68; Saunders, Social History, 150–56; ANC, PNH, ER, 1598, fol. 547; 1587, fol. 584v.

59. ANC, PNH, ER, 1600, fol. 83; 1605, fol. 810; 1601, fol. 635; 1609, fol. 385v. For examples of blacks who continued to give alms to other confraternities, see the wills of Catalina Bran (1603, fol. 263) and Catalina Garay (1607, s/f, 5 July).

60. Ibid., 1601, fols. 67v, 552; 1604, fol. 557v; 1606, fol. 515v. Opisbo Gerónimo de Lara a SM, no date, 1635, AGI, SD, leg. 150, ramo 3; "Relación del Obispado de Cuba," 1636, BNM, MS 3000.

61. ANC, PNH, ER, 1604, fol. 318; 1600, fol. 83; 1629, fol. 88.

62. Pike, "Sevillian Society," 345, 357–58; ACAH, January 1568; Benzoni, Historia, fol. 93. For further references to the election of kings, see Thornton, Africa, 202–3, and Bernand, Negros, 79–83.

63. Bradley, *Slavery*, 155–63, Epstein, *Speaking*, 172; Queirós Mattoso, *To be a Slave*, 145–49; Schwartz, *Sugar Plantations*, 157. For a useful overview see Klein, *African Slavery*, 217–41.

64. ANC, PNH, ER, 1600, fols. 926v, 319, 108v; 1609, fol. 418v.

65. Studies during the past few decades have consistently underlined the importance of children. See Schwartz, "Manumission," 615; Bowser, "Free Person," 350; Johnson, "Manumission," 262; Queirós Mattoso, *To Be a Slave*, 163–64; and Klein, *African Slavery*, 227.

66. ANC, PNH, ER, 1597, fol. 99v; 1602, fol. 48; 1604, fol. 452.

67. Ibid., 1600, fol. 839; 1609, fol. 418. The gender imbalance in manumissions is well documented. For a summary, see Klein, *African Slavery*, 227.

68. Among the African slaves freed by mistresses, 92 percent were women. Among those freed by men, women represented 68 percent. The owners' gender made no difference, however, in the manumission of criollos. For a discussion of gender and manumissions, see Higgins, "*Licentious Liberty*," and Proctor, "Gender."

69. Klein, *African Slavery*, 227.

70. ACAH, January 1559; Wright, *Historia* (1927), 1:73; Diego Fernández de Quiñones a SM, 12 December 1582, ANC, AH, leg. 82, no. 110.

71. Article 53 of the ordinances in Marrero, *Cuba*, 2:437.

72. ANC, PNH, ER, 1579, in Rojas, *Indice*, 1:286, 320; 1592, fol. 182; 1591, s/f; 1585, in Rojas, *Indice*, 1:531.

73. These life sketches are constructed out of our databases from the notarial records, the parish registries, the town council records, and fiscal sources from AGI, Contaduría.

74. ANC, PNH, ER, 1579, in Rojas, *Indice*, 1:410.

75. ACAH, June 1561.

76. Saunders, *Social History*, 141–47; Franco Silva, *Esclavitud*, 261–72; González Díaz, *Esclavitud*, 92–105.

77. Stella, *Histories*, 55–58; Parrilla Ortiz, *Esclavitud*, 50–53; Izco Reina, *Amos*, 34–36.

78. ACAH, January 1554, December 1550.

79. ACAH, January 1553, January 1561, January 1585, November 1612.

80. ACAH, February 1556, June 1551, August 1565, September 1570, July 1599, February 1621, October 1589.

81. ACAH, September 1565, June 1623, January 1603.

82. Marrero, *Cuba*, 5:25–28; RC of 21 July 1623, in Konetzke, *Colección*, 2:278; El gobernador Francisco Venegas a SM, 12 August 1622, AGI, SD, leg. 100, ramo 1.

83. ACAH, April 1557, November 1565, November 1577.

84. ACAH, February 1556.

85. For just a few examples that are very similar to the Havana regulations, see Saunders, *Social History*, 76, 78, 106, 120–25; Franco Silva, *Esclavitud*, 216, 223; Pike, *Aristocrats*, 181, 185; and Malagón Barceló, *Código*, 128–43.

86. Marrero, *Cuba*, 2:438.

87. The traditional principles are contained in Law 6, Título 21, Partida 4. See articles 22 and 23 of the Ordinances of 1528 and article 34 of the Ordinances of 1535 in Malagón Barceló, *Código*, 134, 141; Cáceres's views are in a letter to Licenciado Juan de Ovando, 1570, in CODOIN I, 11:55.

88. Franco, *Palenques*, 51; Marrero, *Cuba*, 1:364.

89. The issue is mentioned in the session of 28 February 1569 and prompted the cabildo to send four Spaniards and twelve Indians for their capture, but this did not lead to any sustained institutional effort against runaways. See ACAH, February 1569.

90. Proceso de oficio contra Andrés de Niz, 1558, AGI, Justicia, leg. 35, no. 4; ANC, PNH, ER, 1604, fol. 464; 1595, fol. 890v; 1609, fol. 757; 1603, fol. 222; 1605, fol. 143.

91. Debien, *Esclaves*, 422; Thornton, *Africa*, 274–79.

92. There are several copies of these "Ordenanzas redactadas por el cabildo habanero para la reducción de negros cimarrones" dated 14 July 1600. The original is in the original series of ACAH in volume 1603-9, fol. 3v, which is reproduced in the copied ("trasuntadas") series, vol. 1599-1604, fol. 4. There are additional copies in AGI, SD, leg. 116, and in ANC, AH, leg. 31, no. 289.

93. ACAH, June 1599, July 1600, October 1618. On the runaways in the sixteenth-century circum-Caribbean, see Vidal Ortega, *Cartagena*, 219–34; Mena García, *Sociedad*, 400–427; Deive, *Esclavitud*, 2:429–63; Palmer, *Slaves*, 52–53; Klein, *African Slavery*, 202–3.

94. See article 4 of the ordinances and subsequent modifications and discussions in ACAH, July 1600, September 1600, November 1602, December 1602, January 1610, January 1611.

95. Traslado de las Ordenanzas, 1611. ANC, AH, leg. 31, no. 289. For complaints about lack of cooperation by slaveholders, see ACAH, October 1600, November 1600, February 1602, April 1602, November 1602, May 1603, January 1610.

Chapter Seven

1. Law 2, Título 23, Partida 4. I have used here the translation of Samuel Parson Scott, in the edition by Burns, *Siete Partidas*, 4:987.

2. See an excellent discussion of this process in Ruiz, *Spanish Society*, 3–7.

3. See Góngora's 1601 letrilla "Verdad, mentira" in *Obras*, 36, and Quevedo, *Antología*, 113–15.

4. A point that historians of colonial cities have made; see Borah, "Trends"; Morse, "Urban Development"; Socolow and Johnson, "Urbanization"; and Knight and Liss, *Atlantic Port Cities*.

5. Los inquisidores al Real y Supremo Consejo, Mexico, 31 March 1595, AHN, Inquisición, libro 1049, fol. 51; Luján to Juan Ibarra, 14 August 1588, quoted in Marrero, *Cuba*, 2:335.

6. El cabildo a SM, 9 June 1552, AGI, Justicia, leg. 19, no. 2, registro 3.

7. Testimonio de la visita de Juan del Castillo, Obispo de Cuba, August 1569-April 1570, ANC, Donativos y Remisiones, leg. 209, no. 395. On the Council of Trent's mandate and the quality of the parish registries in the colonies, see Borah, *Demografía*, 35.

8. El gobernador Valdés a SM, 15 April 1607, AGI, SD, leg. 100, ramo 3; El gobernador Vitrián de Biamonte a SM, 18 January 1631, ibid., leg. 101; ACAH, January 1571, January 1568. See also article 12 of the Cáceres ordinances in Marrero, *Cuba*, 2:430.

9. This reconstruction was done with a data set from the annual elections of the town

council, as they appear in ACAH in 1550–78 and 1584–1610 (the years 1579–83 are missing) and cross-referenced with data sets from the parish registries and the notary records to identify family links. The discussion that follows draws heavily on a database of petitions to the town council as well.

10. Marrero, *Cuba*, 2:330; Sentencia del Consejo contra Juan Bautista de Rojas, 18 July 1591, AGI, Escribanía de Cámara, leg. 1184.

11. Expediente de Alonso de Rojas (1573), AGI, Santo Domingo, leg. 124; The reference to "los cayos de Alonso de Rojas" appears in the manuscript of Barrozo, "Derrotero."

12. RC of 5 June 1581, AGI, SD, leg. 99.

13. El Lcdo. Diego Cabrera vs. Juan de la Parra, 1567, AGI, Justicia, leg. 979, no. 9, ramo 5; Informaciones presentadas por Gómez de Rojas Manrique, 19 May 1575, ibid., leg. 41, no. 4; ANC, PNH, ER, 1579, fol. 548, in Rojas, *Indice*, 1:223.

14. ANC, PNH, ER, 1598, fol. 129; Marrero, *Cuba*, 2:248, 330; Wright, *Historia* (1927), 1:82–83. The quotation is from Vargas Machuca, *Milicia*, 2:97.

15. Marrero, *Cuba*, 2:335; ANC, PNH, ER, 1587, fol. 162v; 1602, fol. 67.

16. Marzahl, "Creoles," 640, 648; Ferry, *Colonial Elite*, 23.

17. ANC, PNH, ER, 1595, fol. 635; 1602, fol. 104.

18. On Morales, see ACAH, January 1567, September 1569, January 1570, February 1574, October 1575, April 1576, May 1578. The dowry of Orellana and the commission of Gómez de Rojas are in ANC, PNH, ER, 1589, fol. 943v, and 1595, s/f. On a prior marriage to Isabel Pineda, see Rojas, *Indice*, 1:121. See also Marrero, *Cuba*, 2:221–28.

19. On Rodríguez's family, see ANC, PNH, ER, 1600, fol. 982; 1609, fol. 240. Rodríguez died between 1595 and 1600.

20. ACAH, May 1569. Recio had purchased the office in 1564. See AGI, Justicia, leg. 999, no. 2.

21. ANC, PNH, ER, 1595, fol. 869; 1600, fol. 982.

22. Ibid., 1598, fol. 612; 1599, fol. 76v; 1600, fols. 359, 555; 1604, fol. 441v.

23. On marriage and dowry practices in the Iberian colonies, see Lavrín and Couturier, "Dowries"; Nazzari, "Parents"; Powers, *Women*, 116–17; and Socolow, *Women*, 60–77. For an excellent overview of this literature, see Caulfield, "History of Gender."

24. Compare with Lavrín and Couturier, "Dowries," 288–90.

25. ANC, PNH, 1602, fol. 500.

26. Ibid., 1598, fol. 612; 1579, fol. 176, in Rojas, *Indice*, 1:87.

27. ANC, PNH, 1579, fol. 613, in Rojas, *Indice*, 1:178; 1590, fol. 313; 1600, fols. 38, 148, 404.

28. ANC, PNH, ER, 1590, fol. 285. On this see Lavrín and Couturier, "Dowries," 297; Powers, *Women*, 114–17; Socolow, "Acceptable Partners," 209–10; and Nazzari, "Parents," 652.

29. For an example, see ANC, PNH, ER, 1588, in Rojas, *Indice*, 3:188.

30. See Law 23, Título 11, Partida 4, in Burns, *Siete Partidas*, 4:941; ANC, PNH, ER, 1595, fol. 1077. For a discussion of the so-called *adulterinos*, see Twinam, *Public Lives*, 128, 220.

31. See Laws 54, 55, 56, and 57 of Toro, in *Códigos*, vol. 6; Lavrín and Couturier, "Dowries," 282–87; and Powers, *Women*, 119–20.

32. ANC, PNH, ER, 1590, fol. 114; 1591, fol. 313v; 1592, fol. 134.

33. Ibid., 1595, fol. 844; 1596, fol. 635; 1599, fol. 59; 1600, fol. 404. ASCH, Libro Barajas de Matrimonios de Españoles, 1584–1622, fol. 68v.

34. ACAH, September 1551, November 1551, December 1575, March 1558, January 1573, January 1609.

35. ACAH, February 1576, December 1575.

36. Memoria y capítulos del cabildo de la Habana, 1552, AGI, Justicia, leg. 19, no. 2; Residencia del Dr. Angulo, 1556, ibid., leg. 89; Residencia del Dr. Mazariegos, 1566, ibid., leg. 89; El Alguacil Mayor con el Dr. Zayas, 1569, ibid., leg. 980, no. 2; Sentencia del Consejo, 1604. AGI, Escribanía de Cámara, leg. 1185A; Gerónimo de Quero a SM, 29 December 1606, AGI, SD, leg. 100, ramo 2; Información ante el Alcalde Ordinario de Santiago, 1619, AGI, SD, leg. 156, ramo 1; Residencia de García de Osorio, 1568, AGI, Justicia, leg. 95.

37. Villalón, Tratado, fol. 38. See also the distinction that Cáceres makes between merchants and retailers in article 43 of his ordenanzas in Marrero, Cuba, 2:434, and Ruiz, Spanish Society, 3–6, on merchants' noble lifestyles.

38. The reconstruction of these mercantile activities is based on our databases from the notarial records. The "merchant" references are taken from Antón Recio y consortes con el Fiscal de SM, 1568, AGI, Justicia, leg. 1000, no. 1, and ANC, PNH, ER, 1589, fol. 316.

39. Luján a SM, 31 March 1583, AGI, SD, leg. 153; Luján a SM, 14 August 1588, in Wright, Historia (1927), 2:130–31; Marrero, Cuba, 2:248, 335.

40. These designations appear in a variety of documents, most frequently in legal disputes or reports. See El Cabildo a SM, 9 June 1552, AGI, Justicia, leg. 19, no. 2; El Alguacil Mayor con el Dr. Zayas, 1569, ibid., leg. 980, no. 2; El Lic. Diego Cabrera contra Juan de la Parra, 1567, ibid., leg. 979, no. 9; Informaciones presentadas por Gómez de Rojas Manrique, 1575, ibid., leg. 41, no. 4.

41. ANC, PNH, ER, 1602, fol. 745v; Ruiz de Pereda a SM, 3 September 1608, AGI, SD, leg. 100, ramo 3; Petition of Martín Calvo de la Puerta, July 1607, ANC, PNH, ER, 1607, s/f.

42. See examples in ANC, PNH, ER, 1595, fol. 626; 1602, fol. 630; Alonso de Chávez con Alonso de Hurtado, sobre ciertas palabras, 1550, AGI, Justicia, leg. 978, no. 3.

43. Informativo realizado en la villa de Cedillo sobre la limpieza de sangre de Gómez de Rojas Manrique, 1571, AGI, Justicia, leg. 41; Informaciones presentadas por Gómez de Rojas Manrique, 1575; Luján a SM, 30 April 1583, and Luján a SM, 4 March 1583, AGI, SD, leg. 99.

44. We have been unable to identify the link between Hernán Manrique, his brothers Gómez de Rojas Manrique and Juan de Rojas, and their sister Inés Manrique with the brothers Alonso de Rojas and Diego de Soto. Santa Cruz y Mallén, Historia, 1:316, mentions Manrique and his brother as "members of the family" but fails to establish their links to the other Rojas on the island. It is noteworthy that when Governor Gabriel de Montalvo, then in Bayamo (1575), named Diego de Soto his deputy in Havana, the latter appointed Gómez de Rojas Manrique for the position, a clear indication of strong bonds between the two. More on this below.

45. About Manrique's trip to Florida, see AGI, Contaduría, leg. 1174, and Lyon, Enterprise, 40–61. Concerning Manrique's activities in Drake's times, see Luján a SM, 4 May 1586, AGI, SD, leg. 99, no. 138.

46. Morales Padrón, Jamaica, 130; Wright, Historia (1927), 1:77.

47. The reconstruction of these activities is based on Juan de Parra con Hernán Manrique, por haber tratado y contratado con extranjeros (1567), AGI, Justicia, leg. 979, no. 9, ramo 2; Don Luis de Colón para que la Audiencia envíe preso a Hernán Manrique, ibid., leg. 1001, no. 2; and Marrero, Cuba, 2:261.

48. Marrero, Cuba, 2:33; Juan de Tejeda a SM, 30 May 1593, AGI, SD, leg. 99. The accounts of Manrique's administration of the sisa are in AGI, Contaduría, leg. 1011.

49. ANC, PNH, ER, 1600, fol. 1036v; 1604, fol. 294v.

50. This discussion is largely based on the extensive testimony of Gómez de Rojas in Informaciones presentadas por Gómez de Rojas Manrique, 1575. See also Marrero, Cuba, 2:195–99. On the War of Granada, see Harvey, Muslims, 204–37.

51. Tithe collection figures in AGI, Contaduía, legs. 1174, 1088–89, 1091–93, 1100; "Memoria de los Obispados."

52. ACAH, May 1574; Juan del Castillo a SM, 3 June 1574, AGI, SD, leg. 150, ramo 1; ANC, PNH, ER, 1606, fol. 584v; 1608, fol. 473.

53. ANC, PNH, ER, 1579, fol. 776, in Rojas, Indice, 1:169.

54. ANC, PNH, ER, 1596, fols. 49–51, 101–111.

55. Ibid., 1585, fol. 41, in Rojas, Indice, 1:539.

56. Cervantes, Quijote, 2:148. References to these religious functions are scattered throughout the notarial records and usually appear in contracts that they made on behalf of those institutions.

57. ACAH, March 1601, September 1603, September 1606; Cabezas Altamirano a SM, 23 September 1603, AGI, SD, leg. 150.

58. Cabezas Altamirano a SM, 22 September 1608, AGI, SD, leg. 150, ramo 2; El gobernador Ruiz de Pereda a SM, 20 September 1608, ibid., leg. 100, ramo 3; ACAH, August and September 1608, September 1610; ANC, PNH, ER, 1598, fol. 870; Marrero, Cuba, 5:112–19. For examples of vecinos who bequeathed sums to endow "doncellas," see ANC, PNH, ER, 1595, fol. 1077.

59. Nalle, "Literacy," 65–95; Ruiz, Spanish Society, 32, 75; Cervantes, Quijote, 2:148; Quevedo, Historia, 4.

60. For examples of contracts with instructors, see ANC, PNH, ER, fol. 807, in Rojas, Indice, 1:291; 1601, fol. 285v; 1602, fol. 706v; 1607, fol. 39; 1608, fol. 175. The 1582 reference is in Diego Fernández de Quiñones a SM, 12 December 1582, ANC, AH, leg. 82, no. 110.

61. ACAH, September 1603, September 1606; Simón de Valdés a SM, 14 February 1604, ANC, AH, leg. 86, no. 334; El Cabildo a SM, 1606, ANC, AH, leg. 86, no. 339.

62. ACAH, March 1607, March 1616. ANC, PNH, ER, 1608, fol. 292; Ruiz de Pereda a SM, 16 March 1611, ANC, AH, leg. 87, no. 396.

63. ANC, PNH, ER, 1602, fol. 706v.

64. Ibid., 1604, fol. 390. For a discussion of the accuracy of signatures as indicators or literacy see Nalle, "Literacy," 95–96.

65. Socolow, Women, 167. Concerning gender differentials in literacy in Castile, see Nalle, "Literacy," 69–71. The rates for Havana were calculated using information for 357 women and 4,360 men who appear in the notarial records between 1578 and 1610.

66. El cabildo de la Habana a SM, 9 June 1552, AGI, Justicia, leg. 19, no. 2.

67. Diego Fernández de Quiñones a SM, 12 December 1582; ACAH, November and December 1576.

68. Díez's will in ANC, PNH, ER, 1579, fol. 721, in Rojas, *Indice*, 1:268.

69. No reference to this marriage appears in the parish registries, but Hernán Rodríguez makes reference to it in his will. See ANC, PNH, ER, 1604, fol. 76.

70. Marrero, *Cuba*, 2:319; ANC, PNH, ER, 1607, s/f.

71. ANC, PNH, ER, 1598, fol. 550; 1601, fol. 464.

72. These confraternities are mentioned in ACAH, May 1609.

73. These are the typical apprenticeship conditions. For examples, see ANC, PNH, ER, 1579, fols. 609, 920, in Rojas, *Indice*, 1:176, 357; 1598, fol. 467v; 1595, fol. 1135.

74. ANC, PNH, ER, 1596, fol. 480.

75. Quevedo, *Libro*, 6; Molina, *Pretendiente*, 3.

76. In 1589, for instance, a "famous" doctor from Peru stayed in town for several months. See Marrero, *Cuba*, 2:158.

77. ACAH, August 1552, February 1569; ANC, PNH, ER, 1587, fol. 417, in Rojas, *Indice*, 2:416; 1597, fol. 389; 1598, fol. 196; 1586, fol. 565v; Marrero, *Cuba*, 2:41.

78. Valdés a SM, no date, BNM, MS 3047, "Papeles varios," fols. 224–32; El cabildo a SM, 14 February 1604, ANC, AH, leg. 86, no. 334; Ruiz de Pereda a SM, 24 November 1609, AGI, SD, leg. 100, ramo 4; ACAH, September 1610.

79. ANC, PNH, ER, 1599, fol. 281; 1602, fol. 350v. On the development of this trade in Havana, see Romero, "Orfebrería."

80. Unfortunately no samples of his work seem to have survived. For references, see ANC, PNH, ER, 1601, fol. 67v; 1602, fol. 372; 1603, fol. 193; 1606, fol. 533; ACAH, March 1599. See also Veigas and Romero Estébanez, "Fichero ilustrado."

81. ANC, PNH, ER, 1596, fol. 51; ACAH, February 1576; ASCH, Libro Barajas de Matrimonios de Españoles, 1584–1622, fol. 35.

82. ANC, PNH, ER, 1608, fol. 160.

83. Ibid., 1609, fol. 254.

84. Ibid., fol. 257. For examples of wills of these artisans, see ibid., 1592, fol. 4v; 1599, fol. 281; 1600, fol. 1100.

85. Ibid., 1601, fol. 473; 1605, fol. 959; 1600, fol. 925v; 1586, fol. 337v, in Rojas, *Indice*, 2:60.

86. This characterization is based on the following soldiers' wills: ANC, PNH, ER, 1601, fols. 473, 560; 1602, fol. 530; 1605, fol. 844v; 1607, s/f.

87. Ibid., 1601, fol. 609; 1605, fol. 959; 1604, fol. 406.

88. Ibid., 1605, fol. 477v; 1602, fol. 94; 1604, fol. 287.

89. Ibid., 1596, fol. 211; 1605, fol. 363v; 1591, fol. 243; Pérez-Mallaína, *Spain's Men*, 185–86.

90. Pérez-Mallaína, *Spain's Men*, 123.

91. ANC, PNH, ER, 1595, fols. 444, 10v. Pérez-Mallaína, *Spain's Men*, 75–79, 128–31.

92. ANC, PNH, ER, 1599, fol. 236.

93. For examples, see Rotz, "Book"; Manuel, "Derrotero"; and Oliva, "Portolano."

94. Marrero, *Cuba*, 2:391.

95. Luis de Salas al Real Consejo de la Inquisición, 13 January 1599, AHN, Inquisición,

leg. 2178, no. 2; Los inquisidores de Cartagena al Real Consejo de la Inquisición, 14 July 1612, ibid., libro 1008, fol. 34v; Causa contra Michael Juan, 1572, ibid., libro 1064, fol. 11v.

96. Sentencia del Consejo, 18 July 1591, AGI, Escribanía de Cámara, leg. 1184; El obispo Antonio Díaz de Salcedo a SM, 11 May 1592, AGI, SD, leg. 150, ramo 1; Valdés a SM, 3 August 1606, AGI, SD, leg. 100, ramo 2; ANC, PNH, ER, 1605, fol. 880.

97. Luján a Juan Ibarra, 14 August 1588, quoted in Marrero, *Cuba*, 2:335; Valdés a SM, 3 January 1604, AGI, SD, leg. 100, ramo 2; Demanda en residencia que tomo el Lic. Valdivieso, 1608, AGI, Escribanía de Cámara, leg. 74A, pieza 6.

98. El obispo Díaz de Salcedo a SM, 29 December 1594, AGI, SD, leg. 150, ramo 1; Luján a SM, 24 August 1583, ibid., leg. 99; Marrero, *Cuba*, 2:331.

99. Marrero, *Cuba*, 2:382; Bachiller Andrés de Valdés a SM, 29 December 1568, AGI, SD, leg. 153, ramo 1; Informativo del Bachiller Juan Díaz Aldeano, 1579, AGI, SD, leg. 153, ramo 1; Residencia del Dr. Angulo, 1556, AGI, Justicia, leg. 83; El obispo Alonso Enríquez a SM, 20 April 1612, AGI, SD, leg. 150, ramo 2.

100. This process has not been located at the AGI so far. References to it appear in Maldonado Barnuevo a los Inquisidores de Mexico, 15 March 1598, AHN, Inquisición, leg. 2178, and in the Residencia del Lic. Ronquillo, 1604, AGI, Escribanía de Cámara, leg. 1185A. Another case of sodomy was rerpoted in Simón Fernandez Leyton contra Francisco de Angulo, 1608, AGI, Escribanía de Cámara, leg. 74A, pieza 12.

101. On this process, see the excellent study by Nalle, *God in La Mancha*.

102. Luis de Salas al Real Consejo de la Inquisición, 13 January 1599.

103. Los inquisidores de Cartagena al Real Consejo de la Inquisición, 14 July 1612; Fr. Francisco Carranco a los inquisidores de Mexico, 18 September 1609, AHN, Inquisición, libro 1049, fols. 415–17. I have studied Cuba's inquisitorial cases at the AHN, and they are indeed quite modest compared with the viceroyalties on the mainland. On the impact of the Inquisition in Spain, see Ruiz, *Spanish Society*, 86–90; Nalle, *God in La Mancha*, 56–69; and Kamen, *Inquisition*.

104. Valdés a SM, 3 January 1604, AGI, SD, leg. 100, ramo 2. On jurisdictional conflicts, see Marrero, *Cuba*, 2:330–31; Wright, *Historia* (1927), 1:91–100; and Macías, *Cuba*, 186–96.

105. Castillero-Calvo, "City," 203–4.

106. The precise dates for the celebration of Corpus Christi in the sixteenth century are prescribed in Hera y de la Barra, *Repertorio*, fols. 117v–127. See also Chaves, *Cronographia*, fols. 157–67.

107. Ruiz, *Spanish Society*, 124–25, 150–55. On Corpus Christi in the Spanish world, see Nalle, *God in La Mancha*, 167–69; Dean, *Inka Bodies*, 7–22; and the essays in the excellent collection edited by Molinié, *Celebrando*. On the origins and early development of the feast, see Rubin, *Corpus Christi*.

108. ACAH, May 1554.

109. ACAH, April 1569, May 1570, April 1573, May 1576.

110. Nalle, *God in La Mancha*, 168; Dean, *Inka Bodies*, 9–14. ACAH, June 1590, April 1597, March and May 1598, April 1599.

111. ACAH, November 1569, January 1586, May 1607, June and November 1610.

112. ACAH, July 1557, January, February, and December 1599, February 1600.

113. ACAH, January 1599, June 1623, January 1624. On clothing and difference, see Wheeler, *Complexion*, 12, 17, and Ruiz, *Spanish Society*, 222–27.

Epilogue

1. Marrero, *Cuba*, 2:382.

2. Hardoy and Aranovich, "Urban Scales," 74.

3. Ibid., 79; Jay, *Urban Communities*, 107–14.

4. Chaunu, *Sevilla*, 147; Ward, *Imperial Panama*, 32; Mena García, *Sociedad*, 57.

5. Chaunu, *Sevilla*, 108–9, 142.

6. Ward, *Imperial Panama*, 191; Chaunu, *Sevilla*, 112–13; Hardoy and Aranovich, "Urban Scales," 79.

7. Vidal Ortega, *Cartagena*, 66–68, 167–208; Hardoy and Aranovich, "Urban Scales," 70, 79; Borrego Plá, *Cartagena*, 46–48.

8. Elliot, *Empires*, 105; Knight and Liss, *Atlantic Port Cities*, 3; Socolow and Johnson, "Urbanization."

9. Stein and Stein, *Silver*, 32; TePaske, "Integral to Empire," 38.

10. Morse, "Urban Development," 77.

11. This is what David Armitage, "Three Concepts," has called "cis-Atlantic history." Pioneer examples of this approach can be found in the Knight and Liss volume, *Atlantic Port Cities*.

12. Games, "Atlantic History," 750. The most important exception to this trend is the work done by Africanists such as Thornton, *Africa*; Miller, "Central Africa"; Mann and Bay, *Rethinking the African Diaspora*; and Sweet, *Recreating Africa*.

13. The British emphasis has been noted by several authors, such as Games, "Atlantic History," 750; Bailyn, "Idea of Atlantic History," 39; Gabaccia, "Long Atlantic," 4; and Cañizares-Esguerra, *Puritan Conquistadors*, 218–23.

14. Emmer, "Dutch," 75–96; Cañizares-Esguerra, *Puritan Conquistadors*, 215–33.

15. Elliot, *Empires*, xiii.

Bibliography

Archives

Cuba
    Archivo del Museo de la Ciudad, Havana
        Actas Capitulares del Ayuntamiento de la Habana, 1550–1656
    Archivo del Sagrario de la Catedral de la Habana
        Libro Barajas de Bautismos de Españoles, 1590–1600
        Libro Barajas de Matrimonios de Españoles, 1584–1622
        Libro Primero de Bautismos de Españoles, 1600–1610
    Archivo Nacional de Cuba, Havana
        Academia de la Historia
        Donativos y Remisiones
        Protocolos Notariales de la Habana
            Escribanía Fornari, 1639
            Escribanía Ortega, 1653
            Escribanía Regueira, 1579–1610, 1630, 1652
        Reales Ordenes y Cédulas
Great Britain
    British Library, Manuscript Section, London
Mexico
    Archivo General de la Nación, Mexico
        Archivo Histórico de Hacienda
Spain
    Archivo General de Indias, Seville
        Contaduría
        Contratación
        Escribanía de Cámara
        Justicia
        Santo Domingo
    Archivo Histórico Nacional, Madrid
        Inquisición
    Biblioteca Nacional de España, Sección de Manuscritos, Madrid
United States
    John Carter Brown Library, Providence, Rhode Island

Manuscripts

Barrozo, Benito A. "Derrotero de las Indias Occidentales y compendio de todas sus costas" (1689). British Library, Manuscript Section, London, Add. MS 28496.

Calderón de Salcedo, Diego. "Tratado y compendio breve y sumario de cierta y verdadera relación de la descripción de todos los reinos y dilatados mundos de las Yndias e Islas Occidentales y ponentinas de la China y Philipinas" (1629). British Library, Manuscript Section, London, Add. MS 13977.

Cardona, Nicolás de. "Descripciones geográficas e hidrográficas de muchas tierras y mares del norte y sur, en las Indias, en especial del descubrimiento del Reyno de California" (1632). Biblioteca Nacional de España, Sección de Manuscritos, Madrid, MS 2468.

Escalante de Mendoza, Juan. "Itinerario de navegación de los mares y tierras occidentales" (1575). Biblioteca Nacional de España, Sección de Manuscritos, Madrid, MS 3104.

Fernández de Villalobos, Gabriel. "Grandezas de Indias" (ca. 1670). Biblioteca Nacional de España, Sección de Manuscritos, Madrid, MS 2933

Manuel, Francisco. "Derrotero y sendas de tierra y sondas de la costa de la Nueva España y de Tierra Firme y de vuelta de las Indias a España y regimiento de la declinación del sol" (1583). British Library, Manuscript Section, London, Add. MS 28189.

"Memoria de los Obispados que hay en las Indias, su renta lo más ajustadamente que aca se puede entender y que personas los tienen" (1626). British Library, Manuscript Section, London, Add. MS 13974.

Oliva, Joan de. "Portolano" (1613). British Library, Manuscript Section, London, Eg. MS 819.

Rotz, John. "Book of Hidrography" (1542). British Library, Manuscript Section, London, Royal MS 20EIX.

Printed Primary Sources

Abbeville, Duval d'. Abrege du monde ou discours general de ses parties. Paris: Antoine de Sommaville, 1646.

Abbot, George. A Briefe Description of the Whole Worlde. London: John Brown, 1608.

Acosta, Cristobal. Tractado de las drogas, y medicinas de las Indias Orientales, con sus plantas dibuxadas al bivo. Burgos, Spain: Martín de Victoria, 1578.

Almendáriz, Alonso Enríquez de. "Relación del Obispo Alonso Enríquez de Almendariz a S.M. 12 August 1620." Memorias de la Sociedad Económica de Amigos del País (1847): 188.

Alvarez D'Almada, André. Tratado breve dos rios de Guiné do Cabo-Verde. Porto, Portugal: D. Köpke, 1841.

Anania, Gian Lorenzo. La universal fabrica del mondo. Naples: Giusepe Carchi, 1573.

Arias de Benavides, Pedro. Secretos de chirurgia, especial de las enfermedades de morbo galico y lanparones y mirrarchia. Valladolid, Spain: Francisco Fernandez de Córdova, 1567.

Avity, Pierre d'. Les etats, empires, et principautez du monde. Paris: Pierre Chevalier, 1616.

Benzoni, Girolamo. La historia del Mondo Nuovo. Venice: Francesco Rampazetto, 1565.

Boemus, Johann. El libro de las costumbres de todas las gentes del mundo, y de las Indias. Antwerp: En casa de Martin Nucio, 1556.

Botero, Giovanni. *Delle relationi universali.* 2 vols. Rome: Giorgio Ferrari, 1591–92.

———. *Relaciones universales del mundo.* Valladolid, Spain: Herederos de Diego Fernandez de Córdova, 1599.

Burns, Robert I., ed. *Las Siete Partidas.* 5 vols. Philadelphia: University of Pennsylvania Press, 2001.

Calle, Saravia de la. *Instrucción de mercaderes muy provechosa.* Medina del Campo, Spain: Antonio de Vrueña, 1547.

Cano, Tomé. *Arte para fabricar, fortificar, y apareiar naos de guerra y merchante.* Seville: En casa de Luis Estupiñán, 1611.

Cárdenas, Juan de. *Problemas y secretos maravillosos de las Indias.* 1591. Madrid: Ediciones Cultura Hispánica, 1945.

Cervantes Saavedra, Miguel de. *El Ingenioso hidalgo don Quijote de la Mancha.* 2 vols. Salamanca, Spain: Ediciones Universidad de Salamanca, 2005.

Champlain, Samuel de. *Narrative of a Voyage to the West Indies and Mexico in the Years 1599–1602.* London: Printed for the Hackluyt Society, 1859.

Chaves, Jerónimo de. *Cronographia e repertorio de los tiempos.* Seville: En casa de Alonso Escribano, 1572.

Codogno, Ottavio. *Nuovo itinerario delle poste per tutto il mondo.* Venice: Lucio Spineda, 1611.

Colección de documentos inéditos, relativos al descubrimiento, conquista y organización de las antiguas posesiones españolas de América y Oceanía. 1st ser. 42 vols. Madrid: M. B. de Quirós, 1864–84.

Colección de documentos inéditos relativos al descubrimiento, conquista y organización de las antiguas posesiones españolas de ultramar. 2d ser. 25 vols. Madrid: Establecimiento Tipográfico "Sucesores de Rivadeneyra," 1885–1932.

Connor, Jeannette T. *Colonial Records of Spanish Florida.* 2 vols. Deland: Florida State Historical Society, 1925.

Dapper, Olfert. *Description de l'Afrique.* Amsterdam: Chez Wolfgang, Waesberge, Boom et van Someren, 1686.

Dassié, F. *Description generale des costes de l'Amerique, havres, bancs, ecueils, basses, profondeurs, vents & courans d'eau.* Rouen, France: Bonaventure le Brun, 1677.

Dudley, Robert. *Arcano del mare.* 2 vols. 1646. Florence: Giuseppe Cocchini, 1661.

Echagoyan, Felipe de. *Tablas de reduciones de monedas.* Mexico City: Henrico Martínez, 1603.

Elvas, Fidalgo de. *Relaçam verdadeira dos trabalhos que ho governador don Fernando Soutoe y certos fidalgos portugueses pasarom no descobrimento da provincia da Frolida. Agora novamente feita per un fidalgo Delvas.* Evora, Portugal: Andres de Burgos, 1557.

Encinas, Diego de. *Cedulario indiano.* 4 vols. 1596. Madrid: Ediciones Cultura Hispánica, 1945–46.

Farfán, Agustín de. *Tractado breve de medicina y de todas las enfermedades.* Mexico City: Pedro Ocharte, 1592.

Fernández de Enciso, Martín. *Suma de geographía que trata de todas las partidas y provincias del mundo en especial de las Indias.* Seville: Juan Combrenger, 1530.

———. *Suma de geographía que trata de todas las partidas y provincias del mundo en especial de las Indias.* Seville: Andres de Burgos, 1546.

Fernández de Oviedo y Valdés, Gonzalo. *Historia general y natural de las Indias*. 4 vols. Madrid: Imprenta de la Real Academia de la Historia, 1851–55.

Figueiredo, Manoel de. *Roteiro e navegaçáo das Indias Occidentais ilhas, antilhas do mas Oceano Occidental: com suas derrotas, sondas, fundos, & conhecenças*. Lisbon: Pedro Crasbeeck, 1609.

Fragoso, Juan. *Discurso de las cosas aromáticas*. Madrid: Francisco Sánchez, 1572.

García de Palacio, Diego. *Instrución náutica, para el buen uso, y regimiento de las naos, su traza, y gobierno conforme a la altura de Mexico*. Mexico: En casa de Pedro Ocharte, 1587.

García de Palacios, Juan. *Sínodo diocesano*. Havana: Oficina de Arazoza y Soler, 1814.

García Icazbalceta, Joaquín. *Relaciones de viajeros ingleses en la ciudad de México y otros lugares de la Nueva España, siglo XVI*. Madrid: Porrúa, 1963.

Girava, Jerónimo. *Dos libros de cosmographía*. Milan: Maestro Juan Antonio Castellon y Maestro Cristobal Caron, 1556.

Gómez, Duarte. *Discursos sobre los comercios de las dos Indias*. [Madrid]: n.p., 1622.

Góngora, Luis de. *Obras. Tomo II [Manuscrito]*. Alicante, Spain: Biblioteca Virtual Miguel de Cervantes, 2005.

González de Mendoza, Juan. *Historia de las cosas mas notables, ritos y costumbres del gran reyno de la China*. Madrid: En casa de Pedro Madrigal, 1586.

Hakluyt, Richard. *The Third and Last Volume of the Voyages, Navigations, Traffiques, and Discoveries of the English Nation*. London: George Bishop, Ralph Newbery, and Robert Barker, 1600.

Hera y de la Barra, Bartolomé V. de la. *Repertorio del mundo particular, de las spheras del cielo y orbes elementales*. Madrid: Casa de Guillermo Druy Impresor, 1584.

Hernandez, Francisco. *Quatro libros de la naturaleza, y virtudes de las plantas, y animales que estan recevidos en el uso de la medicina en la Nueva España*. Mexico: En casa de la viuda de Diego López Dávalos, 1615.

Hevia Bolaños, Juan de. *Labyrintho de comercio terrestre y naval*. Lima: Francisco del Canto, 1617.

Heylyn, Peter. *Cosmographie in Foure Bookes Contayning the Chorographie & Historie of the Whole world*. London: Henry Seile, 1657.

Konetzke, Richard, ed. *Colección de documentos para la historia de la formación social de Hispanoamérica, 1493–1810*. 3 vols. Madrid: CSIC, 1953.

Laet, Jean. *L'Histoire du Noveau Monde ou description des Indes Occidentales*. 1625. Leiden: Bonaventure & Abraham Elseviers, 1640.

Leblanc, Vincent. *The World Surveyed*. London: Printed for John Starkey, 1660.

Linda, Luca di. *Le descrittioni universali et particolari del mondo, & delle republiche*. Venice: Combi & La Nou, 1660.

Linschoten, Jan Huygen van. *His Discours of Voyages into Easte and West Indies*. London: John Wolff, 1598.

Llaverías, Joaquín, ed. *Papeles existentes en el Archivo General de Indias relativos a Cuba y muy particularmente a la Habana*. 2 vols. Havana: Imprenta El Siglo XX, 1931.

Lobo Guerrero, Bartolomé, and Fernando Arias de Ugarte, eds. *Sínodos de Lima de 1613 y 1636*. Madrid: CSIC, 1987.

Lopez, Duarte, and Filippo Pigafetta. *Relaçao do Reino de Congo e das terras circunvizinhas*. 1598. Lisbon: Agencia Geral do Ultramar, 1951.

López de Gómara, Francisco. *Historia general de las Indias.* 2 vols. Madrid: Espasa, 1941.

López de Haro, Damián, ed. *Sínodo de San Juan de Puerto Rico de 1645.* Madrid: CSIC, 1986.

López de Velasco, Juan. *Geografía y descripción universal de las Indias.* Madrid: Fortanet, 1894.

Los códigos españoles concordados y anotados. 12 vols. Madrid: La Publicidad, 1847–51.

Mármol y Carvajal, Luis de. *Segunda parte y libro séptimo de la descripción general de Africa.* Málaga, Spain: Iuan René, 1599.

Mercator, Gerardus. *Atlas ou representation du monde universel.* 2 vols. 1595. Amsterdam: Henrici Hondius, 1633.

Molina, Tirso de. *El pretendiente al revés y Del enemigo, el primer consejo.* Madrid-Pamplona: Instituto de Estudios Tirsianos, 2005.

Motolinía, Toribio de Benavente. *Motolinía's History of the Indians of New Spain.* Washington, DC: Academy of American Franciscan History, 1951.

Münster, Sebastian. *A Treatyse of the Newe India, with other New Founde Landes and Islandes.* London: By Edward Sutton, 1553.

Ogilby, John. *America: Being the Latest, and Most Accurate Description of the New World.* London: Printed by the author, 1671.

Ordoñez de Cevallos, Pedro. *Viage del mundo.* Madrid: Luis Sanchez, 1614.

Quevedo, Francisco de. *Antología poética.* Madrid: Espasa Calpe, 1967.

———. *Historia de la vida del Buscón llamado don Pablos, ejemplo de vagamundos y espejo de tacaños.* Madrid: Espasa-Calpe, 1997.

———. *Libro de todas las cosas.* Madrid: Cátedra, 1993.

Ramusio, Giovanni Battista. *Delle navigationi et viaggi.* 3 vols. Venice: Nella Stamperia de Antonio Giunti, 1554–65.

Recopilación de leyes de los reynos de las indias. 4 vols. Madrid: I. de Paredes, 1681.

Rojas, María Teresa de. *Indice y extractos del archivo de protocolos de la Habana.* 3 vols. Havana; Imprenta Ucar, García y Cía, 1947.

Román, Gerónimo. *Republicas del mundo.* 3 vols. Salamanca, Spain: Juan Fernandez, 1594–95.

Sandoval, Alonso de. *Un tratado sobre la esclavitud.* 1627. Madrid: Alianza Editorial, 1987.

Solórzano y Pereyra, Juan de. *Política indiana.* 5 vols. 1648. Madrid: Compañía Ibero-Americana, 1930.

Stafford, Robert. *A Geographicall and Anthologicall Description of All the Empires and Kingdoms, both of Continent and Islands in this Terrestriall Globe.* London: Nicholas Okes, 1618.

Thevet, André. *La cosmographie universelle.* 2 vols. Paris: Chez Pierre l'Huillier, 1575.

Vargas Machuca, Bernardo. *Milicia y descripción de las Indias.* 2 vols. 1599. Madrid: V. Suárez, 1892.

Veitía Linage, Joseph de. *Norte de la contratación de las Indias occidentales.* 1672. Buenos Aires: Fomento Interamericano, 1945.

Villalón, Cristóbal de. *Provechoso tratado de cambios y contrataciones de mercaderes y reprobación de usura.* Valladolid: n.p., 1546.

Voisin, Lancelot. *Les trois mondes.* Paris: Pierre l'Huillier, 1582.

Books and Articles

Acosta Saignes, Miguel. *Vida de los esclavos negros en Venezuela*. Havana: Casa de las Américas, 1978.

Aguirre Beltrán, Gonzalo. *La población negra de México: Estudio etnohistórico*. Mexico City: Fondo de Cultura Económica, 1972.

Altman, Ida. "A New World in the Old: Local Society and Spanish Emigration to the Indies." In *"To Make America": European Emigration in the Early Modern Period*, edited by Ida Altman and James Horns, 30–58. Berkeley: University of California Press, 1991.

———. "Spanish Society in Mexico City after the Conquest." *Hispanic American Historical Review* 71, no. 3 (1991): 413–45.

Andrés-Gallego, José, and Jesús M. García Añoveros. *La iglesia y la esclavitud de los negros*. Pamplona: EUNSA, 2002.

Andrews, Kenneth R. *Elizabethan Privateering: English Privateering during the Spanish War, 1585–1603*. Oxford: Oxford University Press, 1964.

———. *The Spanish Caribbean: Trade and Plunder, 1530–1630*. New Haven, CT: Yale University Press, 1978.

———. *Trade, Plunder and Settlement: Maritime Enterprise and the Genesis of the British Empire, 1480–1630*. New York: Cambridge University Press, 1984.

Angulo Iñiguez, Diego. *Bautista Antonelli: Las fortificaciones americanas del siglo XVI*. Madrid: Hauser y Menet, 1942.

Armitage, David. "Three Concepts of Atlantic History." In *The British Atlantic World, 1500–1800*, edited by David Armitage and Michael J. Braddick, 11–27. New York: Palgrave Macmillan, 2002.

Atwell, William S. "Ming China and the Emerging World Economy, c. 1470–1650." In *The Cambridge History of China*, edited by Frederick W. Mote and Denis Twitchett, 8:376–418. Cambridge: Cambridge University Press, 1998.

Bailyn, Bernard. "The Idea of Atlantic History." *Itinerario* 20, no. 7 (1996): 19–44.

Balard, Michel. "Coastal Shipping and Navigation in the Mediterranean." In *Cogs, Caravels, and Galleons: The Sailing Ship, 1000–1650*, edited by Robert Gardiner, 131–38. Edison, NJ: Chartwell Books, 2003.

Barret, Ward. *The Sugar Hacienda of the Marqueses del Valle*. Minneapolis: University of Minnesota Press, 1970.

Barry, B. "Senegambia from the Sixteenth to the Eighteenth Century: Evolution of the Wolof, Sereer and 'Tukuloor.'" In *Africa from the Sixteenth to the Eighteenth Century*, edited by B. A. Ogot, 262–99. Paris: UNESCO, 1992.

Bazant, Jan. "Evolution of the Textile Industry of Puebla, 1544–1845." *Comparative Studies in Society and History* 7, no. 1 (1964): 56–69.

Benedict, Philip. "Rouen's Foreign Trade during the Era of the Religious Wars (1560–1600)." *Journal of European Economic History* 13, no. 1 (1984): 29–74.

Bennett, Herman L. *Africans in Colonial Mexico: Absolutism, Christianity, and Afro-Creole Consciousness, 1570–1640*. Bloomington: Indiana University Press, 2003.

Bergad, Laird. *Cuban Rural Society in the Nineteenth Century: The Social and Economic History of Monoculture in Matanzas*. Princeton, NJ: Princeton University Press, 1990.

Berlin, Ira. *Many Thousands Gone: The First Two Centuries of Slavery in North America.* Cambridge, MA.: Belknap Press, 1998.

Bernand, Carmen. *Negros esclavos y libres en las ciudades hispanoamericanas.* Madrid: Fundación Histórica Tavera, 2001.

Berthe, Jean-Pierre. "Xochimancas: Les travaux et les jours dans une hacienda sucrière de Nouvelle-Espagne au XVIIe siècle." *Jahrbuch fur Geschichte von Staat, Wirtschaft und Gesellschaft Lateinamerikas* 3, no. 3 (1966): 88–117.

Blackburn, Robin. *The Making of New World Slavery: From the Baroque to the Modern, 1492-1800.* London: Verso, 1997.

Blanes Martín, Tamara. *Castillo de los Tres Reyes del Morro de La Habana: Historia y arquitectura.* Havana: Editorial Letras Cubanas, 1998.

Bonnassie, Pierre. *From Slavery to Feudalism in South-Western Europe.* New York: Cambridge University Press, 1991.

Borah, Woodrow. *El siglo de la depresión en Nueva España.* Mexico City: Ediciones Era, 1982.

———. *La demografía histórica en América Latina: Fuentes, técnicas, controversias, resultados.* Bogotá: Universidad Nacional de Colombia, 1972.

———. *Silk Raising in Colonial Mexico.* Berkeley: University of California Press, 1943.

———. "Trends in Recent Studies of Colonial Latin American Cities." *Hispanic American Historical Review* 64, no. 3 (1984): 535–54.

Borah, Woodrow, and Sherburne F. Cook. *Price Trends of Some Basic Commodities in Central Mexico, 1531-1570.* Berkeley: University of California Press, 1958.

Borrego Plá, María del Carmen. *Cartagena de Indias en el siglo XVI.* Seville: EEHA, 1983.

Bottin, Jacques. "Structures et mutations d'un espace protoindustriel a la fin du XVIe siècle." *Annales ESC* (July-August 1988): 975–95.

Bowser, Frederick P. *The African Slave in Colonial Peru, 1524-1650.* Stanford, CA: Stanford University Press, 1974.

———. "The Free Person of Color in Mexico City and Lima: Manumission and Opportunity, 1580-1650." In *Race and Slavery in the Western Hemisphere: Quantitative Studies*, edited by Stanley L. Engerman and Eugene D. Genovese, 331–68. Princeton, NJ: Princeton University Press, 1975.

Boyajian, James C. *Portuguese Trade in Asia under the Hapsburgs, 1580-1640.* Baltimore: Johns Hopkins University Press, 1993.

Boyd-Bowman, Peter. *Indice geobiográfico de cuarenta mil pobladores españoles de América en el siglo XVI.* 2 vols. Bogotá: Instituto Caro y Cuervo, 1964.

———. "Patterns of Spanish Emigration to the Indies until 1600." *Hispanic American Historical Review* 66, no. 4 (1976): 580–604.

Bradley, Keith. *Slavery and Society at Rome.* New York: Cambridge University Press, 1994.

Braude, Benjamin. "The Sons of Noah and the Construction of Ethnic and Geographical Identities in the Medieval and Early Modern Periods." *William and Mary Quarterly* 54 (1997): 103–42.

Braudel, Fernand. *Afterthoughts on Material Civilization and Capitalism.* Baltimore: Johns Hopkins University Press, 1977.

———. *Civilization and Capitalism, 15th-18th Century.* 3 vols. New York: Harper and Row, 1982–84.

———. *The Mediterranean and the Mediterranean World in the Age of Philip II.* 2 vols. New York: Harper and Row, 1976.

Broeze, Frank, ed. *Brides of the Sea: Port Cities of Asia from the 16th-20th Centuries.* Honolulu: University of Hawaii Press, 1989.

———. *Gateways of Asia: Port Cities of Asia in the 13th-20th Centuries.* London: Kegan Paul International, 1997.

Brunelle, Gayle K. *The New World Merchants of Rouen, 1559-1630.* Kirksville, MO: Sixteenth Century Journal Publishers, 1991.

Calderón Quijano, José A. *Historia de las fortificaciones en Nueva España.* Madrid: CSIC, 1984.

Cañizares-Esguerra, Jorge. *Puritan Conquistadors: Iberianizing the Atlantic, 1550-1700.* Stanford, CA: Stanford University Press, 2006.

Carreira, Antonio. *Cabo Verde: Formaçao e extinçao de uma sociedade escravocrata (1460-1878).* Praia, Cape Verde: Instituto Cabo-Verdeano do Livro, 1983.

Carrera Stampa, Manuel. "The Evolution of Weights and Measures in New Spain." *Hispanic American Historical Review* 29, no. 1 (1949): 2-24.

Casado Soto, José L. "Atlantic Shipping in Sixteenth-Century Spain and the 1588 Armada." In *England, Spain and the Great Armada, 1585-1604,* edited by M. J. Rodríguez-Salgado and Simon Adams, 95-133. Edinburgh: John Donald Publishers, 1991.

Castillero-Calvo, Alfredo. "The City in the Hispanic Caribbean, 1492-1650." In *General History of the Caribbean,* vol. 2, *New Societies: The Caribbean in the Long Sixteenth Century,* edited by Pieter C. Emmer and Germán Carrera Damas, 201-46. London: UNESCO, 1999.

Castillo Meléndez, Francisco. "La emigración de familias canarias a la Isla de Cuba en el último cuarto del siglo XVII." *Anuario de Estudios Americanos* 40 (1983): 411-67.

Caulfield, Sueann. "The History of Gender in the Historiography of Latin America." *Hispanic American Historical Review* 81, nos. 3-4 (2001): 449-90.

Chaunu, Huguette, and Pierre Chaunu. *Séville et l'Atlantique, 1504-1650.* 8 vols. Paris: A. Colin, 1955-59.

Chaunu, Pierre. *Las Filipinas y el Pacífico de los Ibéricos, siglos XVI-XVII-XVIII.* Mexico City: Instituto Mexicano de Comercio Exterior, 1974.

———. *L'expansion européenne du XIIIe au XIVe siècle.* Paris: Presses Universitaires de France, 1969.

———. *Sevilla y América: Siglos XVI y XVII.* Seville: University of Seville, 1983.

Chevalier, François. *Land and Society in Colonial Mexico.* Berkeley: University of California Press, 1963.

Cook, Noble D. *Born to Die: Disease and New World Conquest.* New York: Cambridge University Press, 1998.

Cook, Sherburne F., and Woodrow Borah. *Ensayos sobre historia de la población: México y el Caribe.* 3 vols. Mexico City: Siglo Veintiuno Editores, 1977-80.

Cortés Alonso, Vicenta. "Procedencia de los esclavos negros en Valencia (1482-1516)." *Revista Española de Antropología Americana* 7, no. 1 (1972): 123-51.

Cortés López, José L. *La esclavitud negra en la España peninsular del siglo XVI.* Salamanca, Spain: Universidad de Salamanca, 1989.

Curtin, Philip. *The Atlantic Slave Trade: A Census.* Madison: University of Wisconsin Press, 1969.

———. *The Rise and Fall of the Plantation Complex: Essays in Atlantic History.* New York: Cambridge University Press, 1998.

Davidson, David M. "Negro Slave Control and Resistance in Colonial Mexico, 1519–1650." In *Maroon Societies,* edited by Richard Price, 82–103. Baltimore: Johns Hopkins University Press, 1979.

Dean, Carolyn. *Inka Bodies and the Body of Christ: Corpus Christi in Colonial Cuzco, Peru.* Durham, NC: Duke University Press, 1999.

Debien, Gabriel. *Les esclaves aux Antilles françaises (XVIIe–XVIIIe siecles).* Basse-Terre: Société d'histoire de la Guadeloupe, 1974.

Deer, Noël. *The History of Sugar.* 2 vols. London: Chapman and Hall, 1949.

Deive, Carlos E. *La esclavitud del negro en Santo Domingo, 1492–1844.* 2 vols. Santo Domingo, Dominican Republic: Museo del Hombre Dominicano, 1980.

de la Fuente, Alejandro. "Esclavos africanos en La Habana: Zonas de procedencia y denominaciones étnicas, 1570–1699." *Revista Española de Antropología Americana* 20 (1990): 135–60.

———. "Los ingenios de azúcar en la Habana del siglo XVII (1640–1700): Estructura y mano de obra." *Revista de Historia Económica* 9, no. 1 (1991): 35–67.

———. "Los matrimonios esclavos en La Habana: 1585–1645." *Iberoamerikanisches Archiv* 16, no. 4 (1990): 507–28.

———. "Población y crecimiento en Cuba, siglos XVI y XVII: Un estudio regional." *European Review for Latin American and Caribbean Studies* 55 (December 1993): 59–93.

de Vries, Jan. *The First Modern Economy: Success, Failure, and Perseverance of the Dutch Economy, 1500–1815.* New York: Cambridge University Press, 1997.

Diagne, P. "African Political, Economic and Social Structures during This Period." In *Africa from the Sixteenth to the Eighteenth Century,* edited by B. A. Ogot, 23–45. Paris: UNESCO, 1992.

Dor-Ner, Zvi. *Columbus and the Age of Discovery.* New York: Morrow, 1991.

Duncan, T. Bentley. *Atlantic Islands: Madeira, the Azores, and the Cape Verdes in Seventeenth-Century Commerce and Navigation.* Chicago: University of Chicago Press, 1972.

Elliot, J. H. *Empires of the Atlantic World: Britain and Spain in America, 1492–1830.* New Haven, CT: Yale University Press, 2006.

Ely, Roland T. *La economía cubana entre las dos Isabeles, 1492–1832.* Havana: Librería Martí, 1960.

Emmer, Pieter C. "The Dutch and the Making of the Second Atlantic System." In *Slavery and the Rise of the Atlantic System,* edited by Barbara L. Solow, 75–96. New York: Cambridge University Press, 1991.

Epstein, Steven. *Speaking of Slavery: Color, Ethnicity, and Human Bondage in Italy.* Ithaca, NY: Cornell University Press, 2001.

Escriche, Joaquín. *Diccionario razonado de legislación y jurisprudencia.* Madrid: Librería de Rosa, Bouret y Cía, 1874.

Fernández Alvarez, Manuel, and Ana Díaz Medina. *Los Austrias mayores y la culminación del imperio (1516–1598).* Madrid: Editorial Gredos, 1987.

Ferry, Robert J. *The Colonial Elite of Early Caracas: Formation and Crisis, 1567–1767.* Berkeley: University of California Press, 1989.

Fisher, John R. *The Economic Aspects of Spanish Imperialism in America, 1492–1810*. Liverpool: Liverpool University Press, 1997.

Franco, José L. *Los palenques de negros cimarrones*. Havana: DOR, 1973.

Franco Silva, Alfonso. *La esclavitud en Sevilla y su tierra a fines de la edad media*. Seville: Diputación Provincial, 1979.

Friedländer, Heinrich. *Historia económica de Cuba*. Havana: Jesús Montero, 1944.

Gabaccia, Donna. "A Long Atlantic in a Wider World." *Atlantic Studies* 1 (2004): 1–27.

Galenson, David W. *Traders, Planters, and Slaves: Market Behavior in Early English America*. New York: Cambridge University Press, 1986.

Games, Alison. "Atlantic History: Definitions, Challenges, and Opportunities." *American Historical Review* 111, no. 3 (2006): 741–57.

García Añoveros, Jesús M. *El pensamiento y los argumentos sobre la esclavitud en Europa en el siglo XVI y su aplicación a los indios americanos y a los negros africanos*. Madrid: CSIC, 2000.

García Bernal, Manuela C. *Población y encomienda en Yucatán bajo los Austrias*. Seville: EEHA, 1978.

García del Pino, César. "Ataque de la Habana por Jacques de Sorés." *Revista de la Universidad de la Habana*, no. 218 (1982): 5–16.

———. "¿Dónde se fundó la villa de San Cristóbal de la Habana?" *Revista de la Biblioteca Nacional "José Martí"* (January–April 1979): 5–26.

———. "El obispo Cabezas, Silvestre de Balboa y los contrabandistas de Manzanillo." *Revista de la Biblioteca Nacional "José Martí"* (May–August 1975): 13–54.

García Fuentes, Lutgardo. "El viñedo y el olivar sevillanos y las exportaciones agrarias a Indias en el siglo XVI." In *Primeras Jornadas de Andalucía y América*, 1:17–38. Huelva, Spain: Instituto de Estudios Onubenses, 1981.

———. "La introducción de esclavos en Indias desde Sevilla en el siglo XVI." In *Andalucía y América en el siglo XVI*, edited by Bibiano Torres Ramírez and José Hernández Palomo, 1:249–74. 2 vols. Seville: EEHA, 1983.

———. *Sevilla, los vascos y América: Las exportaciones de hierro y manufacturas metálicas en los siglos XVI, XVII y XVIII*. Madrid: Fundación BBV, 1991.

García Sanz, Angel. "Competitivos en lanas, pero no en paños: Lana para la exportación y lana para los telares nacionales en la España del Antiguo Régimen." *Revista de Historia Económica* 12, no. 2 (1994): 397–434.

Gascon, Richard. *Grand commerce et vie urbaine au XVIe siècle: Lyon et ses marchands (environs de 1520–environs de 1580)*. 2 vols. Paris, SEVPEN, 1971.

Gil-Bermejo, Juana. *La Española, anotaciones históricas (1600–1650)*. Seville: EEHA, 1983.

González, Antonio C. *El marco histórico de la pastoral dominicana*. Santo Domingo, Dominican Republic: n.p., 1983.

González Díaz, Antonio M. *La esclavitud en Ayamonte durante el antiguo régimen (siglos XVI, XVII y XVIII)*. Huelva, Spain: Diputación Provincial, 1996.

González Ferrando, José M. "El dictamen de los hermanos Coronel en materia de 'cambios y contratos' de 6 de octubre de 1517." *Revista de Historia Económica* 7, no. 2 (1989): 267–96.

Goodman, David. *Spanish Naval Power, 1589–1665: Reconstruction and Defeat*. New York: Cambridge University Press, 1997.

Guanche Pérez, Jesús. *Significación canaria en el doblamiento hispánico de Cuba.* La Laguna, Canary Islands: Taller de Historia, 1992.

Guerra y Sánchez, Ramiro. *Azúcar y población en las Antillas.* Madrid: Cultural S.A., 1935.

Hardoy, Jorge E., and Carmen Aranovich. "Urban Scales and Functions in Spanish America toward the Year 1600: First Conclusions." *Latin American Research Review* 5, no. 3 (1970): 93-110.

Haring, Clarence. *El comercio y la navegación entre España y las Indias en época de los Habsburgos.* Paris: Desclée de Brouwer, 1939.

Harvey, L. P. *Muslims in Spain, 1500-1614.* Chicago: University of Chicago Press, 2005.

Hernández Tapia, Concepción. "Despoblación de la Isla de Santo Domingo en el siglo XVII." *Anuario de Estudios Americanos* 27 (1970): 281-319.

Heijdra, Martin. "The Socio-Economic Development of Rural China during the Ming." In *The Cambridge History of China,* edited by Frederick W. Mote and Denis Twitchett, 8:417-578. Cambridge: Cambridge University Press, 1998.

Higgins, Kathleen J. *"Licentious Liberty" in a Brazilian Gold-Mining Region: Slavery, Gender, and Social Control in Eighteenth-Century Sabará, Minas Gerais.* University Park: Pennsylvania State University Press, 1999.

Hoffman, Paul E. *The Spanish Crown and the Defense of the Caribbean, 1535-1585: Precedent, Patrimonialism, and Royal Parsimony.* Baton Rouge: Louisiana State University Press, 1980.

Inglis, Gordon D. "Historical Demography of Colonial Cuba, 1492-1780." Ph.D. diss., Texas Christian University, 1979.

Izco Reina, Manuel J. *Amos, esclavos y libertos: Estudios sobre la esclavitud en Puerto Real durante la Edad Moderna.* Cádiz, Spain: Universidad de Cádiz, 2002.

Jacobs, Auke P. "Legal and Illegal Emigration from Seville, 1550-1650." In *"To Make America": European Emigration in the Early Modern Period,* edited by Ida Altman and James Horns, 59-84. Berkeley: University of California Press, 1991.

Jay, Felix. *Urban Communities in Early Spanish America, 1493-1700.* Lewiston, NY: Edwin Mellen Press, 2002.

Johnson, Lyman L. "Manumission in Colonial Buenos Aires, 1776-1810." *Hispanic American Historical Review* 59, no. 2 (1979): 258-79.

Kamen, Henry. *Empire: How Spain Became a World Power, 1492-1763.* New York: HarperCollins, 2003.

———. *Inquisition and Society in Spain in the Sixteenth and Seventeenth Centuries.* Bloomington: Indiana University Press, 1985.

Kelsey, Harry. *Sir Francis Drake: The Queen's Pirate.* New Haven, CT: Yale University Press, 1998.

Kerridge, Eric. *Textile Manufactures in Early Modern England.* Manchester, England: Manchester University Press, 1985.

Kinsbruner, Jay. *The Colonial Spanish-American City: Urban Life in the Age of Atlantic Capitalism.* Austin: University of Texas Press, 2005.

Klein, Herbert S. *African Slavery in Latin America and the Caribbean.* New York: Oxford University Press, 1986.

Knight, Franklin W., and Peggy K. Liss, eds. *Atlantic Port Cities: Economy, Culture, and Society in the Atlantic World, 1650–1850.* Knoxville: University of Tennessee Press, 1991.

Konvitz, Josef W. *Cities and the Sea: Port City Planning in Early Modern Europe.* Baltimore: Johns Hopkins University Press, 1978.

Kuethe, Allan J. "Havana in the Eighteenth Century." In *Atlantic Port Cities: Economy, Culture, and Society in the Atlantic World, 1650–1850,* edited by Franklin W. Knight and Peggy K. Liss, 13–39. Knoxville: University of Tennessee Press, 1991.

Kuhn, Dieter. *Textile Technology, Spinning and Reeling.* Vol. 5, pt. 9 of Joseph Needham, *Science and Civilization in China.* New York: Cambridge University Press, 1988.

Kula, Witold. *Problemas y métodos de la historia económica.* Barcelona: Península, 1973.

Lavrín, Asunción, and Edith Couturier. "Dowries and Wills: A View of Women's Socioeconomic Role in Colonial Guadalajara and Puebla, 1640–1790." *Hispanic American Historical Review* 59, no. 2 (1979): 280–304.

Le Flem, Jean-Paul. *La frustración de un imperio.* Barcelona: Labor, 1982.

Le Riverend, Julio. *Problemas de la formación agraria de Cuba: Siglos XVI–XVII.* Havana: Editorial de Ciencias Sociales, 1992.

Lester, Katherine M., and Bess Oerke. *An Illustrated History of Those Frills and Furbelows of Fashion Which Have Come to Be Known as Accessories of Dress.* Peoria, IL: Manual Arts Press, 1940.

Lobo Cabrera, Manuel. *La esclavitud en las Canarias Orientales en el siglo XVI: Negros, moros y moriscos.* Santa Cruz de Tenerife, Canary Islands: Ediciones del Cabildo Insular de Gran Canaria, 1982.

Lorenzo Sanz, Eufemio. *Comercio de España con América en la época de Felipe II.* 2 vols. Valladolid, Spain: Diputación Provincial, 1979.

Lufríu, René. *El impulso inicial: Estudio histórico de los tiempos modernos en Cuba.* Havana: Imprenta El Siglo XX, 1930.

Lyon, Eugene. *The Enterprise of Florida: Pedro Menéndez de Avilés and the Spanish Conquest of 1565–1568.* Gainesville: University of Florida Press, 1976.

Macías, Isabelo. *Cuba en la primera mitad del siglo XVII.* Seville: EEHA, 1978.

MacLeod, Murdo. "Spain and America: The Atlantic Trade, 1492–1720." In *The Cambridge History of Latin America,* edited by Leslie Bethell, 1:341–88. Cambridge: Cambridge University Press, 1984.

———. *Spanish Central America: A Socioeconomic History, 1520–1720.* Berkeley: University of California Press, 1973.

Magalhaes Godinho, Vittorino. "Portuguese Emigration from the Fifteenth to the Twentieth Century: Constants and Changes." In *European Expansion and Migration: Essays on the Intercontinental Migration from Africa, Asia, and Europe,* edited by P. C. Emmer and M. Mörner, 13–48. New York: Berg, 1992.

Malagón Barceló, Javier. *Código negro carolino.* Santo Domingo, Dominican Republic: Ediciones Taller, 1974.

Malowist, M. "Struggle for International Trade and Its Implications for Africa." In *Africa from the Sixteenth to the Eighteenth Century,* edited by B. A. Ogot, 1–22. Paris: UNESCO, 1992.

Mann, Kristin, and Edna G. Bay, eds. *Rethinking the African Diaspora: The Making of a Black Atlantic World in the Bight of Benin and Brazil.* London: F. Cass, 2001.

María y Campos, Teresa de, and Teresa Castelló Yturbide. *Historia y arte de la seda en México: Siglos XVI-XX.* Mexico City: Banamex, 1990.

Marrero, Leví. *Cuba: Economía y sociedad.* 15 vols. Madrid: Editorial Playor, 1972-92.

Martin, C. "The Ships of the Spanish Armada." In *God's Obvious Design: Papers for the Spanish Armada Symposium,* edited by P. Gallagher and D. W. Cruickshank, 39-68. London: Thamesis Books, 1990.

Marzahl, Peter. "Creoles and Government: The Cabildo of Popayán." *Hispanic American Historical Review* 54, no. 4 (1974): 636-56.

———. *Town in the Empire: Government, Politics, and Society in Seventeenth-Century Popayán.* Austin: University of Texas Press, 1978.

Masó y Velázquez, Calixto. *Historia de Cuba.* Miami: Ediciones Universal, 1976.

Mauro, Frédéric. *Europa en el siglo XVI: Aspectos económicos.* Barcelona: Nueva Clío, 1969.

———. *Le Portugal, le Bresil et l'Atlantique au XVII siècle (1570-1670).* Paris: Fondation Calouste Gulbenkian, 1983.

Mazzaoui, Maureen Fennell, ed. *Textiles: Production, Trade, and Demand.* Brookfield, VT: Ashgate/Variorum, 1998.

McNeill, John R. *Atlantic Empires of France and Spain: Louisbourg and Havana, 1700-1763.* Chapel Hill: University of North Carolina Press, 1985.

McPherson, Kenneth. *The Indian Ocean: A History of People and the Sea.* New York: Oxford University Press, 1993.

Mellafe, Rolando. *Breve historia de la esclavitud en América Latina.* Mexico City: Secretaría de Educación, 1973.

Mena García, María del Carmen. *La sociedad de Panamá en el siglo XVI.* Seville: Diputación Provincial, 1984.

Miller, Joseph C. "Central Africa during the Era of the Slave Trade, c. 1490s-1850s." In *Central Africans and Cultural Transformations in the American Diaspora,* edited by Linda M. Heywood, 21-69. New York: Cambridge University Press, 2002.

Minchinton, Walter. "Patterns and Structures of Demand, 1500-1750." In *The Fontana Economic History of Europe,* edited by Carlo M. Cipolla, 2:83-176. Sussex, England: Harvester Press, 1977.

Minguijón Adrián, Salvador. *Historia del derecho español.* Barcelona: Labor, 1943.

Miño Grijalva, Manuel. *La manufactura colonial: La constitución técnica del obraje.* Mexico City: El Colegio de Mexico, 1993.

Molá, Luca. *The Silk Industry of Renaissance Venice.* Baltimore: Johns Hopkins University Press, 2000.

Molinié, Antoinette, ed. *Celebrando el Cuerpo de Dios.* Lima: Pontificia Universidad Católica del Perú, 1999.

Montgomery, Florence M. *Textiles in America, 1650-1870.* New York: Norton, 1984.

Morales Padrón, Francisco. *Jamaica española.* Seville: EEHA, 1952.

Moreno Fraginals, Manuel. "Claves de una cultura de servicios." *La Gaceta de Cuba,* July 1990, 4-6.

Morineau, Michel. "Revoir Seville: Le Guadalquivir, l'Atlantique et l'Amérique au XVIe siècle." *Anuario de Estudios Americanos* 57 (January-June 2000): 277-93.

Morris, Thomas. *Southern Slavery and the Law, 1619-1860.* Chapel Hill: University of North Carolina Press, 1996.

Morse, Richard. "The Urban Development of Colonial Spanish America." In *The Cambridge History of Latin America*, edited by Leslie Bethell, 2:67-104.Cambridge: Cambridge University Press, 1984.

Moya Pons, Frank. *Historia colonial de Santo Domingo.* Santiago, Dominican Republic: UCMM, 1977.

Nalle, Sarah T. *God in La Mancha: Religious Reform and the People of Cuenca, 1500-1650.* Baltimore: Johns Hopkins University Press, 1992.

———. "Literacy and Culture in Early Modern Castile." *Past and Present* 125 (November 1989): 64-96.

Nazzari, Muriel. "Parents and Daughters: Change in the Practice of Dowry in São Paulo (1600-1770)." *Hispanic American Historical Review* 70, no. 4 (1990): 639-65.

Nieto-Galán, Agustí. *Colouring Textiles: A History of Natural Dyestuffs in Industrial Europe.* Dordrecht, Netherlands: Kluwer Academia, 2001.

Ortega Pereyra, Ovidio. *La construcción naval en la Habana bajo la dominación colonial española.* Havana: Academia de Ciencias de Cuba, 1986.

Ortiz, Fernando. *Contrapunteo cubano del tabaco y el azúcar.* Havana: Consejo Nacional de Cultura, 1963.

Palmer, Colin A. *Slaves of the White God: Blacks in Mexico, 1570-1650.* Cambridge, MA: Harvard University Press, 1976.

Parrilla Ortiz, Pedro. *La esclavitud en Cádiz durante el siglo XVIII.* Cádiz, Spain: Diputación, 2001.

Parry, J. H. *The Spanish Seaborne Empire.* Berkeley: University of California Press, 1990.

Peraza de Ayala, José. *El régimen comercial de Canarias con las Indias en los siglos XVI, XVII y XVIII.* Seville: Servicio de Publicaciones de la Universidad, 1977.

Pérez, Louis A. *Cuba: Between Reform and Revolution.* New York: Oxford University Press, 1988.

———. *Winds of Change: Hurricanes and the Transformation of Nineteenth-Century Cuba.* Chapel Hill: University of North Carolina Press, 2001.

Pérez-Beato, Manuel. *La Habana antigua, apuntes históricos.* Havana: Seoane, Fernández y Cía, 1936.

Pérez Bustamante, Ciriaco. "Las regiones españolas de la población de América (1509-1534)." *Revista de Indias* 2, no. 6 (1941): 81-210.

Pérez de la Riva, Francisco. *Origen y régimen de la propiedad territorial en Cuba.* Havana: Imprenta El Siglo XX, 1946.

Pérez de la Riva, Juan. "Desaparición de la población indígena." *Revista de la Universidad de la Habana*, nos. 196-97 (1972): 61-84.

———. *El barracón y otros ensayos.* Havana: Editorial de Ciencias Sociales, 1975.

Pérez Herrero, Pedro. "La estructura comercial del Caribe a mitad del siglo XVI." *Revista de Indias* 47, no. 181 (1987): 777-810.

Pérez-Mallaína, Pablo E. *Spain's Men of the Sea: Daily Life on the Indies Fleets in the Sixteenth Century*. Baltimore: Johns Hopkins University Press, 1998.

Pérotin-Dumon, Anne. *La ville aux îles, la ville dans l'isle: Basse-Terre et Point-à-Pitre, Guadeloupe, 1650–1820*. Paris: Edition Karthala, 2000.

Phillips, Carla R. "The Growth and Composition of Trade in the Iberian Empires, 1450–1750." In *The Rise of Merchant Empires: Long-Distance Trade in the Early Modern World, 1350–1750*, edited by James D. Tracy, 34–101. New York: Cambridge University Press, 1990.

———. *Six Galleons for the King of Spain: Imperial Defense in the Early Seventeenth Century*. Baltimore: Johns Hopkins University Press, 1986.

———. *Spain's Golden Fleece: Wool Production and the Wool Trade from the Middle Ages to the Nineteenth Century*. Baltimore: Johns Hopkins University Press, 1997.

Phillips, William. *Historia de la esclavitud en España*. Madrid: Playor, 1990.

———. *Slavery from Roman Times to the Early Transatlantic Trade*. Minneapolis: University of Minnesota Press, 1985.

———. "Sugar in Iberia." In *Tropical Babylons: Sugar and the Making of the Atlantic World, 1450–1680*, edited by Stuart B. Schwartz, 27–41. Chapel Hill: University of North Carolina Press, 2004.

Pichardo Viñals, Hortensia. *La fundación de las primeras villas de la isla de Cuba*. Havana: Editorial de Ciencias Sociales, 1986.

Pike, Ruth. *Aristocrats and Traders: Sevillian Society in the Sixteenth Century*. Ithaca, NY: Cornell University Press, 1972.

———. "Sevillian Society in the Sixteenth Century: Slaves and Freedmen." *Hispanic American Historical Review* 47, no. 3 (1967): 344–59.

Pino-Santos, Oscar. *Historia de Cuba: Aspectos fundamentales*. Havana: Editorial Nacional, 1964.

Powers, Karen V. *Women in the Crucible of Conquest: The Gendered Genesis of Spanish American Society, 1500–1600*. Albuquerque: University of New Mexico Press, 2005.

Proctor, Frank "Trey," III. "Gender and the Manumission of Slaves in New Spain." *Hispanic American Historical Review* 86, no. 2 (2005): 309–36.

Putnam, Lara. "To Study the Fragments/Whole: Microhistory and the Atlantic World." *Journal of Social History* 39 (Spring 2006): 615–30.

Queirós Mattoso, Katia M. de. *To Be a Slave in Brazil, 1550–1888*. New Brunswick, NJ: Rutgers University Press, 1986.

Quezada, Sergio. "Tributos, limosnas, y mantas en Yucatán, siglo XVI." *Ancient Mesoamerica* 12 (2001): 73–78.

Rambert, Gaston. *Histoire du commerce de Marseille*. 7 vols. Paris: Plon, 1949–51.

Ramos Tinhorao, José. *Os negros em Portugal: Uma presença silenciosa*. Lisbon: Editorial Caminho, 1988.

Rapp, Richard T. *Industry and Economic Decline in Seventeenth-Century Venice*. Cambridge: Harvard University Press, 1976.

Rodríguez Arzúa, Joaquín. "Las regiones españolas y la población de América (1509–38)." *Revista de Indias* 8, no. 30 (1947): 695–748.

Rodríguez Morel, Genaro. "Esclavitud y vida rural en las plantaciones azucareras de Santo Domingo, siglo XVI." *Anuario de Estudios Americanos* 49 (1992): 89–117.

———. "The Sugar Economy of Española in the Sixteenth Century." In *Tropical Babylons: Sugar and the Making of the Atlantic World, 1450-1680*, edited by Stuart B. Schwartz, 85-114. Chapel Hill: University of North Carolina Press, 2004.

Roig de Leuchsenring, Emilio. *Los monumentos nacionales de la República de Cuba.* 3 vols. Havana: Junta Nacional de Arqueología y Etnología, 1957-60.

Romero, Leandro. "Orfebrería habanera en las islas Canarias." *Revista de la Universidad de la Habana* 222 (1984): 390-407.

Rubin, Miri. *Corpus Christi: The Eucharist in Late Medieval Culture.* New York: Cambridge University Press, 1991.

Rubio Serrano, José L. "Las unidades de medida españolas en los siglos XVI y XVII." *Revista de Historia Naval* 6, no. 20 (1988): 77-93.

Ruiz, Teófilo. *Spanish Society, 1400-1600.* Harlow, England: Longman, 2001.

Saco, José A. *Historia de la esclavitud desde los tiempos más remotos hasta nuestros días.* 4 vols. Havana: Imprenta Alfa, 1936.

Sagra, Ramón de la. *Historia física, política y natural de la isla de Cuba.* 2 vols. Paris: A. Bertrand, 1842.

Salim, A. I. "East Africa: The Coast." In *Africa from the Sixteenth to the Eighteenth Century,* edited by B. A. Ogot, 750-75. Paris: UNESCO, 1992.

Salvucci, Richard J. *Textiles and Capitalism in Mexico: An Economic History of the Obrajes, 1539-1840.* Princeton, NJ: Princeton University Press, 1987.

Sánchez-Albornoz, Nicolás. *La población de América Latina desde los tiempos precolombinos hasta el años 2000.* Madrid: Alianza Editorial, 1973.

Santa Cruz y Mallén, Francisco Xavier de. *Historia de familias cubanas.* 9 vols. Havana and Miami: Editorial Hércules and Universal, 1940-1988.

Saunders, A. C. de C. M. *A Social History of Black Slaves and Freedmen in Portugal, 1441-1555.* New York: Cambridge University Press, 1982.

Scelle, Georges. *La traite négrière aux Indes de Castile, contrats et traités d'assiento.* 2 vols. Paris: L. Larose & L. Tenin, 1906.

Schneider, Jane. "The Anthropology of Cloth." *Annual Review of Anthropology* 16 (1987): 409-48.

Schurz, William Lytle. *El galeón de Manila.* Madrid: Ediciones Cultura Hispánica, 1992.

Schwartz, Stuart B. "The Manumission of Slaves in Colonial Brazil: Bahia, 1684-1745." *Hispanic American Historical Review* 54, no. 4 (1974): 603-35.

———. *Sugar Plantations in the Formation of Brazilian Society: Bahia, 1550-1835.* New York: Cambridge University Press, 1985.

Sella, Domenico. "European Industries, 1500-1700." In *The Fontana Economic History of Europe,* edited by Carlo M. Cipolla, 2:354-426. Sussex, England: Harvester Press, 1977.

———. *Il Ducato di Milano dal 1535 al 1796.* Turin, Italy: UTET, 1984.

———. "Rise and Fall of the Venetian Woollen Industry." In *Crisis and Change in the Venetian Economy in the Sixteenth and Seventeenth Centuries,* edited by Brian Pullan, 106-26. London: Methuen, 1968.

Serrano Mangas, Fernando. *Función y evolución del galeón en la carrera de Indias.* Madrid: MAPFRE, 1992.

Sluiter, Engel. *The Florida Situado: Quantifying the First Eighty Years, 1571-1651*. Gainesville: University of Florida Libraries, 1985.

Soares Pereira, Moacyr. *A origen dos cilindros na moagem da cana: Investigaçao em Palermo*. Rio de Janeiro: Instituto de Açucar e do Alcool, 1955.

Socolow, Susan M. "Acceptable Partners: Marriage Choice in Colonial Argentina, 1778-1810." In *Sexuality and Marriage in Colonial Latin America*, edited by Asunción Lavrín, 209-46. Lincoln: University of Nebraska Press, 1989.

———. *The Women of Colonial Latin America*. New York: Cambridge University Press, 2000.

Socolow, Susan M., and Lyman L. Johnson. "Urbanization in Colonial Latin America." *Journal of Urban History* 8, no. 1 (1981): 27-59.

Sorhegui, Arturo. "El surgimiento de una aristocracia colonial en el occidente de Cuba durante el siglo XVI." *Santiago* 37 (March 1980): 147-209.

Stein, Stanley J., and Barbara H. Stein. *Silver, Trade, and War: Spain and America in the Making of Early Modern Europe*. Baltimore: Johns Hopkins University Press, 2000.

Stella, Alessandro. *Histoires d'esclaves dans la péninsule Ibérique*. Paris: Editions de L'Ecole des Hautes Etudes en Sciences Sociales, 2000.

Subrahmanyam, Sanjay. *The Portuguese Empire in Asia, 1500-1700: A Political and Economic History*. New York: Longman, 1993.

Sung, Ying-Hsing. *T'ien-Kung K'ai-wu: Chinese Technology in the Seventeenth Century*. University Park: Pennsylvania State University Press, 1966.

Sweet, James H. "The Iberian Roots of American Racist Thought." *William and Mary Quarterly* 54 (1997): 143-66.

———. *Recreating Africa: Culture, Kinship, and Religion in the African-Portuguese World, 1441-1770*. Chapel Hill: University of North Carolina Press, 2003.

TePaske, John J. "Integral to Empire: The Vital Peripheries of Colonial Spanish America." In *Negotiated Empires: Centers and Peripheries in the Americas, 1500-1820*, edited by Christine Daniels and Michael Kennedy, 29-41. New York: Routledge, 2002.

Thornton, John. *Africa and Africans in the Making of the Atlantic World, 1400-1680*. New York: Cambridge University Press, 1998.

Twinam, Ann. *Public Lives, Private Secrets: Gender, Honor, Sexuality, and Illegitimacy in Colonial Spanish America*. Stanford, CA: Stanford University Press, 1999.

Unger, Richard. *Dutch Shipbuilding before 1800: Ships and Guilds*. Assen, Netherlands: Van Gorcum, 1978.

Vansina, J. "The Kongo Kingdom and Its Neighbors." In *Africa from the Sixteenth to the Eighteenth Century*, edited by B. A. Ogot, 546-87. Paris: UNESCO, 1992.

Vaughan, Alden T. "The Origins Debate: Slavery and Racism in Seventeenth-Century Virginia." In *The Worlds of Unfree Labour: From Indentured Servitude to Slavery*, edited by Colin A. Palmer, 25-68. Aldershot, England: Ashgate, 1998.

Vaughan, Alden T., and Virginia M. Vaughan. "Before Othello: Elizabethan Representations of Sub-Saharan Africans." *William and Mary Quarterly* 54 (1997): 19-44.

Vázquez de Prada, Valentín. *Los siglos XVI y XVII*. Vol. 3 of *Historia económica y social de España*. Madrid: Confederación Española de Cajas de Ahorro, 1978.

Veigas, José. "Fichero ilustrado." *Revolución y Cultura* 32 (April 1975): 24-25.

———. "Fichero ilustrado: Resumen del siglo XVI." *Revolución y Cultura* 30–31 (February–March 1975): 68–70.

Veigas, José, and Leandro S. Romero Estébanez. "Fichero ilustrado: Período de 1584 a 1600." *Revolución y Cultura* 23 (July 1974): 66–68.

Vicens Vives, Jaime. *An Economic History of Spain*. Princeton, NJ: Princeton University Press, 1969.

Vidal Ortega, Antonino. *Cartagena de Indias y la región histórica del Caribe, 1580–1640*. Seville: University of Seville, 2002.

Vieira, Alberto. "Sugar Islands: The Sugar Economy of Madeira and the Canaries, 1450–1650." In *Tropical Babylons: Sugar and the Making of the Atlantic World, 1450–1680*, edited by Stuart B. Schwartz, 42–84. Chapel Hill: University of North Carolina Press, 2004.

Vila Vilar, Enriqueta. *Hispanoamérica y el comercio de esclavos*. Seville: EEHA, 1977.

———. *Historia de Puerto Rico, 1600–1650*. Seville: EEHA, 1974.

———. "Los asientos portugueses y el contrabando de negros." *Anuario de Estudios Americanos* 30 (1973): 557–609.

Viqueira, Carmen, and José Ignacio Urquiola. *Los obrajes en la Nueva España, 1530–1630*. Mexico City: Consejo Nacional para la Cultura, 1990.

Ward, Christopher. *Imperial Panama: Commerce and Conflict in Isthmian America, 1550–1800*. Albuquerque: University of New Mexico Press, 1993.

Weiss, Joaquín. *La arquitectura colonial cubana*. Havana: Editorial Letras Cubanas, 1979.

Wheeler, Roxann. *The Complexion of Race: Categories of Difference in Eighteenth-Century British Culture*. Philadelphia: University of Pennsylvania Press, 2000.

Wilson, Charles. "Cloth Production and International Competition in the Seventeenth Century." *Economic History Review* 13, no. 2 (1960): 209–21.

Wondji, C. "The States and Cultures of the Upper Guinean Coast." In *Africa from the Sixteenth to the Eighteenth Century*, edited by B. A. Ogot, 368–98. Paris: UNESCO, 1992.

Woronoff, Denis. *Histoire de l'industrie en France: Du XVIe siècle à nos jours*. Paris: Editions du Seuil, 1998.

Wright, Irene A. *Historia documentada de San Cristobal de la Habana en el siglo XVI*. 2 vols. Havana: Imprenta El Siglo XX, 1927.

———. *Historia documentada de San Cristóbal de la Habana en la primera mitad del siglo XVII*. Havana: Imprenta El Siglo XX, 1930.

———. *Santiago de Cuba and Its District (1607–1640)*. Madrid: Felipe Peña Cruz, 1918.

Wrigley, E. A., and R. S. Schofield. *The Population History of England, 1541–1871: A Reconstruction*. Cambridge: Cambridge University Press, 1981.

Index

Africans, 5, 6, 35, 70, 107, 108, 124, 147, 161, 167–68, 169–70, 227; cultural practices of, 161, 164; ethnonyms of, 37, 39, 103–6, 150, 167; images of, as inferior, 147–48; skills of, 150, 152, 156. *See also* Slaves

Agriculture, 94, 117, 118, 127, 150, 224; crops, 124, 125, 141

Alaminos, Antón de, 4, 217

Alfonso de Flores, Luis (general), 64

Almendares River, 4

Altman, Ida, 88

Amsterdam, 17

Anania, Gian Lorenzo, 69

Andalusia, 12, 24, 25, 27, 32, 34, 87, 88, 137, 178, 206, 210, 213

Andrews, Kenneth, 71

Anglería, Pedro Mártir de, 87

Angola, 11, 38, 39, 41, 42, 90, 94, 99, 103, 105, 147, 150, 151, 170, 183

Antonelli, Juan Bautista (military engineer), 71, 73, 74, 76

Aqueduct. See *Zanja, la*

Aramburu, Marcos de (general), 64

Arias Maldonado, Pedro (merchant), 197, 207

Artisans, 21, 26, 28, 29, 70, 80, 93, 95, 98, 100, 128, 129–30, 132, 133, 134–35, 150, 152, 156–57, 208–13; and contracts of apprenticeship, 208–10

Asia, 18, 28, 29, 30, 31, 106, 227

Audiencia de Santo Domingo, 12, 97, 190, 192

Azores, 98, 101, 106, 192

Ballesteros, Francisco (master smelter), 134, 135, 209

Baltic supplies, 26, 34, 227

Baracoa, 15, 50

Bayamo, 15, 49, 83, 132, 201, 202, 207

Bazán, Alvaro de (admiral), 68, 72

Beas, Francisco de (master shipwright), 132, 209

Benzoni, Girolamo, 89, 170

Berlin, Ira, 99

Blacks, 1, 2, 82, 134, 220, 221; black women, 177, 179, 180, 181, 213, 222; and *cofradías*, 111, 168–70, 175, 176, 181, 211; discrimination against, 178–81; and housing, 116; land petitions of, 177, 178; and militias, 175, 181; occupations of, 78, 99, 125, 152, 154, 158, 175–76, 179, 198, 213; population of, 174–75; wages of, 126. *See also* Africans; Slaves

Borah, Woodrow, 29

Borja, Juan de (general), 130, 132

Botero, Giovanni, 69

Braudel, Fernand, 6, 21, 81

Brazil, 40, 94, 139, 140, 141, 143

Brotherhoods. See *Cofradías*

Cabezas Altamirano, Juan de las (bishop), 143, 204, 205

Cabildo, 10, 54, 66, 98, 111, 124, 207, 223; control of, 186–87, 188, 189; and currency regulations, 57–59; house for, 112; and education, 205; and festivities, 220–21; and land distribution, 114, 116, 120, 121–22, 189, 198, 226; and metrological regulations, 55–57, 122; and military preparations, 71–73, 78–79; and regulations on blacks, 179–81; and regulations on forests, 127; and regulations on prices, 55, 61–62; and regulations on runaway slaves, 183–85; and regulations on urbanization, 116; and sugar production, 136–37

Cáceres, Alonso de (judge, Audiencia de

Santo Domingo), 114, 121, 124, 154, 175, 182, 183, 184

Calvo de la Puerta, Martín (councilman and notary), 142, 144, 208

Camargo, Juan (retable maker and painter), 169, 211

Campeche (neighborhood), 116, 129

Canary Islands, 11, 12, 15, 17, 21, 22, 24, 34, 35, 36, 40, 64, 84, 88–93, 97, 99, 100, 128, 132, 138, 142, 143, 148, 150, 156, 157, 159, 183, 192, 199, 206, 207, 213, 214

Cañizares-Ezguerra, Jorge, 226

Cano, Tomé (master shipwright), 128

Cape Verde, 11, 41–42, 103, 150, 151, 172, 197

Cárdenas, Bartolomé (physician), 210–11

Cárdenas, Juan de (physician), 149

Carreño, Francisco de (governor), 110

Carreño, Nicolás (councilman, son of Rodrigo Carreño), 189

Carreño, Rodrigo (councilman and landowner), 126, 189, 191, 203

Cartagena de Indias, 12, 35, 37, 39, 44, 46, 60, 72, 73, 76, 91, 98, 102, 106, 137, 147, 184, 214, 219, 224

Carvajal, Pedro de (merchant and councilman), 91, 138

Casas, Bartolomé de las, 138

Casas, Melchor (sugar mill owner), 138, 144, 197, 208

Castile, 4, 10, 25, 27, 31, 57, 59, 87, 90, 93, 96, 97, 136, 182, 186, 187, 197, 198, 204, 205, 212, 219

Castillero-Calvo, Alfredo, 219

Castillo, Juan del (bishop), 48, 110, 111, 188, 218

Cattle, 3, 49, 53, 92, 94, 120, 135, 137, 150, 205; cattle farms, 121, 122–23, 124

Cervantes, Miguel de, 204, 205

Ceylon, 9, 17

Champlain, Samuel de, 20, 54, 69

Charles V, 100, 221

Chaunu, Huguette, 37

Chaunu, Pierre, 3, 12, 37, 47, 224

Chilton, John, 53

China, 28, 29, 30, 31, 32, 44, 45, 227

Chorrera, La. See Zanja, la

Cochineal, 19, 224

Cofradías, 98, 208, 211, 217. See also Blacks: and cofradías

Coloma, Francisco de (armada general), 55, 64, 78

Congo, 41, 42, 105, 150, 167, 168, 170

Contraband, 21, 24, 39, 40, 44, 46, 48, 49, 50, 71, 79, 153, 198, 200–201

Convent, 108, 112, 204

Copper, 80, 89, 118, 119, 135, 137, 140, 142, 143, 150, 201

Corpus Christi, 168, 181, 219–20, 221

Corral, Francisco del (general), 85

Corsairs. See Pirates

Cortés, Hernando, 2, 93

Council of the Indies, 3, 72, 98, 185, 200, 211

Council of Trent, 162, 164, 188

Couturier, Edith, 196

Curtin, Phillip, 39

D'Abbeville, Duval, 22

Dapper, Olfert (geographer), 105

Dassié, F. (geographer), 128

Díaz de Salcedo, Antonio (bishop), 218

Díaz Ferrera, Diego (merchant), 92

Díaz Pimienta, Francisco (merchant), 90, 91, 129, 207

Drake, Francis, 68, 72, 74, 78, 79, 184, 200, 224

Education, 204–6, 223

Elite, 10, 95, 98, 107, 110, 115, 156, 179, 181, 185, 186, 188–206; and Catholic Church, 111, 187, 202–4; and dowries, 194–98; and marriage alliances, 190, 194, 196; merchants as members of, 192–93, 206; participation of, in commerce, 198–202

Elliot, John, 225

Elvas, Fidalgo de, 82

Emmer, Pieter, 226

England, 20–31 passim, 40, 41, 42, 67, 68, 69, 70, 71, 72, 76, 77, 85, 95, 129, 132, 201, 217

Enriquez, Isabel, 96, 99

Española, La. See Santo Domingo

Espinar, Hernando de (sugar mill owner), 140

Estancias. See Agriculture

Fabrics, 9, 18, 24, 25-33, 43, 44, 46, 47, 126, 150
Family networks, 88, 89, 90, 91, 95-97, 99
Farfán, Agustín de (physician), 149
Fernández de Enciso, Martín (geographer), 4, 26, 69
Fernández de Oviedo, Gonzalo, 86, 87, 138
Fernandez Leyton, Simón (merchant), 96-97, 98
Fernández Pacheco, Sebastián (merchant), 98, 132, 157, 177, 192
Ferrera, Alonso de (merchant), 90, 91, 99, 157, 207
Fisher, John, 17
Flanders, 24, 25, 26, 27, 28, 32, 34, 49, 69, 85, 100, 132
Fleets, 5, 6, 7, 8, 10, 12, 13, 17, 19, 24, 44, 67, 69, 81, 83, 85, 95, 98, 110, 111, 113, 140, 154, 183, 225, 226; effects on local economy, 9, 51-55, 62, 64, 65, 118, 124, 224-25
Florida, 4, 15, 45-46, 58, 72, 73, 82, 128, 137, 194, 198, 200, 217
Foodstuff, 2, 3, 12, 19, 22, 44, 45, 47, 53, 54-55, 56-57, 62, 64, 73
Forts, 1, 2, 5, 7, 10, 19, 70, 73, 74, 80, 101, 102, 110, 151-53, 223. See also Fuerza, La; Morro, El; Punta, La
Foundry, 80, 116, 118, 119, 133-35, 137, 143, 223
France, 1, 5, 10, 21-34 passim, 40, 41, 45, 49, 69, 71, 72, 77, 85, 95, 100, 101, 132, 201, 217
Fuerza, La (fort), 58, 71, 73, 74, 76, 78, 93, 101, 102, 108, 110, 111, 113, 115, 129, 154, 192, 201, 202, 206, 221

Gama, Antonio Matos da (sugar master), 98, 143, 208
Gamboa, Inés de (landowner), 191, 194, 198
Games, Alison, 226
Garay, Catalina (free black woman), 169, 177
Garrison, 1, 5, 6, 10, 45, 51, 58, 72, 77, 78, 81, 100, 101, 107, 108, 213, 225
Germany, 32, 34, 35, 85, 100, 217

Gold, 3, 57, 58, 67, 95, 202, 222, 224
Gomez Reinel, Pedro (asiento holder), 42, 92, 137
Góngora, Luis de, 187
Gonzalez Cordero, Pedro, 92, 144, 208
Guanabacoa, 1, 72, 83, 101, 127, 135
Guatemala, 15, 30, 106
Guinea, 11, 36, 37, 38-39, 41, 42, 102, 103, 105, 150, 151, 167
Gutiérrez Navarrete, Francisco (master shipwright), 129, 130, 132, 209
Guzmán, Antonio de (governor of La Punta), 98

Hakluyt, Richard, 68
Hamilton, Earl, 137
Hernández, Diego (slave, ship carpenter), 157, 177
Hernández, Luis (sugar mill owner), 141, 142
Hides, 18, 20-21, 40, 47, 48, 49, 61, 67, 92, 99, 129, 150, 201, 207
Hoffman, Paul, 46
Holland, 9, 21, 25, 26, 28, 31, 35, 40, 42, 49, 69, 70, 92, 100
Honduras, 15, 19, 20, 43, 46, 67, 99, 106
Hospital, 5, 108, 110, 111, 169, 176, 200, 203, 211, 223
Housing, 9, 62-63, 78, 91, 93, 94, 96, 108, 113-16, 127, 150, 194, 212, 223

Immigration, 86-101
India, 26, 29, 31, 69, 106, 227
"Indians," 1, 2, 3, 5, 6, 48, 72, 83, 101, 108, 116, 120, 124, 175, 187, 191, 201, 202; protector of, 126-27, 200; wages of, 126
Indigo, 18-19, 46, 224
Inestrosa, Juan de (treasurer), 189, 196
Inquisition, 94, 98, 219
Intercolonial trade, 11-21 passim, 37, 38, 39, 43-47, 53, 63, 65, 106, 225
Italy, 25, 28, 31, 32, 34, 35, 69, 70, 85, 100, 101, 132, 148, 150, 159, 227

Jail, 110, 112, 202, 223
Jamaica, 15, 39, 40, 45, 67, 101, 106, 200, 201

Jews, 94, 96, 98, 178, 186, 200, 217
Johnson, Lyman, 225
Jolofa, Juana (African freedwoman), 169, 170, 173

Knight, Franklin W., 225
Kuethe, Alan, 7
Kula, Witold, 56

Labor contracts, 21, 125-26, 128, 157, 176
Laet, Jean (geographer), 69
Land, 8, 66, 94, 120, 194, 195; sales of, 122-24, 208
Lara, Diego de (merchant and silversmith, native of Antwerp), 132, 197, 203, 211, 212
Lavrín, Asunción, 196
Leather. See Hides
Le Clerc, François, 1
Leyes de Toro (1505), 197
Leyes Nuevas (1542), 3-4
Linschoten, Jan Huyghen van, 69, 128
Liss, Peggy K., 225
Lobera, Juan de, 1, 2
Lopez, Duarte, 105
Lopez, Gregorio (mason), 93-94, 95
López de Piedra, Francisco (merchant, factor of slave asiento), 92, 143, 204
López de Velasco, Juan (cosmographer), 48
Lorenzo, Gaspar (shipmaster), 129, 130
Lorenzo, Luis (merchant), 38, 90, 91-92, 129
Luján, Gabriel de (governor), 188, 191, 199, 200, 201, 217

Madeira, 35, 99, 106, 138, 139, 143, 156, 208
Maldonado, Juan "el mozo" (nephew of Juan Maldonado Barnuevo), 142, 144, 145
Maldonado Barnuevo, Juan (governor), 64, 78, 122, 134, 136, 138, 139, 140, 144, 145, 152, 156, 157, 158, 218
Manila, 28, 29, 30, 31, 42, 44, 45
Manrique, Mariana (daughter of Hernán Manrique de Rojas), 193, 195, 198
Manrique de Rojas, Hernán, 110, 138, 144, 173, 192, 193, 195, 199, 200-201, 202, 203
Margarita, 15

Mariel, 129, 130
Mármol, Luis de, 103
Matanzas, 24, 40, 72, 125
Mazariegos, Diego de (governor), 61, 74, 102, 200
Medical attention, 81, 100, 152, 208, 210-11. See also Hospital
Mendes de Noronha, Enrique (merchant), 95-96, 97, 98, 144
Menéndez de Avilés, Pedro (governor), 45, 72, 198
Mercator, Gerardus, 69
Mexico, 2, 3, 4, 10, 12, 15, 19, 20, 28, 29, 31, 43, 44, 45, 47, 48, 51, 57, 60, 62, 64, 70, 72, 75, 77, 78, 93, 101, 106, 112, 132, 136, 138, 139, 184, 187, 191, 197, 202, 210, 211, 217, 219
Miranda, Francisca de (slave), 78, 154
Miranda, Gutierre de (governor of Florida), 194, 198
Molina, Tirso de, 210
Monasteries, 5, 111-12, 129, 143, 153, 169, 203, 211, 212, 217, 223
Montalvo, Gabriel de (governor), 201, 202
Moors. See Muslims
Morales, Bartolomé de (merchant and councilman), 61, 192-93, 199, 212
Moreno Fraginals, Manuel, 108
Morro, El (fort and observation post), 1, 71, 72, 73, 74, 76, 77, 78, 101, 152, 219
Morse, Richard, 225
Motolinía, Toribio Benavente, 29
Mozambique, 41, 42, 106
Muslims, 36, 87, 96, 102, 103, 105, 106, 148, 178, 186, 200, 210

New Spain. See Mexico
Nizardo, Beatriz (free black), 116, 126, 176
Nombre de Dios, Panama, 1, 44, 64, 70, 224
Nuñez, Francisco, 126, 129
Nuñez, Isabel (free black woman), 158, 169, 177

Oñate, Pedro de (sugar mill owner), 138, 145
Ordenanzas de Cáceres. See Cáceres, Alonso de

Orta Yuste, Ginés de (sugar mill owner), 206, 207

Ortigosa, Río, 129

Panama, 15, 106, 184, 202, 224

Pardo Osorio, Sancho (general), 64

Parroquial Mayor (parochial church), 5, 39, 108, 111, 115, 162, 169, 187, 202, 211, 219, 223

Paz, Carlos de (free black), 172, 176, 177

Pérez, Louis A., 16

Pérez, Rafael (merchant), 90, 99

Pérez de Angulo, Gonzalo (governor), 1, 2, 5, 58, 83, 198

Pérez de Borroto, Gaspar (notary and councilman), 176, 196

Pérez de Borroto family, 188, 190, 208, 212

Pérez de la Riva, Juan, 47

Pérez-Mallaína, Pedro, 215

Perú, 3, 4, 15, 48, 57, 67, 98, 106, 138, 140, 187, 202

Philip II, 34, 221

Philip III, 204, 221

Phillips, Carla Rahn, 22, 34

Physician, 110

Pigafetta, Filippo, 105

Pirates, 1–2, 5, 10, 52, 71, 73, 79, 201, 215

Population, 3, 5, 6, 14, 40, 45, 53, 55, 58, 81, 82–86, 100, 103, 106, 107, 113, 114, 120, 122, 136, 181, 204, 222, 223, 224–25. *See also* Immigration

Portobelo, 17, 44, 224

Portugal, 1, 15, 18, 26, 29, 32, 35, 36, 37, 40, 41, 42, 43, 92, 93–100, 101, 105, 106, 137, 142, 148, 150, 159, 168, 178, 201, 206, 209, 212, 213

Poyo Valenzuela, Juan del (merchant), 144, 145

Prieto, Gonzalo (slave ship master), 38, 90, 148, 149

Puercos, Río de, 129, 132, 133

Puerto Príncipe, 15, 48, 49, 61, 211, 214

Puerto Rico, 15, 45, 67, 73, 78, 91, 101, 106, 138, 147, 215

Punta, La (fort), 73, 74, 77, 78, 98, 134, 202

Quevedo, Francisco de, 187, 205, 210

Quirós, Tomás Bernardo de (captain and councilman), 192, 199

Recio, Antón, 57, 191, 193, 195, 203

Recio, Juan, 62, 93, 129, 154, 156, 191–92, 195, 199, 203

Recio, Martín, 188, 191

Recio family, 190, 191, 193, 203

Remedios, 15, 47–48, 214

Ribera, Antonio de (sugar mill owner), 138, 141, 143, 162, 163, 164

Rocha, Gonzalo de la (master carpenter), 134, 137, 209, 211

Roda, Cristóbal de (engineer), 76

Rodríguez, Isabel (free black woman), 169, 177

Rodríguez, Jusepe (landowner), 141, 156

Rodríguez, Melchor (merchant), 129, 192, 193, 212

Rodriguez Coutino, Juan (*asiento* holder), 42, 92, 151

Rodríguez Tavares, Hernán (merchant), 96, 140, 206, 207

Rodríguez Tavares, Jorge (merchant), 96, 97, 99, 207

Rojas, Alonso de (councilman and landowner), 188, 189, 190, 193, 201–2, 203

Rojas, Baltasar de (councilman and landowner), 140, 143, 189, 190

Rojas, Juan de (the elder, brother of Hernán Manrique de Rojas and Gómez de Rojas Manrique), 108, 111, 173, 198, 202

Rojas, Lucas de (councilman and landowner), 144, 189, 190

Rojas, Magdalena de (daughter of Juan de Inestrosa), 195–96, 197

Rojas, Manuel de (governor), 3, 189, 196

Rojas Avellaneda, Gerónimo (councilman and landowner), 93, 111, 202, 204

Rojas family, 190–91, 193

Rojas Manrique, Gómez de (councilman and landowner), 173, 176, 193, 200, 201–2, 212

Rojas Sotolongo, Juan de (son of Alonso de Rojas, councilman), 189, 190

Romero, Leandro, 107
Ruiz, Teófilo, 220
Ruiz de Pereda, Gaspar (governor), 97

Sánchez de Moya, Francisco (captain of
    artillery), 134, 135, 137, 210
Sancti Spíritus, 15, 48, 176, 214
Sandoval, Alonso de, 103, 150, 151, 161
Santiago de Cuba, 1, 3, 15, 49–50, 83, 89, 99,
    134, 135, 137, 140, 143, 145, 201, 202, 204, 214
Santo Domingo, 3, 15, 20, 39, 44, 46, 50, 52,
    60, 67, 71, 72, 73, 79, 90, 101, 120, 132, 138,
    147, 159, 166, 170, 181, 182, 183, 184, 190,
    192, 201, 215
São Tomé, 11, 35, 42, 106, 143
Sarmiento, Diego (bishop), 83
Saunders, A. C. de C. M., 159
Seamen, 5, 9, 15, 20, 21, 45, 51, 55, 85, 95, 99,
    100, 135, 173, 213–17, 222
Sella, Domenico, 17
Seville, 11–27 passim, 32, 34, 35, 36, 37, 38, 39,
    44, 51, 64, 71, 80, 84, 85, 87, 88, 89, 90, 91,
    95, 96, 97, 99, 128, 135, 142, 145, 148, 159,
    168, 170, 178, 192, 197, 207, 210, 211, 214, 215,
    217, 225
Shipping: and seasons, 15–17, 51, 52, 55, 62,
    63–64, 65–66; shipping routes, 4, 5, 11–17,
    43; and supplies, 24, 32, 34, 64, 90, 192. See
    also Shipyards
Shipyards, 10, 21, 79, 80, 90, 108, 116, 119, 135,
    208, 223; location of, 128–29; and pro-
    duction, 130; reputation of, 127–28, 130;
    and supplies, 32–33, 128, 130, 132, 133; and
    workers, 128, 129–30, 132, 133
Sicily, 86, 119
Siete Partidas (thirteenth-century code), 166,
    186, 196, 197
Silver, 17, 19, 29, 30, 44, 46, 51, 57, 58, 67, 80,
    95, 126, 194, 199, 202, 224
Sisa (local tax), 55, 109–10, 112, 201
Situados, 18, 46, 58, 65, 75, 77, 78, 79, 119, 132,
    134
Slaughterhouse, 54, 57, 112, 116, 186, 223
Slaves, 6, 9, 14, 18, 32, 35, 59, 93, 96, 107, 119,
    194, 195, 197, 199, 222; autonomy of, 153–

56, 161, 179–80, 181, 182; baptism of, 38, 39,
    106, 147, 161–65, 167; children of, 172–73;
    diet of, 141, 145–46, 152; and diseases, 101,
    149, 152; female slaves, 152, 154, 157, 159–
    60, 173–74, 179–80; and freedom, 160, 161,
    170–74, 176, 177, 180, 181; ladino slaves, 36,
    37, 39; male slaves, 159–60; marriages of,
    165–68, 176; in Mediterranean societies,
    148, 159, 168, 178; occupations of, 80, 81,
    93, 94, 102, 118, 123, 125, 133, 134, 137, 141,
    151–59, 179–80; prices of, 148, 149–50, 151,
    159–60; royal slaves, 102–3, 134, 151–53,
    157; treatment of, 182; runaways, 146, 166,
    183–85, 201. See also Africans; Blacks
Slave trade, 35–43, 46, 91–92, 98, 101, 105, 137,
    145, 147
Socolow, Susan, 206, 225
Sodomy, 218
Solórzano Pereyra, Juan de, 164
Sorés, Jacques de, 1, 2, 4, 5, 6, 9, 10, 65, 70, 81,
    83, 100, 108, 110, 111, 119, 174, 181, 202, 222,
    223, 227
Soto, Diego de (the elder), 189, 190, 193, 195,
    201–2, 203
Soto, Diego de (the younger), 189, 191
Soto, Hernando de, 3, 82, 83
Soto or Sotolongo family, 191, 193
Suárez de Toledo, Alonso (councilman and
    landowner), 125
Sugar, 3, 19, 35, 94, 118–19, 124, 136–46, 199,
    202; prices of, 137; production in Cuba,
    137, 145; production in La Española, 20,
    46–47; sugar masters, 92, 95, 99, 142, 156,
    208
Sugar mills: construction of, 119, 137, 201;
    investments in, 143, 144–45; and land,
    140–41; owners of, 96, 136, 206, 207, 208;
    prices of, 122; and slaves, 142, 144, 145–46,
    158; and supplies, 127, 135, 140, 142–43;
    and technology, 119, 136, 138–40

Tavares, Antonio Manuel (merchant), 96
Taverns, 9, 57, 61, 62, 95, 108, 111, 154, 173
Tejeda, Juan de (governor), 75, 130, 132, 133,
    156

TePaske, John J., 225
Thornton, John, 105
Tierra Firme, 3, 12, 51, 60, 62, 64, 72, 86, 140, 184
Tithes, 136, 202
Tobacco, 20, 124
Trinidad, 15, 47, 48
Turks, 102, 106, 178

Vaez Coutino, Gonzalo (*asiento* holder), 42, 92
Valdés, Pedro de (governor), 79, 89, 95, 98, 134, 135, 198, 210, 211, 217, 219
Valencia, 27, 87, 119, 178, 217
Velázquez, Diego, 2, 4, 195
Velázquez de Cuellar, Alonso (councilman and landowner), 176, 195, 197
Venezuela, 105, 184, 194, 202
Venice, 21, 28, 69
Veracruz, 15, 17, 19, 44, 45, 64, 72, 73, 76, 91, 92, 128, 184, 224

Viera, Baltasar de (fisherman), 94, 95
Vila Vilar, Enriqueta, 42
Vizcaya, 34, 133, 215

Ward, Christopher, 224
Wine, 9, 18, 22, 24, 25, 32, 43, 45, 47, 55, 56, 57, 59, 62, 89, 90, 91, 95, 100, 133, 150, 179, 192, 198, 201, 213
Women, 8, 82, 89, 90, 99, 174, 186, 194, 196, 204; literacy among, 205-6; participation in mercantile activities, 197-98; and petitions for land, 198. *See also* Blacks: black women; Elite: and dowries; Slaves: female slaves
Wood, 18, 19, 20, 47, 50, 118, 127, 130, 132, 133, 135, 136, 140, 153, 157, 198

Yucatan, 4, 15, 19, 30, 43, 44, 45, 112, 116, 137, 194, 204

Zanja, la, 108, 109-10, 137, 201, 205, 223

ENVISIONING CUBA

Alejandro de la Fuente, *Havana and the Atlantic in the Sixteenth Century* (2008).

Reinaldo Funes Monzote, *From Rainforest to Cane Field in Cuba: An Environmental History since 1492* (2008).

Matt D. Childs, *The 1812 Aponte Rebellion in Cuba and the Struggle against Atlantic Slavery* (2006).

Eduardo González, *Cuba and the Tempest: Literature and Cinema in the Time of Diaspora* (2006).

John Lawrence Tone, *War and Genocide in Cuba, 1895–1898* (2006).

Samuel Farber, *The Origins of the Cuban Revolution Reconsidered* (2006).

Lillian Guerra, *The Myth of José Martí: Conflicting Nationalisms in Early Twentieth-Century Cuba* (2005).

Rodrigo Lazo, *Writing to Cuba: Filibustering and Cuban Exiles in the United States* (2005).

Alejandra Bronfman, *Measures of Equality: Social Science, Citizenship, and Race in Cuba, 1902–1940* (2004).

Edna M. Rodríguez-Mangual, *Lydia Cabrera and the Construction of an Afro-Cuban Cultural Identity* (2004).

Gabino La Rosa Corzo, *Runaway Slave Settlements in Cuba: Resistance and Repression* (2003).

Piero Gleijeses, *Conflicting Missions: Havana, Washington, and Africa, 1959–1976* (2002).

Robert Whitney, *State and Revolution in Cuba: Mass Mobilization and Political Change, 1920–1940* (2001).

Alejandro de la Fuente, *A Nation for All: Race, Inequality, and Politics in Twentieth-Century Cuba* (2001).